THE HEALTHY
HORSE

THE HEALTHY
HORSE

CARING FOR YOUR HORSE – IN SICKNESS
AND IN HEALTH

JANET L. ELEY
BVSc MRCVS

SWAN·HILL
PRESS

Title page photograph: C. L. Hocking

Copyright © 2000 Janet L. Eley

First published in the UK in 2000
by Swan Hill Press, an imprint of Airlife Publishing Ltd

British Library Cataloguing-in-Publication Data
A catalogue record for this book
is available from the British Library

ISBN 1 85310 964 9

Typeset by Servis Filmsetting Ltd.
Printed in Italy.

Swan Hill Press
an imprint of Airlife Publishing Ltd
101 Longden Road, Shrewsbury, SY3 9EB, England
E-mail: airlife@airlifebooks.com
Website: www.airlifebooks.com

DEDICATION

To my Mother

ACKNOWLEDGEMENTS

Thanks go to Gillian Jenkinson for all the illustrations.

I would like to thank:
The Blue Cross; Robert Eustace FRCVS, Chris Hocking and Phil Russell of Smith and Nephew for use of their photographs as credited.

Gary Khahkian M/Eq.D for providing the dental numbering chart on page 25 and for his expert dental work.

John Preece RSS., Steve Aldford and all the farriers who have allowed me to photograph their work.

John Brentnall BVSc, MRCVS and William Rosie BVM&S, MRCVS for allowing me to photograph them at work.

All the friends and clients who assisted by handling and providing horses for photography, especially; Vivienne Davies, Mynderley Stables; Petra Archer, Redwood Stables; The Wyke, Deb Dudley, Stuart Deane, Thomas Hollinshead, James Stimpson, Don Pearce, Hilary Holmes, Joy Humphreys, Sandra Hughes, Linda Morris, Oonagh O'Neil, Joan Rogers and Kelly Williams.

CONTENTS

PART ONE

KEEPING YOUR HORSE HEALTHY

It is necessary to recognise the signs of good health in order to detect the first signs of illness. Every horse is an individual so it is important to make a record of each animal's basic details. These can include normal temperature, pulse and respiratory rate, any existing scars or blemishes, feeding and exercise details, preventive medicine programmes and any known health problems. A horse in good health should be alert and interested in its immediate surroundings. It should have a shiny coat free from sores, and the skin should be supple and move freely over the underlying tissues. The eyes are normally bright and free from discharges or swelling of the lids, the nostrils also should be clean and the breathing regular, slow and quiet. The breath should not smell offensive. A healthy animal does not normally cough or have enlarged glands below the ears.

It is not healthy to be over or underweight. It is advisable to monitor the body condition regularly. The amount of faeces and urine

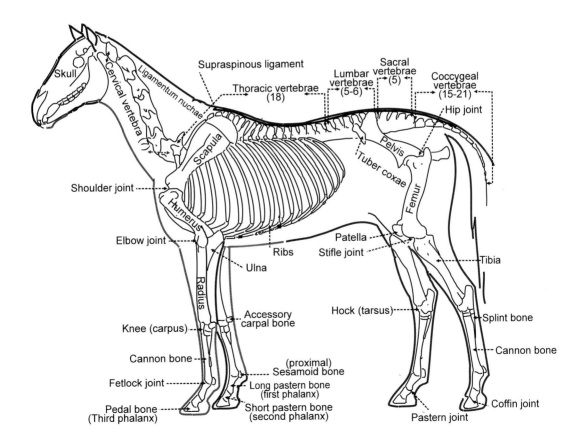

Fig.1. The skeleton of the horse.

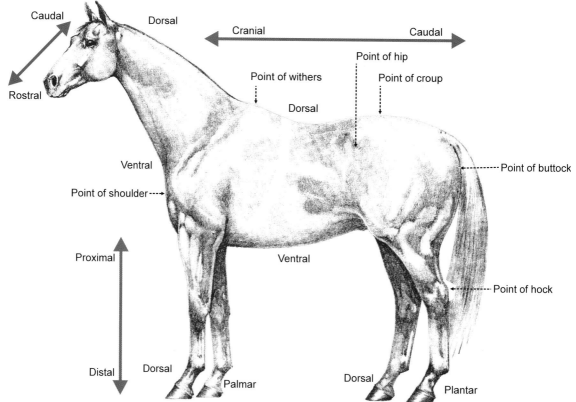

Fig.2a. *Terminology used to describe direction and position.*

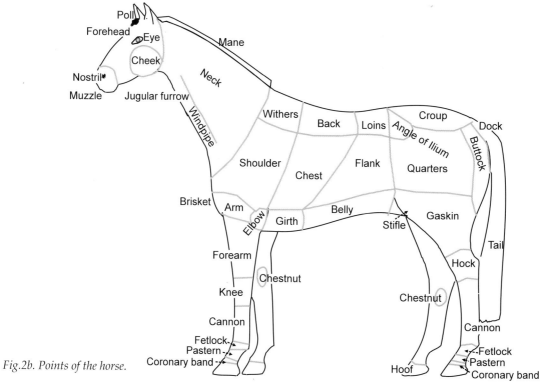

Fig.2b. *Points of the horse.*

2

passed obviously depends on the type and amount of feed given. A horse on a set feeding regime can be expected to pass similar amounts each day so it is easy to detect any differences which may be the early signs of disease. The horse should have a good appetite, be interested in its food and show no difficulty in chewing or swallowing. The horse should stand square and hold its head in a normal position, and when moving all the steps should be regular in length. It should move willingly and freely. The wear on the horse's shoes should be even.

It is important to know your own animal's pattern of behaviour. Some horses usually lie down in the field and stable whereas others only get down to roll. Often the owner notices quite subtle changes in behaviour which may be the early signs of illness. This is the time to check the horse's T.P.R.

NORMAL VALUES for an adult horse at rest:

TEMPERATURE (T)	37–38°C (98.5–100.5°F)
PULSE RATE (P)	25–40 per minute
RESPIRATION RATE (R)	8–16 per minute
CAPILLARY REFILL	less than 2 seconds
SKIN PINCH	less than 1½ seconds

The normal T.P.R. values for foals, young animals and ponies are higher than the adult horse values and those for donkeys are in the lower range.

HEALTH CHECKLIST

* behaviour
* eyes
* nostrils
* coat
* body condition
* posture
* appetite
* thirst
* faeces
* urine

ASSESSING BODY WEIGHT

There is a variety of methods available to calculate body weight if a weighbridge is not available. A weight tape measure designed for horses can be used (Spillers or Daltons).

When the height and condition score is known the weight can be read off a nomogram. (See opposite.)

Alternatively the following formula may be used:

$$\text{Weight (kg)} = \frac{\text{Length (cms)} \times \text{Girth (cms)}^2}{11877}$$

The length is measured from the point of the shoulder to the point of the buttock (Carroll and Huntington 1988).

There is another formula using heart girth squared multiplied by length from the point of the shoulder to the hip and divided by 8,717. The heart girth circumference of the horse is measured by passing a tape over the withers and behind the elbows. The measurement is taken as the horse breathes out. This heart girth circumference is a useful measurement to take at weekly or monthly intervals to detect weight loss or gain.

Condition scoring is a method used to assess the amount of body fat under the skin. The neck, the ribcage and back and the pelvis are examined visually and by palpation. The condition of the horse is then given a score from 0 to 5.

Condition scoring

0 = emaciated
1 = poor
2 = fair
3 = good
4 = fat
5 = very obese

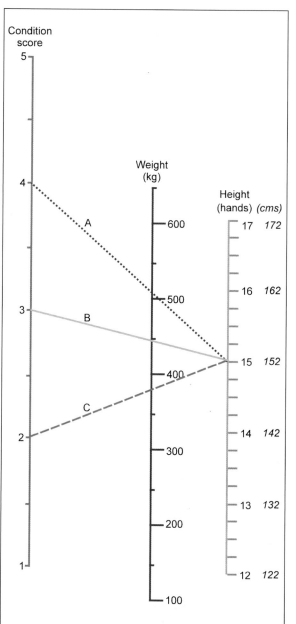

Fig.3. Weight nomogram e.g. Line C. 15 hh horse CS 2 weighs 380 kg. Line B CS 3 weighs 450 kg. Line A CS 4 weighs 500 kg.

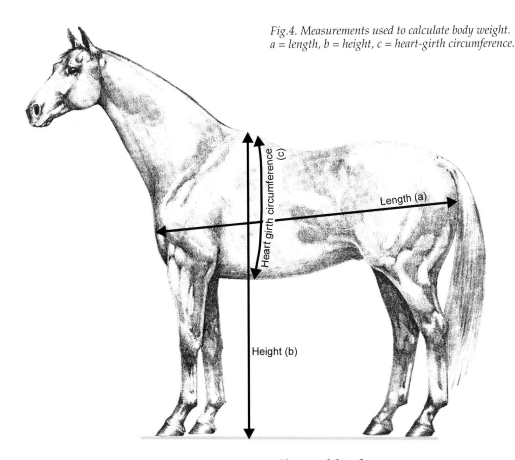

Fig.4. Measurements used to calculate body weight.
a = length, b = height, c = heart-girth circumference.

Neck

This is examined from the side to look at the general shape. Not all horses with a poor top line are thin, they may just lack muscle. It is best to feel just in front of the withers to get an idea of the firmness and width of the neck. Stallions tend to be cresty but are not necessarily fat. Fat horses will have folds of fat at the base of the neck and pads of fat in front of the shoulders.

Some animals with a poor conformation are ewe necked but not thin:

0 marked ewe neck; base of neck narrow/slack.
1 ewe neck; base of neck narrow/slack.
2 no top line; base of neck narrow/firm.
3 top line good but not cresty (NB stallions); base of neck firm.
4 crest starting fat folds; base wide/firm.
5 marked crest and fat folds; base very wide and firm.

Ribs and back

This area is examined from the side to see if the ribs and spine are visible. The mid ribcage is felt to assess the amount of fat covering the ribs. The vertebrae are well covered in the fat animal and it will have a table-top back. In obese cases a gutter runs along the backbone. It is not possible to feel the ribs even with firm pressure in very obese animals.

0 ribs and backbone easy to see and feel, skin drawn tightly over ribs, back bone sharp.
1 ribs and vertebrae well defined.
2 ribs just visible, backbone covered but easily felt.
3 ribs and vertebrae covered, ribs easily felt.
4 ribs felt only on firm pressure, gutter along backbone.
5 ribs buried in fat, table-top back with deep gutter.

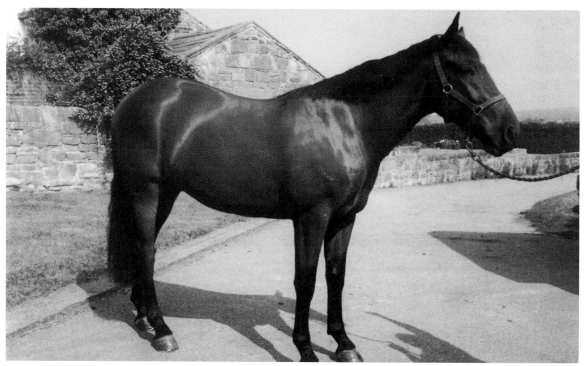

CS = 3 (Condition score 3: good) (C. L. Hocking)

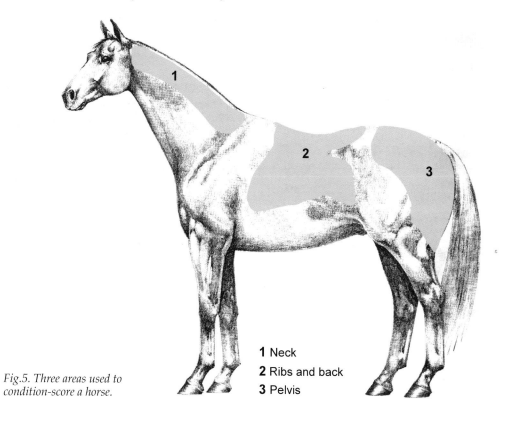

1 Neck
2 Ribs and back
3 Pelvis

Fig.5. Three areas used to condition-score a horse.

CS = 2 (Condition score 2: fair).

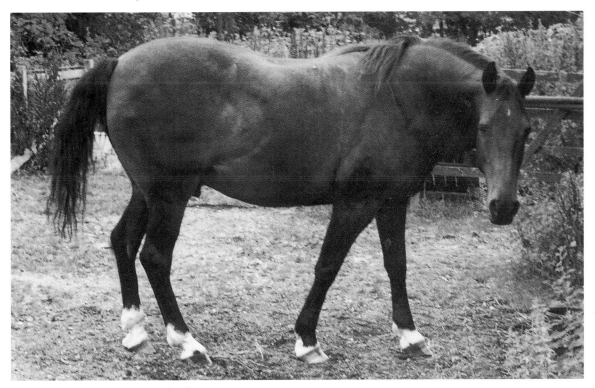

CS = 5 (Condition score 5: very obese).

Pelvis

The pelvis is best viewed from behind to assess the amount of flesh covering the bones. Thin animals will appear angular, with hollow flanks and a deep depression under the tail. The pelvis and croup will be easy to palpate. An obese horse will have a round rump, the inner thighs will touch and the gutter at the base of the tail will be deep. Remember that a hairy coat may be hiding a thin or fat animal so use your hands!

0 angular pelvis, hollow flanks, deep cavity under tail, skin tight.
1 pelvis/croup well defined, deep cavity under tail, skin supple.
2 rump flat, pelvis easily felt, cavity under tail.
3 pelvis covered, rump rounder, skin smooth.
4 pelvis well covered, only felt with firm pressure, gutter at root of tail.
5 pelvis buried in fat, deep gutter, skin distended.

To calculate the condition score, score each of the three sites separately. If the pelvis score differs from the neck or rib score by one point or more adjust it by 0.5 to give the correct score, e.g. neck score 3, rib and back 2, pelvis 3, actual score = 2.5.

In order to keep the horse in good health we usually have a health programme to include:

> vaccinations
> worming
> external parasite control and skin care
> routine dental checks
> farriery and hoof care
> correct nutrition
> exercise

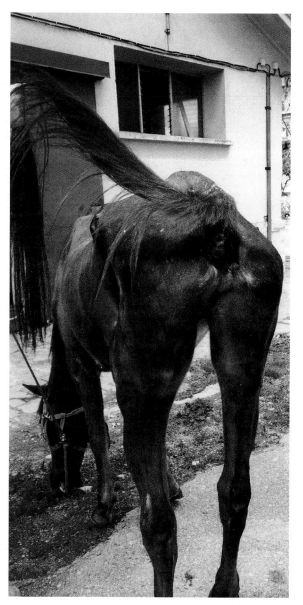

CS = 0 (Condition score 0: emaciated).

VACCINATIONS

It is important only to vaccinate animals which are in good health and are not stressed. They should not be travelled, competed or worked hard immediately before or after vaccination. Any animal which develops side effects or swelling at the vaccination site should be re-examined by the vet and the manufacturers of the vaccine informed. It is very uncommon to have a problem due to vaccination if the recommended procedure is followed.

Equines can be protected against tetanus, equine influenza virus and equine herpes virus 1 and 4.

It is sensible to vaccinate all horses. Tetanus is usually fatal in the horse and often animals which become infected with the influenza or herpes virus are ill for many months and are left with respiratory problems and poor performance when exercised. Tetanus vaccine is available as a combined vaccine with influenza or as a separate vaccine.

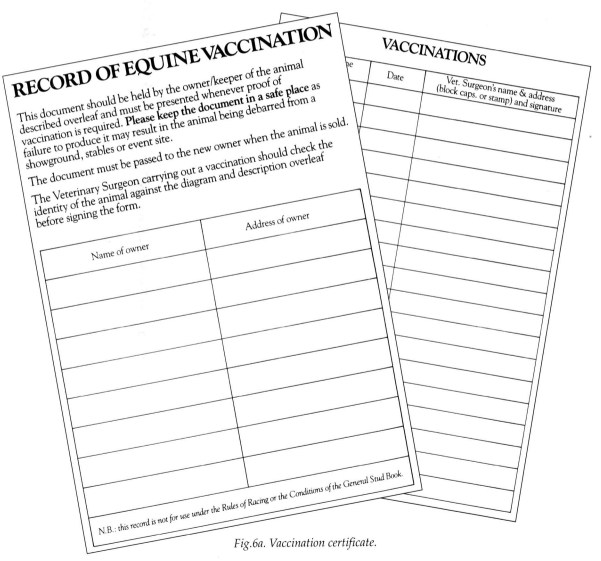

Fig.6a. Vaccination certificate.

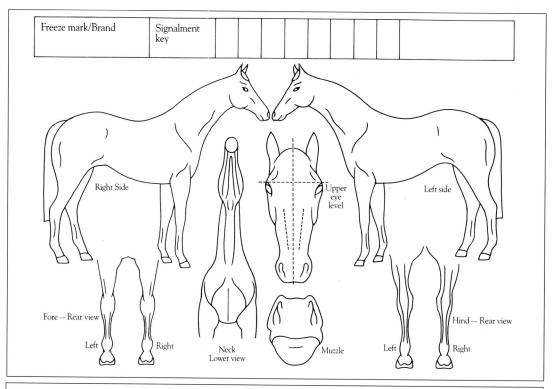

Freeze mark/Brand	Signalment key							

Right Side

Left side

Upper eye level

Fore — Rear view

Left   Right

Neck
Lower view

Muzzle

Hind — Rear view

Left   Right

Name of animal		No.		
Colour	Sex	Date of Birth	Approx. Adult Height	
Head				
Neck				
LEGS LF				
RF				
LH				
RH				
Body			V.S. Stamp and signature:	
Place and Date				

Identification procedure: The above identification must be completed by a Veterinary Surgeon only.

The recommended procedure for identification is described in the F.E.I. booklet 'Identification of Horses'.

The diagram and written description must agree and must be sufficiently detailed to ensure the positive identification of the animal in future. White markings must be shown in red and the written description completed using **black ink in block capitals or typescript.** If there are no markings, this fact must be stated in the written description.

All head and neck whorls should be marked ("X") and described in detail. Other whorls should be similarly recorded in greys and in animals lacking sufficient other distinguishing marks. Acquired marks (" ") and other distinguishing marks, e.g. prophet's thumb mark ("△"), wall eye, etc., should always be noted.

Age: In the absence of documentary evidence of age, animals older than 8 years may be described as "aged".

Please leave blank: 'signalment key' top right hand box and 'No'.

Fig.6b. Vaccination certificate, reverse

Fig.7. Landmarks for intramuscular injection sites in the neck and rump.

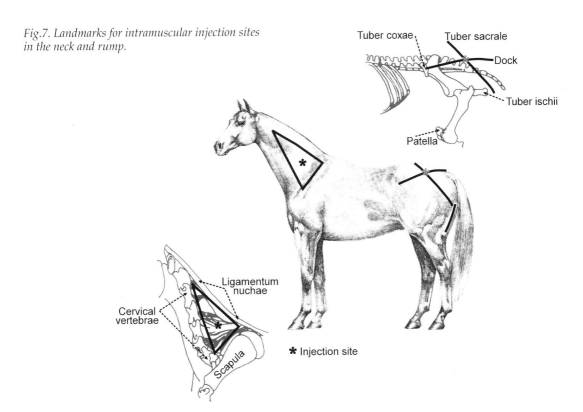

Tuber coxae

Tuber sacrale

Dock

Tuber ischii

Patella

Ligamentum nuchae

Cervical vertebrae

Scapula

✲ Injection site

Intramuscular injection in the neck.

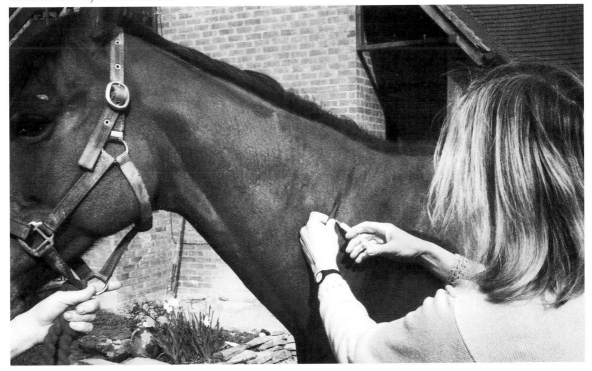

RECOMMENDED VACCINATION PROGRAMME

Vaccine	Trade name	Primary course
Tetanus	Duvaxyn T Equip T Tetanus Toxoid	2 doses 4–6 weeks apart Booster after one year and then every 18–36 months
Equine Influenza strains A Equi/2 (Suffolk 89) A Equi/1 (Prague 56) A Equi/2 (Miami 63) A Equi/2 (Newmarket 2/93) A Equi/1 (Newmarket 77) A Equi/2 (Brentwood 79) A Equi/2 (Borlange 91)	Duvaxyn IE Plus and Prevac Pro EQUIP F	Primary course 2 doses 4–6 weeks apart 1st and 2nd booster at 6 month intervals then yearly Primary course 2 doses 6 weeks apart 1st booster 5 months after 2nd dose. Next boosters at 12 to 15 month intervals
Equine Herpes virus EVH-1 and EVH-4 EVH-1	DUVAXYN EHV 1, 4 Pneumabort K	Primary course 2 doses 4–6 weeks apart. Booster every 6 months
Equine Viral Arteritis (EVA)	Artervac	Primary course 2 doses 4 weeks apart and completed at least 3 weeks before the start of breeding. Annual boosters. This vaccine is used to protect stallions from infection and to prevent them becoming viral shedders and infecting the mares they serve at mating.

All vaccinations have a primary course followed by boosters. Some authorities, e.g. *Fédération Équestre Internationale* (FEI) and the Jockey Club require that booster vaccines are given at specific times in order for a horse to compete on their premises and under their rules. As an owner it is wise to check on these rules if there is any chance that you may wish to ride on a race-course.

Foals usually start their primary vaccination course at three to five months of age, when the passive immunity they received from their dam wanes. These maternal antibodies pass to the foal in the colostrum (first milk produced at foaling time). Pregnant mares are given boosters three to six weeks prior to foaling so that the foal will receive the maximum protection.

Vaccination certificates are signed by the vet and are proof that the animal is vaccinated. They have a diagram and written description of the animal. If you purchase a new horse it is wise to check that the vaccination certificate matches the horse! If no certificate is available presume the animal is not vaccinated. If you fail to have the required booster within twelve months of the last booster the horse will have to start the course again. It is best to keep a record of when the boosters are due so they are not forgotten. The manufacturers advise that vaccine boosters are given at set intervals so that the horse's immunity to that disease remains high, i.e. the horse is protected.

The success of vaccination depends not only on the correct administration of the vaccine but also on the health, nutritional status and age of the animal. Animals already on medication or with illnesses will not produce a good immunity to vaccines. Vaccines are used in disease control in combination with good animal husbandry and management.

WORMING

Internal parasites are present in all equines. They cause a variety of clinical diseases in their hosts depending on the species of worm and the numbers involved. The effect may be:

weight loss	emaciation
colic	diarrhoea
staring coat	tail rubbing
anaemia	jaundice
swollen legs	sheath swelling
debility	nasal discharge
coughing	poor performance
ill thrift	anorexia
bowel obstruction	death

Animals which are heavily infested are debilitated which makes them prone to other diseases.

As you can see from the table below, most of the adult worms are in the horse's gut where they damage the bowel wall. They shed eggs which pass out in the horse's faeces to contaminate the pasture. Infective larvae hatch out of the eggs and are then eaten by the grazing horse. The life-cycle of the parasite depends on the species. The worm larvae migrate through various tissues and organs causing damage before emerging as young adult worms in the gut lumen. The migration path and the time taken for the parasite to complete its life-cycle varies with the species. The stable and grassland management system has to be considered before a worming programme can be designed to suit the individual. Your vet is the best person to advise on worming as he knows your particular situation. All animals on the same premises which share the grazing must be treated as a herd. Fields which are overgrazed and overstocked and small turn-out paddocks will have more problems than those which are better managed. Pasture management methods which include removal of dung twice weekly, alternate grazing, destocking or resting fields will all reduce re infestation and therefore the number of treatments needed.

Harrowing should only be done in dry, hot weather when the parasites will be desiccated; at any other time it just spreads the larval worms all over the pasture.

Horses do not like to graze the areas they have dunged and so create roughs and lawns. If dung clearing is practised, more of the pasture can be grazed. Small paddocks can be cleared daily; larger areas at least twice a week during the grass growing season and once a week in frost and cold winter conditions. Pasture larval counts when considered with local temperature and rainfall will show the efficacy of the worming programme and warn of potential problems.

MAIN INTERNAL PARASITES OF THE HORSE		
Type	Species	Location of adult worm in host
Large redworm	Strongylus vulgaris	Caecum/Colon
	Strongylus edentatus	Caecum/Colon
Small redworm	Cyathostomes	Caecum/Colon
Roundworm	Parascaris equorum	Small intestine
Bots	Gastrophilus	Larvae in stomach (adult=fly)
Threadworm	Strongyloides westeri	Small intestine
Seat/Pinworm	Oxyuris equi	Colon/Rectum
Tapeworm	Anoplocephala perfoliata	Ileum/Caecum
Lungworm	Dictyocaulus arnfieldi	Lung/Bronchi

The drugs (anthelmintics) used to worm horses in the U.K., are in one of the following chemical groups:

1 Benzimidazole: Panacur, Telmin, Bayverm, Equivurm plus and Equitac
2 Ivermectin: Eqvalan, Panomec and Furexel
3 Pyrantel: Strongid P and Pyratape P
4 Moxidectin: Equest

These drugs kill the parasite in different ways:

Benzimidazoles interfere with the uptake of food by the worm.
Ivermectins cause a non-spastic paralysis of the worm.
Pyrantel causes a spastic paralysis.
Moxidectin causes paralysis

Some drugs have a specific action against certain worms and some kill the adult parasite in the gut lumen along with the immature migrating larvae.

The inter-dosing interval differs for each of the groups of drugs:

Drug	Dosing interval
Ivermectins	8–10 weeks
Benzimidazole	6–8 weeks
Pyrantel	4–6 weeks
Moxidectin	13 weeks

In order to use the correct drug at the correct dose rate it is necessary to have the following information:

1 The age and weight of the horse(s) to be treated
2 Is it pregnant?
3 Is it healthy?
4 Is it on medication?
5 Does it have worms?

By examining faeces samples at the laboratory using a variety of tests the number and types of worms present will be known. Blood tests can detect anaemia and raised beta globulins in gut damage due to strongyle infestation; there is also a blood test specifically for tapeworm infestation. Some horses appear healthy, but have a high worm burden and are contaminating the pasture with millions of eggs a day.

The faecal egg reduction test is used to test for drug resistant parasites. Faeces samples are taken seven to twenty-one days after worming, and the results compared with the pre-worming sample. This shows how effective the wormer has been. Small strongyles (cyathostomes) have become resistant to many of the drugs in the benzimidazole group at the normal dose rate. This has been caused by overuse of these drugs at incorrect dose rates and dosing intervals.

WORMING PROGRAMMES Spring and summer routine					
Year	APR	MAY	JUN	JUL	AUG
1	Ivermectin every 8–10 weeks				
2	Benzimidazoles every 6 weeks				
3	Pyrantel every 4 weeks				
4	Moxidectin every 13 weeks				

WINTER WORMING PROGRAMME		
Month	Parasite	Treatment
Sep	Tapeworm	Pyrantel (2 x dose)
Oct	nil	nil
Nov	Small redworm	Fenbendazole (5 day)
Dec	Bots	Ivermectin/Moxidectin
Jan	nil	nil
Feb	Small redworm	Fenbendazole (5 day)
Mar	Tapeworm	Pyrantel (2 x dose)

The conditions needed for grass to grow, warmth and moisture, are also ideal for worm larvae to hatch from the eggs passed out in the dung. At temperatures over 7°C the eggs hatch. The infective third stage larvae move out of the dung onto blades of grass where they can be eaten by any grazing animal. Most horses spend more time at grass from spring to autumn and ingest many larvae. It is necessary to worm regularly in the spring and summer.

Choose one of the drug groups and use that wormer at its correct dosing interval for the entire season. The next year a different drug is used, i.e. rotate the wormers on an annual basis during the spring to autumn grazing season. Between March and September most animals will be routinely wormed every four to thirteen weeks depending on the chemical used that particular year.

Horses which are grazed individually, or where pasture hygiene is rigidly practised may need fewer treatments, assessed by the results of faecal worm egg counts (WEC).

Selective dosing can be used all year round if monthly WECs are done on all the herd. Only those animals with a positive count need treatment.

If a new horse is introduced onto a system, it should be wormed with a five day course of Fenbendazole (Panacur equine guard) prior to going onto the pasture. This will prevent contamination of the grazing with new worm strains which may have anthelmintic resistance.

All horses should be wormed before moving onto new grazing. Elderly and debilitated animals should have a faecal WEC and the results discussed with your vet prior to any drugs being given.

Tapeworm

The mature tapeworm sheds segments full of eggs in the dung. The eggs are eaten by the forage mite (oribatid mite). The mite lives on grassland, hay and bedding. The cysticercoid stage larvae are eaten by the horse and take six to ten weeks to develop into egg laying adults. The adults attach by suckers to the gut wall at the ileocaecal junction (where the small intestine meets the caecum) and can cause impactions (blockages), ruptures and peritonitis. They are responsible for about 20% of surgical colics and also chronic recurrent colic (abdominal pain).

A blood test, the Elisa method IGGT test can detect animals with a large number of tapeworms. These animals are at great risk of developing gut damage.

Pyrantel at double the normal dose rate is the only drug available to treat tapeworm infestation in equines. As part of a worming programme it is used in March and September. Infestation is greatest in heathland areas and acid soils – a favoured environment for the intermediate host, the oribatid mite. Animals which are debilitated or have a history of laminitis should not be treated with pyrantel (double dose) unless they have a tapeworm burden and should be carefully monitored. It is recognised that some drugs can precipitate a laminitis attack in high risk animals.

Bots

Horse bot flies (Gastrophilus intestinalis) lay eggs on the legs and abdomen of grazing horses in the summer. They are licked off by the horse and the larvae hatch and burrow to the stomach where they stay for about ten months before passing out in the dung. The adult fly emerges from the pupa to complete the life-cycle. Ivermectin or Moxidectin are used to treat bots in December after the frost has killed the flies and

Worming drugs

Fig.8. Life-cycle of the tapeworm.

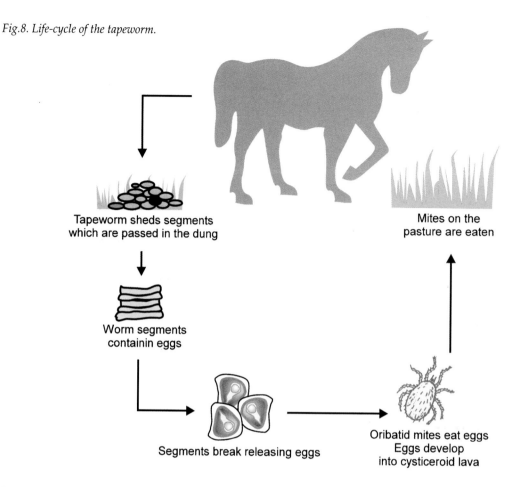

Tapeworm sheds segments
which are passed in the dung

Mites on the
pasture are eaten

Worm segments
containin eggs

Segments break releasing eggs

Oribatid mites eat eggs
Eggs develop
into cysticeroid lava

the bots are in the stomach. Insecticides/fly repellents applied to the horse in the summer will stop the flies laying eggs on the horse. The eggs can be removed from the horse's coat with Sellotape or special bot fly combs or knives.

should be wormed in November and February with a five day course of fenbendazole to remove small redworm. Many small strongyle strains show resistance to other drugs in the benzimidazole group.

Small redworm

This is the most important parasite because of its ability to delay development as larval cysts within the walls of the caecum and colon in the autumn. The larvae continue to develop in the spring when large numbers emerge from the gut. Both the encysted stage and the emerging larvae can cause serious disease, even death. Elderly animals and those under six months of age are particularly at risk, the highest risk occurring from late autumn to early spring. Animals

Large redworm

This used to be the most important parasite affecting the horse's gut. The larvae migrate through various tissues and some species damage the walls of arteries in the gut. This causes death to the part of the bowel supplied by the thrombosed vessel and acute colic. The incidence of this infection decreased when ivermectins became available in the U.K. as these are effective against both the larval and adult stages of large redworm.

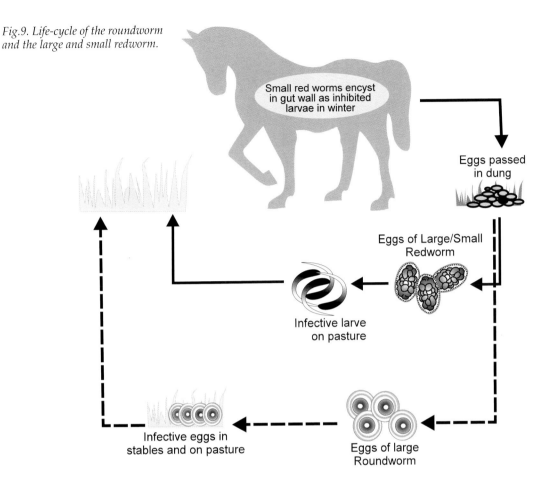

Fig.9. Life-cycle of the roundworm and the large and small redworm.

Small red worms encyst in gut wall as inhibited larvae in winter

Eggs passed in dung

Eggs of Large/Small Redworm

Infective larve on pasture

Infective eggs in stables and on pasture

Eggs of large Roundworm

Lungworm

Lungworms cause respiratory problems in adult horses and ponies, usually coughing and ill thrift. The infected larvae are passed out in the dung of affected donkeys and foals which may not show signs of the disease. The larvae are eaten by grazing horses and migrate through the bloodstream to the lungs. They rarely develop into egg-laying adults in the horse. In the donkey the larvae do mature to adults and eggs are coughed up, swallowed and pass out in the dung. Faeces can be used to test for lungworm in the foal and donkey but not in the horse, washings from the lungs of horses will detect the infection. Ivermectin is the drug of choice to treat lungworm infestation. It has become less common both in the donkey and horse over the last few years, but it is always wise to dose donkeys prior to moving them onto new pasture. Lungworms can survive for a long time on pasture and infect grazing animals for years to come.

Threadworm and roundworm

Threadworms live in the small intestines of young foals. They become infected soon after birth, either through the dam's milk or by the larvae penetrating the skin. Foals develop an immunity to this infection after six months of age. Heavy infestations cause diarrhoea, dullness and loss of appetite. Ivermectin is the drug of choice for threadworm, the alternative being fenbendazole at seven times the standard dose. Foals should be treated from four weeks old.

Roundworms are very large when mature and

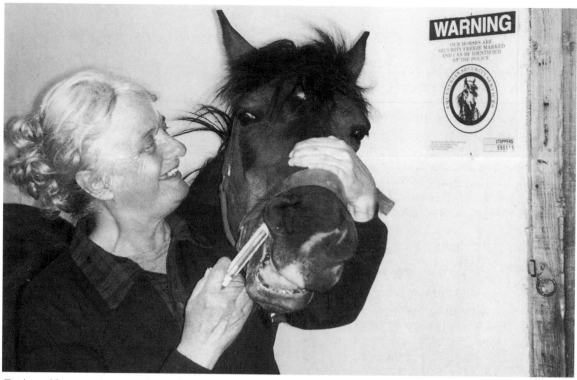

Dosing with a worming paste in a syringe

may cause blockages in the small intestine, failure to gain weight and emaciation. The female can lay millions of sticky, thick shelled eggs which can survive for years on stable walls and floors. These eggs containing infective larvae are picked up by the foal. The larvae migrate via the blood to the liver and lungs; this stage causes fever, coughing and anorexia. Yearlings develop an immunity at eighteen months old. Mares should be wormed prior to foaling, their udders washed to remove any eggs, and be provided with a clean pasture. Stables should be power cleaned and disinfected before being used as foaling boxes. All three groups of drugs are effective against ascarids.

Anthelmintics are available as pastes in dosing syringes and in feed additives as powder or liquid. Whichever preparation is used the animal must swallow the whole dose. If the drug is mixed in food you must watch while it is eaten and replace any spillages. All the products have full instructions for use and worming advice. It is advisable to wash your hands before and after handling medicines, and do not allow children to handle these products. Owners can always seek veterinary advice if they do not understand the instructions or there are any problems.

WORMING CHECKLIST

* follow the instructions on the product leaflet
* use the correct dose and dosing interval
* use a programme to suit your management system
* remove dung from the pasture 2 x week
* treat all the herd at the same time
* monitor results with WECs
* treat all foals and youngsters from 4 weeks old
* treat all newcomers before mixing with the herd
* treat all the herd before moving onto new pasture
* dispose of all packaging correctly
* do not treat sick or debilitated animals without seeking veterinary advice

Skin Care

The skin and coat need daily care and inspection. Grooming includes washing the dock region and the udder or sheath. Tack, rugs and grooming equipment must be correctly cleaned and maintained to prevent the spread of infection and injury. All tack and rugs must be properly fitted or the skin can be damaged, e.g. girth galls, saddle sores and biting injuries (at the corners of the mouth and the bars). Back muscles may also be damaged by poorly fitting saddles. Animals which gain or lose a lot of weight may need their saddles changed if they no longer fit correctly.

Grooming is the ideal time to check for any skin disorders and new injuries. It also means the horse is tied up and is being handled in a relaxed and calm way. Grooming should be a pleasant experience and a confidence builder for both horse and groom. There are many grooming aid products on the market, horse shampoos, sprays to make the coat shine, sheath cleaners etc. These are not really necessary when elbow grease and plain soap and water will normally do the job. There are a wide range of detergents for washing machines and many tack cleaning and leather preserving products. Many horses and people show skin irritation to modern cleaners, and simple soap and warm water is often the safe option. Before using any new product on the horse's skin it is best to do a spot test. A small amount of the substance is placed on a non-hairy area (inner thigh) and examined after a couple of hours to see if there is any inflammation (redness).

Flies are a seasonal problem. They annoy the animal by swarming around its head and feeding on the discharges from the eyes and nostrils. Some give painful bites and are blood sucking. Horses may be allergic to the bites of certain insects, the commonest being the allergy to midge bites, Sweet itch.

It is important to use fly repellents and/or insecticides before the horse is bitten. Horses can be stabled when the flies are most active. Fly

Acquired marks shown as patches of white hair

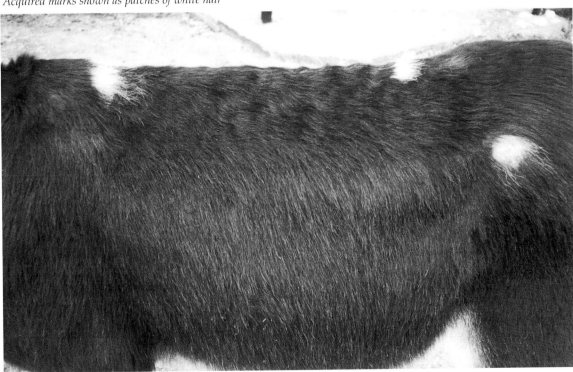

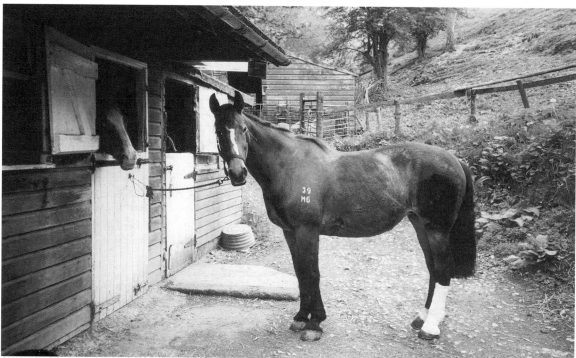

A freeze mark on the shoulder

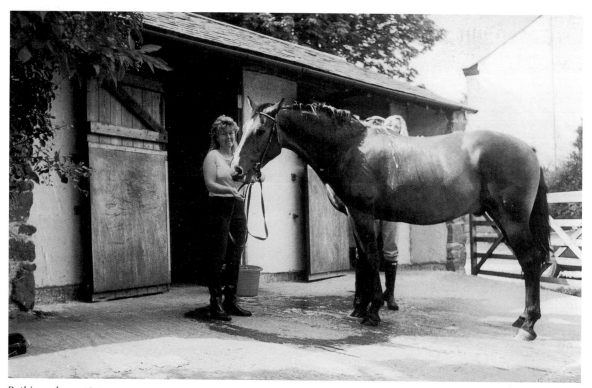

Bathing a horse (C. L. Hocking)

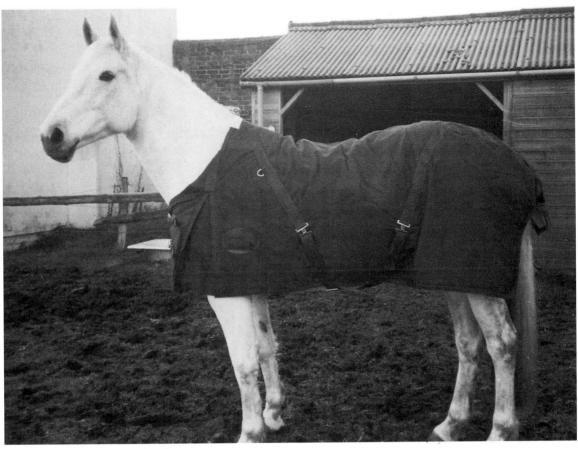

A horse wearing a waterproof outdoor rug

fringes and veils are useful but may become caught on fencing or branches, so must be used with care and closely supervised. Lightweight rugs (summer sheets) will keep the flies off the horse while it is in the stable and the removal of manure heaps from stable areas will also reduce the number of flies. Some insecticides are oily, pour-on products (permethrin) which are active for several weeks providing they are not washed off. These also kill lice so are used in the autumn/winter. The aromatic fly repellents tend to be short acting so these have to be frequently applied.

Shelter should be provided from strong sunlight as well as flies. Animals with unpigmented muzzles are prone to sunburn and need protection with a high factor sun screen.

Wet cold weather can also cause problems for the skin, e.g. rainscald and mud rash. These can be prevented by providing a field shelter with a hard standing and by using waterproof rugs and avoiding turn-out pastures which are poorly drained.

GROOMING AND SKIN CARE CHECKLIST

* look for injuries and first signs of disease
* wash grooming kits frequently
* keep tack clean and in good repair
* wash rugs and numnahs in non-detergents and rinse well
* test shampoos and sheath cleaners before use
* use fly and external parasite control
* use sunscreen on unpigmented skin
* prevent the skin becoming too wet

ROUTINE DENTAL CHECKS

Domesticated horses need routine dental care. They are given diets which modify their eating patterns. They have bits in their mouths from a young age and are not selectively bred for good dentition or even wear of cheek teeth. Animals which have slight abnormalities at eight years old may have a serious problem by their mid teens if they do not receive corrective dentistry at a young age. Preventive dentistry is vital as the condition of the horse's teeth is very important with regard to its health and welfare. The equine evolved as a grazing animal, normally spending eight to fourteen hours daily eating plant material. The silicates in grass are abrasive and normally wear down the teeth, acting like pumice as the horse chews. The lower jaw (mandible) of the horse is narrower (30%) than the upper jaw (maxilla). As the horse chews the sideways movement favours wear on the outside edge of the lower cheek teeth and the inside edge of the upper cheek teeth. Sharp enamel points tend to form on the outer (buccal) edge of the upper cheek teeth and on the inside (lingual) edge of the lower cheek teeth which can cause ulceration of the cheeks and tongue. Tight nosebands press the cheeks against the sharp points and cause pain and discomfort when tacked up.

The horse has both deciduous (milk) and permanent teeth. At about nine months old the foal will have a full set of deciduous teeth; these include six front (incisor) teeth and six premolar (cheek) teeth in the maxilla and mandible. The gap between the incisors and the cheek teeth is the interdental space or bars. The incisors are small and white and rounded at the gum margin. The middle incisors are referred to as the centrals, the teeth on either side are the laterals and

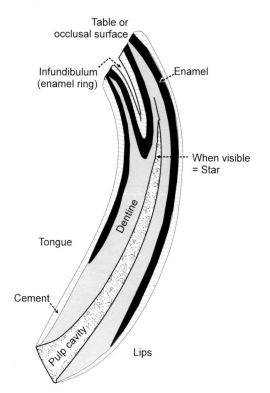

Fig.10. Section through lower incisor tooth.

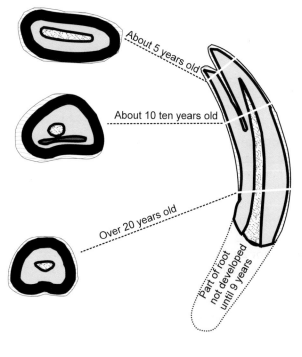

Fig.11. The occlusal surface changes shape with age. The infundibulum becomes shallow and the dental star appears.

A healthy horse at grass

the teeth on the outside of these are the corner incisors.

The eruption times for temporary teeth in foals are:

0–1 week	central incisors
4–6 weeks	lateral incisors
6–9 months	corner incisors
0–2 weeks	1st, 2nd and 3rd premolars (left and right side upper and lower jaw)

There are twenty-four milk teeth.

The bones of the head expand during the next two years and allow room for thirty-six to forty-four adult teeth. The changes continue at a slower rate throughout the horse's life as the permanent teeth continue to erupt their reserve crowns. These are hypsodont teeth, i.e. most of the crown (80 to 90 mm) is under the gum in the jaw bone in the young horse. The root is short and slow to form (six to nine years). The teeth continue to erupt 2 to 3 mm per year as the occlusal (biting) surface wears away. Because of this continuous wear and eruption any misalignment or disease can affect the function of the cheek teeth.

The permanent (adult) incisor teeth erupt at specific times in most horses. The centrals at $2\frac{1}{2}$ years, the laterals at $3\frac{1}{2}$ years and the corners at $4\frac{1}{2}$ years. The teeth in the upper jaw are larger and erupt before those in the lower jaw. They are in wear (attrition) with those of the opposite jaw approximately six months after erupting. The permanent incisors are large teeth, yellow in colour and square at the gum margin. The eruption times for the larger breeds, e.g. shires, Warmbloods are later than the thoroughbred.

Traditionally, horses have been 'aged' by examining the incisor teeth but recent research

A four-year-old

Fig.12. Four-year-old.

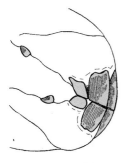
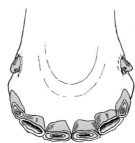

Fig.13. Five-year-old.

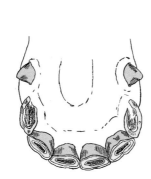

Fig.14. Eight-year-old.

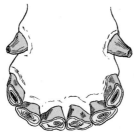

Fig.15. Nine-year-old.

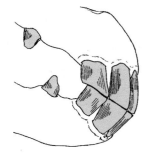
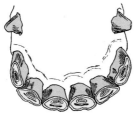

has revealed that this is an inaccurate method of ageing animals over six years of age. The eruption of the permanent incisor teeth gives a fairly accurate correlation with the actual age of the horse but the ageing of older animals becomes less precise with increasing age and is no more than an 'informed' guess!

There are twenty-four cheek teeth in the permanent dentition, six on either side of the upper and lower jaws, three premolars and three molars. The premolars (PM) and molars (M) of the upper jaw are broad and square; the lower cheek teeth are narrower and rectangular. The grinding surfaces have ridges of cement, enamel and dentine which are sharp and serrated.

The cheek teeth are numbered 1 to 6 from the bar to the angle of the jaw. They erupt at $2\frac{1}{2}$ years, 3 years, 4 years, 1 year, 2 years and $3\frac{1}{2}$ years. The first three permanent cheek teeth may have the remains of the temporary premolar teeth (retained caps) stuck on top of them.

Male horses normally have two upper and two lower canine teeth which erupt at four years of age in each interdental space. Canines are absent or rudimentary in mares.

Some horses have a small vestigial tooth (wolf tooth) just in front of the first cheek tooth. They vary in position, root length and angle. There may be one to four of these teeth. Occasionally wolf teeth cause a problem in which case they are removed.

The eruption times for permanent teeth are:

$2\frac{1}{2}$ years central incisors
$3\frac{1}{2}$ years lateral incisors
$4\frac{1}{2}$ years corner incisors
4–5 years canines

PERMANENT CHEEK TEETH

1	2	3	4	5	6
PM2	PM3	PM4	M1	M2	M3
$2\frac{1}{2}$yr	3yr	4yr	1yr	2yr	$3\frac{1}{2}$–4yr

As you can see the first cheek tooth is the second premolar, the wolf tooth is the first premolar tooth.

There is a method used to number the teeth so that there is no confusion about which tooth is

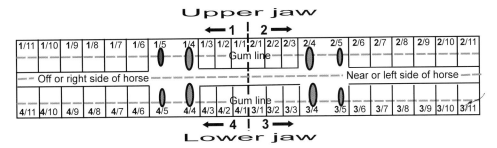

First number (**1 - 4**) defines Quadrant

Second number (1 - 11) defines tooth ⟶ 1 - 3 = incisors
4 = canines
5 = wolf teeth
6 -8 = premolars
9 - 11 = molars

Fig. 16. Dentition numbering system

under treatment. The mouth is divided into quadrants, i.e. upper right is number 1, upper left is number 2, lower left is number 3 and lower right is number 4. When facing the horse the numbers go clockwise. Each tooth is then given a number 1 to 11. The central incisor being 1 and the last cheek tooth 11 in each quadrant. To locate a tooth first state the number for the jaw and then the tooth number, e.g. 3.4 is the canine tooth on the lower left.

See chart above.

The dental examination

All horses require a dental examination every six months with any required dental maintenance carried out. Foals should be examined for congenital defects of the lips, palate and tongue. Some foals have dental malocclusions of the incisor teeth (parrot mouth), i.e. the upper jaw is longer than the lower jaw so the incisor teeth are not opposed. This condition should be corrected in the young foal to prevent problems later on. A bracing apparatus is used to slow down the growth rate of the upper jaw allowing the lower jaw to catch up in length. At six to eight months old all the incisors will have erupted and the occlusion of incisors and premolars should be checked. The premolars must be checked for sharp points and the tongue and cheeks for ulcers.

Over the next four years all sorts of changes are occurring in the mouth of the young horse. Teeth are erupting and being lost. Up to 60% of two to four year olds will suffer from gingivitis (gum inflammation). The mouth should be examined for wolf teeth; bit injuries on the bars and corners of the mouth; enamel points on cheek teeth; hooks on PM2 and M3; retained

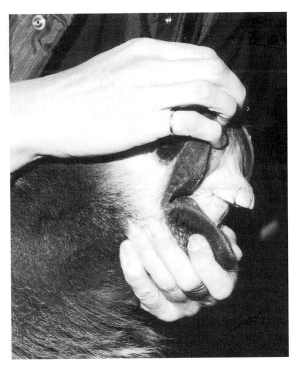

Overshot jaw – parrot mouth in a foal

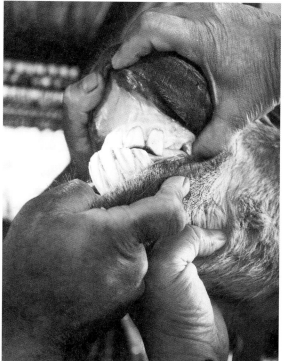

Undershot jaw

An injury to the inside of the upper lip

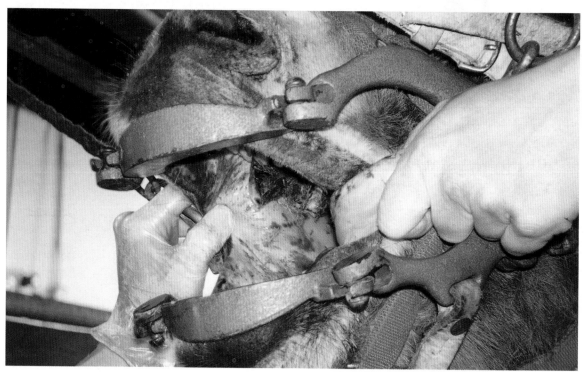

A large hook on the 1/6 right upper cheek tooth

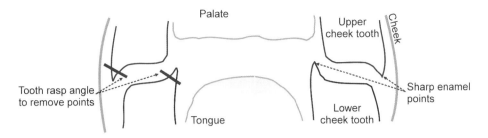

Fig.17. Sharp enamel points on the outer edge of the upper molars and the inner edge of the lower molar teeth.

caps. Incisors should be checked for retained or extra teeth. By five years all the incisors and canines should have erupted so they can be visually examined and palpated for sharp edges and tartar. Occasionally too many teeth may be present or teeth can erupt in the wrong position. The molar teeth also must be checked for good alignment and proper eruption. Horses with small dished heads have more curve to the jaws and are more prone to overcrowding of teeth than horses with long roman noses and straight dental arcades.

The horse's diet plays a major role in the wear of the cheek teeth. The amount of lateral movement of the lower jaw depends on the length of forage. Feeding pellets and short length forage

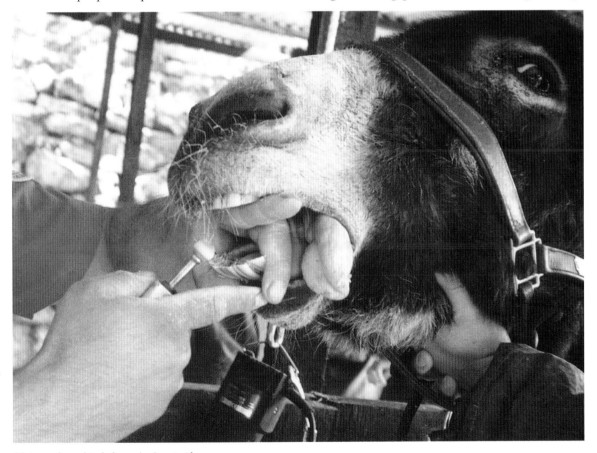

Using a dremel to balance incisor teeth

27

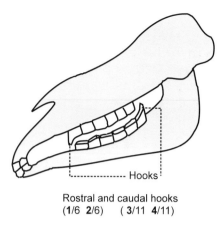

Rostral and caudal hooks
(**1**/6 **2**/6) (**3**/11 **4**/11)

Fig.18. Rostral and caudal hooks on 1/6, 2/6, 3/11, 4/11.

limits the jaw movement and causes the formation of sharp points. Horses at pasture or fed hay or straw have a wide range of jaw movement. Malocclusions of incisors and molars will cause abnormal patterns of wear which lead to serious dental problems. Hooks can occur on the first upper cheek tooth and the last lower cheek tooth. These can become long and pointed and meet the opposite soft tissue and lock the jaws as any sideways movement is painful.

Pain will alter chewing movements so abnormal wear occurs. Food material may become packed around the molar teeth causing gingivitis and peridontitis (inflammation of the tooth socket). The teeth may become loose especially in elderly horses. If a tooth is lost the opposing tooth becomes too long and prevents normal chewing. Overlong teeth have to be cut off with shears or rasped frequently.

Infection of the tooth roots of the upper cheek teeth may result in facial swelling and an offensive nasal discharge if the tooth root abscess bursts into the sinus cavity. Abscess of the lower molar roots causes a swelling and pus/scabs on the lower jaw bone. Young horses often have a bumpy lower jaw when the teeth are erupting.

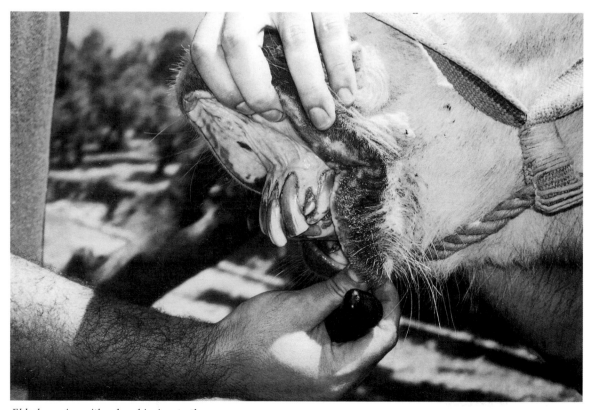

Elderly equine with splayed incisor teeth

Fig.19. Late teens.

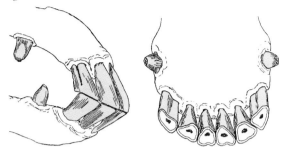

Fig.20. Twenty plus.

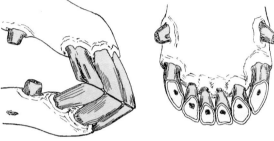

Teeth with root abscesses used to be removed but recently drilling out the root and using amalgam has been tried as an alternative treatment, which if successful saves the tooth. Signs of dental disease are:

poor bodily condition
slow to finish food
quidding (dropping chewed food out of mouth)
food pouched in the cheeks
salivating
abnormal chewing action
facial swelling
smelly nasal discharge from one nostril
halitosis (bad breath)
colic and choke due to inadequately chewed feed
abnormal head carriage when ridden, headshaking
reluctance to drink cold water
whole grain or long stems in faeces

Usually a gag (a full mouth speculum) is placed in the horse's mouth so that all the teeth can be fully inspected. The horse has to be adequately restrained or in some cases sedated. If

Sinus infection treated by trephining (C. L. Hocking)

A dental gag is used to hold the mouth open

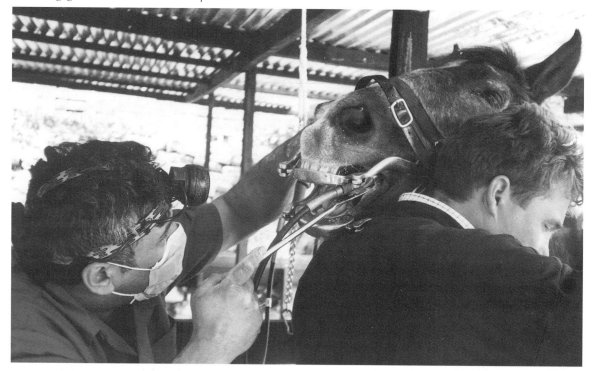

The use of a dental rasp

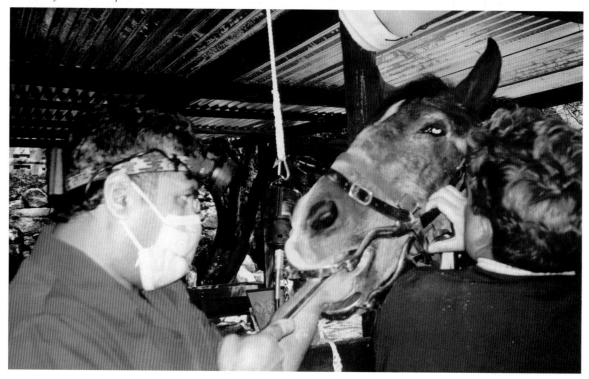

Failure of teeth 4/2 and 4/3 to erupt

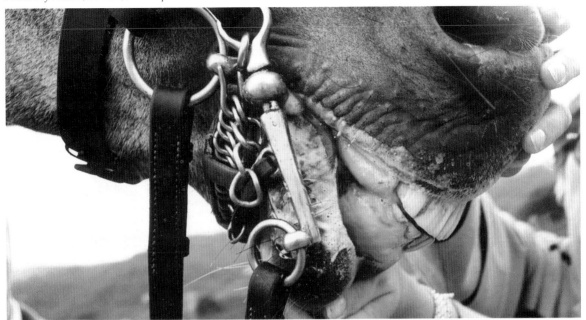

extensive surgery is required the horse will be anaesthetised. X-rays of the head are useful if infection of the sinuses is suspected or the position of a root has to be located in an abnormal eruption site.

Only veterinary surgeons are qualified and legally allowed to remove teeth and sedate horses. Many lay dental technicians rasp teeth but some have no training while others have qualified and trained in the U.S.A. There will be a recognised training course with certification in the U.K. for Equine Dental Technicians in the near future.

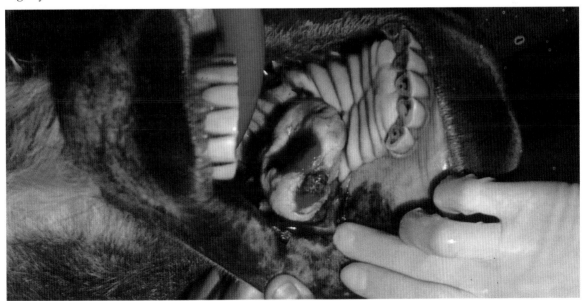

A tumour on the palate

FOOT CARE

The foot is a common site of disease and injury. Feet should be carefully inspected every day. They should be picked out morning and evening and before and after exercise. Horses out at grass need to have their feet attended to at least once a day. Hoof picks which have a brush at one end are useful.

The horse should be tied up and standing square with its weight taken equally on all limbs. If the feet are picked out in the same order each time the horse will soon learn the routine and there will be no reluctance to have the feet picked up. The limb joints should bend easily in a normal healthy animal. The clean hoof wall is checked for damage, e.g. cracks or horn deficits. The sole is cleaned and should be free of any sensitive or sore areas. The grooves on either side of the frog and the central sulcus are easy to clean with a brush. Any grit is removed from the white line. The heels and the coronary band are checked for injuries. The temperature of the feet will vary throughout the day and warm feet do not always signify disease (a consistently hot foot with a bounding digital pulse is a sign of inflammation within the hoof).

If the horse is shod the position and wear on the shoe is checked, and the clenches are felt to make sure they are tight against the hoof wall.

Raised clenches can cause injuries to the opposite limb especially in animals who do not have a straight action. Any soil or stones are removed from under the shoe at the heels and between the shoe and the sole.

In dry, hot conditions the hoof dries out so it is important to wet the feet to prevent the horn becoming brittle and cracked. In wet conditions the hoof can become saturated, however wet feet will soon dry out in a clean shavings bed.

> ### FOOT EXAMINATION CHECKLIST
>
> Examine wall for defects
> Examine frog and sole for injuries
> Check heels and coronary band
> Note position of shoe, state of wear and feel the clenches

The horse's diet, state of health, environmental factors, climate, and farriery all affect the quality and rate of hoof horn growth. Horn growth rate slows down in cold, dry conditions and increases in warm, moist conditions. Good quality horn can withstand environmental challenges and protect the pedal bone from concussion. Some animals inherit poor quality horn, with crumbly

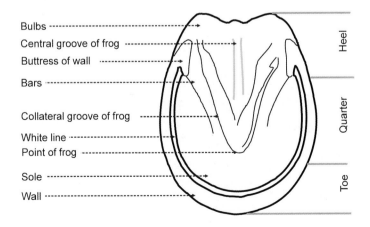

Bulbs
Central groove of frog
Buttress of wall
Bars
Collateral groove of frog
White line
Point of frog
Sole
Wall

Heel
Quarter
Toe

Fig.21. Structures on the ground surface of a hind foot.

walls and thin soles; these animals should not be bred from. Poor quality horn is susceptible to many diseases and also predisposes to pedal bone damage (pedal osteitis).

Dietary factors

Ideally a horse on a balanced diet which includes good quality forage should have all the necessary nutrients to grow good horn. Often diets which lack calcium and protein result in poor horn tubule formation. Occasionally inadequate levels of biotin will cause horn defects. Feeding bran was historically a common cause of calcium deficiency in the diet, however today bran is not such a popular part of the horse's diet, being replaced by forage such as chopped hay, straw and alfalfa mixes. Alfalfa is a good source of both calcium – in a form which can be absorbed by the horse's gut – and protein. Sugar beet and carrots are also a good source of calcium. The calcium in limestone is not as easily absorbed and is therefore not the best way of giving extra calcium to equines. There are a number of dietary supplements on the market which are supposed to promote hoof horn growth rate and quality. They have not all been scientifically tested so it is best to ask veterinary or farriery advice before purchasing such products.

Environmental factors

Horses kept in very wet conditions with no chance for the feet to dry out will be prone to horn infections, e.g. thrush or hollow hoof disease. Wet horn is weaker than dry horn and the hoof loses its shape. The walls flare and separate, the heels collapse and the sole becomes flatter and thicker. The toes become long and the minerals are leached out of the hoof. Keratolytic (horn destroying) bacteria and fungi can enter the hoof through defects in the horn.

Ammonia from urine in deep litter beds will damage the horn, chemicals like formalin, copper sulphate and strong disinfectants are all detrimental to hoof horn and should be avoided.

Hoof oils, creams and tars will trap the excessive moisture in the hoof and provide an ideal environment for anaerobic infections.

Ideally the hoof should not need any dressing other than to be washed with clean water. The outer surface of the hoof is naturally shiny and protects the inner layers. The modern hoof dressings are designed to allow air and moisture in and out of the horn and protect it from ammonia in the bedding, so maintaining good quality horn.

Farriery

Many domesticated horses live in a confined area so that hoof growth rate exceeds hoof wear. The hoof wall grows 8 to 10 mm per month on average. Horses in work are shod to prevent excessive wear on the hoof wall. Most horses will need their hooves trimmed at four to six week intervals. The farrier will advise on the trimming interval for each individual animal and this may alter from summer to winter when climatic and diet changes affect horn growth rate.

Overlong feet cause lameness and distortion of the hoof. The bones, joints, ligaments and tendons

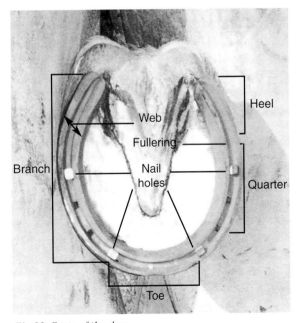

Fig.22. Parts of the shoe

Fig.23. Section through a horse's foot.

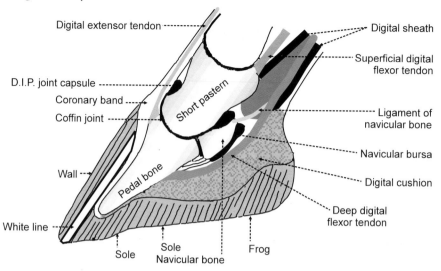

higher up the limb are also put under abnormal stresses which can result in long-term lameness. Shoes which are left on too long will have raised clenches. The shoe moves off the wall onto the sole, causing bruising and corns. The shoe may be pulled off and cause further damage if areas of wall are torn away or if the horse punctures the foot on a nail.

It is the responsibility of the owner to make regular appointments with the farrier. In order for the farrier to do a professional job he needs certain conditions to work in:

A clean dry horse with the feet picked out
The horse should be correctly restrained and be used to having its feet handled
A well lit shoeing area with a smooth flat surface to walk the horse on to check foot balance

The farrier is trained to trim the feet, to prepare them for shoes and to fit the shoes. They are trained in the anatomy of the limbs and feet, horsemanship and metal-work. Many are experienced in radiology, lameness diagnosis and disease processes. Some farriers specialise in surgical shoeing when they work closely with their veterinary colleagues. Many foot lamenesses involve both veterinary and farriery expertise as well as owner co-operation. Often the farrier is the first person to detect a problem. Abnormal wear on the shoe may be the first sign of an alter-

ation in gait due to a lameness. Reluctance to bend a joint during shoeing may be an early sign of arthritic pain. As the farrier sees the horse at frequent intervals he will notice weight changes and will also be aware of any infectious diseases in the area.

Shoes may be metal or plastic, handmade or machine-made (keg), they may be attached to the wall by nails or by glues. Aluminium shoes are lighter than steel shoes but not as hard wearing. The farrier decides which type of shoe to use on a particular animal. The amount and type of work has to be considered as well as the quality of the hoof wall and its ability to hold the nails. Horses with abnormal foot flight patterns or those which forge, overreach or brush may need special shoeing to prevent further problems. By careful foot balance and shoeing some toe-in or toe-out conformation can be improved.

Foot balance

In order to balance the feet the farrier assesses the conformation of the horse, paying special attention to the limbs and the hooves. The shape of the hoof capsule, the length of the toe and the thickness of the horn on the sole, frog and bars must all be considered prior to trimming to a

Fig.24. Assessing foot balance.

(a) *a perpendicular line from the point of shoulder should bisect the knee, fetlock pastern and hoof.*

(b) *The hoof pastern axis is parallel to the heel and the middle of P1, P2 and P3. A line from the centre of the coffin joint divides the hoof in half.*

(c) *A line down the centre of the cannon bone is at right angles to the pastern and heels if the foot is balanced medio-laterally.*

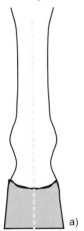
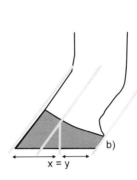

x = y

correct shape. The front feet should be a matching pair, as should the hind feet. The front feet are rounder than the hind feet. The soles should be concave and thick enough to prevent bruising under normal conditions. The wall is thickest at the toe, and thinner at the heels.

When viewed from the side the hoof wall at the toe should be parallel to the hoof wall at the heel and parallel to the slope of the shoulder. The hoof pastern axis should be a straight line and not broken. If the hoof pastern axis is broken the slope on the pastern is not the same as the slope on the hoof wall. A broken hoof pastern axis should be restored by correctly trimming the hoof.

The normal angle between the hoof wall and the ground is 45 to 50 degrees for front feet and 50 to 55 degrees for hind feet. There is a lot of individual variation but the angle should be the same as that of the pastern and shoulder in the normal horse. Horses with long, sloping pasterns put more strain on their suspensory ligament, flexor tendons and sesamoid bones. Horses with upright pasterns suffer from increased concussion to their pastern and fetlock joints and are predisposed to arthritic conditions and navicular disease.

Medio-lateral balance (inside-outside) means that the foot lands flat on the ground as the walls are the same height. This is checked by picking up the foot and letting the leg hang under the horse in a natural way, holding the leg by the front of the cannon bone. By viewing across the heels it is easy to see if they are the same height

Fig.25. Broken back hoof pastern axis (HPA).

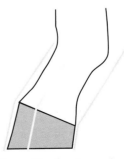

Fig.26. Broken forward hoof pastern axis.

and at right angles to a line down the centre of the flexor tendons. A 'T' square placed over the middle of the flexor tendons should have the right-angled bar level with the weight-bearing surface of a correctly balanced foot. (See page 102.)

Medio-lateral imbalances are common and cause quarter cracks and twisting of the hoof capsule, arthritic lower limb joints and dishing. In the front feet the outside toe quarter is often left long so the horse lands on this part of the wall and then crushes down onto the inside heel. The inside wall becomes straighter and the heel becomes jammed up. The outside wall will eventually become convex and the heels may shear apart so the feet appear pigeon-toed. In the hind feet the converse is true with the inside wall left long so the outside heel is the second impact site and the hind feet will turn out. It is very impor-

tant that the feet are balanced correctly otherwise the horse will show lameness due to foot and limb pain.

When viewed from the front the feet should not turn inwards (pigeon-toe) or point outwards (splay foot). The whole limb may deviate or the problem may occur low down, e.g. deviation at the fetlock or pastern. With a toe-in conformation the foot usually swings outwards (paddles); with toe-out the foot swings inwards (wings) and damages the opposite leg.

The horse should be walked and trotted in hand so that the limb flight patterns can be assessed. Sometimes the limbs interfere with each other, causing brushing and overreach injuries. Animals with poor limb conformation will have poor foot conformation due to abnormal stresses on the hoof capsule.

FEEDING

Horses and ponies are herbivores. They evolved to eat plants like grasses and coarse vegetation, not lush fertilised pasture land. Feral horses spend up to 16 hours a day grazing. Their teeth and digestive tract are designed to utilise a forage diet. They also have a psychological need to spend time searching for and chewing forage. Animals fed on concentrate diets which can be eaten three to six times faster than the same weight of fibre are more likely to exhibit stereotypic behaviour (boredom vices). Forage is an essential part of the equine diet to maintain the teeth and guts in good order and for the mental well-being of the animal. Although many animals only require a forage diet, those in hard work, young growing animals, breeding stock, the ill or elderly may require concentrates and supplements in addition to the forage.

Horses are fed forage (grass, hay, straw), cereals (oats, barley, maize) and other straights like soaked sugar beet and compound feeds such as pellets and coarse mixes.

Water is also an essential nutrient and without it a horse will soon become dehydrated, seriously ill and may die. The volume of water required by a horse depends on the moisture content of the feed, the size of the animal, the amount of exercise taken and the weather conditions.

Foods vary in their water content; grass contains 80% water, compounds and hay may only

Fig.27. Common varieties of grasses.

Italian rye grass

Perennial rye grass

Cocksfoot

Timothy grass

Bent

Meadow fescue

Offering water during a fun ride

salts like electrolytes to water may stop a horse from drinking. Insufficient water will lead to a depressed appetite and weight loss and dry gut contents which may cause impactions and colic. The basic nutrients provided by a balanced feed are carbohydrates as starch and fibre; protein and fat. Vitamins and minerals are also needed in small amounts for a variety of bodily functions. Forage such as grass and hay can provide all the nutrients a horse needs. The composition of grass alters through the growing season. Young grass is high in nutrients, especially soluble carbohydrates and only has a small amount of fibre. As the grass matures it has longer stems and less leaf and has a lower nutrient value.

The feed value of hay will vary depending on how well it was made and what species of grass it contains. Once the grass has been cut for hay it may deteriorate if it is rained on and it can become mouldy if it takes a long time to dry. Barn dried hay will contain more minerals, vitamins and other nutrients than hay made on the field.

There are alternative packaged feeds to hay which may be more expensive but have the advantage of being dust free, clean and of known nutritional value. These include haylage, short chop hay and straw chaffs, high fibre pellets and alfalfa.

Horses that need more energy than a forage diet can supply require energy feed such as cereals, either fed as individual grains (straights) or mixed in commercial compound feeds as pellets or coarse mixes.

Cereals can be fed as whole grains, rolled, extruded or micronised. Cereals commonly fed to horses are oats, barley and maize. Wheat by-products, bran and breadcrumbs are also fed. Cereals are usually mixed with other ingredients to give a balanced diet. As most owners are not experts in nutrition it is safer to use a commercially formulated compound feed to supplement the forage ration. There are compound feeds to suit all age groups and types of performance horse. These have been expertly designed by the equine nutritionist employed by the manufacturer. Most companies have an advice helpline for their customers and as with all products you get

contain 15% moisture. Horses on a high protein diet will drink more water and produce more urine.

A 500 kg horse at rest requires 25 lit (5 gal) of water. Exercise in hot conditions may increase the water requirement three-fold to 75 lit (15 gal). Water is lost from the body in urine, faeces, sweat and from the respiratory tract.

Horses should always have access to clean, fresh water and this must be checked twice a day. Water may be provided in clean buckets, troughs, automatic drinking bowls or from streams or ponds. Natural supplies may dry up in summer-time or become stagnant. In the winter water may freeze over and access to streams may be very muddy and dangerous. Many horses have been stuck in ponds and streams. Bucket handles and sharp edges on troughs can cause injuries. Old baths are often used as water containers and can cause horrific injuries, especially when headcollars are caught on taps. The newer rubber-type water troughs are the safest option in fields. Most horses prefer cool, clean water and are reluctant to drink tainted water. Adding

Filling hay nets in the feed store

Feed scoops come in various shapes and sizes so you need to know how much by weight each scoop holds.

The horse's gut contains billions of friendly bacteria that assist the digestion of plant material. These bacteria can be destroyed by sudden changes in the diet, especially high cereal and starch rich food which alter the acidity of the gut contents. This can cause laminitis, colic and digestive upsets such as diarrhoea and flatulence. All changes in diet should be made slowly and for a good reason – do not swap and change your horse's diet just to feed what happens to be in fashion! If your horse is healthy, the correct weight, i.e. condition score 3 and works well you do not need to change the diet. If you need advice related to feeding ask the expert, not the next door neighbour! Remember over 75% of the horses in the UK are overweight so a lot of money is being wasted on feed.

The amount that the horse needs to eat depends on a number of factors. Firstly the size of the horse, not only its height and present weight but also the condition score. The type of work done or exercise taken and the frequency of exercise will affect its energy requirements. It is a common fault to overestimate workload. Most animals are at maintenance or a light level of work. This would be hacking three or four times a week and out at pasture each day. Show jumping and dressage competition horses that are worked six days a week would have a medium workload. Hunting, endurance work and eventing would be classed as hard work. The daily ration is then divided into a percentage of roughage and a percentage of concentrates depending on workload.

Horses on maintenance exercise need 100% of the ration as forage. Horses in light work need 80 to 85% ration as forage and 15 to 20% as concentrates. Horses in medium work need 75% forage and 25% concentrates.

The horse's management system also has to be considered. The horse may have access to grazing all or part of the day, which may be a lush meadow or poor scrubland. Horses that are rugged up and provided with a field shelter require less calories to maintain their body

what you pay for. It is false economy to go for the cheaper feeds which may contain poor quality ingredients and may not be as accurately analysed and formulated.

The vitamin and mineral supplements are added to the mixes and pellets and providing they are consumed before the 'use by' date on the label do not add further supplements to a balanced feed. The label will also list the nutrients in the feed and the batch number, 'sell by' date and suggested amounts to feed.

Horses have small stomachs and are naturally trickle feeders, which means that they need frequent small feeds. Roughage is given to dilute the compound feeds and prevent digestive disturbances. All food should be fed by weight. Hay can be weighed in a net using a balance scale.

weight than those without rugs and shelters. Animals that are clipped out may be stabled most of the time. Weather conditions will also affect the way food is utilised. The digestion of roughage is thermogenic, i.e. it produces heat. If a number of animals are fed hay in the field it may be difficult to monitor the amount each individual receives. Obviously animals on an inadequate worming programme and those with dental problems will not utilise the food properly. Animals that are debilitated, stressed or in pain may lose weight on what seems to be an adequate ration. The temperament of the horse should also be considered as this may affect the type of feed you use.

As a rough rule of thumb and a starting point in calculating the amount of food your horse requires, first calculate its body-weight. There are a number of weight bands on the market that give an estimated weight on the heart girth measurement. These vary in accuracy depending on the height and type of horse; most are accurate to

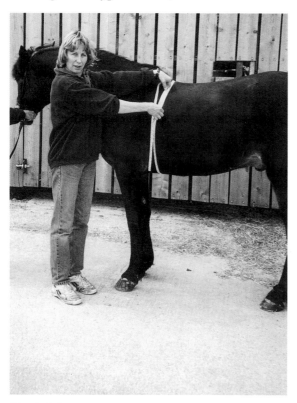

Heart girth measurement

within 3 to 10% of the actual body weight. Horses normally eat 2 to 2½% of their body weight each day. A 500 kg horse will require 10 to 12½ kg per day. Donkeys and native ponies require less than 2% to remain at their present weight. If your horse or pony is overweight it is getting too much food and in order to lose weight it needs less calories and more exercise. Calculate its ideal weight and feed at 75% requirement for that weight in order to lose some kilos. It is a lot easier to put weight on than to lose it. It is important to recognise small fluctuations in weight so the diet can be altered before the animal is grossly under or overweight. Heart girth measurements taken at fortnightly intervals are an easy way to monitor body-weight changes. All animals are individuals so the diet that suits one may not suit another.

Feeding guidelines:

1. Fresh clean water should always be available.
2. Feed according to body-weight and work load.
3. Feed small amounts at regular intervals. Keep to a routine.
4. Feed hay before and after concentrates. Mix chaff with concentrates.
5. Weigh all food and keep a record.
6. Changes in diet must be gradual to allow the gut bacteria to adjust and prevent illness.
7. Use good quality food and avoid dusty, mouldy hay.
8. Store feed in vermin-proof, labelled bins in a cool, dry building. Store hay and straw on pallets.
9. Keep all utensils, buckets and mangers clean. Provide each horse with its own equipment.
10. Monitor body-weight and condition score frequently.
11. Feed balanced rations. Do not overdose vitamins and minerals.
12. Do not feed or give large volumes of water immediately before or after exercise.
13. Give carrots or apples to stabled horses that have no grass.

Vitamins

Vitamins belong to the water-soluble group, e.g. B complex and C or the fat soluble group, e.g. A, D, E, K which are stored in the liver and body fat. The bacteria in the horse's gut make the B vitamins and vitamin K. Vitamin C is produced in

Vitamin	Source	Required for
A	Grass new hay, carrots Green food, alfalfa	Nerve function, immune system, eye sight
B	Forage and grains, synthesized in the gut	General metabolism of fats, carbohydrates and protein, skin repair and haemoglobin
C	Synthesized in the body	Muscle function, immunity
D	Sun cured forage, fish oil, synthesized in the skin	Bone formation, calcium and phosphorus metabolism
E	Green forage and cereals	Muscle function, fat metabolism

the liver and Vitamin D is formed in the skin when it is exposed to sunlight. In the winter Vitamin A and D reserves may be depleted and supplementation may be needed. The horse is unlikely to need extra B vitamins unless the gut flora is upset after antibiotic treatment or sudden changes in diet. Young, sick and stressed animals need an increased level of vitamins. Healthy adult horses fed on good quality, correctly stored rations are unlikely to need extra vitamins. Excess amounts of water-soluble vitamins are excreted from the body, unlike the fat-soluble vitamins which are toxic if overdosed.

Minerals

Minerals, unlike some of the vitamins cannot be synthesised in the animal's body; they have to be supplied in the diet. The main minerals are Calcium, Phosphorus, Magnesium, Sodium,

Potassium and Chlorine. There are a number of trace elements which are needed in small amounts. These include Iron, Copper, Zinc, Manganese, Cobalt, Iodine and Selenium.

Compound feeds already contain minerals and trace elements in the correct proportions. Horses that are on a purely forage diet of grass and hay can be given a forage balancer. Salt licks can also contain minerals as well as sodium chloride.

There are a plethora of herbal and other supplements or additives on the market, all claiming to have beneficial effects, but most have never been scientifically tested. They are not subject to rigorous analysis like medicines and may contain unwanted impurities. They are sometimes thought to cure conditions or alleviate symptoms but this is based mainly on results on human experience. Think carefully before you buy supplements for your horse, be sure that it is needed and that it is safe to use.

Mineral	Source	Used for
Calcium	Alfalfa Sugar beet Carrots Milk	Bone structure, muscle and nerve function
Phosphorus	Cereals	Same as above
Magnesium	Bran Vegetables Milk	Bones and teeth structure, muscle function Electrolyte balance
Sodium Chlorine Potassium	Forage Hay Grass	Maintaining pH, electrolyte balance, nerve and muscle function

EXERCISE

Exercise is important for both the physical and mental well-being of the horse. This may be unsupervised walking in the field while grazing or, at the opposite end of the scale, the hard work and high level of schooling performed by the elite athlete. Most equines are kept for pleasure and leisure pursuits, not serious competition, so their workload is light. It is good to consider where, when and how much work you should give your horse. The work should not cause injuries like sprains or strains nor cause exhaustion or illness. Animals that are inadequately prepared for exercise by not having been properly warmed up, or those which become tired are more likely to sustain injuries. Most injuries occur due to unfitness; poor conformation; incorrect tack; poor conditions underfoot; rider inexperience and accidents. The correct tack should be used for the type of work and it should fit correctly. Badly fitting tack causes pain and injuries and affects the horse's attitude to work. Interference injuries like brushing and over-reaching are seen in young unbalanced animals, tired animals and those with poor limb conformation. Exercise boots must be fitted carefully to avoid them slipping down or causing pressure injuries if too tightly applied.

The ability of the rider will reflect the type of terrain and activity the horse can cope with. An inexperienced rider may cause an accident by poor balance, errors in judgement and physically hindering the horse. They will certainly come to grief on a novice or young horse if they overestimate their riding prowess. Inexperienced riders on inexperienced horses can spell disaster for the horse and ruin it for the future. Horses under four years old may not be used in riding establishments nor competed in any sport other than racing. Many horses raced as two year olds never reach maturity as they are injured.

Badly fitting boots cause injury

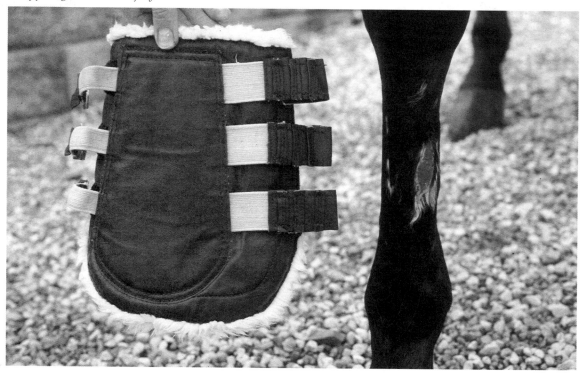

Horses wearing knee boots (C. L. Hocking)

There are advantages and disadvantages to riding on all types of terrain. Roads tend to be smooth but are a hard surface and cause concussion to the limb joints, especially in trot work. In winter the surface may be icy. Anyone who exercises horses on public roads should be aware of the Highway Code relating to horses. The British Horse Society holds training courses and Road Safety tests for horse-riders. It is important to be clearly visible to other road users by wearing reflective and fluorescent clothing and it is not advisable to ride on the highway at dusk or in the dark, even with stirrup lights. Horses should wear knee boots for road work and be well shod. Worn shoes should be replaced. The volume of motorised traffic even on country lanes means that the rider has to pay attention at all times to avoid accidents.

Bridleways and tracks avoid the hazards of traffic but the surfaces may be very muddy, uneven, rocky and hard. Horses may stumble, especially if ridden at speed on an unsuitable surface. Prepared surfaces like sand and wood chip are ideal for schooling the horse. They should not be too deep nor too hard. Some surfaces are springy and others are 'dead'. Pastureland is fine to ride on at certain times of the year, when it is not baked hard or waterlogged. The type of terrain will dictate what pace you can ride at. Occasional ridden exercise should be slow and for short periods to avoid sore muscles, tendon and ligament injuries. The aim of training or fitness programmes for horses and humans is to prepare the musculoskeletal system and the heart and lungs for athletic work. The training will increase muscle strength, increase

Lungeing is a useful training aid

endurance and improve flexibility. Hill work is introduced gradually into a fitness programme. As the horse becomes fitter it can do faster and more collected work. Before commencing on a training programme it is a good idea to have a veterinary check-up and perhaps blood sample analysis. The horse must be in good health prior to work. Animals that are overweight or have respiratory or musculoskeletal problems will show exercise intolerance and loss of performance. Obesity can be avoided by correct feeding. Respiratory disease can be minimised by avoiding contact with infected animals, feeding

clean forage and keeping the environment free from dust, ammonia fumes and fungal spores and using vaccines and worming programmes. Muscle, tendon, ligament and other joint or bone disease should be diagnosed by a veterinary surgeon who will treat the condition. Sometimes the farrier or physiotherapist will work with the veterinary surgeon to rehabilitate the horse after an injury. The same performance tests used on human athletes are available for horses. Heart rate monitors are used to assess response to exercise, recovery time and fitness. Horses are worked on treadmills to check oxygen uptake,

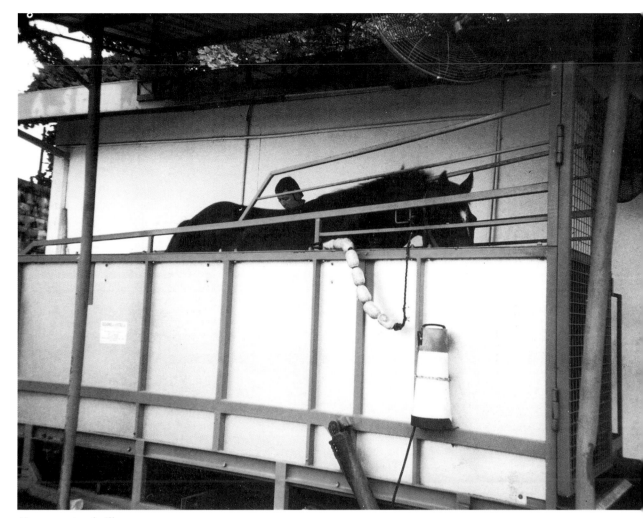

Horse on a treadmill

respiratory and heart rate response to graded work, and to diagnose problems. Blood is analysed for muscle enzymes and lactate levels. The horse's gait can be studied using video cameras and force plates to detect lameness. Tendons are scanned using ultrasound to detect minute injuries. Swimming pools are also available for training and convalescing animals.

Grooming and massage to increase muscle tone followed by warm-up exercise prepares the horse for more vigorous work. A warm-up may include using heat lamps or a solarium or brisk walking and stretching exercises. Muscles work more efficiently when they are warm and when the weather is hot the horse will warm up faster.

Heart rate monitors have become more popular during training to assess improved fitness and work level. The heart rate can be measured at rest, before and after exercise using a stethoscope or by palpating a superficial artery (taking a pulse). These methods cannot be used while the horse is exercising so a heart rate monitor is used. As the horse becomes fitter the heart rate will be slower at a given running pace and will recover to the pre-exercise level in a shorter time.

After strenuous exercise there should be a period that allows the horse to stretch and relax. The horse should not show signs of dehydration, fatigue, exhaustion or exertional myopathies

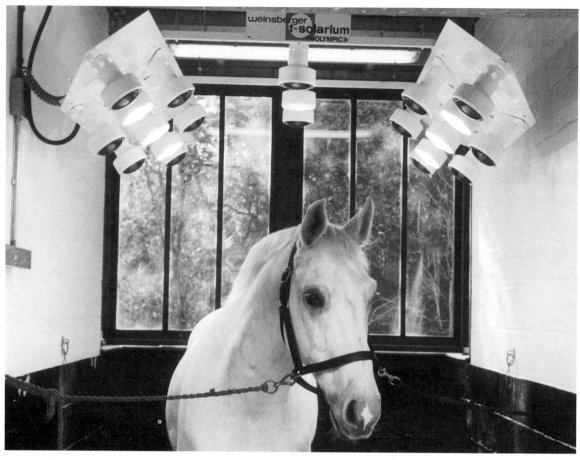

In a solarium

(tying-up). The capillary refill test and the skin pinch test, TPR and the presence of gut sounds can all be monitored.

Signs of heat stress/exhaustion/dehydration syndrome:

Reluctance to move, inco-ordination, muscle weakness and cramps
Rectal temperature over 40°C
Colic
Unwillingness to eat or drink
Sunken eyes
Depression
Rapid respiration
Pulse over 70 beats per minute
Diaphragmatic flutter (thumps)

These are all serious signs that urgent veterinary attention is needed.

Research undertaken before the Olympic games in Atlanta has shown how to cool a horse efficiently after exercising in a hot climate. The horse's normal rectal temperature at rest is 37° to 38°C (98.6° to 100.4°F). You should know your own horse's temperature. In the resting animal under moderate climatic conditions, heat is lost from the body by radiation and convection. Muscle activity during exercise produces a lot of heat which has to be removed to prevent the animal overheating. This heat is normally lost by radiation, convection and the evaporation of sweat. About 15% of heat is lost through breathing, hence the increased respiratory rate after exercise. When horses exercise in hot conditions the heat loss by radiation and convection is reduced. High humidity prevents sweat evaporating, so reducing heat loss. Excessive sweating leads to dehydration and salt imbalances. Travelling long distances can cause dehydration

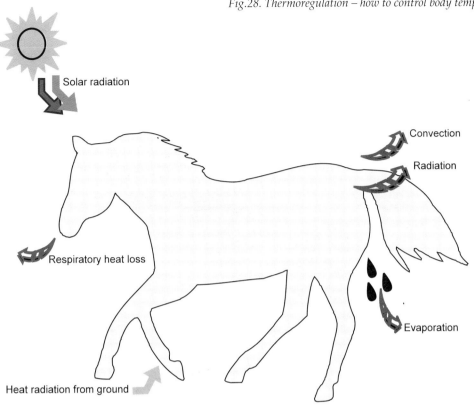

Fig.28. Thermoregulation – how to control body temperature.

Solar radiation

Convection

Radiation

Respiratory heat loss

Evaporation

Heat radiation from ground

A heart-rate monitor

so the horse may be dehydrated before exercise commences. Horses should have access to water up to 15 minutes before exercise and have hay with a hard feed at least four hours before strenuous work.

Any animal that is hot and working in a hot environment will benefit from cold water cooling. There is no evidence that cold water cooling causes tying-up.

During hot conditions you should be prepared to cool your horse and have the necessary equipment. You will need:

40 to 50 lit of ice cold water
several small buckets and large sponges
a rectal thermometer
three assistants

One person holds the horse and the other two stand either side to commence pouring cold water on all parts of the body including the hindquarters.

Horse dressed for travel (C. L. Hocking)

The tack can be left on and the temperature taken while cooling has started. Apply cold water for 30 seconds and then walk the horse for 30 seconds and then cool again, the walking between cooling is necessary as it aids evaporation and improves skin blood flow. Try to do this procedure in the shade. The horse can be offered small amounts of water to drink. The rectal temperature should decrease by 1°C every 10 minutes. When the rectal temperature reaches 38° to 39°C, the respiratory rate is less than 30 per minute, and the skin over the quarters feels cool after walking, the cooling process can stop.

There has been an increase in all types of competitions, long pleasure rides and endurance riding during the summer months so heat stress in horses is becoming more common. It is important that owners recognise this problem can occur and make every effort to avoid it. Horses and ponies that are overweight will heat up more quickly than those with less insulating fat under the skin.

PART TWO

COMMON AILMENTS

THE RESPIRATORY SYSTEM

Anatomy

The respiratory tract begins at the nostrils and ends at the alveoli (air sacs) where gaseous exchange occurs. The inspired air passes along the nasal chambers, the pharynx and larynx into the trachea. The hairs on the nostrils trap dust and dirt and prevent large particles from entering the tract. The air is also warmed and moistened as it passes over the highly vascular epithelial lining of the nasal chambers. The trachea is easy to palpate on the lower side of the neck, it is held open by a series of incomplete cartilaginous rings and is lined by a membrane which has fine hair-like projections (cilia) and mucus producing cells. Inhaled particles stick to the mucus which is propelled to the pharynx by the cilia. Obviously in the grazing animal this is also aided by gravity as the head is low. Conversely when the horse is tied with its head held up for long periods of time this reduces the clearance rate of mucus. There are also groups of lymphoid cells scattered throughout the airways. These cells maintain the lungs' defence mechanism to infectious diseases. The trachea divides into the two main bronchi inside the chest at the level of the fifth rib above the heart. The right lung is larger than the left as the heart is situated on the

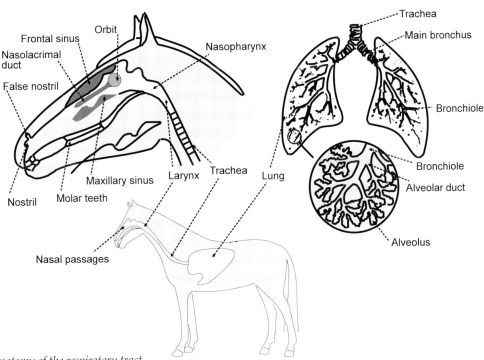

Fig.29. Anatomy of the respiratory tract.

left side of the chest. Each bronchus further divides into progressively smaller branches, the bronchioles, which end at the thin walled alveoli. The alveoli contain cells called macrophages which mop up tiny particles that reach the air sacs, e.g. bacteria and dust. The alveoli are surrounded by a dense network of capillaries. The oxygen in the inhaled air diffuses from the air sacs into the blood stream and is carried mainly in the red blood cells to all tissues of the body. Carbon dioxide diffuses out of the capillaries into the air sacs and is exhaled.

The muscular diaphragm separates the chest from the abdominal cavity. During inspiration the muscles of the diaphragm and those between the ribs (intercostal muscles) contract, causing the chest to expand. Air is drawn into the lungs. When the muscles relax, air is expelled from the lungs and the abdominal muscles assist in pushing air from the lungs. In the healthy resting horse movement of the nostrils, chest wall and abdomen are slight. The respiratory centre in the brain controls the frequency of breathing via the peripheral nerves to the respiratory muscles. The nerve receptors in the blood vessels and the respiratory tract respond to chemical changes. The normal resting rate is 8 to 16 per minute depending on the age and size of animal. At rest the average 500 kg horse takes in 5 lit of air and breathes 12 times per minute.

Management and disease

Respiratory disease is common in equines. The incidence of disease and the type of recovery is greatly influenced by the horse's management system.

Stables should be positioned so that full benefit can be gained from sunlight, making use of windows and skylights where possible to allow sunlight into the building. Ultra-violet light kills many bacteria, viruses and parasites. Stables should be well ventilated without being draughty. Even in well ventilated buildings horses may inhale small fungal spores from contaminated bedding and feed.

The bedding material should be clean and dust free. Straw, however clean, contains more fungal spores than shavings, paper and synthetic bedding material. Deep litter beds should be avoided as mould can easily form and a build-up of bacteria and parasitic larvae will develop. Ammonia in bedding is an irritant to the respiratory tract.

Poorly insulated buildings, especially those with a metal roof can cause condensation and raise humidity. Condensation is also a sign of poor ventilation.

Muck heaps should be positioned well away from stables. Decomposing plant material is a source of mould spores which are easily inhaled. Flies and vermin are attracted to these areas and can spread infections.

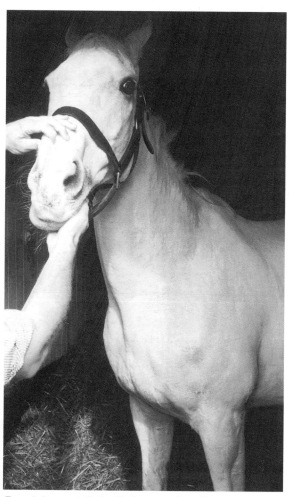

Examining nostrils for discharge and smell

Only good quality, clean forage should be used. Musty or dusty hay will contain millions of spores and is unsuitable for use. Hay barns should be positioned carefully. It is not advisable to store hay in lofts over stables as it is a fire hazard.

Horses need shelter at pasture from driving wind and rain and, depending on climatic conditions, may also need rugs. Animals that are on a poor plane of nutrition or are suffering from other debilitating diseases are more susceptible to respiratory infections. Young animals may have no immunity to certain diseases and are more sensitive to cold. Stress due to overcrowding, hard training and travelling long distances may increase the incidence of disease. The owner can reduce the likelihood of disease by using a high level of care and avoiding conditions that cause poor air quality and contamination of the horse's environment by mould spores.

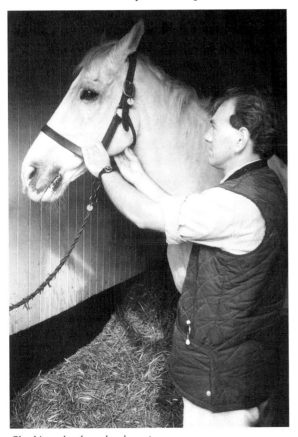

Checking glands and pulse rate

Respiratory disease may affect the upper or lower respiratory tract and be caused by infectious or non-infectious agents. Infections may be viral, bacterial, fungal or parasitic. Allergies, anatomical problems and injuries also cause disease.

Signs of disease

The owner usually notices that the horse's respiratory pattern and rate has altered. There may be exercise intolerance, i.e. unexpected tiredness. There may be a fever, swollen glands, nasal discharge and coughing.

Veterinary assistance is needed if any of the above signs of disease are noticed.

The vet will take a full history of the horse and all the management details before doing a thorough examination. The owner can provide the following information:

Number of animals affected
Age and breed
Stable management
Diet, bedding and grazing routine
Appetite and thirst
Worming and vaccinational history
Exercise routine
Contacts with other equines, e.g. at shows or sales
Duration and signs of illness
Weight loss

The clinical examination will include:

Taking the rectal temperature, pulse and respiratory rate
Observing the depth and type of breathing
Listening to the respiratory tract with a stethoscope
Observing the amount and type of nasal discharge
Palpating the lymph nodes in the throat
The frequency and type of cough e.g., dry or moist, will be noted
Endoscopy of the upper respiratory tract to detect abnormalities.

In order to determine the cause and give the correct medication and an accurate prognosis the vet may need to take samples for laboratory examination.

Blood samples are taken for haematology, to determine the number and types of blood cells

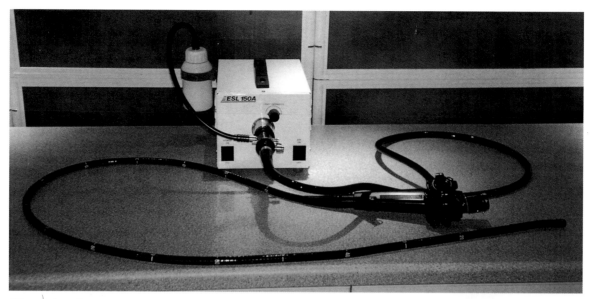

Fibre-optic endoscope

present, and biochemistry and serology to show tissue damage and the presence of antibodies to infectious agents.

Nasal and pharangeal swabs are used to detect and grow organisms on culture plates. Tracheal washes and bronchial/alveolar washes are obtained using an endoscope with a sterile catheter to flush and collect samples. These samples are examined for white blood cells associated with infections and bacteria, fungi and parasites. Faecal samples are used to detect parasites and their eggs. Further techniques involve radiography, diagnostic ultrasound and thermal imaging. .

Viral disease

Many owners refer to any horse showing signs of respiratory disease as having 'the virus' or 'the cough'. In fact many viruses are responsible for these infections, either singly or in combination, e.g.

Equine influenza

This is a highly infectious disease of all equines and is caused by several strains of influenza virus. Both the upper and lower tract are affected and the heart and liver may be inflamed. The incubation period is short, only one to three days so infection can spread rapidly through a susceptible group of animals. Infected animals shed virus for six days. The virus is spread by contact with infected discharges and inhaling droplets propelled into the air by coughing.

The virus causes the following clinical signs:

Depression due to high fever (39° to 40°C [103° to 106°F])
Watery nasal discharge which may become purulent (thick and yellow)
A severe dry harsh cough
Conjunctivitis
Painful glands
Loss of appetite

Secondary bacterial infections of the nose, throat and lungs may complicate the recovery. Chronic obstructive pulmonary disease (COPD), an allergy to fungal spores, may follow a viral infection. The inflamed tissues may be hyper-sensitive to inhaled particles during the course of viral disease which leads to COPD in later life. (See page 55.) The vet should attend any coughing or feverish horse. Clinical signs, nasopharyngeal swabs to isolate the virus and serology to detect antibody levels will confirm a diagnosis.

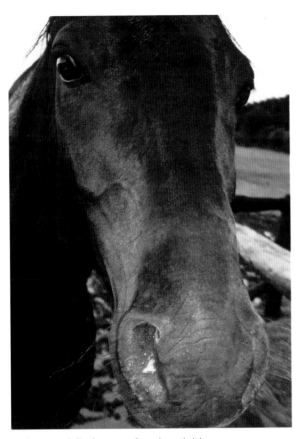

White nasal discharge and conjunctivitis

Treatment involves medication, good nursing and hygiene.

MEDICATION
1 Antibiotics are used to treat secondary bacterial infection.
2 Antipyretics will reduce the fever and improve the appetite.
3 Mucolytics reduce the viscosity of the secretions.
4 Bronchodilators open up the airways and reduce muscle spasm in the walls

NURSING
See page 137.

HYGIENE AND MANAGEMENT
All affected and in contact animals should be isolated and closely monitored.

The horse must stop work and have complete rest for at least a month after all clinical signs have disappeared.

A fresh air regime is important. The horse must be kept in a well ventilated box with minimal access to dust and fungal spores.

PREVENTION
Avoid contact with infected animals and premises with known infections.

Good hygiene and management, i.e. clean stables, bedding and feed. Avoid using other animals' tack and equipment and have individual feeding and watering utensils.

Isolate new horses and those that have travelled long distances or returned from events coughing.

Avoid sharing transport with horses of unknown disease status

Follow a vaccination programme to give the best possible level of immunity to all equines on each premises. (See page 12.)

Equine Herpes Virus 1

There are two forms of this virus; sub-type one EHV 1 and sub-type two also called EHV 4.

EHV 1 can cause abortion in mares, paralysis, respiratory disease and serious disease in new born foals.

EHV 4 mainly causes respiratory disease in young horses. Infection is spread by inhaling virus coughed out from infected animals or from symptomless carriers or from aborted material.

Respiratory signs include:

Upper tract infection
Coughing more common in young animals
Nasal discharge rapidly becoming purulent and may last for three weeks
Fever
Enlarged lymph nodes
Depression and loss of appetite

Diagnosis and treatment of the respiratory forms of the disease are as discussed for equine influenza.

Blood and tissues from aborted or dead foals can be cultured for virus. Horses showing incoordination, dribbling urine or paralysis will need intensive care if they are to recover.

Avoid stress in carrier animals.

All aborting mares and foal deaths must be investigated.

All movement of animals on/off the premises must stop until a diagnosis is made. Presume all in-contact animals are infected.

PREVENTION
Isolation of infected animals and disinfection of the contaminated area.

VACCINATION
See page 12.

Equine Viral Arteritis

This disease was first seen in the U.K. in 1993 and was traced to an imported stallion from Poland. Mares were infected via semen and developed a respiratory disease. EVA infection is spread by contact with any of the body secretions, e.g. urine, faeces, nasal discharge, saliva and milk and aborted foetuses/foetal membranes. Following infection the virus is excreted in all body fluids for up to a month. Stallions may become carriers and shed virus for years in their semen.

The virus can cause:

Fever for many days
Discharge from eyes and nose
Inflamed conjunctiva 'pink eye'
Depression
Swollen legs, head and genitalia
Skin plaques and rashes
Diarrhoea
Coughing
Abortion in mares
Disease in new born foals

There is a Common Code of Practice covering this disease and the importation of horses into the U.K.

Quarantine and blood samples are necessary from horses arriving from EVA infected countries. Horses are blood tested prior to vaccination to see if they have already been infected. Stallions that are free from EVA are vaccinated to prevent them becoming infected and being viral shedders. All suspect cases need veterinary investigation and strict isolation as with EHV 1 abortions.

Bacterial disease

Strangles (Streptococcus equi)

Strangles is a common, highly infectious and contagious disease of all equines, it can occur in any age group but may be more serious in the young, debilitated and elderly animal. Animals develop some immunity after recovery from the disease but many become symptomless carriers and intermittently excrete the bacteria for months. The animal's environment becomes contaminated and handlers can easily spread the infection on hands, clothing and utensils. The incubation period is three to ten days. The clinical signs are those of an upper respiratory tract disease with abscess formation in the lymph nodes and a profuse nasal discharge.

The early signs include:

High fever with depression
Loss of appetite (anorexia) and reluctance to swallow
Watery discharge from nose and eyes
Soft moist cough due to pharyngitis
Slightly swollen glands

Within a few days the signs become more obvious:

Thick copious yellow nasal discharge
Large, painful glands that eventually burst to discharge pus
Difficulty in breathing as the airway is obstructed, often the head and neck are outstretched
Coughing becomes more frequent
Fever persists
Loss of weight

Early treatment is necessary with good nursing care and strict hygiene is needed to avoid spread of infection. Isolation procedures should be carefully followed according to veterinary advice. In contact animals should be closely watched for early signs and their temperatures monitored twice daily.

There may be complications due to abscess formation in lymphoid tissue of internal organs 'bastard strangles'.

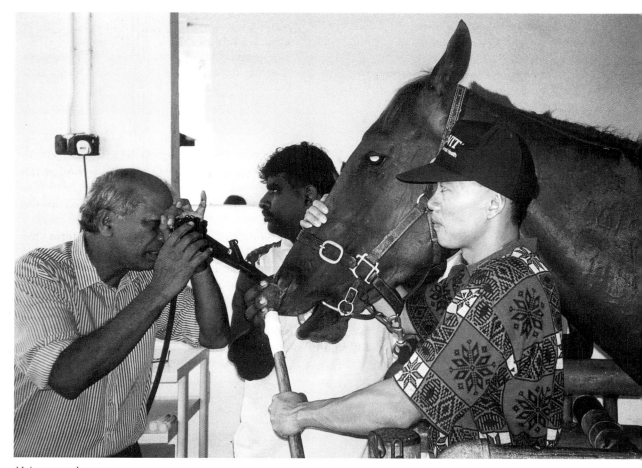

Using an endoscope

Purpura Haemorrhagica can occur one to three weeks after the horse has apparently recovered from strangles. This is an allergic reaction to the bacterial antigens in which the blood vessels are damaged and there is oedema of the limbs, head and ventral body wall. Haemorrhages occur and serum oozes from the skin weals. Intensive nursing and treatment gives only a 50% recovery rate from these complications.

Other bacteria may be involved, both primary and secondary to virus disease of the respiratory tract. They can cause bronchitis, pneumonia and pleurisy. They include: Streptococcus zooepidemicus, Streptococcus pneumoniae, Rhodococcus equi, Bordetella bronchiseptica, Klebsiella sp., Salmonella sp., Pseudomonas sp., E. coli., Pasteurella sp. and various Mycoplasma organisms.

Parasitic disease

Lungworm and roundworm infestation can cause coughing in equines. The diagnosis and treatment is described in Part one, page 17. Animals on the correct management and worming programme should not suffer from these parasite infestations.

Allergic disease

Chronic Obstructive Pulmonary Disease (COPD)

This is a small airway disease of domesticated equines. This allergic disease is also known as emphysema, 'heaves' and 'broken wind'. It may be seen after a viral or bacterial infection and is associated with a hypersensitivity to inhaled airborne dust and fungal spores. The presence of ammonia from urine in stables also damages the airways. Some fungal spores are small enough to avoid being filtered out in the upper airways and reach the small airways where they cause inflammation, excessive mucus production and smooth muscle spasm of the small airway walls. The affected animals show marked respiratory signs at rest; these include a chronic cough, flared nostrils, forced abdominal breathing, increased respiratory rate and depth and some nasal discharge. Advanced or severe cases will be unable to work and show weight loss; milder cases will show variable degrees of exercise intolerance and respiratory distress if worked. The condition is more likely to develop in animals that are not completely rested and allowed to convalesce after an infection. It takes a month for the cilia lining the airways to recover following equine influenza. Animals with a respiratory infection take longer to recover in a dusty environment than in a fresh air regime. Veterinary examina-

tion, early management and treatment may control COPD cases before they become severe. Diagnosis is made on the clinical signs, response to a dust-free environment and therapeutic treatment, endoscopy and examination of tracheal/bronchial washes.

DUST-FREE ENVIRONMENT

This means keeping the horse away from the allergens. If possible the animal should be out at pasture with access to a field shelter. If stabling is necessary, the design and ventilation may need improvement. The main sources of mould spores in the stable are from feed and bedding. The horse should be bedded on shavings, paper or rubber matting. Beds must be cleaned daily and the horse should be removed from the stable area at mucking out time. The stable must be a good distance from the muck heap and straw bedding should not be used in neighbouring stables.

COPD cases should be transported in clean

Using a nebuliser and face mask (C. L. Hocking)

vehicles with no access to hay and straw and should be frequently untied to allow postural drainage of mucus.

Hay of good quality may be fed as long as it is soaked in clean water for up to 30 minutes, drained and fed damp in a container at ground level. Any wet hay landing on the bedding can dry out and the spores will seed the clean bed. The horse will inhale these if it lies down or sniffs the bed. If the hay is allowed to dry out before it is eaten the spores will become airborne again and may be inhaled. Soaking the hay swells the spores and sticks them to the hay. It is important that fresh water is used, otherwise it may ferment. It is not advisable to soak the hay for longer than 30 minutes as this will greatly reduce the nutritional value and turn the soak water into a potent, sewage-like liquid.

There are many alternative forms of forage to hay available for animals with COPD. Haylage; preserved, baled, semi-wilted grasses; treated chaffed hay and straw; complete cubed diets and grass nuts.

Various pharmacological agents are used to alleviate the symptoms of COPD:

1 Mucolytics breakdown secretions and thick mucus blocking airways
2 Bronchodilators open airways, stop broncho-spasm and stimulate mucociary clearance
3 Antibiotics are required to remove bacterial agents
4 Anti inflammatory agents to reduce acute inflammation
5 Nebulisation with desensitising agents

Nebulisers have been used regularly in humans with asthma and are now used to treat and prevent respiratory disease in horses. The medication is converted into an aerosol of fine droplets which are inhaled using a face mask.

Summer pasture associated obstructive pulmonary disease (SPAOPD)

This condition is seen in horses at pasture without exposure to hay and straw. They show the same clinical signs as COPD cases. They are allergic to a variety of plant pollens and if possible they should be moved to a new location away from blossom and pollen. A fresh air regime and medication to alleviate the symptoms is needed.

Conformation, anatomical problems

Respiratory distress (dyspnoea), exercise intolerance, abnormal respiratory noise during exercise, and difficulty in swallowing and inhalation pneumonia may occur due to abnormalities in the anatomy of the respiratory tract.

Common problems are conditions of the pharynx and larynx, which are diagnosed by endoscopy, e.g.

1 Foals are occasionally born with cleft palates, which require surgical intervention
2 ILH (idiopathic laryngeal hemiplegia). Horses with paralysis of the left vocal chord make a roaring or whistling inspiratory noise at canter or gallop. This condition is normally treated surgically
3 DDSP (dorsal displacement of soft palate). This condition occurs when the soft palate moves over the epiglottis and interferes with airflow during fast work. Gurgling sounds are heard
4 Epiglottic cysts may also cause displacement of the soft palate and the epiglottis.
   Epiglottic entrapment may occur if there is a large fold of mucosal membrane over the epiglottis

Injuries

Accidental injuries may involve and damage any area of the respiratory tract and cause dyspnoea. These injuries are potentially life threatening and require urgent veterinary assistance. Puncture wounds may cause air to leak under the skin or the collapse of a lung. Foreign bodies occasionally block airways and have to be surgically removed. Horses may also suffer from smoke inhalation after stable fires.

THE DIGESTIVE SYSTEM

Anatomy

The digestive tract starts at the mouth and ends at the anus. Horses select their food with their lips, bite off lengths with the incisor teeth and grind it into small 1 mm to 2 mm particles with the cheek teeth (mastication). Dental disease will affect this process.

Saliva is produced when the horse chews and this lubricates the food. It contains bicarbonate ions that buffer the food when it passes into the stomach.

The food bolus, once it is in a suitable form, is moved to the back of the mouth, swallowed and propelled down the muscular oesophagus and into the stomach by waves of peristalsis. This takes 10 to 12 seconds. The oesophagus can be located on the left side of the horse's neck immediately above the trachea in the jugular groove. Inadequately lubricated food can block the oesophagus (see *Choke, page 60*).

The stomach lies in the abdomen against the diaphragm and within the ribcage. The stomach can only hold a small amount, about 2½ kg of food (10 lit). Horses cannot vomit and dilation of the stomach can lead to rupture. The food is mixed with the acidic gastric juices and some protein is broken down. Bacterial fermentation begins in the stomach and the food is physically broken down. The food enters the small intestine and is mixed with the bile and pancreatic juice. The enzymes convert the protein to amino acids and the fats to fatty acids. Some carbohydrates (starch) are converted to simple sugars. Small nutrient molecules are absorbed through the gut wall into the bloodstream. The small intestine is about 21 metres long and food takes less than an hour to pass along it as the smooth muscle walls contract (peristalsis). The digestion of all but insoluble fibre is completed here. Undigested food, mainly fibre enters the large intestine at the ileocaecal junction which is the site where tapeworms attach. The caecum is a large pear-shaped organ on the right side of the abdomen, it is a large fermentation vat containing millions of micro-organisms which break down insoluble

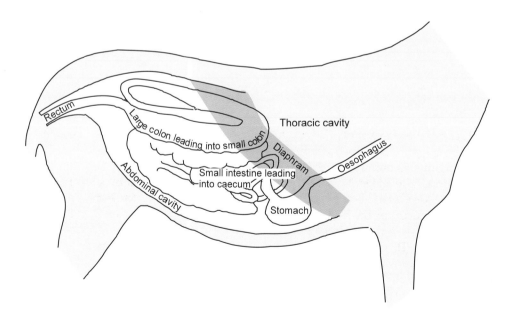

Fig.30. The digestive tract.

Fig.31. The length and capacity of the digestive tract.

Organ	Average length		Average capacity	
	Metric	Imperial	Metric	Imperial
Stomach			10 lts	3 gals
Duodenum	1 metre	3 ft		
Jejunum	20 m	65 ft		
Ileum	1.5 m	4.5 ft		
Caecum	70 cm	2.5 ft	30 lts	7 gals
Large colon	3 - 5 m	12ft	100 lts	22 gals
Small colon	3 - 5 m	12 ft	55 lts	12 gals

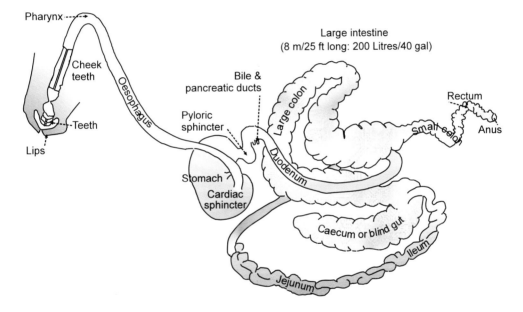

fibre to produce volatile fatty acids (VFAs), and continue the digestion of protein, carbohydrate and fat. These organisms manufacture the B vitamins and vitamin K. The fermentation of fibre is thermogenic, i.e. produces heat, and VFAs provide an energy source for the horse. The caecum opens into the large looped colon where fermentation continues. The food material may remain in the large intestine for two to three days. Water is extracted as the food contents pass along the large bowel. Any dysfunction of the colon, e.g. colitis, will result in diarrhoea. Undigested contents, mainly lignin and waste products, pass into the rectum and are voided as faeces through the anus. Abnormal faeces indicate a bowel disorder.

If the stable bacterial population of the large intestine is disturbed by sudden changes in diet or dietary excesses the horse may develop colic, diarrhoea, azoturia, excitability or laminitis. These are common consequences of overloading the gut with soluble carbohydrates, e.g. spring grass or grain/cereal feed, which pass undigested from the small intestine into the large intestine, where rapid fermentation produces lactic acid.

The friendly bacteria may die due to the alteration in pH of the gut contents. They then release endotoxins that further damage the gut wall, enter the bloodstream, and the resulting tox-aemia can kill the horse.

Disorders of the digestive tract

Mouth

Dental disease and the need for regular dental care is discussed in part one, page 22.

Injuries to the incisors, lips and tongue will affect prehension (intake of food). Dysphagia, the inability to eat or swallow may be caused by sharp teeth, mouth ulcers, arthritis of the tem-poromandibular joint, soft palate abnormalities and paralysis of tongue or pharynx. Neurological conditions which affect swallowing include tetanus, botulism, lead poisoning and grass sickness.

Oesophageal obstruction (Choke)

Choke refers to a blockage in the gullet usually caused by food. This can happen if dry food is bolted, not chewed thoroughly and not lubricat-ed by saliva. Hungry or greedy animals are more likely to bolt their food. Accidentally feeding unsoaked sugar beet cubes is a common cause of choke. Occasionally large pieces of carrots and apples may lodge in the gullet or there may be a narrowing of the oesophagus due to scar tissue or an abscess or tumour. Any reduction in diameter of the oesophagus may predispose to blockage by dry or inadequately chewed food. Obstructions may cause necrosis of the mucosal lining if left for a prolonged time, e.g. 48 hours. This may heal with excessive scar-ring and narrowing (stricture) of the oesopha-gus.

Signs of choke are:

Usually a sudden onset after starting a feed
Saliva and food material will drool from the mouth
 and nostrils
The neck will be alternately extended and arched
The horse may cough and grunt
Dysphagia
Nasal regurgitation of food
Possible inhalation of food and saliva will cause an
 aspiration pneumonia

Cervical oesophageal obstructions can be seen and palpated over the left jugular groove

All food and water should be removed from the stable and the horse observed for a few minutes. Many cases clear up without veterinary help within 10 minutes.

Animals that do not self cure or are distressed should have veterinary treatment. In the mean-time, provide an inedible bed or stay with the horse, prevent it from eating its bed and do not offer any food.

Veterinary treatment includes: sedation, pain relief and muscle relaxation of the oesophageal wall; passing a stomach tube to locate and move

Passing a stomach tube

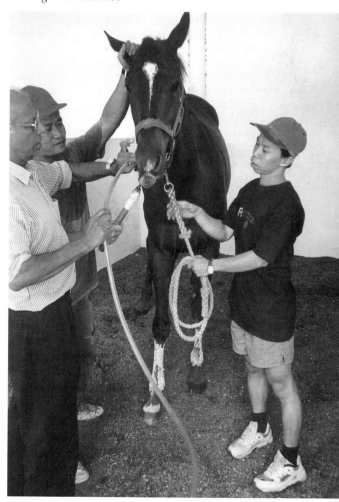

the obstruction by water irrigation down the tube; endoscopy to detect any damage or abnormality.

Most cases recover with conservative treatment within 24 hours but sometimes the obstruction is so firmly impacted that the horse may need to be anaesthetised. The vet will advise on the aftercare.

Obviously after the obstruction has been removed the horse must not be given its usual diet for several days. Grass and small soaked feeds and water may be offered. Wet hay can be introduced after a couple of days if no grazing is available.

It is important to prevent the condition recurring and this may involve changes in management, for example:

Avoid dry cubed feeds
Always offer hay before feeding concentrates
Do not allow animals access to food while they are heavily sedated or recovering from sedation
Avoid peer pressure at feeding times, by feeding separately
Routine dental maintenance

Colic

In the equine world colic simply means abdominal pain. Colic has many different causes and is classified in a variety of ways. Most colics respond to medical treatment but about 10% require prompt surgical intervention if they are

Sugar-beet shreds should be soaked in a jug. Apples and carrots should be chopped into small pieces

to survive. The signs of colic exhibited by the horse depend on the severity of the pain.

Signs of colic are:

Curling upper lip
Flank watching
Restless behaviour as pain increases
Digging and pawing the ground
Repeatedly lying down and rolling
Lying on back
Lying down for long periods
Backing into a corner
Grinding teeth
Sweating
Kicking at abdomen
Straddled position as if to urinate and straining
Anorexia
Alteration in faeces, e.g. constipation or diarrhoea
Flatulence
Elevated pulse and respiratory rate

CAUSES OF COLIC

Parasites
Large redworm, small redworm and tapeworm are all responsible for causing spasmodic colics. They damage the gut mucosa and affect gut motility. Large adult roundworms can block the intestines, especially after worming. Parasite infestation is easy to control by good pasture hygiene and correct use of worming drugs, see page 15.

Environmental factors
Lack of water or inadequate water intake can cause impacted colic as the horse becomes dehydrated. This is exacerbated by hot weather and strenuous exercise and is preventable by allowing free access to water at all times.
Horses grazing on sandy pastures may ingest sand which irritates the gut.
The horse may also eat large amounts of bedding resulting in an impacted colic. This may be avoided by using inedible bedding and providing good quality forage.
Poisonous weeds are usually eaten when grass is in short supply and may cause colic. All poisonous plants should be removed from horse pasture and hay provided there is insufficient grass.

Feeding
High concentrate diets, insufficient forage and sudden changes in diet all have a detrimental effect on the normal bacterial flora of the intestine. Poor quality, spoilt and inappropriate feed such as that intended for sheep, pigs or cattle can cause intestinal upsets. Poor feeding practices such as irregular or over-large meals should be avoided.

Ulcers
Gastric ulceration may cause colicky pain. Ulcers are also associated with colic involving other

Ragwort – a poisonous plant (C. L. Hocking)

parts of the tract. There may be an association between gastric ulcers and intestinal problems.

Enteritis

Infections caused by salmonellosis, intestinal clostridiosis and coccidiosis cause enteritis and colitis. The inflamed gut is painful and the animal will show signs of colic.

Tumours

Tumours of the intestine are not common. They may occasionally cause surgical colics. They are seen in the older equine.

Dental disease

Impactions are common in animals with poor dentition. Regular dental care is important.

Drugs

Several drugs cause bowel dysfunction. Some anti-inflammatory drugs cause gastrointestinal ulceration if used for long periods at high dose rates.

Some sedatives/painkillers used prior to surgery reduce gut motility and in horses that have been starved or are anorexic these may also contribute to post-operative intestinal problems.

Antibiotic therapy, especially the tetracyclines are associated with colitis and diarrhoea as they disturb the gut flora. Horses on oral antibiotics are often given probiotics to help reseed the gut.

Chemical toxins may be inadvertently eaten and cause colic, e.g. arsenic, organophosphorus compounds, monensin.

Other abdominal but non-intestinal causes of colic do occur. The liver, kidneys and reproductive organs are also located inside the abdomen and may be the source of pain. A foaling mare may show colic signs.

Horses with chest pain, e.g. pleuritis, or muscle pain, e.g. azoturia, or acute lameness e.g. laminitis may exhibit some colic-like signs. Frequently the cause of colic is not positively identified or diagnosed but the case responds to symptomatic medical treatment. In surgical cases the reason for a twisted gut is not always obvious.

All cases of colic should be examined by an equine vet. This examination will include:

Taking a detailed case history
Temperature, pulse and respiratory rate
Listening for gut activity
Capillary refill and skin pinch tests
Examination of mucous membranes
Rectal examination

Passing a stomach tube, blood samples and samples of peritoneal fluid may also be required.

Ultrasound may be used, e.g. to detect tumours and X-rays also aid diagnosis, especially in smaller animals including foals.

Colics can be grouped into medical or surgical colics. Medical colics are amenable to medical treatment. After a thorough examination of the horse, the vet will select the appropriate medication for that animal. Treatment is tailored to each case. Types of medical colic are:

Spasmodic colic
This is the commonest form of colic, about 70% are in this group. The normal regular peristalsis is disrupted. The movement becomes irregular and violent. Parasites and feeding problems are often the underlying cause.

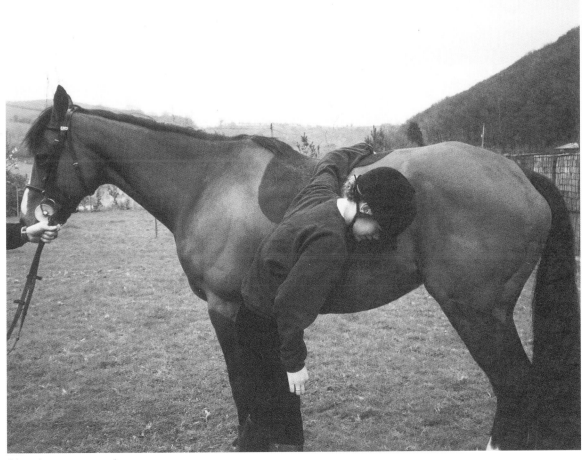

Listening to gut sounds

The horse shows pain relating to gut spasms interspersed with normal behaviour.

These cases respond to antispasmodic medicines and analgesia (pain relief)

Tympanitic/flatulent colic

This is caused by gas distending the gut due to over fermentation of unsuitable food, usually grass cuttings, fruit or clover. This problem may resolve untreated or the gut may need to be decompressed. Analgesia is often required together with anti-fermentative drugs. Gas-filled portions of gut may float out of their normal position.

Impactions of the large intestine

This is usually caused by dry and coarse food material completely or partially blocking the gut lumen. Affected animals usually have a history of dental problems, water shortage, unsuitable diet and irregular exercise. The common sites this occurs in are those where there is a sudden reduction in diameter of the gut, such as at the pelvic flexure of the left colon and at the junction of the large and small colon.

This usually is treated with fluids and lubricants given by stomach tube. Colic drinks/drenches should not be used on equines. Large volumes of fluid can only be given safely by stomach tube. The ingredients in colic drenches are not suitable for all types of colic and may be harmful.

Gastric and small intestinal impactions require prompt surgery.

Surgical colic

These are either simple cases where the bowel is obstructed without compromising the blood supply or complex ones where the bowel is twisted or strangulated and the blood supply is cut off. In the first condition the displaced bowel has to be returned to its normal position. The horse will be in pain and shocked but not suffering from toxaemia. When the blood supply has been obstructed the section of dead bowel is resected and the healthy tissue on either side joined up. These animals rapidly develop endotoxic shock as the dead bowel wall leaks its contents into the peritoneum.

Colic surgery

This is a specialised procedure and is performed in an equine operating theatre by a team of surgeons, nurses and an anaesthetist. The horse will require specialised post-operative nursing with careful monitoring and fluid therapy.

If the equine hospital is a long distance away or the animal is unlikely to survive the journey or the case is inoperable the only alternative is humane euthanasia. It is wise to insure all equines for veterinary fees as colic surgery is expensive. Horses that receive prompt veterinary attention,

an early diagnosis and specialist care are likely to make a good recovery from surgery. Some surgical teams hope for a 70 to 80% success rate and full return to athletic work.

What the owner can do while waiting for the vet to arrive

It is important that no one is injured, so great care must be taken in handling a horse that is in pain. Animals that are lying quietly should be observed from a distance. Buckets and mangers should be removed in case the horse rolls. It is safer to leave animals that are rolling violently in a flat field or menage, rather than in a stable where they may injure themselves. Traditionally all colic cases were prevented from rolling as this was thought to twist the guts but it is now accepted that normal horses roll without such a mishap. Horses may injure their head or limbs or may become cast when rolling repeatedly. Colicky animals used to be force walked for hours, this is harmful as it tires the animal who may actually be more comfortable lying down.

Animals with colic should not be offered food or water before they have been assessed by the vet. Colic drenches should not be given.

The owner could monitor pulse and respiratory rate, gut sounds, the passing of urine/faeces, flatulence, colour of mucous membranes and capillary refill at regular intervals, if the horse is calm. This information will be useful for the vet.

Movement of other horses and people should be kept to a minimum as this may disturb the patient.

Grass sickness

Grass sickness or equine dysautonomia has killed hundreds of equines since 1909 when it was first described. The causal agent has not been isolated despite extensive scientific research, but a fungal toxin is thought to be the possible agent. In this condition the digestive tract is paralysed as the autonomic nerve supply degenerates.

Grass sickness can affect any breed of horse, pony or donkey. It occurs in mares, geldings and stallions. Animals in the two to seven year age range are more commonly affected.

The disease is most frequently seen between April and July and often follows a week or more of cool and dry weather.

Most cases occur in grazing animals. Frequently the animal has grazed on the same pasture for less than two months. Certain fields are known to have a high incidence of grass sickness cases. Stress, surgery, travel and mixing with new animals on a new premises may be predisposing factors to this disease. These are common factors in the clinical history notes.

Depending on the degree of gut paralysis, grass sickness may be an acute, a sub-acute or a chronic disease.

Acute cases have a high pulse rate, sweat, muscle tremors and severe colic with a distended abdomen. They salivate and often stomach contents reflux down their nostrils. They are constipated and pass small amounts of hard faecal pellets. They die within two days so these cases should be euthanased as soon as possible.

Sub-acute cases survive for two to seven days. They have a mild to moderate colic with patchy sweating, muscle tremors, dysphagia and obvious weight loss. Those that do not die progress to the chronic stage.

Chronic grass sickness cases have varying difficulty in swallowing both food and water. They chew slowly and pouch food in the mouth, often quidding. They 'fake' drinking, playing with water, so froth is seen on the water and over buckets and the surrounding area. They have mild episodes of colic.

The nostrils become dry and crusty and the eye lids droop. These animals are depressed, have a poor appetite and rapid weight loss. They look 'tucked up' with a greyhound shape to their abdomen.

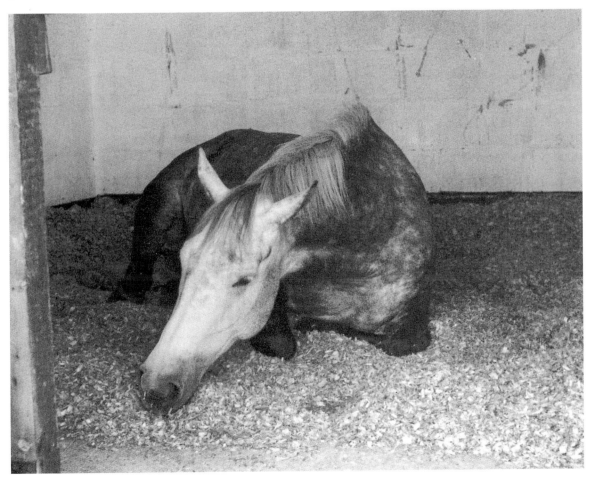

A colicky horse lying down (C. L. Hocking)

The diagnosis is difficult as other causes of colic appear clinically similar. Thorough examination and specific blood tests are needed to make a diagnosis.

Histological examination of gut biopsy samples taken from the ileum (area of small intestine) is a reliable confirmatory test. In grass sickness the damaged nerve cells are detected in strained microscopic sections using an electron microscope.

TREATMENT

A small number of chronic cases will respond to treatment. Careful screening and selection of cases is mandatory. Animals must be able to swallow soft food and drink and have enough body fat to survive for the first two to three weeks with a poor appetite. They should still have an interest in life. Animals that fill this criteria will then require intensive nursing by experienced staff. Recovery is slow in cases that respond to treatment. Cisaprid is used eight hourly to stimulate gut activity. Major setbacks like pneumonia, choke and colic episodes may occur at any time. Inhalation pneumonia is an early complication. About 50% of chronic cases recover but may still experience sweating and changes in their coat. Care in feeding is needed to prevent choke. These animals should be kept stress free and not over exercised. They can be ridden once they return to the correct body weight. See nursing pages 138–9.

PREVENTION

Until the causal agent is found it is not possible to prevent grass sickness. It is advisable not to graze animals on high risk pasture land. Avoid grazing after periods of dry cool weather, especially from April to July. Try to make moves to new premises stress free.

THE SKIN

Anatomy

The skin or integument is the largest organ of the body, covering the entire body surface. It varies in thickness from 1 to 6 mm. Areas liable to greater wear and tear have thicker skin. The condition of the skin and coat is a good indicator of the health, level of hydration and nutritional status of the horse (see skin pinch test and condition scoring pages 8, 118). The surface layer, the epidermis covers the deeper dermis which lies over the subcutaneous fascia, a loose connective tissue containing nerves and blood vessels. The skin has many important functions. It is a protective barrier to physical injury and infective agents and prevents water and salt loss. It relays information from the animal's environment by sensory nerve receptors that detect changes in temperature, pressure, touch and pain. It synthesises vitamin D when exposed to sunlight and acts as a storage organ for fat and water. It is part of the body's thermoregulatory system, e.g. secretion of sweat to lose heat; erection of hair to conserve heat. The pigment in skin protects the tissues from harmful sun rays. It produces specialised structures such as hoof horn, chestnuts, ergots and hair.

The epidermis has a hard, keratinised waterproof surface made up of tightly bonded cells which are constantly worn away to be replaced by the next layer of cells. The base layer of the epidermis produces new cells which take about two weeks to migrate to the surface. The epidermis also contains the pigment producing cells, the melanocytes.

The dermis consists of a protein matrix with elastin and collagen fibres to give strength and pliability to the skin. It has an intricate blood and nerve supply and also contains hair follicles, sweat and sebaceous glands. The hair follicles and sweat glands are formed by invaginations of the epidermis. Each hair follicle produces a single hair, which grows at an angle to the skin surface so the hair normally lies flat. Hair is continually falling out and being replaced by a new hair that goes through a growing stage followed

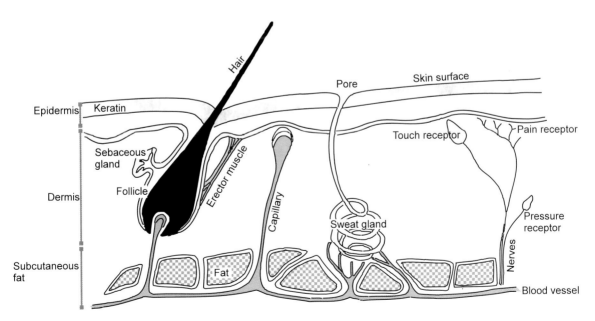

Fig.32. The structure of the skin.

by a resting stage. Hair protects the skin and provides insulation.

Whorls are a hair pattern created by follicles being at different angles. They are used on diagrams as part of the identification of the horse along with colour and non-pigmented hair, skin and hoof wall. Hair colour is inherited and genetically controlled. Acquired marks are areas of white hair resulting from skin damage, such as saddle sores, boot or bandage rubs and girth galls. Unpigmented skin is more susceptible to sunburn, and cream hooves are thought to be weaker than black hooves.

The shedding of the coat is under environmental and hormonal control in the spring and autumn, when the thick, winter coat is replaced by a fine, summer coat and vice versa. The mane and tail hairs are coarser, permanent hairs. There are long, tactile hairs around the muzzle and finer hairs on the teats and inside the ears. Eyelashes are specialised hairs.

The sebaceous gland secretes sebum onto the hair to make it pliable and acts as a waterproofing agent. Sebaceous glands produce the waxy surface on the udder, sheath and around the anus and dock. The muscle attached to the hair erects the hair when the horse is cold which helps to empty the sebaceous gland.

Sweat glands open onto the skin surface where sweat evaporates causing heat loss. They are found in most areas of the horse's skin. The greatest numbers are on the flank, the mammary gland and beside the nostrils. They are essential for electrolyte balance, excretion of waste products and temperature control.

Management

Normally horses keep their skin and coat in good condition by self-grooming, e.g. rolling, shaking, licking, nibbling, scratching and rubbing. They also perform mutual grooming with a close companion.

Domestication can make self-grooming difficult for the horse. Stables may be too small for the horse to roll safely and it may roll on faeces which it would normally avoid. Rugs, boots and hoods make it impossible for the horse to groom itself. They also prevent the synthesis of vitamin D. Horses that are tied up are unable to reach most of their body with their mouths, so cannot lick or nibble those areas. Animals with neck pain, lameness and those that are ill often stop self-grooming so their coats soon look neglected.

Grooming

Horses should be groomed every day in a manner to suit their management system. This means that the horse is handled regularly, whether it is in work or not. Grooming should be a pleasant experience for the animal if done in the correct way. Heavy handed grooming or using hard brushes on sensitive areas will upset the horse. Grooming stimulates the circulation, disperses sebum from the sebaceous glands and massages the skin and underlying muscle masses such as the hindquarters. Cleaning the eyes, nose and dock are included in the grooming process. The udder or sheath may need washing with separate sponges used for each area. The feet should be picked out as part of this routine.

The grooming equipment needs regular cleaning as do rugs, boots clippers, tack etc. Detergents should not be used on horse clothing. There are a number of bactericidal and fungicidal shampoos which can be used on both the horse and its equipment. The owner can check the horse for signs of injury and skin disease while grooming.

Signs of skin disease are:

Behavioural signs of irritation, e.g. excessive rubbing/scratching
Restless, stamping feet, tail swishing, head tossing. There may be self-inflicted injuries
Broken hair, dull, staring coat, scurf
Bald areas
Abnormal amount of hair, e.g. long, curly coat
Failure to sweat or excessive sweating
Inflamed skin, scabs, pustules, open wounds, ulcers
Abnormal swelling, e.g. skin wheals, areas of thickened skin, abscesses and tumours
Alteration in skin pigment
Presence of parasites, e.g. lice, ticks, mites, bot eggs.

Housing and shelter

Shelter should be available to protect the horse from inclement weather and strong sunlight as well as nuisance insects. Animals with unpigmented muzzles are prone to sunburn and may also require the added protection of a high factor sunscreen. Wet weather can also cause rain scald and mud rash. These can be prevented by providing a field shelter with a hard standing, by using waterproof rugs and avoiding turn-out pastures which are poorly drained. Muddy, poached areas of fields can be electric fenced to allow the ground to recover.

Clipping

Animals who fail to shed their coat (Cushing's disease) should be clipped out, otherwise they become sweaty, uncomfortable and prone to skin infections.

Animals in regular hard work may also require clipping, to prevent heat stress and allow them to dry quickly after work. There is no point in clipping a horse just to be fashionable. Electrical clippers should be quiet, have sharp blades and be properly cleaned, well maintained and used by a competent person. Battery operated and mechanical hand clippers are suitable for small areas and on horses that are nervous of electrical clippers. Some horses require sedation by the vet before clipping. Animals that are clipped should be provided with correctly fitting rugs in the stable and at pasture.

Each animal should have its own equipment, i.e. rugs, tack and grooming kit to avoid inadvertently transmitting skin diseases to other equines.

Fly problems

Flies are a seasonal problem and many species can cause problems to the horse and rider. House flies annoy the animal by swarming around its head and feeding on the discharges from the eyes, nostrils and sheath. They are attracted to wounds where they spread infection.

The Habronema larvae cause summer sores. Sores near the eyes can cause conjunctivitis as the animal rubs its face to remove the insects. Older and long-coated geldings seem to attract flies around their sheaths. Urine splashes onto the hair in front of the sheath. Geldings should have their sheaths cleaned to remove discharges which are attractive to flies. The hair should be clipped from the abdomen in front of the sheath.

Flies cause inflammation of sensitive skin and serum oozing from the wounds attracts more flies. Wounds in summer time can quickly become infested with maggots (myiasis or fly strike). This is why routine surgical procedures like castrations are avoided in the summer. Accidental wounds should be covered with a dressing whenever possible, or a wound ointment, which will repel/kill insects, may be used on the skin surrounding the injury.

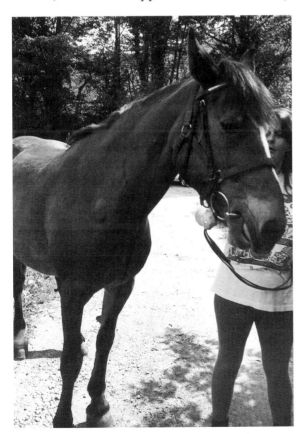

Swelling caused by a fly bite at the base of the neck

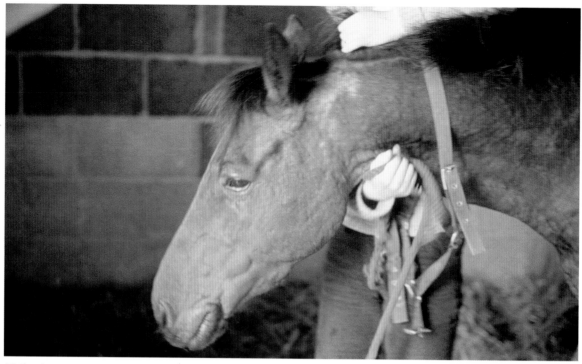

Urticaria (C. L. Hocking)

Stable and horse flies give painful bites which distress the horse and can make it difficult to control. The horse may accidentally kick the handler when it is bitten. Large painful swellings may appear at the site of the bite. Swellings in areas where tack is placed may prevent the animal being ridden under saddle for a few days. Horses may be allergic to the bites of certain insects, and produce very large swellings which require treatment. Some develop hard nodular swellings that remain for months as a reaction to the original bite.

Many horses, ponies and donkeys have an allergy to midge bites, this is called Sweet itch. The bite of the Culicoides midge is painful and the saliva causes a hypersensitivity in some animals. This causes intense irritation and the animal rubs itself raw if left unprotected.

Fly control

There are a variety of methods used to control and reduce the fly problem. It is best to start a control programme early in the spring. In order to breed the insects need warm, moist conditions where there is a plentiful supply of food. Flies congregate around manure heaps so these should be sited away from animal housing and removed weekly. Stable hygiene is important and deep litter beds must be avoided. Pools of urine and water should not be allowed to gather in front of shelters and stables.

Chemical protection

It is important to use fly repellents and/or insecticides before the horse is bitten. Insecticides kill adult flies and can be used on stable walls, manure heaps and applied to the horse's coat. Fly papers and insecticide blocks can be hung from the ceiling. All insecticides should be used according to the manufacturer's instructions. Horses that are frequently bathed or washed after exercise will need insecticide chemicals reapplied. The oily permethrin pour-on products are spread over the body on the grease on the skin and usually last for two to four weeks, providing they are not washed off. Permethrins also kill lice, forage and harvest mites. Fly repellents do not kill flies but deter them from landing on the horse. They are usually only effective for a few hours and then have to be reapplied. Some contain natural oils like citronella. Repellents are applied prior to riding the horse so the animal is not constantly annoyed by flies. The flies can continue to breed and multiply if only repellents are used. Whenever a new product is used on the horse it is important to do a test spot first, on a small area of skin to make sure that there will be no adverse reaction. The manufacturer's instructions should be carefully followed and any adverse reaction reported to the veterinary supplier. Adding garlic to the horse's feed is supposed to help keep flies away, although this has not been scientifically proven.

Physical protection

Horses can be stabled during the day, when the flies are most active. Fly fringes, veils and hoods must be used with care and the horse closely supervised. Lightweight summer sheets will keep the flies off the horse while in the stable, field and when travelling. Well sited field shelters positioned away from trees, water and manure heaps provide a cool, shady place away from the flies during hot weather.

No one method will totally control flies; it is necessary to use good management combined with repellents and insecticides.

Parasitic skin diseases

Lice

Equines may be infested by biting lice, Damalinia equi, which feed on scurf and skin debris or by sucking lice, Haematopinus asini, which feed on blood and tissue fluid. Lice are a seasonal problem seen in mid to late winter when animals have long coats. Both lice and their eggs (nits) are visible to the naked eye, adult lice are grey, about 3 mm long and live on the host. They lay cream-coloured nits onto the base of hairs, especially the mane and forelock. The life-cycle takes two to three weeks.

Louse infestation is transmitted by direct contact with infested animals, their grooming equipment, tack and rugs. Debilitated animals and those suffering from immune suppressive disorders, e.g. Cushing's disease, may be severely affected.

Signs of infestation are easy to detect. Lice cause irritation and rubbing, so the animal's coat has a moth-eaten appearance with bald patches and broken hairs. Some animals are very sensitive to lice infestation and do not need to harbour large numbers of the parasite before they show pruritis. The head, neck, flanks and croup are usually affected. Severe cases will lose condition and become anaemic.

Animals can be treated with permethrin preparations at two weekly intervals to kill newly hatched lice. All in-contact animals and equipment must be treated at the same time. The ivermectin wormer medicines may help to control lice as these chemicals circulate in the blood to the skin.

Harvest mites (Trombicula) and forage mites (Acarus spp)

Both harvest and forage mites can produce skin disease in equines. The adult and nymph stages of these parasites are free living (non-parasitic), it is only the larval stage that feeds on mammals. The more usual host is a small rodent, but they may parasitise horses. Animals at pasture are infested in late summer and autumn by larvae of harvest mites; the limbs, head and trunk being commonly affected. They cause small papules with hair loss and intense irritation. Preserved hay and bedding straw may harbour numerous forage mites that induce disease at any time of the year in the stabled animal.

Mite infestations also cause intense pruritus in some individuals and, like lice, can be treated with pour-on permethrin preparations.

The infested straw and forage should be removed from the patient's environment and preferably burned.

Mange mites

Chorioptic mange is seen on the lower limbs of heavy horses and those with 'feather', especially in winter. The mite has a two to three week life-cycle and is able to live off the host for a couple of days. The mite burrows into the skin of the cannon, fetlock and pastern causing pruritus, leg stamping and self mutilation. There is usually scab formation and scaly skin. Neglected cases may result in Greasy heel, a form of dermatitis that is difficult to treat. Diagnosis is made on clinical signs and skin scrapings from the affected areas should contain parasites which can be identified under the microscope. Treatment involves removing all the feather (leg hair) and applying ectoparasiticides.

Psoroptic mange is seen on the head, ears, mane and tail. It causes pruritus and head shaking. Papules, moist scabs and bald areas are commonly seen.

The mite can live off the host for a couple of weeks on grooming utensils etc.

A diagnosis is made on examining skin scrapings.

Treatment involves clipping and cleaning the affected areas and using ectoparasiticides. Headcollars and other equipment should be thoroughly cleaned.

Ticks

These are blood sucking parasites and can transmit diseases from one host to another, e.g. Lyme's disease.

In the U.K. sheep ticks can parasitise equines. They are found in heathland and bracken areas. Ticks are large, round and usually seen in groups on the horse's abdomen. Ticks are firmly attached to the skin while they are feeding and are difficult to remove without leaving their mouthparts in situ. They can be killed by applying an acaricide directly on to the tick.

PREVENTION
Keep equines off tick infested land. Sheep that are dipped after shearing and in the late summer are less likely to carry ticks. Bracken should be removed from grazing areas as it is poisonous to livestock and carcinogenic.

Oxyuris (Pinworm)

The adult pinworm lays its eggs on the perineum of the horse causing anal irritation and tail rubbing.

DIAGNOSIS
The eggs can be removed on clear sticky tape and identified microscopically.

TREATMENT
Wash perineum and treat skin lesions as wounds. Use any anthelmintic preparation as advised.

Stables and fittings should be periodically steam cleaned.

Fungal disease

Ringworm

Ringworm is the commonest fungal infection seen in equines. It is highly contagious and spreads easily in four to seven days in humid conditions and four to five weeks in a dry, cold winter. There are a number of fungal species that can infect horses and also humans. Care should be taken when handling and treating ringworm patients! Although the condition is not serious it is unsightly, expensive and time consuming to treat. Once a premises has become infected it is difficult to eliminate the ringworm spores. The spores are resistant to most environmental conditions and disinfectants and can survive for years on wooden fences and in buildings.

Trichophyton and Microsporum species are usually responsible for equine ringworm. Other species not specific to horses can spread to other animals e.g. cattle, dogs and cats.

Ringworm is seen in areas where there is friction or abrasions, so under tack and boots are a common site for lesions, e.g. saddle, girth, martingale. Riders' boots can spread infections from one horse to another. Ringworm is more common in winter time, which may be due to spread by clipping and hard grooming to remove mud. The active spores will penetrate abraded skin. In winter horses tend to be stabled and kept in closer proximity to each other and possible infection.

SIGNS OF RINGWORM

Unfortunately the skin lesions are variable in appearance and may be confused with other skin diseases. Some cases show spherical areas of dry, scaly skin and hair loss, while others form a crusty scab around tufts of hair. The horse soon develops more lesions and the original area may become a large irregular shaped patch. The lesions may appear anywhere on the body and only cause mild irritation. If left untreated the signs usually disappear in eight to twelve weeks but by then the highly resistant spores will be widely disseminated and many animals may be affected. Whole yards may be involved in an outbreak.

DIAGNOSIS AND TREATMENT

If ringworm is suspected it is important to have an early diagnosis and prompt treatment to prevent contamination of the horse's environment and infection spreading to other animals.

The diagnosis is made on the clinical signs and the history of other infected animals. Skin, hair and scabs are examined microscopically for fungal spores and hyphae. The fungi can also be cultured on special media plates in an incubator which may take a couple of weeks.

The horse is usually given in-feed medication and antifungal/sporicidal washes at three to five day intervals. The horse's environment and all equipment also has to be cleaned with a sporicidal/fungicidal disinfectant. Woodwork can then be creosoted. Strict hygiene measures are necessary to avoid infection of handlers and other horses. The handler should wear overalls to prevent contaminating their clothes.

All at-risk animals should be carefully inspected each day for a couple of weeks after the last new case. Avoid grooming or clipping the horse as this spreads the spores. An easily cleaned cotton sheet may be used under a rug to avoid having to repeatedly wash thick rugs. Horses with ringworm obviously should be isolated and not

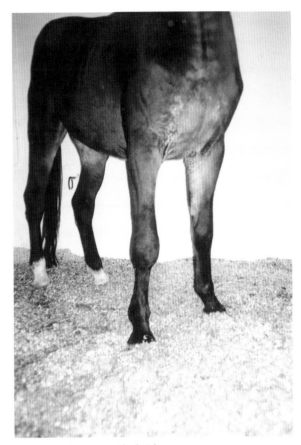

Ringworm lesions on the brisket

travelled or competed. If the lesions are under the saddle or girth the horse should not be exercised under saddle.

The treatment involves care of the patient and care of the equipment and stable which is very time consuming. The horse will be resistant to that species of ringworm for six to twelve months.

Bacterial skin diseases

A number of bacteria found on the skin surface and in the horse's environment may cause inflammation of the skin (dermatitis), or the hair follicles (folliculitis) or the dermis, (furunculosis), (acne). If the skin surface is injured, the resulting wound allows bacteria to enter the tissues to form an abscess or cellulitis.

Dermatophilosis

The commonest cause of dermatitis is Dermatophilus congolensis. This bacterium causes mud rash and rainscald in areas of skin that are continually wet. The skin feels lumpy with the hair matted into typical paintbrush lesions. Attached to the hair tufts are scabs that are moist on the skin surface. The skin is usually inflamed and may be painful. The skin over the pasterns may crack and ooze serum. Mud rash affects the lower limbs while rainscald is seen on the neck, back and rump. It is usually seen in mild, wet winters but can occur at other times of the year when the ground or pasture is wet. The organism penetrates skin that is damaged and then softened by wet conditions. Animals with thick coats and feathered legs are more prone to mud fever as they take longer to dry than fine coated animals.

Secondary bacterial infection with Staphylococcal spp may complicate mud rash and these cases will require swabs and samples to be taken to establish the cause. The horse may become systemically sick with fever and swollen lymph nodes. These animals will resent their legs being handled and be lame. Treatment of the milder cases involves clipping the hair and using antibacterial washes on the affected skin. This must be thoroughly dried and antibiotic cream applied. It is important not to use strong antiseptics or shampoos as these will inflame the skin and make the condition worse.

The horse must be kept dry so in most cases this means stabling. The bedding should be clean and dry and the legs bandaged using a non-adherent dressing, gamgee and wool stable bandages. This will prevent bedding from sticking to and abrading the damaged areas. If the horse is not lame it may be exercised on dry roads or tracks. If possible the horse can be tied up on the yard or placed in an empty stable, so the legs may be left uncovered for a short time each day. Severe cases may require antibiotics given systemically as well as pain relief. Lame animals should not be ridden.

Mud rash may be prevented by carefully inspecting the horse's legs each day and avoiding excessive wetting of the skin. Hairy legs need clipping so that they dry more easily. Muddy legs should be allowed to dry and then the mud brushed off with a soft body brush. The legs should not be hosed as this does not remove all the mud and makes the legs very wet. They can be properly washed to remove all traces of mud and then thoroughly dried. Wool leg wraps or Thermatex wraps which wick moisture to the surface may be used, or alternatively a hairdrier on a cool setting. Avoid using muddy areas in the winter and provide a hard standing in the field shelter. Remember to clean all the grooming equipment and boots frequently.

Rainscald will normally resolve if the horse's skin is kept dry. The horse should be stabled, the scabs gently removed and the area washed with a mild antibacterial solution and dried. Once the condition has resolved the horse should be provided with a waterproof rug and shelter from wet weather.

Cotton sheets are easy to wash and may be placed under all other rugs. With good hygiene and stable management these conditions are usually preventable.

Skin tumours

Skin tumours are the most common type of tumour seen in horses. They can be benign like the lipoma and fibroma or malignant like squamous cell carcinoma and melanoma. It is important that all tumours are properly investigated using biopsy techniques with laboratory diagnosis. A prognosis is then made depending on the type of tumour, its position and growth rate.

The most common skin tumour is the equine sarcoid. This is thought to be caused by a virus. There are six types of sarcoid seen in horses. These are found on the inner thigh, sheath or udder, neck, head, elbow and girth areas. They are commonly seen on the ventral body wall. Types of sarcoid are:

1 Occult sarcoid. Circular grey scaly patches
2 Verrucous sarcoid. Crusty, wart-like irregular shaped growths
3 Nodular sarcoid. Smooth, nodular swelling under normal looking skin

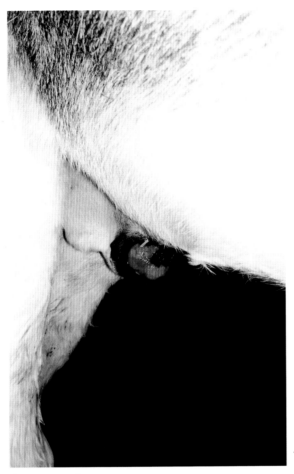

A tumour on the prepuce

4 Fibroblastic sarcoid. Very aggressive mass often ulcerated. May complicate skin wounds
5 Malevolent sarcoid. Invasive tumour which infiltrates the lymphatic system
6 Mixed sarcoid. Contains a mix of the other types

Affected animals usually have multiple tumours of various sizes. They are thought to be spread by biting flies and may spread to other in-contact equines. They can spread locally and be difficult to treat. They often recur at the original site or develop at a new site, making treatment expensive and time consuming. Animals with only a few small tumours that are not likely to be rubbed by tack or rugs may not require treatment, only close observation after initial veterinary diagnosis. Severe cases are not treatable. Tumours that fall between these two groups may

require early treatment. The options available are:

1 Surgical removal
2 Radiation therapy
3 BCG vaccine
4 Cryosurgery
5 Topical chemotherapy
6 Implants and injections into the tumour with cytotoxic chemical

Sarcoids are a serious disorder and need to be diagnosed early if treatment is to be effective.

Allergic skin diseases

The most common skin allergy in equines is Sweet itch. This is due to a hypersensitivity to the bites of midges (Culicoides). Other insects such as the black fly (Simulium) occasionally cause a similar condition. Animals may also develop a skin reaction to food allergies, contact allergies or skin parasites including pinworm infestation.

Although Sweet itch is seen in all types and breeds of horse and pony it is more common in certain breeds, e.g. the Welsh pony and shire-horse which suggests that there is a genetic influence. It is not sensible to breed from animals with Sweet itch. It is not normally seen in animals under two years of age. Affected animals react to the midge bites by rubbing at the bitten areas, causing open wounds and further problems from other insects attracted to the wounds.

The culicoid midges are blood sucking; their bites are painful and annoy the animal, causing intense irritation. Depending on the species of midge, the horse may be bitten on the head, neck, back or ventral midline. Animals who show an allergic reaction to the bites gradually over the years develop grossly thickened skin and hairloss in the affected areas. These animals are very distressed and spend hours rubbing and scratching.

The midges are most active at dawn and dusk. They like warm and moist conditions and congregate around muck heaps, under trees and near open water. They do not like exposed and windy conditions. Sweet itch is a seasonal

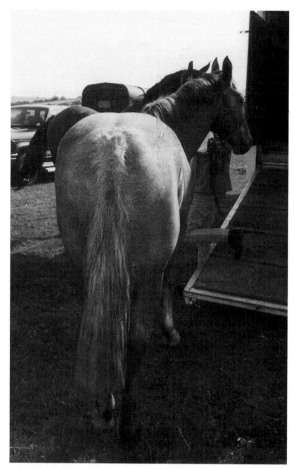

A sign of Sweet itch – a badly rubbed tail

insecticidal sprays can be used as previously described. (See page 70.) No one preparation can be expected to protect a highly sensitised animal unless there are management controls. At present there is no cure and no single effective form of prevention.

Photosensitivity

Horses at pasture can develop sunburn-like lesions due to photosensitivity caused by eating certain plants, e.g. St John's Wort. These plants contain photodynamic chemicals which are absorbed from the gut into the blood. On reaching areas of unpigmented skin they react with sunlight and cause blistering of the skin. This is painful and may become infected by

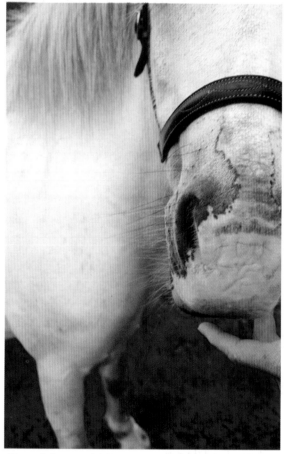

condition seen from spring to autumn but if the climate continues to change we may see midges in the winter months. Good management is the key to success with this condition. It is important to identify the early signs to prevent unnecessary suffering.

Treatment with antihistamines or corticosteroids is not usually successful and cannot be used in the long-term. Long-acting steroids may precipitate acute laminitis.

The sensitised animal must be kept away from the midges and every effort should be made to achieve this. The horse should have an insect-proof stable and a protective rug with a hood. The horse can be stabled at times when the midges are most active. Fly repellents are useful in combination with housing the horse and

Signs of photosensitivity

bacteria. The areas must be kept clean by careful bathing and covered in an antibiotic cream. Lesions on the muzzle and lips will make eating difficult. Forage may be damped and fed from a shallow bowl rather than a net or rack.

These animals have to be housed during daylight and not allowed to graze on pasture where these plants grow.

Photosensitisation is also a symptom of liver disease.

Phylloerythrin, a light sensitive chemical, accumulates in the skin of animals with liver dysfunction. This is a normal product of plant digestion which is normally removed from the circulation by the liver and excreted in the bile. Blood tests are needed to diagnose liver disease. Ragwort poisoning is a common cause of chronic liver damage.

For prevention of sunburn see page 69.

Sores and galls

Saddle sores, girth galls and pressure sores all result from friction and abnormal pressure on areas of skin. They are a result of poor stable management and are caused by tack, rugs, bandages and insufficient bedding.

Saddle sores are seen on the horse's back as

Sunburn around the eyes

Girth gall

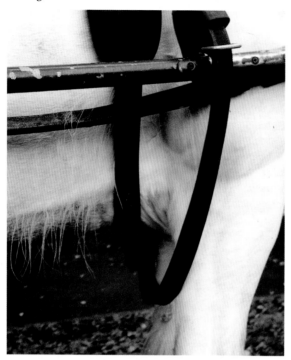

raised areas of skin, painful to touch and usually covered with broken hairs. Sites of old sores will have white hair (acquired marks). They are caused by poorly fitting saddles, bad riding, dirty saddles and numnahs, incorrectly positioned rollers and surcingles.

Saddle sores must be allowed to heal completely before the horse can be ridden again. The tack should be cleaned and saddles inspected by a saddler to prevent further problems.

Girth galls are injuries to the girth area and have similar causes to saddle sores. They are prevented by keeping girths clean and using a protective sleeve over the girth. It is important to check the girth is not too loose or too tight as both situations will damage the skin.

Pressure sores are commonly seen over bony prominences in recumbent animals and under incorrectly applied bandages. Animals that are stabled need sufficient bedding to prevent injury being caused by contact with hard floors.

All these conditions should be treated as wounds. (See page 126.)

The Eye

Anatomy

The horse's eyes are positioned on the side of its head, which gives good all-round vision except for the area directly behind its quarters. The eyeball is slightly flattened so both near and far images can be in focus at the same time. The horse has to move its head up or down to focus clearly on a particular image.

The eye consists of the eyeball, the eyelids and the muscles to move the eye.

The lacrimal apparatus produces tears which coat the surface of the eye. The tears drain through a series of ducts which join together and open onto the floor of each nostril at the junction of the skin and the pink mucous membrane inside the nose. Tears can be seen running from the nostrils. If the ducts are blocked or the horse is producing an excessive volume of tears they will overflow down the face. Tears kill bacteria and wash away debris. The horse has both upper and lower eyelids covered by the conjunctiva on the inside and skin on the outside with lashes on the rim. The eyelashes filter large particles and help to protect the eye. There is a third eyelid at the corner of the eye, this moves across the eye to spread the tears and remove dust particles. The third eyelid becomes prominent in horses with tetanus. The eyeball is made up of three layers.

The white of the eye is the tough outer sclera which becomes part of the transparent cornea at the front of the eye. The junction between cornea and sclera is the limbus. Light enters the eye via the cornea. The conjuctiva becomes transparent at the front of the eye to form part of the cornea. The middle layer, the choroid contains blood vessels, and has a central hole or pupil. Surrounding the pupil is the pigmented iris. Muscles in the iris alter the shape of the pupil to allow the correct amount of light to enter the eye. The pupil becomes narrower in bright light and dilated and rounded in poor light. The edges of the iris have irregular shaped projections, the corpora nigra, which hang over the pupil. Behind the iris is the ciliary body which contains the muscles that alter the shape of the lens. The transparent lens is attached to the ciliary body by the suspensory ligament.

The lens and ciliary body divide the eye into the anterior and posterior chambers which contain two distinct forms of fluid. The anterior chamber contains a watery aqueous humour and the posterior chamber has a thick fluid, the vitreous humour.

The retina is the thin, inner light-sensitive layer containing many nerves and blood vessels. The nerve fibres leave the eye, via the optic discs, in the optic nerve. The rods and cones, light sen-

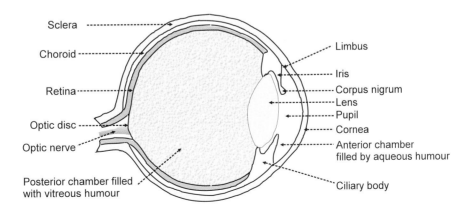

Sclera
Choroid
Retina
Optic disc
Optic nerve
Posterior chamber filled with vitreous humour
Limbus
Iris
Corpus nigrum
Lens
Pupil
Cornea
Anterior chamber filled by aqueous humour
Ciliary body

Fig.33. The internal structure of the eyeball.

sitive cells in the retina, release chemicals to cause nerve impulses that are translated into images by the brain.

Common conditions of the eye

Inflammation

Inflammation to any structures of the eye will result in swelling and pain. The eye will close when it is painful and there will be an increase in tear production (epiphora). Inflammation may be a result of an injury, a foreign body or infection.

Conjunctivitis

Inflamed conjunctiva will be swollen and red. The eye may be closed and painful with tear overflow. There are many causes including respiratory diseases when both eyes will be involved. Foreign bodies such as grass awns or dust and trauma may affect one eye. Allergies and infections are usually bilateral. Wind and flies may cause irritation and conjunctivitis.

Keratitis

Keratitis, inflammation of the cornea, may follow conjunctivitis or be a primary infection or secondary to injury of the cornea. This is extremely painful as the cornea is well supplied with sensitive nerves. There will be clouding of the cornea and the eye will be closed. Usually there is a copious occular discharge which may become purulent. Early treatment is needed to prevent permanent scarring and reduction in vision.

Uveitis

Uveitis is an inflammation of the uveal tract, (iris, ciliary body and choroid) and is serious. It is commonly caused by trauma and the cornea may also be involved.

Equine recurrent uveitis (Periodic Ophthalmia or Moon Blindness)

This is one of the most important disorders of the eye. It is found in all breeds and ages

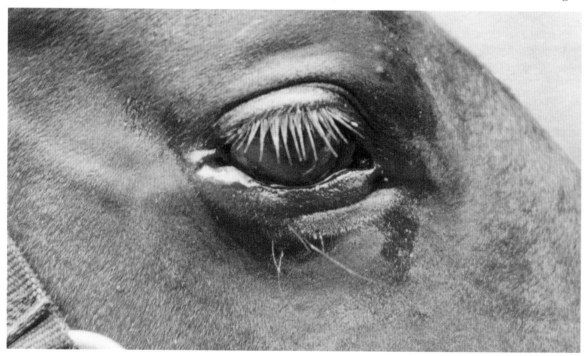

Epiphora plus an eyelid injury

of equine and occurs in all countries. The actual cause is not known but it is thought to be a response to an immune-mediated inflammation. Both eyes may be affected alternately or at the same time and the condition recurs at irregular intervals. The consequence of repeated attacks is a distorted iris due to adhesions between the iris and the lens. The eyeball becomes shrunken and covered by the third eyelid and the animal will be blind. In the acute phase the eye is extremely painful due to the corneal swelling (oedema), keratitis, uveitis and inflammatory debris in the aqueous humour.

Prompt treatment is needed to limit the damage to the eye. Unfortunately it is not possible to predict when the next attack will occur so the prognosis is guarded. Partially sighted animals require special care when handling.

Corneal injuries

Injuries to the cornea are common due to the prominence of the eye. Even though the horse has a good blink reflex it can still injure the eyes in hedges, and on sharp pieces of

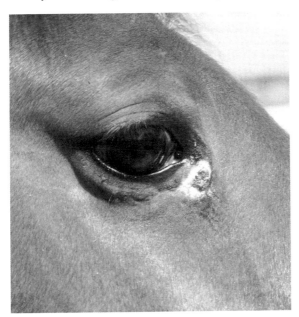

Eyelid tumour

bedding or forage. Chemical irritants like ammonia and sprays may damage the cornea. Dust and grit may be blown into the eye on a windy day. Signs of a corneal injury are:

pain
profuse lacrimation
partially closed eye
sensitivity to light
cloudy cornea with prominent blood vessels

The eye needs to be thoroughly examined and treated according to the diagnostic findings.

Eyelid injuries

Damage to the eyelids will result in corneal problems if they are not treated promptly. They often require suturing to prevent distortion of the lids and to enable them to function correctly.

Blocked tear-ducts

The upper part of the tear-duct is enclosed in a bony canal in the maxillary bone. Swelling of the bones or inflammation of the duct will cause narrowing or blockage resulting in epiphora (tear overflow).

Occasionally horses are born with incomplete tear ducts and no opening into the nostril. Injuries to the head may also damage the tear-duct.

The patency of the duct can be tested by placing a dye into the eye and waiting for it to appear from the nasal ostium (opening in nostril).

A catheter can be placed into the nasal ostium and flushed with warm saline solution which should appear at the eye.

It may be possible to flush out debris while using this method to test if the duct is blocked.

Tumours

Masses on the eyelids and surrounding tissues are relatively common. It is important to diagnose which type of tumour is present as this will affect the treatment and prognosis. They may distort the eyelid and prevent its normal function resulting in other eye disorders. Eyelid tumours are serious as they will become larger and cause complications. The commonest tumours at this site are sarcoids, squamous cell carcinoma, melanoma and neurofibroma. They may be treated surgically, by radiation therapy, chemotherapy and immune methods depending on the tumour.

Cataracts

Cataracts are opacities in the lens. Some animals are born with cataracts, i.e. congenital cataracts, but more usually they are a result of uveitis, trauma or old age. Some are small, non-progressive and of no consequence. Mature cataracts in adult horses usually progress and eventually result in blindness. Progressive loss of sight will result in behaviour changes and clumsiness and be noticed by the owner. Diagnosis can be made by the veterinary surgeon.

Examining the eye

A horse with a painful eye will resent examination of the eye. It will usually be sedated and given analgesia (pain relief). This may be adequate in some cases but others will require an

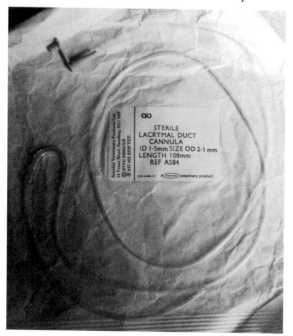

A catheter

auriculo-palpebral nerve block with local anaesthetic. This block is used to overcome the eyelid closure which prevents detailed examination of the painful eye. Local anaesthetic drops may also be instilled onto the eye surface.

The horse is usually placed in a darkened stable and all the eye structures are examined through an ophthalmoscope. Fluorescent drops are placed on the eyeball to illuminate areas of corneal damage. The dye fluoresces bright green in ulcers or blemishes. The lids and surrounding area are also inspected. Where infection is suspected, swabs from the corneal surface and from any occular discharges can be tested at the laboratory. Biopsies may be taken from tumours for histological analysis.

Treatment and medication

It may be difficult to apply medication either as drops or ointments to the eye if the patient will not co-operate. Solutions give a high level of drug release for a short period of one to two hours. Ointments give a low level of drug release for about four hours. In the acute stage it may require treatment every hour and the horse may become fractious. It is difficult to open tightly closed eyelids.

There are two types of indwelling catheters used in the horse so that there is no need to handle the eye and distress the animal. These are remote ways of delivering drugs onto the eye surface. One system is placed into the tear-duct, i.e. a nasolacrimal catheter, and the other, a subpalpebral lavage system is attached under the upper lid. The vet will normally fit a catheter system after examining the horse and while it is sedated.

Antibiotics and anti-inflammatory solutions can be injected into the catheters. Horses with profuse epiphora will wash the drugs away or at least dilute them. The presence of pus may prevent some drugs from being absorbed.

In cases of corneal injury the eyelids may be sutured together or the third eyelid sutured across the eye to promote healing. (See nursing, page 138.)

THE MUSCULOSKELETAL SYSTEM

The musculoskeletal system includes all the structures involved in movement, i.e. the bones of the limbs and spine and the associated muscles, tendons and ligaments with their blood vessels and neurological supply. Disorders of this system result in alteration in gait and movement, i.e. lameness.

Anatomy

The horse has evolved over millions of years to walk on the tip of a single digit. The bones of the middle toe, the third digit in prehistoric horses, elongated and became the specialised structure we know today. The equine digit comprises the third metacarpus/metatarsus, the first, second and third phalanx with the proximal and distal sesamoid bones. The second and fourth metacarpal/metatarsal bones (medial and lateral splint bones) are all that remains of the second and fourth digit along with the ergots. The chestnut is the rudimentary first digit. See figure 1 page 1 and figure 23 page 34.

The foot

This consists of the hoof capsule and the structures within it. The pedal bone is suspended within the hoof by interdigitating sensitive and insensitive laminae. The pedal bone articulates with the second phalanx and the navicular bone (distal sesamoid) at the distal interphalangeal joint (coffin joint). The pedal bone is semicircular in the front feet and oval in the hind feet in horses and ponies. In the donkey all four feet are staple shaped. Ligaments bind the bones together. The deep digital flexor tendon (DDFT) attaches to the pedal bone and is separated from the navicular bone by the navicular bursa. The bursa contains synovial fluid and facilitates the movement of the DDFT over the navicular bone. The common digital extensor tendon attaches to the extensor process of the pedal bone. Cartilages are attached to the medial and lateral side of the pedal bone and can be palpated above the coronary band at the heel. The fibro elastic digital cushion lies above the frog and between the collateral cartilages.

The hoof wall, the sole, frog and bulbs of the heel are a type of modified epidermis. The horn tubules are produced at the coronary band from the dermal papillae, and with the intertubular horn, form the hoof wall. The wall is thickest at the toe and becomes thinner and more flexible over the quarters and heel. The heels expand when the foot is weight bearing. The heel wall turns inwards to form the bars of the foot. The sole, formed from the solar corium, is concave to prevent bruising and is often more vaulted in the hind feet than the front feet. The solar horn is softer and flakier than the wall due to a higher moisture content. The triangular frog is made of a more elastic, rubbery horn than the sole. It is separated from the bars by the collateral grooves and has a central sulcus.

The white line is the junction between the wall and the sole on the underside of the foot. It allows some movement between these structures and can be stretched in certain conditions which allows infection to enter the hoof capsule.

The hoof wall can be divided into three layers:

The stratum externum or the periople is composed of tubular and intertubular horn and has a high lipid content. It controls the moisture content of the hoof and protects the underlying layers.

The stratum medium is the largest layer and has zones of tubules and intertubular horn.

The stratum internum is composed of the interlocking laminae (leaves) of the epidermal (horn) and dermal (sensitive/vascular) tissues. The dermal laminae are attached to the pedal bone. Factors which affect horn quality and growth rate are discussed in part one, page 33. Incorrect foot balance and foot trimming can distort the hoof capsule, cause lameness and predispose the foot to certain diseases.

Conditions of the foot

Pedal sepsis

Infections in the foot are caused by a variety of organisms. Foot abscesses are a common cause of lameness in all equines. The animal becomes progressively lame over several hours. The foot may be hot with a strong digital pulse. Sometimes the lower limb becomes filled (swollen) and the horse will rest the foot with just the toe on the ground.

Infection may gain entry through a damaged white line or puncture wounds to the sole of the foot. If the infection is trapped between the horny sole and the sensitive tissue it causes pain as the pus accumulates and undermines the sole. The subsolar abscess can be drained and in most cases the horse will soon recover. The overlying horny sole is pared away to allow drainage and the foot tubbed in hot water and covered in a foot dressing. (See pages 131–2). A rubber or plastic boot will protect the dressing. The farrier will usually remove the shoe as it tends to cut through the foot dressings or he may alternatively reshoe the foot with a hospital plate under the

A removable hospital plate under the shoe

shoe, which allows access to the injury for inspection and replacing dressings. When the horse is sound it may be exercised on a dry surface. Animals will need tetanus antitoxin if they are not vaccinated with tetanus toxoid. Infections of the white line tend to track up the wall and burst out at the coronary band if untreated. This condition is known as gravel.

Deep penetration or puncture to the middle area of the foot is, however, very serious as vital structures, e.g. the navicular bursa, coffin joint

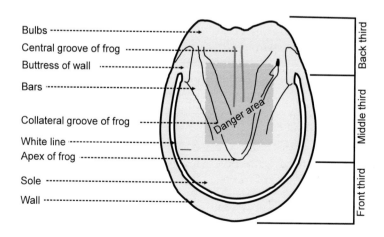

Fig.34. The ground surface of a foot to show the danger area for penetrating injuries.

Fig.35. Sagittal section of the foot.

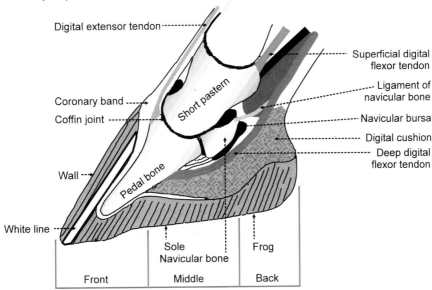

DDFT may be involved. Infections in these structures are difficult to drain and control and often result in euthanasia on humane grounds. All cases of puncture wounds need prompt attention by a vet with the correct treatment. Deep penetrations will involve surgery in order to save the patient. Cases are more likely to respond if treated early, i.e. within two days. Cases with an injury that is over seven days old have a poor prognosis.

It is important to know the anatomy of the foot so that the possible consequence of any injury is realised. If the horse is found with a nail stuck in the foot, the location, depth and angle of the nail should be noted as it is removed. This will be valuable information for the vet. In cases where the cause of penetration is unknown, deep punctures will be probed and X-rayed to locate the tract. The foot may be anaesthetised with local nerve blocks to allow more detailed exploration of the tract. Samples of synovial fluid from the digital tendon sheath and the coffin joint can be examined for signs of sepsis.

Broad spectrum antibiotics and analgesics will be needed with surgical drainage and foot dressings.

Although injuries to the foot cannot always be prevented, daily foot care will mean early detection of any potential problem.

Quittor

Injuries to the back third of the coronary band over the quarters and heel may result in quittor, which is an infection of the collateral cartilages. Pus discharges from tracts in the heel area above the coronary band. The cartilages have a poor blood supply so antibiotic therapy is not normally successful and it is difficult to get adequate drainage. Surgery is normally necessary to remove all the infected and necrotic tissue. Any injuries in the region of the cartilages that do not respond to conservative treatment should be investigated for quittor.

Thrush

Thrush is an anaerobic infection of the frog horn and the collateral grooves. The organisms destroy the horn tissue and produce a black, foul smelling discharge. In severe cases the horse will

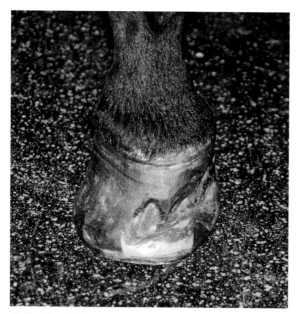

Hollow hoof disease

be lame as the sensitive tissue under the frog and sole is exposed. Commonly the hind feet are most badly affected. Thrush is a result of poor foot care, poor stable hygiene and poor management.

Both the veterinary surgeon and the farrier may be involved in the treatment. All the necrotic material is pared from the infected area which is then cleaned and dressed. It is important to keep the feet dry and replace the dressings daily. Grease, tar and oils should not be applied to the feet as they trap moisture in the hoof and prevent air reaching the tissues.

The stable floor should be power cleaned and a new, dry bed supplied. This should be mucked out every day and the unaffected feet picked out twice daily.

Onychomycosis (hollow hoof disease)

A variety of anaerobic organisms which destroy horn are responsible for this condition. The first signs are seen as grey or brown powdery areas in the stratum medium. If these areas are not removed the infection will invade the wall, creating large cavities, hence the name hollow hoof disease. It may be necessary to remove large areas of the overlying wall to gain access to the infected horn. This condition is potentially serious as the organisms are resistant to many topical antiseptics. Often animals have lesions in all their feet and will be lame. If hoof walls are resected, glue-on surgical shoes may be used once the disease is under control. Synthetic hoof fillers are not used as they may trap organisms in the foot.

A high standard of stable hygiene is required with continual foot care for many weeks. This is a time consuming and expensive condition to treat.

Poor foot care and poor stable hygiene may predispose animals to onychomycosis. Some animals have a history of seedy toe, chronic founder and white line separation, all conditions which result in poor quality horn. It is necessary to treat any concurrent disorders and provide a good diet with supplementation to promote horn growth. Animals that have genetic horn defects are susceptible to this condition and have a very poor prognosis.

Shoeing and related problems

Nail bind and nail prick are both caused by incorrectly placed horseshoe nails by the farrier. These are normally removed and repositioned immediately but occasionally they are missed and the horse is lame after shoeing. Nail bind is caused by pressure when a nail is placed too close to the sensitive laminae. A nail prick is caused by a nail puncturing the sensitive laminae and may lead to a foot abscess.

Corns

Corns occur on the sole between the wall and the bar. They are caused by abnormal pressure on the sole and are usually due to poor shoeing and long shoeing intervals. As the hoof wall grows the shoe is pulled onto the sole at the heel. Corns are normally found in the front feet, especially if the feet are shod with a shoe that is too small and too short. Feet that are not balanced and those with lowered heels are also prone to corns. Studs

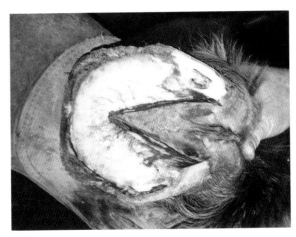

A dry corn

cause a mediolateral imbalance and corns may occur on the second impact side as this side takes more weight. Animals with mediolateral imbalance may eventually develop sheared heels. Stones may jam under the shoe at the heel and cause trauma at the seat of corn. Shoes with pencil heels are more likely to cause corns. On examining the seat of corn, i.e. the area of sole between the wall and the bar, three different types of corn may be seen:

1 Dry corn. Red staining of the sole due to haemorrhage of the underlying dermal tissue.
2 Moist corn. Serum accumulates beneath the damaged horn.
3 Septic corn. The horn is infected and the area becomes necrotic.

Corns are treated by removing the shoes and paring away infected and damaged horn. The horse should not be ridden until it is sound and correctly shod, i.e. wide at the quarters and heels with plenty of length. The horse should be reshod every four to five weeks or as often as the farrier advises. It is false economy to leave long shoeing intervals but a common fault with many owners.

Bruised sole

The sole may be easily bruised if the horse is flat footed or has thin soles. Animals working on rough terrain can bruise their feet on stones. This can occur in shod and unshod animals. The area

of sole will be discoloured and may become infected. The horse will be lame. Repeated bruising to the horny sole will eventually damage the pedal bone. This can be diagnosed radiographically.

Collapsed heels

Collapsed heels and long toes are a common fault in certain breeds that have a low heel, flat foot conformation. They can be a result of incorrect trimming and fitting shoes which are too short. The hoof pastern axis is broken back. The horn tubules at the heel will be curved under the foot and no longer parallel to those at the toe. The horse will bruise its sole and tear the laminae apart at the toe. The horse's weight will be shifted onto the heels, causing further damage and putting strain on the flexor tendons.

The foot balance has to be corrected and surgical shoeing may be required.

Cracks in the hoof wall

Cracks may be found in the hoof wall of both shod and unshod feet. Cracks that start at the

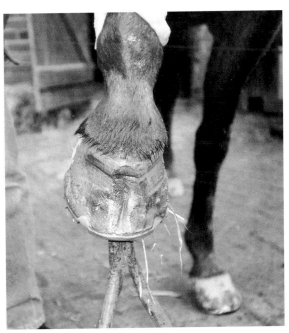

A crack in the hoof wall at the toe

ground surface are called grass cracks and those that start at the coronary band are sand cracks. Superficial cracks do not cause lameness. Deep cracks may involve the sensitive laminae, become infected and will result in lameness. The horn at the ground surface at the toe is both older and thicker than that at the heel, so the prognosis will differ depending on the position and depth of the crack.

· Cracks may be a result of an injury, especially at the coronary band, or due to irregular trimming and overlong feet. Brittle feet and thin walls are more susceptible to cracks.

Cracks caused by neglect can be prevented. Horses with brittle feet should be frequently trimmed and the feet watered and washed each day to encourage retention of moisture. Glue-on shoes are preferable to metal shoes as the nails cause further damage to the walls.

Superficial cracks can deteriorate into deeper, serious cracks and require early treatment by corrective trimming and shoeing to remove tension across the crack. Both the vet and the farrier will be required to treat deep cracks. They will remove infected horn, place filler in the defect and stabilise the hoof capsule with a surgical shoe.

Laminitis

Laminitis is a condition of the domesticated equine. It is a serious, painful disease of the foot which affects all ages and breeds of horse, pony, donkey and mule. Any number of feet may be involved and it may occur at any time of the year.

Trigger factors cause the lamellar attachments that suspend the pedal bone within the hoof wall to disintegrate. They activate metalloproteinase enzymes (MMPs) which destroy the basement membrane. This is the layer of cells which connects the epidermal cells of the inner hoof wall to the connective tissue of the pedal bone. The capillaries that supply the lamellae are also damaged and anoxia (lack of oxygen) causes more cells to die. The remaining blood supply is diverted away from the capillary network and shunted through arteriovenous anastomoses which dilate in response to the damage. The horse will have a pounding digital pulse in the affected limbs and will show varying degrees of

Founder case – a prolapsed pedal bone fitted with a heart bar shoe (R. A. Eustace)

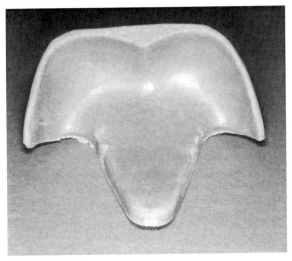

A LILY pad frog support

foot pain depending on the extent of the lamellar damage and the instability of the pedal bone.

A number of conditions appear to trigger laminitis:

1 *Nutritional*
   Carbohydrate overload due to excess cereal starch or excess soluble carbohydrate found in fast growing grass disturbs the gut flora. The normal bacteria die in the acid conditions releasing toxins which are thought to activate MMP.

2 *Trauma and mechanical damage*
   Fast work on a hard surface may precipitate laminitis. Overlong toes cause tearing of the lamellar attachments each time the foot breaks over. Animals that are lame for other reasons, e.g. fracture, may develop laminitis in the opposite foot, which is taking more weight than normal.

3 *Systemic disease*
   Retained placenta, hepatitis, respiratory infections, and diseases of other organs can all precede laminitis.

4 Cushing's disease, hyperlipaemia and steroid therapy all alter glucose metabolism and increase MMP production.

5 Travel stress and other causes of stress, e.g. colic surgery may precipitate laminitis due to release of steroids from the adrenal glands.

6 Certain drugs precipitate laminitis, especially in high risk animals, e.g. steroids.

High risk animals are those who have suffered previous attacks of laminitis, animals that are overweight, animals on free access to lush grazing and those with poor foot care/overlong feet.

The early signs of laminitis are foot pain and a pounding digital pulse. The temperature of the feet is not a reliable sign of laminitis. The coronary band may be painful and the sole is sensitive to pressure.

The animal will be lame. Mild cases will move awkwardly on uneven ground but appear normal on soft level ground. As the pain increases, the horse may shift weight from one foot to another and try to take more weight on the heels of the foot and on the unaffected feet by placing them further forward. Eventually the horse will become rooted to the spot or lie down. Animals in pain will have an elevated pulse and respiratory rate and there will be signs of the disorder which has triggered the laminitic attack.

The pedal bone may tip downwards and leave an obvious depression at the coronary band opposite the toe. This stage is called founder. The pedal bone can prolapse through the sole in front of the point of the frog, which is serious but can be treated. In severe cases the pedal bone becomes detached and the depression is felt all the way around the coronary band. These cases are sinkers and need urgent, specialised treatment within a few hours if they are to survive.

Even the mildest case of laminitis should be treated with some urgency as it can rapidly deteriorate. The horse should not be walked as movement will cause more laminar (lamellar) attachments to breakdown.

In older cases of chronic founder there is distortion of the hoof capsule and diverging growth rings on the hoof wall. The rings are closer together at the toe than the heel. There is reduced blood supply and jamming of the coronary band at the toe so the heel horn grows faster than the toe horn. The white line becomes stretched at the ground surface and is susceptible to infection. Seedy toe is a common sequela to laminitis. The sole becomes flatter and in some cases convex as the tip of the pedal bone rotates downwards.

All laminitis cases should be stabled on a deep, clean, white shavings bed with easy access to hay and water. They should be moved in a trailer to the stable and not forced to walk. They should never be starved but given the correct forage diet

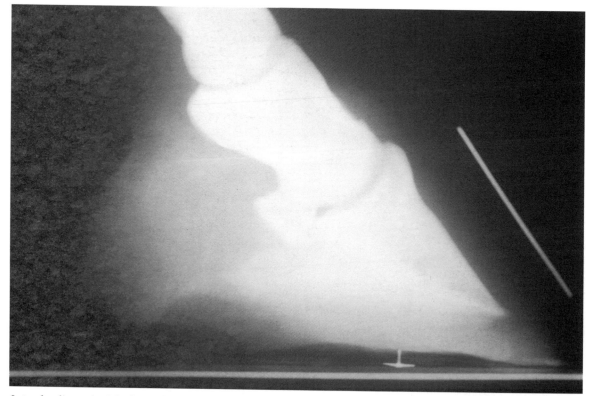

Lateral radiograph of the foot with a metal marker on the dorsal hoof wall and a pin near the point of frog (R. A. Eustace)

with supplements to promote horn growth. Overweight animals need careful dieting using a straw/hay mix. Starving obese animals can precipitate hyperlipaemia, a fatal metabolic disorder. Veterinary assistance should be sought if laminitis is suspected. The vet will provide frog supports to stabilise the pedal bone and give analgesics and medication to improve the circulation to the lamellae. Cases of toxaemia will require antibiotics. Liquid paraffin or bran mashes can be used to move the food quickly through the gut. Blood samples are taken to detect disease in other organs.

Animals with depressions at the coronary band will require foot X-rays to assess the position of the pedal bone. Glue-on adjustable heartbar shoes can then be fitted. Metal heartbar shoes may be used at a later stage when the horse can tolerate nailing on. A large amount of serum can collect under the hoof wall and this can be released by drilling a small hole in the middle of the dorsal hoof wall, which gives pain

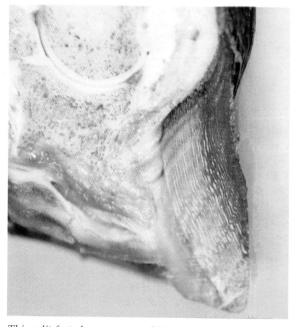

This split foot shows osteomyelitis, crimping of the horn tubules and a loss of pedal bone (R. A. Eustace)

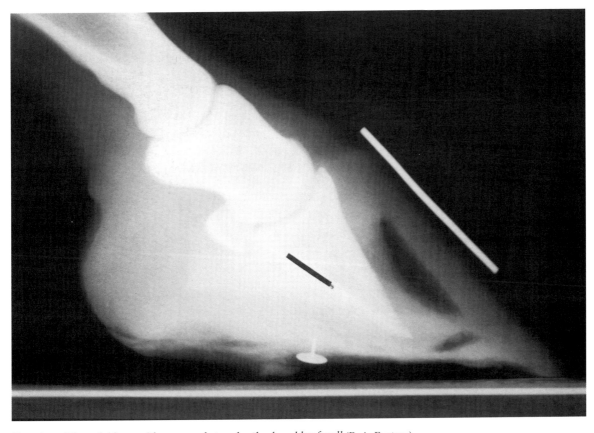

Rotation of the pedal bone with a gas pocket under the dorsal hoof wall (R. A. Eustace)

relief as it reduces pressure. It is sometimes necessary to remove the front of the hoof wall to encourage the new wall to grow parallel to the front of the pedal bone. This also improves the circulation at the coronary band and allows the serum and necrotic debris to escape. Dorsal wall resections are performed by the vet at the old founder stage, e.g. when the acute stage is over.

Animals with rotated pedal bones may have their DDFT cut so that the pedal bone is no longer under tension. These animals are fitted with heel extension shoes after the surgery.

Horses with chronic founder may become permanently lame with loss of pedal bone, osteomyelitis and deep abscess formation. These animals are crippled and are destroyed on humane grounds. All cases of laminitis need a high level of foot care and management for the rest of their lives to avoid another attack. Careful attention to the diet and regular foot trimming are vital. Heart girth and body weight measurements taken at weekly intervals are useful to show fluctuations in weight. Mild cases will need about six weeks' box rest and gradual return to work, with restricted grazing for obese animals.

Severe founders and sinkers can take a year of dedicated veterinary, farriery and nursing care to recover.

Research in Australia on MMP inhibitor substances is underway. Recent studies have suggested monitoring the pH of faeces of grazing animals in order to anticipate carbohydrate overload. The animals are prevented from grazing when the faecal acidity increases.

A number of parameters are used to give an accurate prognosis, especially for founder cases.

The founder distance, that is the distance

the pedal bone has dropped within the hoof capsule, can be measured on X-rays with a metal marker on the dorsal hoof wall. Retrograde venography is used to detect reduced capillary perfusion by injecting dyes into the foot veins before X-rays are taken. Areas without a capillary network cannot survive.

Navicular syndrome

This is a chronic progressive disease which affects the navicular bone, navicular bursa and DDFT in one or both front feet. All breeds and types of horse and pony can be affected, especially those in seasonal or irregular work, e.g. polo, hunting.

This disease has caused confusion and disagreement in its aetiology, pathogenesis, radiographic findings and treatment, and has been used as a dumping ground for undiagnosed forelimb lameness.

The owner often observes that the horse is reluctant to work as there is pain in the back of the foot. At rest the animal may point the affected foot and weight shift. They will prefer to stand with bedding under the heel and the hind feet will be placed further under the body and base wide.

At walk and trot there is an intermittent lameness that increases on a circle. There is an alteration in stride length with the toe landing first. The strides tend to be stilted and hesistant and there may be muscle loss over the shoulder(s).

The farrier may observe an alteration in shoe wear and foot size and shape. The foot becomes more boxy with contracted heels. The horse may become unco-operative when the farrier is clenching up. Often animals with navicular disease have poor mediolateral balance, a broken hoof pastern axis and fetlock valgus or varus. Their shoes are often too short and are not supporting the back of the foot.

On examination a number of clinical tests are performed: foot percussion, hoof testers, pressure on DDFT, extension and flexion tests.

Local analgesia, nerve blocks with local anaesthetics are used to locate the seat of pain. The palmer digital nerves, the coffin joint and the navicular bursa can all be anaesthetised. Radiographs are taken to detect abnormalities in the navicular bone.

The treatment of navicular disease depends on the degree of damage found. Early cases may respond to farriery to correct foot balance and special shoes, e.g. eggbar, rolled toes, heel wedges. A regular exercise regime is important. Medication using drugs to improve the circulation and thin the blood and analgesics have all been tried. Surgery to cut the nerve supply (neurectomy) to the foot was fashionable at one time. Some cases respond to cutting the navicular suspensory ligament.

At present there is no 'cure' for this condition especially for cases that show radiographic changes to their navicular bones. Animals with a low heel and long toe conformation put more strain on the back of their foot and need careful farriery. Good shoeing, foot balance and regular exercise may prevent or slow down the progress of this condition.

Sidebone

The cartilages at the back of the pedal bone are normally springy. Sidebone is ossification of the cartilages so they feel hard and will not move. This may be an ageing process or due to concussion, foot imbalance, or an injury. This usually occurs in the front feet.

Animals are not often lame. Sometimes there is pain if pressure is applied over the developing sidebone. Occasionally they fracture; this will be painful and the horse will be lame. Lame animals should be rested, their feet balanced and the fracture treated as advised by the vet.

Bones

The skeleton has bones of various shapes and types, e.g. long, flat short and irregular. The long limb bones (appendicular skeleton) are a system of levers for converting muscular contraction into movement. The scapula and pelvic girdle contain large flat bones that provide a large surface for muscle attachment and support the axial skeleton and trunk between the four limbs. Sesamoid bones such as the patella, proximal sesamoids and navicular bone alter the pull on tendons and reduce the friction between tendons and bones. The internal organs are protected by the thoracic and pelvic girdles. Bone is an important source of calcium, phosphorus and magnesium. The red bone marrow of young foals produces red blood cells.

The long limb bones are tubular and can resist bending, tension and compression due to their biphasic structure of a mineral component to give strength, and collagen fibres to provide flexibility. Immature bone needs mechanical stimulation provided by normal forces to develop correctly. It has a higher fibrous content than mature bone, and a lower mineral content.

Bones increase in length by the production of cartilage at the growth plate which is converted to bone. The epiphyseal growth plates of each long bone ossify and close at different times. They are all closed by the time the foal reaches maturity at about three years of age. Osteoblasts that line the periosteum are responsible for the increase in diameter of the bone.

Bone consists of an outer membrane, the periosteum, which is well supplied with a network of arteries and veins and it attaches tendons and ligaments to bone. Under the periosteum is compact bone and spongy bone. The shaft of a long bone is mainly compact bone. The centre of the shaft is the medullary cavity which contains bone marrow. Both ends of the long bone have a thin layer of compact bone covering the spongy bone. (See fig. 36 on page 94.)

Bone can be subjected to developmental and nutritional disorders, trauma and infection. Serious trauma results in a fracture. Depending on the age of the animal, the bone involved and the type and site of the fracture, surgical repair or conservative treatment is possible in many cases.

Bone infection is serious and a frequent complication following accidental wounds to limbs. This requires early, aggressive treatment and often surgery to remove infected bone.

Periostitis

Inflammation of the periosteum, periostitis, may result from a blow or infection or tearing of the ligament or tendon attachments, e.g. sprain. There will be heat, pain and swelling over the affected area involving the soft tissues. The bleeding and resultant blood clot is invaded by osteoblasts which produce new bone. The tender, inflamed area over the new bone subsides to leave a firm, painless, hard swelling.

Splints, sore shins and ringbone are all a result of periostitis.

Splints

The splint bones are attached to the cannon bone by the interosseous ligament. Tearing of this ligament in young horses results in a bony enlargement on the splint bone, which is called a splint. Animals with poor conformation, poor action and poor foot balance are more likely to develop splints. They are more common on the medial aspect of the forelimb. Excessive work on hard ground can also predispose to splint formation. Direct blows to the splint bones will also cause a splint. Large swellings at the proximal end of the splint bone may interfere with movement of the knee. Adhesions may involve the suspensory ligament and cause lameness.

During the acute stage of splint formation the animal will be lame to some degree according to the amount of damage. Diagnosis is made on clinical findings and radiographs to show the extent of the injury.

Early treatment by cold therapy and support bandages will limit the inflammation. Non steroidal anti-inflammatory drugs (NSAIDs) and box rest are advisable. Surgery is necessary in cases of fractured splint bones and those that are encroaching on the knee joint or the suspensory ligament.

The horse can gradually be brought back into

Fig. 36. The structure of a synovial joint.

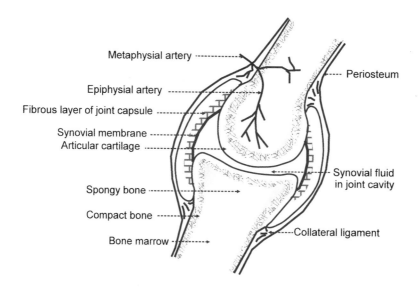

work once it is no longer lame. It should be exercised on a suitable surface and attention paid to foot balance and shoeing. Animals that move badly should wear boots to prevent brushing injuries.

Sore shins

Sore or bucked shins are seen in young horses due to the stress of work on immature bone. The area at the front of the cannon bone becomes inflamed with lifting of the periosteum, haemorrhage and microfractures. The front of the cannon becomes swollen, convex in outline and sore to touch. The horse will be lame and may take several months to recover. Treatment includes rest, cold therapy, NSAIDs to reduce inflammation and pain, and physiotherapy.

Joints

A joint is where bones meet and allows movement.

All the limb joints are synovial joints and most are capable of a large amount of movement. They are susceptible to various injuries and diseases.

The joint capsule has an outer fibrous layer attached to the outer layer of bone (the periosteum) and an inner synovial membrane which is well supplied with blood vessels and nerves. The membrane secretes synovial fluid to lubricate the joint and nourish the articular cartilage. The cartilage protects the ends of the bones forming the joint and is thickest at areas of greatest pressure.

Ligaments stabilise the joint. They can be part of the fibrous capsule and are composed of collagen and elastic fibres.

Joint sprain

The ligaments and the fibrous capsule can be torn due to twisting or turning awkwardly. In severe cases the periosteum may also be torn leading to new bone formation (callus). There will be varying amounts of heat, swelling, loss of function and pain depending on the amount of damage. There may be increased production of synovial fluid and the joint capsule will be distended. This may happen as a result of low grade trauma without causing lameness or pain, e.g. articular windgalls and bog spavin.

Articular windgalls are a distension of the fetlock joint capsule seen on either side of

A sacroiliac strain shows as an obvious bump on the croup

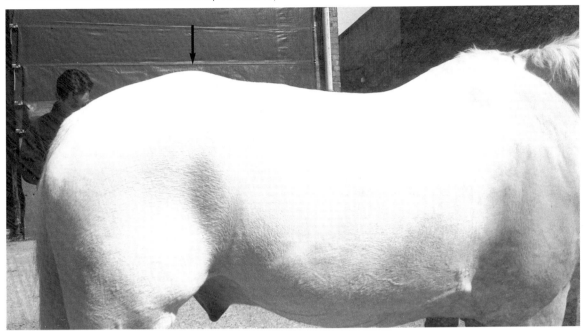

the fetlock between the cannon bone and the suspensory ligament.

Bog spavin is a distension of the tibiotarsal joint of the hock and is seen as a large swelling on the inside of the hock with a smaller swelling above the hock on the lateral side. Pressure on either swelling increases the size of the other.

They are sometimes confused with a thoroughpin. A thoroughpin is a distension of the tarsal sheath of the Achilles tendon (DDFT) above the point of the hock.

Treatment of sprains includes cold therapy, support bandages, rest, and NSAIDs. Radiographs are taken to assess periosteal damage and ultrasound scans for soft tissue damage. Physiotherapy techniques aid recovery and the prognosis is good providing the ligaments are not ruptured. Dislocation occurs when all the joint tissues are disrupted, the limb will be an abnormal shape and will be unable to bear weight.

Sacroiliac strain

The sacroiliac ligaments stabilise the sacroiliac joint between the pelvis and the sacrum. This joint is rigid in adult horses but allows a small amount of movement in young animals. It may be strained or sub-luxate due to an injury, commonly jumping. The tuber sacrale and the tuber coxae will be asymmetrical when viewed from behind. After a period of rest the injury will heal and the pelvis become stable, but horses are often left with a bump over the croup. Often animals return to work with a slight alteration in gait but are not lame.

Joint infections

Joint infections are serious and very painful with an obviously distended joint capsule. They require early treatment to avoid a septic arthritis and destruction of the articular cartilage. Bacterial infection usually follows an accidental wound but in foals may be a result of a navel infection (joint ill). Lyme's disease causes joint distension in older animals. Animals with joint infections resulting from bacteraemia will be sick, have a fever and be depressed. The diagnosis is made on clinical signs, radiography and examination of synovial fluid. The prognosis is grave unless early aggressive treatment with antibiotics and flushing the joint is effective.

Osteoarthritis or degenerative joint disease (DJD)

Osteoarthritis is a common cause of lameness especially in the distal interphalangeal joint – ringbone, and the tarsal/tarsal metatarsal joints – spavin. There are often large firm swellings around these joints due to new bone formation which are easy to see and palpate. The cause of DJD involves many factors which result in loss of a constituent, proteoglycan, from the articular cartilage. The cartilage loses its stiffness and the increased friction between the joint surfaces causes the collagen network in the cartilage to break down. Animals with conformational faults such as toe-in or toe-out or poor foot balance may contribute to the wear and tear on the joints. Certain drugs may affect the breakdown of protoeglycans and so hasten the destruction of the cartilage. Animals in irregular work or working on a poor surface are more likely to suffer joint trauma.

DJD may follow a sprain or a fracture or infection but often there is no history of such an obvious traumatic incident.

Bone spavin

This is a common cause of hindleg lameness. Usually the distal intertarsal and tarsometatarsal joints are affected. Animals with sickle hocks or cow hock conformation are predisposed to bone spavin.

Most cases have a gradual onset of lameness and present as a stiffness and reluctance to work. They are worse after hard work and after a prolonged period of rest. Usually both hocks are affected to some degree with the animal appearing to be lame on the worse leg. The horse will be shorter striding and often drag the toe which shows as abnormal wear on the shoe. It may become more difficult to shoe and resent the leg being held in a flexed position. Trotting on a hard surface will exacerbate the lameness. There may

be an obvious bony swelling on the inside of the hock. Radiographs of the hock will confirm the disease. Animals in the early stages of DJD will not show radiographic signs and these cases will be confirmed by giving articular nerve blocks to abolish the lameness and analysing synovial fluid.

Treatment for spavin can vary depending on the state of the joints. Exercise, corrective shoeing, surgery and medication are all possible forms of treatment. The joints will eventually be destroyed, being replaced by bone, and will fuse together. This can take a long time but when it occurs the horse is no longer lame. Surgery aims to hasten this fusion by drilling out the joints. Some of the pain may be related to inflammation of the cunean tendon as it passes over the joint. This tendon can be cut under local or general anaesthesia. Alternatively the horse can be worked on analgesics in the hope that this will accelerate the fusion process.

Acutely inflamed joints with obvious synovial distension will require rest and further investigation.

Some horses with bone spavin will be able to do light work but will probably never return to their former athletic use.

Ringbone

This may occur in any limb but is more common in the front legs. DJD of the pastern joint is known as high articular ringbone and that of the coffin joint is known as low articular ringbone. False ringbone is new bone formation on the distal end of the first phalanx or the proximal end of the second phalanx that does not involve the joint. Horses with false ringbone may be lame initially but usually become sound once the inflammation has settled down, when they will develop a hard swelling over the affected area. Ringbone may be caused by injury to the periosteal attachment of the joint capsule and ligaments or by trauma to the periosteum. Horses with poor conformation and those in fast work involving twisting and turning are more commonly affected.

Horses with articular ringbone are lame and

Fig.37. The tendons and synovial structures of the lower limb.

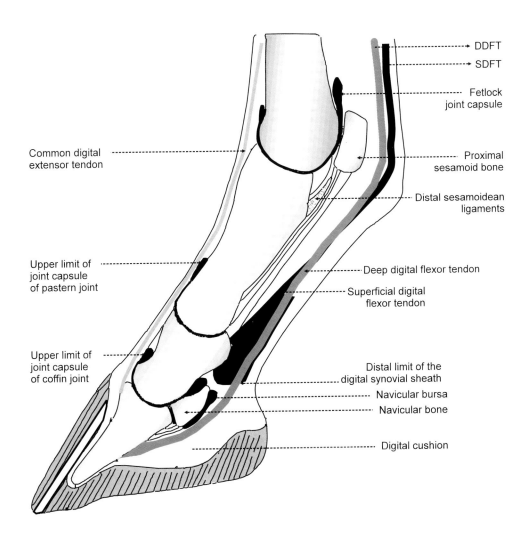

DDFT

SDFT

Fetlock
joint capsule

Common digital
extensor tendon

Proximal
sesamoid bone

Distal sesamoidean
ligaments

Upper limit of
joint capsule
of pastern joint

Deep digital flexor tendon

Superficial digital
flexor tendon

Upper limit of
joint capsule
of coffin joint

Distal limit of the
digital synovial sheath

Navicular bursa

Navicular bone

Digital cushion

will resent flexion and extension of the joint. The lameness will be exacerbated by turning sharply. There may be some heat and swelling over the pastern.

Early cases can be diagnosed on clinical examination, using nerve blocks and radiographs. Treatment by intra-articular injections of sodium hyaluronate or polysulphated glycosaminoglycan (PSGAG) in the early stages of the DJD can reduce the lameness and in the case of PSGAG, prevent further destruction of the cartilage and stimulate the repair process.

Tendons and ligaments of the lower leg

All the muscles of the horse's limbs are above the carpus (knee) and the tarsus (hock). They extend and flex the limb with virtually no rotation of the limb.

The extensor and flexor tendons attached to these muscles run parallel to the bones of the lower limb. The musculotendinous unit is responsible for limb movement and weight bearing.

There is little soft tissue protecting the lower

limb; the bones and tendons are just under the skin and are easily injured. The suspensory ligament lies behind the cannon bone; it is composed of modified muscle. It is attached to the distal row of carpal bones and the metacarpus and at the distal end to the proximal sesamoid bones (fetlock). At the fetlock it divides and passes forward to the front of the limb onto the first phalanx (pastern) where it joins the common digital extensor tendon. The suspensory ligament supports the fetlock joint.

The deep digital flexor tendon (DDFT) and the superficial flexor tendon (SDFT) are behind the ligament.

A synovial sheath surrounds the flexor tendons from above the carpal joint to the mid-

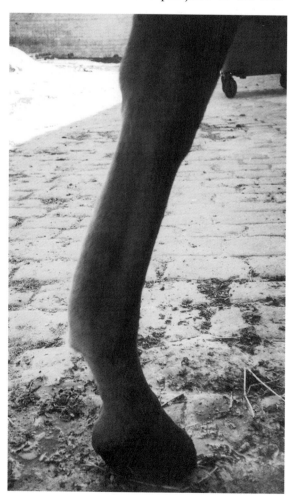

An example of a bowed tendon

metacarpal region to protect them from friction as they pass through the carpal canal at the back of the knee.

The digital synovial sheath protects and lubricates the flexor tendons as they pass over the fetlock, it extends from the distal quarter of the cannon to the middle of the second phalanx. If the digital synovial sheath becomes distended with synovial fluid the swelling can be felt above the fetlock between the suspensory ligament and the flexors. This is a tendinous windgall.

Tendons join muscle to bone. Ligaments usually join bone to bone, e.g. around joints.

The inferior check ligament (accessory ligament of DDFT) attaches the DDFT to the cannon bone. The superior check ligament attaches the SDFT to the distal radius. The check ligaments take some of the strain off the DDFT and SDFT and their muscles. They assist the suspensory ligament in supporting the fetlock joint and prevent it touching the ground when the limb is weight bearing. Any of these soft tissue structures can be overstretched, causing a strain to a tendon (tendonitis) or a sprain to a ligament (desmitis). The complete tendon or ligament may rupture or individual collagen fibres may be damaged. Haemorrhage and inflammation follows rupture of collagen fibres. White blood cells remove the damaged tissue and blood clot. Fibroblasts produce new collagen and start the repair process. This collagen is poorly aligned in the tendon and is weak. Remodelling occurs to replace the weak fibres with stronger, axially aligned collagen. This stage is assisted by controlled exercise. The collagen matures, becoming thicker and stronger. Tendons are slow to repair, taking up to fifteen months, so repeated micro injuries that occur during training can accumulate to produce quite large core lesions in apparently sound horses. These are detected by routine scanning of tendons of horses in training by ultrasound. These lesions may be due to overheating of the tendon core during fast exercise. The accumulation of micro injuries predisposes the tendon to further damage unless they are given adequate time to heal. Horses that do athletic work are prone to tendon and ligament injuries, especially the superficial flexor tendon over the mid-cannon where the tendon is at its narrowest.

Wild horses had no need to gallop for long distances as their predators were only able to sustain small bursts of speed for thirty to forty seconds. Racehorses may be required to gallop for eight or nine minutes with the extra weight of a jockey on their backs. This is expecting a lot of a structure never designed to cope with such forces. Factors that increase the mechanical overload of the tendons, will increase the incidence of injury.

Strains and sprains often occur when the horse is tired, or when the ground conditions are poor. Animals with poor conformation, poor foot balance, inappropriate shoeing and who are overweight are more likely to sustain injuries. Unfit and poorly trained horses and poor rider ability may also contribute to injury. Road work does not harden tendons but will reduce body weight.

The signs of tendonitis and desmitis will depend on the severity of the injury, e.g. mild, moderate or severe. The classic signs of inflammation, heat, swelling and pain will be apparent to some degree. These may be slight but should not be ignored: even minor strains should be treated as potentially serious. When mild injuries are not given time to heal the damage accumulates resulting in a severe injury. Animals with mild injuries may not be lame but the area will be painful on palpation and the injury will be detected using modern techniques. Ultrasound scanning, thermography, scintigraphy and magnetic resonance imaging are used to detect the site and severity of soft tissue injuries.

Animals with moderate tendon/ligament damage will be lame. Treatment is aimed at reducing the amount of swelling and inflammation and controlling pain.

Ice cold therapy with ice packs, applied over gamgee to prevent thermal burns, are used for up to three 30 minute cycles with 30 minutes of firm bandaging in between the cold treatment. The ice packs may be bandaged into place or the horse's limb placed in a cold water boot containing iced water.

Animals with severe injuries are very distressed and often cannot tolerate cold therapy. These horses should have the limb supported and immobilised to reduce swelling and prevent further injury. A Robert Jones bandage, a cast or a monkey splint may be used to keep the digits in alignment. (See page 132.)

Non steroidal anti-inflammatory drugs are used to reduce the swelling and inflammation associated with the initial injury. Other medication will reduce adhesions between the tendon and surrounding tissue such as polysulphated glycoaminoglycans. These drugs may increase the rate of healing and the quality of repair. BAPN, a scar remodelling drug is used in some cases.

Initially the horse will be on box rest with support bandages or a cast on the affected limb. Legs that are taking extra weight need checking daily. Animals with ruptured/lacerated tendons will require surgical repair and have a guarded to poor prognosis.

Therapeutic ultrasound, magnetic field therapy, laser therapy and Transcutaneous Electrical Nerve Stimulation (TENS) machines are used by physiotherapists during the repair phase. Ultrasound scanning three weeks after injury will show the extent of the injury and enable a prognosis to be given. Some cases require surgical removal of blood clots during the first week post injury and the cutting of the superior check ligament after a month.

As the tendon repairs, axial alignment of the collagen fibres is encouraged by a six to nine month graded exercise programme, initially walking in hand or on a horse walker. The time spent walking will increase by five minutes per day and build up gradually to suit the individual case over the first month. By the second month a thirty to forty minutes session in walk will be possible in most cases. The horse will be confined to a small yard or stable at all other times. After three months mild cases may start ridden exercise in walk depending on their progress. Most animals that show good progress should be back in full work in twelve to eighteen months.

Recovery is monitored by regular clinical

examination, measurement of limb diameter, gait analysis using a force plate and ultrasound scanning. Attention must be paid to the animal's diet (to prevent obesity), and to foot care.

Muscles

Muscular problems are common in the performance horse. They may be difficult to diagnose without the use of sophisticated tests to complement clinical examination and gait analysis.

Muscular injuries may be due to trauma or tearing, e.g. muscle strain, muscle rupture, muscle soreness and fibrosis. Metabolic conditions may also affect muscles, e.g. nutritional disorders, azoturia (equine rhabdomyolysis syndrome).

Diagnostic tests include blood samples to measure muscle enzyme activity and thermography to detect the site of inflammation.

Back pain

Back pain may be caused by muscle soreness or strains due to a fall or overexertion. Badly fitting saddles and poor rider ability may also result in a sore back. The skin as well as the underlying muscle may be damaged. Painful muscles will go into spasm when palpated. The horse should be rested and given NSAIDs for pain control and to reduce inflammation. Physiotherapy, heat treatment and therapeutic ultrasound will assist the recovery.

Azoturia or equine rhabdomyolysis syndrome (ERS)

This is a syndrome that affects the muscles of working horses. Exercise, diet, electrolyte imbalance and stress are thought to trigger the disease which can occur in all breeds and ages of horse. The disease tends to recur, especially if the management and diet are inappropriate. Horses with ERS show varying degrees of muscle stiffness, usually in the hindlimbs, and are distressed due to the pain. Animals may be unable to walk in severe cases hence the common name 'set fast'

which is given to this condition. Some animals will become recumbent and some will die. The horse may have hard, swollen muscles and be sweating. Urine will often be discoloured and reddish due to the presence of myoglobin, muscle pigment. Blood samples show elevated muscle enzymes in the plasma, creatine kinase (CK) and aminotransferase (AST).

It is important to prevent further muscle damage and the animal must be rested as soon as the first signs of stiffness appear. It must not be forced to walk. Often the condition appears after a short rest in the middle of an exercise session or at a competition. The horse should be transported to the nearest stable and long journeys should be avoided.

Animals with ERS may develop kidney failure so treatment involves maintaining fluid balance. Fluids may be given by mouth or intravenous drip to prevent renal failure. Urination needs to be carefully monitored and catheterisation may be necessary. The horse also needs analgesia and NSAIDs. Distressed animals require sedation so that they can be treated.

Recumbent animals need deep beds and protection from injury to prominent areas, e.g. elbows or hips. Bandages and blankets may be used for this. All cases should be kept warm and dry and fed a low energy, high fibre diet. They should have easy access to hay and water. Animals must remain stabled until they can move easily, are passing normal urine, and are free from pain on palpation of the muscles. The CK/AST levels should be monitored and the horse must not be transported long distances or put back into work until the levels are within the normal range. The horse will be allowed in a small paddock for part of each day for a week or two before ridden exercise begins. Animals that are recovering from ERS must not be given high levels of cereal grains or too much soluble carbohydrate. The energy intake must be kept lower than expected for the workload. The mineral and vitamin supplement should be analysed to make sure that a balanced diet is fed and the horse should be kept at the correct body weight. The animal must be kept warm when out at pasture with suitable rugs and shelter.

Work should start slowly with a warm-up period. Exercise on a regular basis with a slow increase in speed and intensity is important. Horses recovering from this condition will need careful monitoring in the future to avoid another bout.

Tetanus

Tetanus is a serious disease causing muscle spasm, stiffness and terminal paralysis. Tetanus is one of the earliest known diseases and over 100 years ago a Japanese scientist studied the causative organism, Clostridium tetani, in pure culture in a laboratory. The organism produces spores which can survive for years in the environment. It is found in soil, faeces and the gut of mammals. The organism cannot survive in healthy tissue; it needs anaerobic conditions to survive, so is found in damaged tissue. Wounds, however small, are a common site for the organism to multiply and release the toxin that is responsible for the muscle spasms. The toxin affects the central nervous system and the symptoms of the disease take up to fourteen days to appear.

The horse is the most susceptible of our domestic species to this life-threatening disease.

The signs of tetanus in the horse are those of a progressive stiffness and inability to eat. There is stiffness of the limbs, back and neck. The jaw muscles go into spasm hence the common name of 'lockjaw'. There is prolapse of the third eyelid and the horse will have an anxious expression with pricked ears. The nostrils will be flared and food material may be regurgitated. As the condition progresses the horse takes on a rocking horse stance, stiff legged, neck stretched out, and the tail will be raised. The horse will have a fast heart and respiratory rate and be sweating. These cases are very sensitive to noise, touch and light and the smallest stimulus will result in muscle spasm or convulsion. The horse is unable to urinate or defaecate and it rapidly loses weight due to malnutrition and dehydration. Eventually it will be unable to stand and will die of respiratory or heart failure. This disease is very difficult to treat and only animals diag-nosed while showing the mildest signs, in the earliest stages of the condition are likely to recover. Intensive nursing in a controlled environment with sedation, antibiotics, antitoxin and fluid therapy will be required.

Prevention of tetanus is by an inexpensive vaccination course of two injections given four to six weeks apart, followed by regular boosters at one to three year intervals. The booster interval after the primary course depends on which product is used. All owners of horses, ponies, donkeys and mules should protect their animals by vaccination as they are all at risk from tetanus.

Detecting lameness

Lameness affects the posture when standing and the way a horse moves at walk and trot. It is caused by pain or discomfort somewhere in the musculoskeletal system.

Lameness may be slight, mild, moderate or severe. It may be graded from 0 to 5 where 0 is sound (not visibly lame) and 5 is severe lameness. All lame animals should receive veterinary attention. The more severe the lameness the sooner this should be provided. A lame animal is in pain, although many owners prefer to say that the horse is unlevel or stiff or 'pottery', this is avoiding the issue. Some even say the horse is stiff or unlevel but not in pain!

The vet will require details of the horse's history before examining it. These will include the age, breed or type and:

1 How long has the horse been in the owner's possession?
2 What is the exercise and management regime?
3 How long has it been lame?
4 Has it had an injury, e.g. a kick or fall?
5 When was it shod?
6 Has the lameness altered in severity?
7 Has the behaviour altered?

Lameness may be obvious when the horse is weight-bearing or when the limb is moved and the joints are flexed or extended, i.e. swinging leg lameness.

Normally 60% of the animal's body-weight is on the forelegs and the horse should stand

Using a T-bar to check mediolateral balance

ing the extra weight being handled. It may prefer to stand on a soft surface and may be reluctant to walk in the field or stable so all the faeces are in one spot. The horse may lie down if severely lame.

Moderate and severe lameness will be easy to detect in the standing horse and certainly at walk. If the horse is obviously lame at rest or walk there is absolutely no point in asking it to trot as this could have serious consequences.

Mild and slight lameness may be difficult to detect and probably the horse will have to be trotted in hand on both a hard and soft surface and on a gradient. The horse may be lunged on a small circle to exacerbate the lameness, turned sharply and backed to detect abnormal gait. It may be necessary to see the horse ridden to detect the problem. Some causes of lameness become progressively worse on exercise while others may wear off or become intermittent.

All the limbs including the feet should be examined for abnormal swellings, heat and pain. Digital pulses should be checked and all the joints flexed and extended to detect resistance or loss of movement. There may be signs of muscle wastage. Special attention should be paid to the wear on the shoes and the type and position of the shoes. Hoof testers may be used to squeeze each area of the sole. Defects in the hoof wall and bruising on the sole should be noted and the nails tapped with a hammer. The shoe may be removed to examine the seat of corn and the white line. In severe lameness it may be easy to locate the site of pain, especially if there is a fracture, a wound or a nail stuck in the foot. Mild and subtle lameness are harder to diagnose and need an experienced person to discover the cause of the problem. Firstly it is important to decide whether the horse is lame and then which limb or limbs are involved and finally the location of the pain.

The vet will require the horse to be handled by a competent person who is familiar with horses and confident. The horse can be held on a head-collar and rope or on a bridle with the reins over the head. The handler should wear strong shoes, gloves and a riding hat and may have to carry a short whip. Any rugs and boots should be

square with the front cannon bones vertical to the ground. The pelvis should be level and symmetrical when viewed from behind. The conformation should be assessed. When standing the horse may be resting the lame leg and only bearing weight on the toe. It may point the affected limb and not stand square. It may be taking more weight on the front or back of the foot according to the site of pain. When more than one limb is affected the horse's posture will be abnormal, the back may be arched and the hindlegs further under the body to take more weight. The horse may resent both the lame limb and the limb tak-

removed from the horse. The surface should be level, hard and non slippery.

The horse will be walked away from and turned, and then towards and past the examiner in a straight line. The handler should walk beside the horse and look straight ahead. They must not walk in front of the animal as this will obscure the observer's view. The lead rope or reins should be held loosely a metre from the horse's head so that it can move its head freely. The head movement must not be restricted in any way and the horse must not be pulled along. The horse should be turned away from the handler to change direction which enables the observer to see the horse turn and avoids it standing on the handler's toes! The foot flight pattern is noted as well as how each foot lands and leaves the ground. The length of each stride and foot height is checked. The fetlocks should all sink on weight-bearing to the same degree in the normal, sound horse.

The procedure is then repeated in trot. The trot should be active and steady. The observer must concentrate on the horse, not the handler, nor any other distractions. Dogs, small children, prams, bikes and traffic make it difficult for the examiner to focus on the horse. First listen to the footsteps. The volume and rhythm of the foot-falls will not be equal in a lame animal. It is sometimes easier to listen to footfalls if you close your eyes. Less weight is taken on a lame limb so its beat will be softer, and the beat of the foot taking extra weight louder. The rhythm will be uneven, the toe of the shoe may catch the ground and this can be heard and seen. The horse is then watched as it walks and trots. The hindlimbs are observed as it goes away and the forelimbs as it comes towards you. A hindlimb lameness is seen when there is sinking or raising of the hindquarter and a shortening of the stride length. Forelimb lameness is detected by a nodding of the horse's head. In trot the nodding of the head corresponds to the sound leg taking more weight

and the hindquarters sinking. The horse is weight-bearing on the lame leg as the head is thrown up and the quarters rise. The horse may be lame on more than one limb so the action is shuffling, stilted or pottery; often the head and neck are stretched out.

Certain lamenesses are more apparent on a soft surface or on a gradient. These facilities are usually available when the lameness examination is conducted at a veterinary premises. The horse may be lunged especially if the lameness is only very slight, at trot in a straight line. Working in a small circle puts more strain on the limb on the inside of the circle and makes the lameness more easily seen. Lungeing can be done on a hard, level, non-slippery surface and on a menage. The lungeing area should be safe and properly enclosed. The horse should be fitted with a lungeing cavesson and a 7 m long lungeing rein. The person lungeing the horse should be experienced and be able to walk, trot, and stop the horse in both directions under control at all times. Some horses are evasive on the lunge and fall in on the circle, turn towards the handler, refuse to move or are difficult to stop.

Flexion tests will exacerbate lameness caused by joint pain. Each limb is held in the flexed position for one to two minutes and the handler is asked to immediately trot the horse away while the examiner looks for lame strides. Interpreting flexion tests can be difficult as more than one joint is being flexed each time. The examiner needs to take notes at all stages of the examination for comparison with any future examinations and for use after further tests, e.g. local or intra articular nerve blocks.

Diagnostic ultrasound, radiography, bone scans, arthroscopy and thermography are all veterinary techniques used in the diagnosis of lameness. Samples of blood and synovial fluid may be examined if an infection is suspected.

Video recordings and force plate analysis may also be useful in obscure cases.

Conditions of the Elderly Equine

The life expectancy of equines varies with each species; donkeys can reach fifty years of age, ponies thirty to forty years and horses twenty to thirty years. The working life expectancy is usually much less. Insurance and feed companies refer to animals over sixteen years as being old. The general state of health and fitness of the older horse will depend on the standard of management and the type and amount of work done in its younger years. Any previous illness may lead to problems in old age. Many competition animals may not be able to pursue their particular discipline as they become elderly but may be schoolmasters or compete at a lower level which is not as physically taxing.

All horses and especially elderly animals benefit from an annual veterinary examination. This should include:

1 Blood samples for a full metabolic profile. The amount of liver and kidney enzymes in the blood are tested to detect any disease in these organs.

   The blood cells are counted to check for anaemia and chronic infections. It is very useful to have regular samples from older horses while they are in good health so that these results can be used as a bench mark to compare with any results obtained when the animal is unwell.

2 The heart and lungs should be auscultated to monitor for deterioration in any existing conditions and to detect any new problems.

3 The eyes should be examined for cataracts. Partially sighted animals should be approached carefully. The eyelids are palpated for growths. The lacrimal ducts may become blocked causing tear overflow and staining down the face. Tear staining is also a sign of vitamin A deficiency. Discharges will attract flies.

4 The teeth must be carefully examined using a gag and a torch to visualise all arcades. Sharp points, hooks and peridontal disease can be detected and treated accordingly. Some elderly equines have wave mouths and abnormalities of the incisors. Loose teeth and root fragments are extracted and tall teeth rasped to prevent them touching the opposing gum. Horses who lack good occlusion of their cheek teeth need special feed, e.g. soaked grass nuts. If the horse is unable to grind its food adequately it is predisposed to impactions of the gut which present as colic. Some horses require dental attention every three months. Most elderly equines suffer from some form of dental disease. Tumours are more common in the older horse. Prior to sedation and surgery a full clinical examination is advisable.

5 The animal should be examined for lameness. Many elderly animals have stiffness and pain in their limbs and neck. Neck pain will affect grazing, self grooming and ability to reach water and feed buckets. It may be difficult to reach and pull hay out of a net. The animal with joint pain becomes more difficult to trim and shoe. The

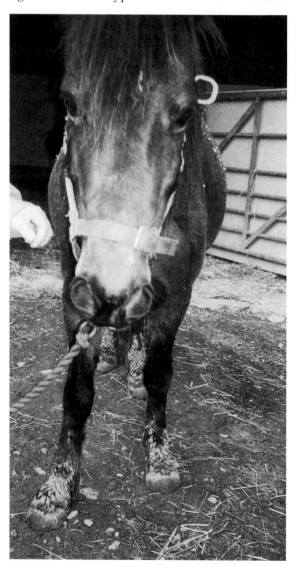

Dilated nostrils seen in COPD, a respiratory disease

pattern of wear on the shoes may alter due to an alteration in gait and limb flight patterns. The hoof horn quality may also become poorer with age, and supplementation of the diet with extra additives may be necessary. Arthritic animals need pain control to improve their quality of life. They may have weaker bone due to low phosphorus levels and are more likely to suffer spontaneous fractures and hip dislocation.

6 The skin is a common site for tumours and older equines may develop a variety of tumours, e.g. lipoma and melanoma. Elderly equines may have excessively long coats and fail to shed their coat in spring. The skin of the elderly tends to be more fragile, prone to infections and trauma, e.g. pressure sores.

7 The animal's body-weight should be regularly monitored. Animals that are inactive may become obese. Overweight animals are putting more strain on their heart and musculoskeletal system. Elderly animals may be in poor body condition due to poor dentition, pain, organ failure, anaemia and low grade infections. Weight loss may be due to gastrointestinal dysfunction. Horses over twenty years may have reduced digestion of protein, phosphorus and fibre compared to younger animals on the same ration. This may be due to previous parasitic damage which has caused scarring of the gut mucosa. There may be altered gut motility as well as reduced absorption of nutrients. Animals on medication may have reduced bacterial digestion and fermentation. Older horses may have lower levels of vitamin C, E and B complex. Prior to altering the diet of the older horse it is important to check their liver and kidney function by blood tests. Animals with hepatic and renal dysfunction will need special diets to prevent further damage to these organs. Those with chronic liver disease require a high carbohydrate, low protein diet, B complex vitamins and glucose. Animals with chronic kidney disease need a higher fat and carbohydrate intake and limited protein.

Soaked sugar beet pulp and increasing dietary fat may improve body condition. There are a number of special formulated compound feeds available for the older horse.

There are several age related conditions seen in equines. Colic caused by colon and caecal impactions are more common in horses over ten years of age. Strangulated gut caused by a fat tumour (lipoma) twisting around the intestine is the commonest surgical colic in the old horse.

Cushing's disease is caused by a tumour of the pituitary gland which is seen in the older horse.

These animals fail to shed their coats, which may be long and curly and they frequently have laminitis. They drink and urinate excessively and often have chronic infections. The diagnosis can be confirmed by blood tests and treated with pergolide or cyproheptadine and good nursing care.

Many geriatric horses have a good quality of life providing that they have the correct management.

It is important to design an exercise regime to suit each animal's capabilities in order to improve suppleness and reduce muscle wastage. Regular exercise is important, avoid fast work on hard surfaces, which jars the joints. Schooling on a prepared surface using large circles can be

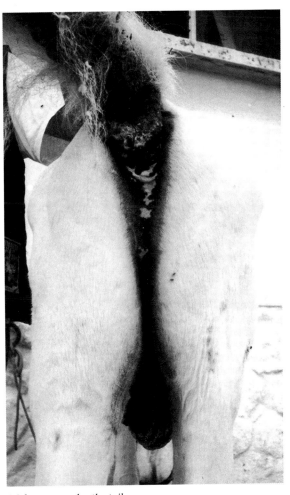

Melanoma under the tail

Pituitary adenoma causes a long, shaggy, curly coat

helpful in keeping the soft tissues supple. If the horse has a tendency to stumble, knee boots should be used for road work. Some animals who can no longer be ridden can be exercised in hand. Pain should be controlled/abolished with analgesic drugs, acupuncture, physiotherapy, massage and warmth. Solaria are very beneficial for older equines, to warm them up prior to exercise and to dry them off after exercise. Non-slip flooring and rubber mats in stables can improve the quality of life as the animal is more confident to lie down. Thick banks and large stables help prevent the animal becoming cast, as do anti-cast rollers. Travelling boots which protect the hocks and lower limbs will prevent pressure sores and rubs on animals that spend a lot of time lying down or have difficulty in getting up. Flat paddocks should be provided for lame animals.

Old horses tend to grow thicker coats and those with pituitary tumours (Cushing's disease) do not cast their coats. They require clipping to

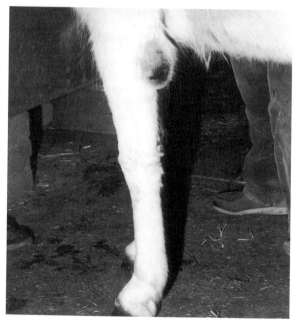

Capped elbow or hygroma

keep the hair clean and the skin healthy. They are more susceptible to skin infections and heavy lice infestation. Grooming is a form of massage and a time to look for bed sores and developing skin growths. The dock, sheath and udder should be kept clean.

Horses should not be allowed to become obese or emaciated. They should be condition scored and their body-weight assessed frequently, e.g. every two weeks. Internal parasites must be controlled, older horses need worming for encysted small strongyles in the autumn and spring and they require regular booster vaccines. They should be fed separately and may require special diets and supplements.

Many older animals appreciate being separated from young, boisterous animals to prevent bullying. They need some peace and quiet and a time to rest. They also require protection from extremes in the climate, e.g. heat stress, cold and wet conditions. They do not tolerate cold as well as younger adults. They need field shelters in summer and winter. Most older horses will be rugged in winter and even native ponies may need to be rugged up as they become older. Stabled animals can have legs bandaged for warmth and to prevent filling of the lower limbs.

Elderly equines need as much, and sometimes more, care and attention than younger animals. They certainly cannot be retired into a field and forgotten about when they are no longer ridden. Most owners will at some time have to face the time when their animal should be put down. This may be because it has a poor quality of life or a terminal illness, or to prevent further suffering due to a serious injury or disease. The veterinary surgeon can advise the owner if the time has come for humane destruction, but the final decision lies with the owner. The horse's welfare should come first so it is wise for all owners to have thought about the subject before it is forced upon them. (See page 143.)

Wounds

Accidental wounds are common and frequently require veterinary attention.

Wounds are usually classified as one of the following types:

1 Bruise or contusion
2 Abrasion or graze
3 Incised wound
4 Lacerated wound
5 Puncture wound

1. Bruise

A bruise is caused by a blow from a blunt object. The skin surface remains intact but there is bleeding into the skin which causes discolouration. There will be pain and swelling and there may be a blood clot (haematoma) under the skin depending on the force of the blow.

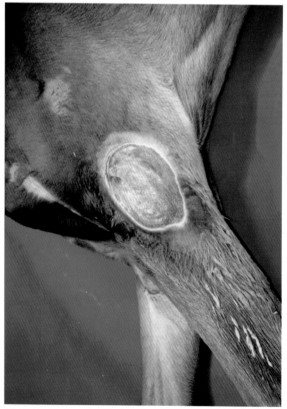

This wound to the forearm of a foal was caused by barbed wire (two weeks ago)

2. Abrasion

Abrasions are caused by friction with a rough surface. They are painful, as a number of superficial nerves are exposed. The surface of the skin is damaged with hair loss and pinpoint haemorrhage. Foreign material such as grit may contaminate the wound.

3. Incised wound

These are usually caused by a sharp flint, metal object, tin or glass. They have full thickness, clear, straight skin edges similar to a surgical incision. They may bleed profusely, especially if a major blood vessel is cut. They are not initially very painful as there is little bruising and inflammation. They may be suitable for primary closure by skin sutures if they are not grossly contaminated. Contaminated wounds must be properly cleaned and may be sutured at a later date (secondary closure).

4. Lacerated wound

These are often caused by barbed wire injuries, impaling on stakes and accidents involving traffic. Lacerated wounds have jagged skin edges, skin flaps and skin deficit. The underlying tissues, blood-vessels and nerves may be damaged and exposed. Fluid and debris collect in pockets. They often bleed profusely and are grossly contaminated. There is often skin loss and tissue death due to a loss of blood supply. These wounds require veterinary attention.

5. Puncture

Puncture wounds often initially appear to be trivial but can be very serious. The small entry hole gives no clue to the depth or direction of the tract beyond it. There can be tissue damage and debris in the tract which travels deep into the underlying tissues. This is the ideal condition for tetanus bacteria to multiply, with possible fatal consequences in the unvaccinated animal.

Puncture wounds are often complicated

A small wound to the pastern

wounds. They may involve synovial structures such as tendon sheaths, joints, or bursa. Body cavities, bones and tendons may be punctured from a small surface wound, these wounds require urgent veterinary attention.

Wounds may appear to be clean or contaminated with hair, soil, faeces etc. All contaminated wounds and even clean wounds will be infected if they do not receive attention within six to eight hours. Infected wounds will be hot, swollen and painful and there may be pus present. Complicated wounds, wounds to the eye or where there is arterial bleeding need prompt veterinary attention.

Wound healing follows certain stages:

1. The inflammatory stage
   This stage lasts from the time of injury to twenty-four hours post insult. The small blood-vessels around and in the wound constrict to limit the bleeding. Within ten minutes small venules dilate and leak blood and serum into the wound. Clots and serum plug the wound. Various types of white blood cells mop up the debris and bacteria. The skin cells at the perimeter of the wound start to multiply at eight to twelve hours. The next stage of repair cannot commence until this stage is completed. A moist environment and a good blood supply is necessary.

2. The repair stage
   This stage takes up to seven days. In most areas where the skin is relatively loose the wound edges start to contract so making the skin defect smaller. In lower limb wounds wound contraction is very slow and starts at day fifteen post injury. The fibrin clot is invaded by fibroblasts which produce collagen fibres and a protein ground substance. The granulation tissue is highly vascular and prone to injury. It continues to be produced until it is covered by the new epithelium.

3. The maturation stage
   This is the final stage of healing. There is a reduction in fibroblasts, capillaries and collagen fibrils. The granulation tissue becomes paler and firmer. As the scar matures it becomes smaller, although it increases in strength over a long time it will never be as strong as the surrounding tissue.

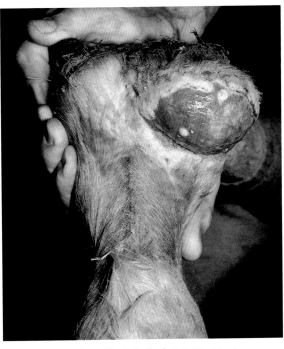

Proud flesh on the bulb of the heel (C. L. Hocking)

109

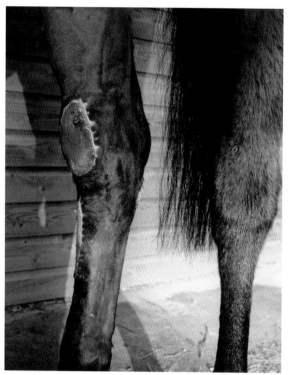

A hock wound which has granulated and is ready to receive skin grafts (C. L. Hocking)

Factors which affect wound healing are:

* The patient's age and physical status
  Elderly and debilitated animals and those with major organ dysfunction heal slowly.

* Nutrition
  The animal's diet is important, especially the protein, vitamin and mineral levels particularly in cases with a large, lacerated wound.

* Therapeutic medicines
  Local anaesthetics and anti-inflammatory drugs delay wound healing. Ointments and wound powders also delay healing.

* Trauma
  Chemicals like antiseptics and physical trauma from bedding materials, insects, or high water pressure from hoses will all delay healing.

* Infection
  Infection at any stage of wound healing will stop the process.

* Movement
  Movement of the wound edges disrupts the epithelial cells that are migrating across the defect.

* Environmental factors
  Wounds require an optimum temperature, pH, blood supply and hydration for cell activity.

First aid for wounds, see page 126.

PART THREE

EQUINE NURSING

REGISTERING WITH A VETERINARY PRACTICE

Every horse should be registered at a veterinary practice for routine health care, e.g. vaccinations, dental maintenance, worming programmes and an annual clinical examination. The practice will also supply and advise on first aid kit and insect control. Animals on the recommended health scheme are less likely to develop serious problems.

The vet will have previous knowledge of the animal, its management, the owner and the location should he be needed in an emergency. This is the advantage in registering with a practice rather than waiting until there is an emergency before making contact with a practice.

The practice will keep a record of all visits, treatment and medication given to the horse. Many practices organise equine clinical evenings on a variety of veterinary topics for their clients' benefit.

Routine visits are booked in advance and during normal office hours. Most practices have set times for arranging such visits. Emergencies may happen at any time and obviously have priority over non-urgent cases. Out of hours visits are reserved for urgent and emergency calls and there may be different phone numbers for day and night calls.

Some practices have their own surgical and hospital facilities whereas others refer cases to colleagues who are specialists in that particular field. When registering with a practice it is advisable to ask about the facilities and the arrangements for surgical or specialised procedures.

Veterinary visit

There are no set rules about when to seek veterinary advice but the owner should be aware of the significance of any signs of ill health. The first sign that something is wrong with the horse may be a change in the animal's normal behaviour and this may be quite subtle. Other signs are an alteration in appetite and thirst and therefore the quantity of faeces and urine. There may be coughing, a nasal and occular discharge and other signs of a respiratory disease. Skin diseases are usually easy to detect when grooming the horse. Digestive problems may present as colic or changes in appetite and faecal content. Lameness will be apparent on ridden exercise or when observing the horse in the field. Once a problem has been noticed, a more detailed examination is required to assess if the condition warrants immediate veterinary attention or can be easily treated by the owner. Veterinary advice can always be sought if there is any doubt and this is preferable to asking the unqualified local horse expert!

Conditions can be categorised into the following groups according to their severity:

1. Emergencies requiring immediate veterinary assistance:

These are cases where the horse is seriously injured or is suffering from a life-threatening disease. The welfare of the animal is of paramount importance and on humane grounds all animals should receive early treatment to avoid unnecessary suffering.

a) Serious injuries are those involving body cavities such as penetrating wounds to the chest or abdomen;
injuries to the eye;
wounds involving synovial structures such as joints and tendon sheaths;

puncture wounds containing a foreign body such as a nail or piece of wood;

fractures to limbs where the animal is not weight-bearing;

continuous bleeding from an injury or body orifice;

injuries to the head, neck and chest causing respiratory distress;

serious burns by fire or chemicals;

smoke inhalation.

b) life-threatening conditions include:

colic where there is an increase in pain and circulatory collapse;

acute laminitis with depressions at the coronary band;

tendon injuries;

difficult foaling;

a collapsed, staggering or unconscious animal;

suspected poisoning;

difficulty in passing urine or faeces or passing blood-tinged urine or diarrhoea;

acute respiratory distress, e.g. allergic response (SPAOAD);

high fever (39°C); heat stroke (40°C);

distress, dehydration or exhaustion after exercise.

In an emergency the vet should be given accurate information about the patient, details of the horse's location and a contact phone number.

The horse should be kept quiet and comfortable and given whatever first aid the vet has advised. While watching the horse, its vital signs can be monitored at regular intervals. It may be necessary to arrange transport for the horse as soon as the vet has examined it. Insurance companies may also need to be notified of the problem.

2. Cases that need veterinary attention the same day.

Wounds that require suturing, or are not responding to first aid or look infected, e.g. swollen and painful. Animals requiring tetanus antiserum.

Animals that are suddenly lame or obviously lame at walk or lame in more than one limb.

Loss of appetite with depression and other signs of illness.

Animals with a fever or hypothermia and other signs of illness.

Increased respiratory rate, coughing and nasal discharge.

Diarrhoea with or without colic.

Eye problems, e.g. partially closed eye, tear over-

flow, cloudy or damaged eye surface, conjunctivitis.

Intense pruritis with self mutilation and distress.

Foaling complications, e.g. retained placenta, weak or sick foal.

Dangerous or bizarre behaviour.

A clean stable with adequate lighting and hot water should be made available for the vet. The horse may need a stable rug and leg bandages and possibly a bridle to be correctly restrained for the examination.

3. Trivial or minor problems should be carefully monitored over the next twenty-four to forty-eight hours and if there is any deterioration or development of other symptoms a veterinary visit should be arranged.

Slight lameness.

Loss of appetite but otherwise bright.

Cough or soft faeces without other symptoms of illness.

Gradual loss of weight.

Non-itchy and non-painful skin lesion.

Preparation

Whenever the veterinary surgeon examines an animal for a routine procedure such as a vaccination he expects the horse to be handled by a competent adult. Children should not handle horses for veterinary procedures as even placid animals can react in an uncharacteristic manner. The horse should be presented in a clean condition and already in a stable with the handler when the vet arrives on the premises. The vet does not want to waste time searching for the animal and a handler, nor waiting for it to be caught in the field. This will make him late for the next appointment. When a routine visit is booked the appointment time will be arranged to fit in with other visits so the vet needs to know in advance how many animals he is examining at each premises. He does not want to be presented with extra animals unless they are genuine emergencies.

In the case of emergencies the animal may have to be examined in a field or on a road if it cannot be moved without veterinary supervision.

Restraint by grasping the skin at the base of the neck

Transport and stabling should be arranged while waiting for the vet to arrive.

Case history and record keeping

A detailed history of the animal is usually required. The age, sex, breed or type of animal and its description including colour, brands or freeze marks are usually kept on the practice records. The length of time it has been owned, what activity it is used for and the type of management will also be recorded. Existing ailments relating to the present problem may also be significant. It is important to know if the animal is on any medication or has a history of allergic or adverse reaction to any products. The onset, duration and progression of the present problem may help in making a clinical diagnosis. The horse may be referred to another clinician or need subsequent examinations so it is essential to have accurate written details of each examination. These details are needed for insurance claims and for calculating the account.

Methods of restraint

The owner or nurse will normally handle the horse for the veterinary examination. The animal may be in unfamiliar surroundings, be distressed, or be in pain and may be unpredictable. It has to be restrained calmly and firmly to prevent injury to itself, the handler and the vet. The handler should wear stout boots, gloves and probably a hard hat. The degree and type of restraint depends on a number of factors: the age and temperament of the patient, the level of training and the treatment/procedure for the injury or disease. The animal should be observed from a distance to assess whether it is calm or nervous, relaxed or agitated. The vet can then decide if physical restraint will be adequate or if chemical restraint should be used. It may require more than one assistant to help the vet and restrain the horse.

The horse should be in a confined area, a stable or small yard. It should be placed beside a wall to prevent it moving sideways. The handler must stand at the same side of the animal as the vet otherwise they may push the horse on top of each other. The horse may be distracted by offering a small feed or by talking quietly to it.

Buildings with a low roof or ceiling should not be used as the horse may bang its head if it panics.

The horse may be held on a headcollar and rope. The rope can be threaded over the nose-band

Restraint using a nose twitch

to apply pressure on the horse's nose if it becomes unruly. If the horse starts to push into the handler they can push the horse away with their elbow while still controlling the head. Some animals are badly trained and pushy but not dangerous and just need firm handling. It is not easy to control the adult horse without controlling its head and a bridle allows more control than a headcollar. A skin pinch or a nose twitch will subdue some horses. Gripping a handful of loose skin on the side of the neck just above the shoulder is a useful method of restraint for a short procedure, especially in horses that are head shy.

THE TWITCH

The top lip can be held by hand or by a humane twitch. This method is used to restrain horses for short periods of time when sedation is not advisable. Applying pressure to the horse's lip causes the brain to release natural endorphins which relax the animal. This takes a few minutes to have the desired effect and some animals will become drowsy so the handler must pay attention. It is not advisable to twitch animals that have been sedated with drugs. Not all horses accept a twitch and some may suddenly become violent after the twitch is applied so care must be taken to avoid injury.

There are two main designs of twitch; a short wooden pole with a loop of soft rope attached to one end, and a metal humane twitch which clamps onto the upper lip and can be clipped to the headcollar. The wooden loop twitch may cut into the horse's nose if it struggles and the wooden handle can swing round which may injure the handler. To apply the twitch the loop is threaded over the hand onto the wrist and the handle held in the other hand. Standing at the side of the horse the top lip is grasped and the loop slipped over the lip. The wooden handle is twisted until the rope is held firm and won't slip off the nose. The twitch can be loosened or tightened as required and the handle must be held securely at all times. The twitch should not be left on for more than twenty minutes. Care should be taken when removing the twitch as the horse may swing its head. The horse's nose should be rubbed and checked for rope marks.

The metal twitch consists of two rounded pieces of metal which hinge together; it is easier to apply. The nose is grasped as before and the twitch is clamped onto the lip. Once in place it can be attached to the headcollar to leave one hand free. Sometimes this type of twitch can cut the nose if the skin is trapped in the hinge as the horse struggles.

THE CHIFNEY BIT

A chifney or anti-rear bit can be used on very strong animals but care must be taken to avoid damaging the animal's mouth. This is a circular bit; the top half goes into the mouth and the bottom half under the chin. A lead rope can be attached to the ring on the bottom of the bit. It should only be used by experienced handlers.

HOLDING UP A FORELEG

This method is used to keep the horse still and to prevent them kicking, especially when treating a limb. It is used in horses that are well handled. As horses are capable of standing on a diagonal pair of legs, when treating a hindleg hold up the foreleg on the same side. If a foreleg is being treated hold up the opposite foreleg. One person should hold the horse and a second person hold the leg. The horse should be stood square and the handler positioned at the shoulder facing the tail. The hand nearest the horse is run down the shoulder and the back of the foreleg to lift the foot off the ground. Horses that are reluctant to

pick up the foot will do so if the chestnut is squeezed. The leg is then held firmly with one hand below the knee and the other on the pastern. The horse must not be allowed to lean on the assistant who is holding the leg. If the horse struggles and the leg has to be released it is vital that everyone is warned to prevent an accident.

Restraining foals

Foals are not always halter broken and cannot be restrained by controlling their heads. They can injure themselves if they panic and tend to rear and rush backwards. The mare should be caught and held quietly with the foal nearby. The foal is then held with one arm around the rump and the other around the brisket and shoulder. They can be carried in this way, size permitting. They respond to having their withers scratched.

Sedation

Chemical restraint or sedation is a very effective method of calming a horse. It is used on fractious animals and for difficult procedures that require the horse to keep still. Sedation is more effective if used before the animal becomes agitated. The animal is clinically examined by the vet; the heart and lungs are auscultated. The type and dose rate of sedative is carefully chosen and usually injected into the jugular vein. The horse is placed in quiet surroundings and allowed a few minutes to become relaxed. Some sedatives cause drowsiness and make the horse unsteady on its feet so care must be taken when moving the animal. The dose rate usually affects the depth of sedation and the length of action of the drug. Sedatives may be given with analgesics.

The horse handler has a responsible job and the vet and other assistants are putting their trust in that person. It is important that they observe the horse's behaviour at all times and do not allow themselves to be distracted.

Basic Nursing Skills

The horse owner is often expected to take on the role of nurse if their horse is sick or injured. Some people do not have the experience, time or facilities; in which case the horse is hospitalised at a veterinary premises.

Basic nursing involves all aspects of horse care including stable management, grooming, feeding, fitting rugs and bandages. The nurse must be able to approach and catch the horse in the stable, fit a headcollar and bridle, tie up correctly and pick out feet. The condition of the patient has to be monitored and this is normally recorded on a day chart. The nurse may be responsible for administering any medication, following veterinary instructions, observing and changing dressings and preparing equipment.

Monitoring the patient

Animals recovering from surgery should be continually observed. Intensive care is needed for colic cases, sick foals and recumbent patients. This will involve a number of people so careful record keeping is vital in order for all the treatments to be given at the correct time and any change in the animal's condition noticed and dealt with immediately. Cases that do not require intensive care may need observation every two or three hours. All observations should be recorded on the day chart. The patient's appetite, food and water intake should be recorded. The amount of urine and faeces passed and the frequency noted. The animal's behaviour, how often it moves, lies down, rolls or shows pain is significant.

The nurse will probably monitor the temperature, pulse and respiratory rate two or three times daily. Other common tests are monitoring digital pulses, capillary refill test, skin pinch test, colour of mucous membranes and monitoring gut sounds. The equipment needed for these tests includes a watch with a second hand, a clinical thermometer, jar of Vaseline, cotton wool or paper towel and a stethoscope.

It is useful to record each animal's normal vital signs when healthy for reference when they are ill. The owner should practise these tests so they are able to monitor their horse's health. The vital signs should be checked when the horse is standing quietly in the stable.

1. *Temperature*
   Do not take the horse's temperature immediately after it has defaecated. The horse can be tied up or held by an assistant. The thermometer is removed from its case and shaken so that the mercury level is lower than the graduated temperature scale. Lubricate the bulb with Vaseline. Stand close to the side of the hindquarters, run your hand over the rump and lift up the tail. Slide the bulb of the thermometer through the anus into the rectum so that it lies against the rectal wall. The

Temperature check

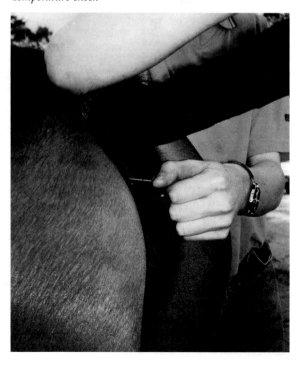

thermometer should not be placed into a faecal ball nor prod the rectal wall. The thermometer is removed after one minute and wiped clean. The temperature is read off the scale. Clean the thermometer in a cold disinfectant solution, dry, shake down the mercury and return to its case. It should be kept in the first aid kit or a cool cupboard.

The average normal temperature for the adult horse is 37° to 38°C (98.5° to 100.5°F). Foals' and ponies' temperatures are normally higher than this, and donkeys' are at the lower end of the range.

When taking a temperature notice if the tail is flaccid and if the anus is slack.

2. *Pulse rate*

The pulse rate is taken when the horse is calm and at rest. The rate increases with exercise,

Checking the pulse rate

excitement, stress, pain and fever. The pulse reflects the heart rate. Any superficial artery can be used; the facial artery as it passes under the lower jaw, the median artery on the inside of the upper forelimb, the coccygeal artery on the underside of the dock, the digital artery on either side of the fetlock joint. The facial artery is commonly used. The horse is held on a headcollar and should not be eating. The artery is located with the finger tips on the lower edge of the mandible, the finger pressure is adjusted until the pulse is easily detected. The number of beats are counted in 15 seconds timed on the watch. This value is multiplied by four to give the pulse rate per minute. The beats can of course be counted for a whole minute if the horse remains perfectly still. Alternatively if a stethoscope is available the heart rate can be counted. The diaphragm end of the stethoscope is placed on the left chest wall behind the point of the elbow with the left foreleg slightly forward.

Normal resting heart-rates vary according to the age, breed, size and fitness of the animal. Normal range is 25 to 45 beats per minute. Large, fit horses will be at the lower end of the range with young and smaller ponies and donkeys at the top end.

3. *Respiratory rate*

The quality, depth and rate of respiration can vary widely among horses. Breathing should be barely noticeable at rest in the healthy animal. The breaths will be even and regular with only slight movement of the chest wall and flanks. Small movements of the nostrils may be detected.

Breathing can be observed from a distance and there is no need to handle the horse. On cold days you can see the exhaled air coming out of the nostrils.

The number of breaths in or out are counted over 15 seconds and multiplied by four to obtain the respiratory rate per minute. If both inspiration and expiration are counted you will have doubled the actual rate. The normal range at rest is 8 to 15 per minute.

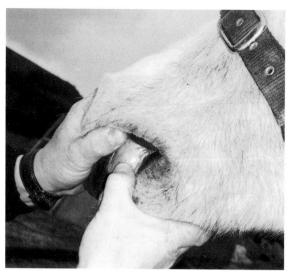

Capillary refill test

4. Digital pulses

The paired digital arteries run down the back of the leg on the lateral and medial side between the suspensory ligament and the DDFT. They can be felt as they pass over the fetlock joint. Digital pulses in all four limbs should be checked as part of the daily grooming routine before picking out the feet, particularly in animals with a history of laminitis. An increase in rate and volume of the digital pulse is an indication of inflammation or laminitis.

5. Capillary refill test and colour of mucous membranes

This is one of the tests used to indicate the state of hydration and the circulatory system.

This test is performed on the gum above the upper incisor teeth. The top lip is lifted and the colour of the gums noted. Normally the gums are pink and slippery to the touch. The gum is then blanched using the thumb and the time taken for the colour to return after releasing the pressure is counted. The capillary refill time should be less than two seconds. An increase in this time indicates a reduction in blood volume or blood pressure due to dehydration, blood loss or shock. Dry mucous membranes can indicate dehydration. The membranes may be an abnormal colour; pale, brick red, jaundiced, blue or purple which warrants further investigation.

6. Skin pinch test

This is a test to check hydration. When the horse is dehydrated water is lost from the skin which becomes less elastic. A fold of skin, usually at the point of the shoulder or the upper eyelid is gently lifted away from the underlying tissue between finger and thumb. It is twisted slightly and released without causing pain, the tent of skin should fall back into place within 1½ seconds. A delay indicates dehydration.

7. Gut sounds

Gut sounds are evaluated by listening over the upper and lower flank on both sides of the abdomen. These sounds vary in frequency, quality and character in the normal horse depending on when it last ate or exercised. Practice is needed to know the normal range of sounds. Absence of sounds or abnormal sounds should be investigated. (See page 63.)

Skin pinch test

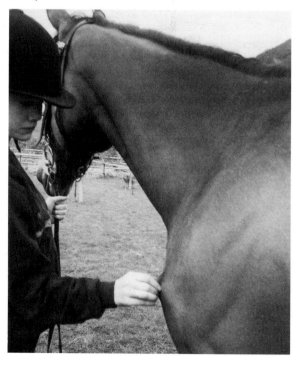

MEDICINES, ADMINISTRATION AND INJECTIONS

Medicines are substances used in the treatment of disease. These may be purchased over the counter by anyone if on the G.S.L. (general sales list), or be P.O.M. (prescription only medicine), prescribed by the veterinary surgeon to treat a specific case. P.M.L. preparations are specially listed veterinary products which may be sold by pharmacists, agricultural merchants or veterinary suppliers.

Certain guidelines should be followed before using any medication:

Check the label to make sure that you are giving the correct medicine to the correct patient. Check the dose rate, the dose interval, and the route of administration. Make sure the medicine has been correctly stored and is within the expiry date. Check it has not been contaminated with other products and that it has not altered in appearance. Read the list of contraindications for use and make sure this drug is compatible with any other treatment the patient is receiving. Some medicines are not suitable for pregnant mares, young foals or animals with liver and kidney disease. There may be competition rules that relate to the drug and a withdrawal period. Some drugs cannot be used on animals intended for meat production and although horse meat is not used for human consumption in the U.K. it is in the rest of the E.U. Follow all instructions carefully and always complete the course of treatment.

Always wash your hands before and after handling medicines. Keep a written record each time you use any medicine and dispose of empty

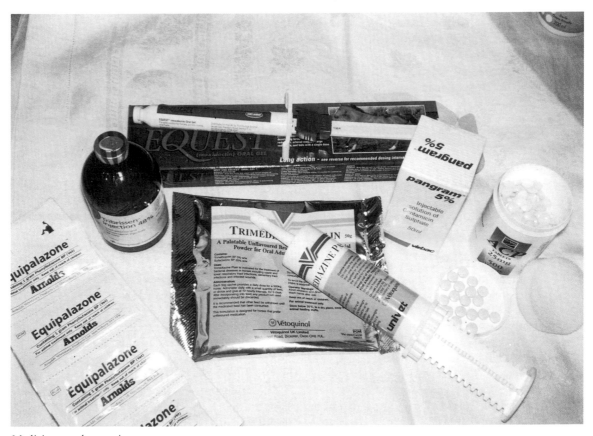

Medicines used on equines

containers and bottles in the veterinary clinical waste. Return all syringes and needles to the vet for disposal.

Medicines may be administered to the animal by a variety of methods:

Topical application

Products used to treat eye conditions and skin diseases are usually applied directly onto the affected area.

Care should be taken when applying drops or ointment to the surface of the eye to avoid further damage. Hold the nozzle parallel to the surface of the eye to prevent stabbing the eye if the horse suddenly moves its head. Animals that need frequent eye medication may become head shy and resist treatment. They will probably be fitted with a lacrimal catheter. The solution is injected into the catheter to avoid handling the horse's painful eye. Care must be taken to prevent contaminating nozzles on tubes of ointment and cream.

Skin preparations such as insecticides are often pour-on formulations. The amount needed is calculated on body-weight and poured down the dorsal midline from the poll to the dock. Washes used to treat fungal and bacterial infections may be concentrated powders or liquids which need to be diluted to the correct concentration before use. Some are left to dry on the coat and others may be rinsed off after a certain time. It may be necessary to clip off a thick coat so that the medicine can be applied to the skin.

Systemic medicines

These include oral and injectable preparations.

Oral products may be powders, pills, pastes or liquids. They may be mixed in the animal's food and the smell and taste concealed by adding treacle, peppermint oil or garlic powder. This method cannot be used on animals with a poor appetite or if you are encouraging them to eat. Good eaters may be put off their food after being offered medicated feeds. The horse has to be watched until it has eaten the complete feed which is time consuming. Pills can easily be lost in a feed so it is safer to feed by hand; push them into the flesh of a ripe pear or apple or fondant mint. Small quantities of powder can be mixed with fruit juice or treacle and spread onto bread; the sandwich is hand fed.

Pastes can be given in a dosing syringe. The animal's mouth must be empty before dosing with the paste. Stand by the horse's right shoulder facing the same direction as the horse. Cradle the head in the left arm with the palm of the hand on the nose above the nostrils. Hold the dosing syringe with the calibrated amount of medicine in the right hand. Place the nozzle of the syringe in the corner of the horse's mouth pointing towards the back of the tongue. Press the plunger to deposit the paste as far back as possible in the mouth. Keep the head up until it has swallowed. (See page 18.)

Small volumes of liquid may be mixed in a feed or made into a paste and squirted into the mouth. Large volumes of liquid should be administered via a nasogastric tube. It is dangerous to drench fluids as they may accidentally be poured into the trachea and cause respiratory problems, e.g. inhalation pneumonia.

Injectable medication

Many equine medicines are only available in an injectable form. The same considerations apply when using injectables as other medicines. Adverse or allergic reactions may occur with any medicine but probably the signs are seen more rapidly with an injectable drug.

The medicine will be injected into the muscle or a vein or under the skin. Each product should be injected into the correct tissue so that it is correctly absorbed and will not cause a reaction at the injection site. The route of injection will be stated on the label.

Injectable preparations are in single or multidose bottles. Horse vaccines tend to be packaged in individual syringes or single dose bottles. Special care is needed when using multidose bottles to prevent contamination of the remaining medicine.

The rubber cap should be cleaned with surgical spirit before and after use. Partly used bottles should be kept in a clean, cool, dark, dry and locked cupboard, preferably in a sealed box, not on a dusty window ledge! They should only be used if the contents are sterile and to treat the animal they were prescribed for. Syringes, needles and catheters are sterilised and individually packaged ready for use and should not be reused.

The size of syringe is determined by the volume of drug to be used. Large volumes may be injected into more than one site. When large amounts of fluid or irritant fluids

Syringes and needles commonly used on equines

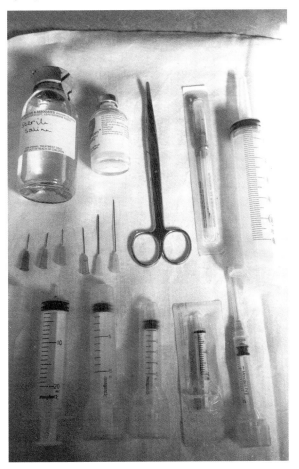

are given intravenously a catheter is used instead of a needle. The gauge of the needle/catheter has to be wide enough to allow the drug through easily and quickly. The thicker the liquid the wider the needle. The needle length is chosen to suit the injection site and size of the animal. Used needles and syringes should be replaced in the containers and returned to the vet to be disposed of in the clinical waste.

Medicines are categorised according to their action on specific tissues or organs, e.g. analgesics, sedatives and anaesthetics act on the central nervous system. Anthelmintics, antifungal drugs and antibiotics are all used to treat different infective agents, i.e., worms, fungi and bacteria. The label will have the brand name and the name of the pharmacological active ingredient and the preservative and any carrier or suspension material. The amount of active ingredient in units per ml is also stated so that an accurate dose can be calculated to treat a specific condition. When using different brands of the same ingredient always check that they contain the same concentration of active ingredient to avoid over- or under-dosing the patient.

Injection techniques

Treatments to be administered by injection are either into a vein (intravenous, I/V), into a muscle (intramuscular, I/M), or under the skin (subcutaneous, S/C). Intravenous injections are performed by the vet, usually into the jugular vein in the neck. Subcutaneous injections are placed where the skin is loosely attached to the underlying tissue, e.g. in front of the shoulder. I/M injections are the most common route used and often nurses, lay staff and owners are trained to perform these injections. Intramuscular injections may be given into any of the large muscle masses; usually the neck, the rump and thigh or the brisket are chosen sites. It is necessary to know the anatomy of the area to be injected and the landmarks used to find the correct location to insert the needle. It is important that the

Fig.38. Landmarks for intramuscular injection sites in the neck and rump

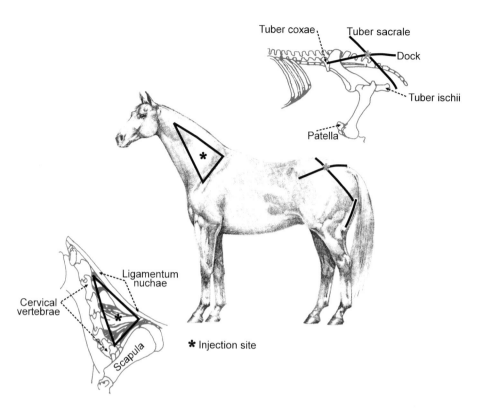

Tuber coxae

Tuber sacrale

Dock

Tuber ischii

Patella

Ligamentum nuchae

Cervical vertebrae

Scapula

✱ Injection site

medicine is injected into the muscle mass and not into a blood vessel or fat tissue, connective tissue, ligament etc. (See photograph, page 11).

There are advantages and disadvantages to all these sites. The injection site is chosen on personal preference, the volume and nature of drug to be injected, the age, size and temperament of animal.

1. The neck

The landmarks are the cervical vertebrae, the shoulder blade and the crest/ligamentum nuchae. These structures form a triangle, bordering the injection site into the splenius muscle. The needle is inserted through the skin into the muscle about a hand's width above the shoulder blade and midway between the vertebrae and the crest. It is easy to restrain the horse for injections into the neck muscle and the skin is thin, so it is easy to insert the needle. The muscle mass is small, so this site is unsuitable for large volumes. The horse may develop a stiff neck if the injection is sited too close to the vertebrae. The drug will be poorly absorbed if injected into the ligament or the fatty crest. Poor or dirty injection technique can result in an abscess which will require draining. This site is unsuitable for young foals or poorly muscled equines except for small volumes of 1 to 2 ml.

2. Rump

The landmarks for injecting into the gluteal muscle are where a line from the top of the croup to the point of the buttocks crosses a line from the point of the hip to the dock. The muscle mass is large and suitable for higher volume of drugs than the neck. It may be difficult to restrain some larger horses for injecting in this site. The skin is thicker so more force is needed to insert the needle and there is poor drainage if an abscess forms.

3. *Thigh*

The hamstring muscles, the semimembranosus and the semitendinosus are situated at the back of the leg. The thigh is the injection site of choice in foals as the muscle mass is large compared to the neck at this age. It is easier to drain an abscess at this site compared to the rump. Needles that are too long may deposit the drug close to the sciatic nerve and cause a temporary paralysis and knuckling of the foot.

4. *Brisket*

The pectoral muscles are easy to locate and used for small volumes of drugs. The skin is thin in this site and there will be good drainage if an abscess forms. Often the site is painful and swollen after injections because of a haematoma formation. The horse has to be adequately restrained – it must not move forwards or strike out as this makes injections at this site difficult.

Preparation of the skin site

Unless the skin area is prepared in the same way as a surgical site skin sterility is not achieved. This would mean clipping the hair and shaving the site before cleaning with an antiseptic solution. This procedure is only used for placement of catheters into veins and injections into synovial structures.

Cleaning the hair over the injection site with surgical spirit is just a token gesture that removes dirt from the hair, it does not kill bacteria on the skin.

Cleaning the area with antiseptic solutions is beneficial if the cleaning is thorough and the solution remains on the skin for a couple of minutes prior to the injection.

Horses often anticipate injections by the smell of surgical spirit or antiseptic as well as the syringe being brandished in front of them!

Most intramuscular injection sites are not sterilised. An area of skin is chosen that is not wet or muddy. The injector should wash their hands prior to selecting a sterile syringe and needle. The top of the needle container is removed and the needle attached to the syringe. If they are not properly attached the drug will spill out of the syringe or air will enter the syringe. The needle cap is left on and the medication label is checked for the drug name, dose and route of injection. The bottle is shaken to mix the contents and inverted. The syringe is then filled and the cap is removed from the needle and inserted through the clean rubber stopper on the bottle. The point of the needle should remain below the fluid level in the bottle while the plunger is withdrawn and the fluid enters the syringe. Slightly more treatment than is needed is drawn into the syringe and then the excess pushed back into the bottle. The needle is then removed from the bottle and a new, sterile needle attached to the syringe for injecting into the horse. The needle used to fill the syringe will be blunt as it has been pushed through the rubber cap on the bottle.

An assistant restrains the horse on a head collar in the stable. The horse's eye can be covered with a cupped hand so that they are unaware of the person with the syringe. They can be offered a small treat like a carrot or apple so that they are relaxed for the injection; it is much harder to inject into tense muscle. Animals that are needle-shy have had a bad injection experience; these animals should be treated sympathetically. Use a different injection site to the one normally used and do not bang the injection site before inserting the needle as this makes the horse tense the muscle. Take the animal outside on a bridle and do not swab the skin with chemicals that forewarn the horse. Use a new, sharp needle to insert through the skin. Make sure the injection fluid is not icy cold. Let the handler speak to the horse to reassure it. The actual injection technique is a matter of personal preference. Some vets bang the muscle with the back of the hand before darting in the needle and then attach the loaded syringe providing no blood is dripping from the needle. If the needle enters a blood vessel it must be repositioned. Other vets prefer to pinch a fold of skin adjacent to the injection site and thrust the needle firmly into the muscle with the syringe attached. The needle must not be allowed to move once in place as this will tear the muscle fibres. The plunger is pulled back to check that no blood enters the syringe in which case the needle is in a vessel and must be removed. When the needle is correctly placed the hub of the syringe and needle are held between finger and thumb and the plunger steadily depressed. The needle is then withdrawn and the cap replaced to avoid accidentally stabbing anyone else.

Sometimes a small amount of blood is seen at the injection site; this should be cleaned.

Different sites or sides of the animal should be used if they are receiving a course of injections. The injection sites should be checked for heat, pain, swelling or abscessation. Animals with stiff necks may be unable to reach food or water. Analgesics may be given to reduce the inflammation and pain.

Some animals develop an allergic or adverse reaction to the drug. This may be because it was injected into the wrong site by mistake. Serious reactions usually occur within a few minutes of the injection and need prompt treatment by the vet.

Occasionally needles are dropped on to the floor and have to be found and destroyed. Needles may break, especially if the horse is struggling. These have to be removed by the vet.

There should be no problems following an I/M injection providing the horse co-operates and a good sterile technique is used. Syringes may be cleaned and resterilised but needles are always destroyed.

FIRST AID

When presented with a sick or injured animal it may be necessary to perform first aid to prevent the condition deteriorating and to improve the chance of recovery. Although most first aid carried out is not life-saving it can make a difference to the prognosis. First aid should improve the prognosis, not make the situation worse. An example of this would be using concentrated antiseptics on a trivial wound and causing a chemical dermatitis. The overuse of poultices is another example of enthusiastic first aid. If it is not broken don't fix it. It is sometimes better to do nothing rather than do the wrong thing. It is far more constructive to seek professional advice as soon as possible. All stables should have a first aid kit in the tack room and probably a second kit for use when travelling. It is also recommended to carry a small kit when hacking. The veterinary surgeon for the premises will advise on first aid equipment. Contents of a first aid kit may include the following items:

Clinical thermometer
Jar of Vaseline
Scissors (round ended, half curved) to clip hair from wounds and cut dressings to size.
Rechargeable electric clippers.
Soap or bacterial hand wash and a towel or kitchen roll.
Plastic measuring jug for accurately diluting irrigating fluid and antiseptic solutions.
Plastic bowl or tray for carrying dressing materials.
Surgical gloves.
Plastic bags for clinical waste and to cover foot dressings.
Twitch.
Surgical boot to fit over the bandaged foot, e.g. barrier boot.
Disposable nappies (these make good foot dressings).
Salt to make a saline solution to irrigate wounds.
Plastic plant spray or a Mills wound irrigator.
Antiseptics, e.g. Pevidine or Hibiscrub.
Cotton wool 1×500 roll.
Roll gamgee tissue.
Cool pack.
Opsite wound spray (permeable plastic skin) for clean trivial wounds.
Poultice, e.g. Animalintex to use on the foot.
Intrasite gel; apply directly onto cleansed wounds.

Wound dressing materials

There are many products that use the moist wound healing system. The kit should contain various sizes of dressings, e.g. 5 cm × 5 cm, 10 cm × 10 cm, 10 cm × 20 cm in the following types:

These may be non-adherent, i.e. do not stick to the wound; non-adhesive, i.e. do not stick to the surrounding hair or skin; absorbent, i.e. absorb wound exudate. There are dressings that encourage debridement, i.e. removal of dead tissue, and promote granulation of tissue.

1 Non-adhesive, non-adherent absorbent dressing, e.g. Allevyn.
2 Non-adhesive, absorbent dressing, e.g. Melolin.
3 Antiseptic dressing, e.g. Inadine with Pevidine or Activate with carbon.
4 Paraffin gauze, a fine mesh impregnated with paraffin.
   Impregnated gauze, an open mesh coated with antibiotic ointment.
5 Kaltostat, a seaweed based dressing that reduces haemorrhage and is incorporated into the wound.

Bandages

Bandages suitable for horses should be $7\frac{1}{2}$ cm or 10 cm wide and 2 to 3 m long.

There are many designs of bandages on the market; they may conform to the limb; they may stick to themselves but not the animal, i.e. cohesive; they may stretch or be elasticated.

1 Polyester orthopaedic padding, a soft bandage that can be used to hold the dressings in place, e.g. Ortho band, Soffban plus.
2 Non-adhesive, stretch, cohesive, conforming bandages, e.g. Vetrap, Co-Plus, Equiwrap.
3 White open weave cotton; these are cheap and strong but non-conforming, non-cohesive and non-stretch.
4 Crepe bandages are washable, easy to use, stretch and conform but are not cohesive.
5 Conforming stretch bandages, e.g. K-BAND or Knit-Firm.
6 Adhesive tape to secure bandages, e.g. surgical tape, zinc oxide tape or insulating tape.

7 Elasticated adhesive tape, e.g. Elastoplast E-BAND, Treplast.
8 Stockinette; elasticated, tubular, conforming bandages useful for knees and hocks and under plaster casts, e.g. Tubigrip, Setonet.

The first aid kit should be kept in a clean container or in a cupboard and checked regularly. Used items should be replaced. It is useful to have a rechargeable torch, wire cutters, a thermos flask and a clean bucket available. The following items can also be kept with the kit:

Controller head collar and lunge line
Exercise and stable bandages
Note-pad and pen
Healthy TPR values for each horse
The vet's and farrier's phone numbers
Contact numbers for all the horse owners on the yard.

First aid kit for travelling should be kept in the vehicle with an adequate amount of water for any weather condition. It should also include:

Thermometer and stethoscope to monitor temperature and heart-rate, to detect heat stress, dehydration and exhaustion.
Aqua spray, an aerosol of sterile saline, or a saline pack.
Antiseptic solution with a large syringe for flushing wounds.
Commercial cool packs or a thermos for ice or a fridge with frozen peas or ice in polystyrene cups.
Curved scissors and tweezers.
Cotton wool or gamgee.
Intrasite gel.
Wound dressings and assorted bandages.
Disposable nappies.
Insect repellent.
Travelling rug, tail bandage, travel boots and poll guard.
Twitch and lunge line.
Hoof pick and barrier boot.
Two 60 cm lengths of wood to make splints.
Mobile phone.

More accidents occur while loading and unloading horses than while actually in transit. Care must be taken if the horse has to be unloaded on a busy road. It is safer to ask the police to stop all traffic and to attach a lunge line to the horse's headcollar or bridle before unloading. Accidents may occur at a sporting venue but hopefully there will be a vet in attendance.

A first aid kit to take out when hacking should fit into a standard size bum bag. It is always advisable to leave directions of your route and your probable time of return at home with a responsible person. Take the following items:

* Money/phone card/mobile phone. Vet's phone number.
* Plastic bag to hold all items. (This could be used on a foot or as a glove.)
* Intrasite gel.
* Allevyn adhesive dressing.
* Soffban and Vetrap bandage.
* Space blanket.
* Plastic waterbottle.

If the horse is injured, dismount immediately and keep the horse as still as possible until you have assessed the extent of the injury. Sudden lameness may be caused by a foot injury, a soft tissue injury to a tendon, ligament or muscle or a bone injury such as a fracture or dislocation. If the condition is serious, get help immediately and do not move the horse. Try to keep calm and avoid exciting the horse with unnecessary movement by other people or horses. Do not put anyone in a dangerous situation. Restrain the horse as quietly as possible and try to reassure it while help is on the way. If the horse can move easily it can be moved from a road to a safer place to wait for help.

Practical wound management

First aid for wounds:

1 Assess the size, depth, site and type.
  The wound may be a simple skin wound, a bruise, graze, incised or lacerated wound. It may be a complicated wound with arterial bleeding or involve tendons or synovial structures or body cavities. Some small puncture wounds have very serious consequences if they involve a joint or a tendon sheath. The tetanus vaccination status of the horse should be checked. It may be decided at this point that assistance is needed.

2 Control the bleeding.

Keep the horse still to stop the blood pressure rising. Arterial bleeding is bright red and squirts out in pulses. A clean cloth or pad is placed directly over the bleeding and held or bandaged into place. Apply direct pressure over the site for at least 10 to 15 minutes. Place second and third dressings with bandages over the site if the bleeding seeps through the first bandage. If the bleeding cannot be controlled seek assistance immediately.

Venous bleeding is dark red or purple and runs out in a steady stream. It will usually clot if covered with a dressing and firm bandage.

Capillary bleeding oozes from the wound and will normally clot.

3 Prevent further damage.

Restrain the horse. Movement increases bleeding and opens the wound edges. Avoid further contamination of the wound. Apply a non-adherent dressing and a bandage to provide support, pressure, and prevent contamination.

Assistance may now be sought.

4 Clean the wound.

Wounds that are simple and not grossly contaminated or bleeding badly may be cleaned.

Antiseptics must be used at the correct dilution otherwise they kill living cells.

Water pressure from hose pipes is too strong to use on wounds. The water forces debris into the depths of the wound and totally waterlogs the tissues so delaying the healing process.

The wound can be flushed with sterile saline solution using a 60 ml syringe with an 18 gauge needle attached; a hand-held plastic indoor plant sprayer; a Mills wound irrigator or an Aquaspray aerosol.

A saline solution is made by adding a teaspoonful of salt to a pint of previously boiled water.

The hair from the skin edges should be removed to allow full inspection of the wound. The wound is filled with intrasite gel or K-Y GEL to prevent the cut hair falling into the wound.

The wound is then irrigated again with saline solution.

The wound is dressed according to the type and status.

First aid treatment for specific types of wound:

1 *Bruise*

Rinse with saline.
Dry on a paper towel.

Apply a cool pack over a sheet of gamgee or wool to control the bleeding for 30 minutes.
Call the vet if the area is very painful or the horse is lame.

2 *Abrasion*

Wash with saline to remove surface contamination.
Apply cool pack over a non-adherent dressing for 30 minutes.
Apply Intrasite gel, Allevyn and bandage to give support.
Call the vet if there is pain, swelling or lameness.

3 *Incised wounds*

Control the bleeding with a pressure pad and bandage.
If the bleeding is not serious clean with saline.
Apply Intrasite gel, a non-adherent dressing and bandage.
Call the vet as the wound may need sutures.

4 *Lacerated wounds*

These wounds always require veterinary attention.
Clean with saline to remove gross contamination.
Apply Intrasite gel, Allevyn dressing and bandage to support and protect limb wounds while waiting for the vet.

Large wounds on the body can be protected with a clean tablecloth, pillow case or cotton sheet. The vet will be required if the wound is to be sutured or if it is grossly contaminated or already infected or if it is a complicated wound.

5 *Contaminated wounds*

Irrigate with warm saline solution providing there is no bleeding.
Dress and bandage to prevent further contamination.

6 *Infected wounds*

Flush with warm saline to remove pus and exudate.
Dress and bandage.

7 *Complicated wounds*

Do not move the horse.
Do not wash the wound.
Apply Intrasite gel, Allevyn dressing and a firm bandage.
A Robert Jones bandage or splints may be needed before the horse can be moved if it has a serious tendon, joint or bone injury.

The horse may be in shock and should be kept warm. A thermatex rug may be placed over the cotton sheet if there is an injury to the chest or abdomen.

Dressings are normally held in place by bandages on limb wounds. All the necessary materials to treat the wound should be prepared before the horse is restrained. Packets should be opened and cotton wool or gamgee cut to size before the treatment commences. The vet may advise on which dressing is to be used at each stage of healing depending on the amount of exudate and sepsis. The frequency at which the bandages are changed should also be under veterinary supervision. Clean wounds with little exudate may need to be redressed every three or four days whereas heavily contaminated wounds may need to be redressed every twelve to twenty-four hours.

Reasons for applying bandages

Bandages are used to hold wound dressings and catheters in place. They protect wounds from contamination with faeces and trauma from bedding materials and prevent the animal licking or biting the wound. Bandages can help control haemorrhage and swelling. They support injured tissue, prevent movement of wound edges and suppress the formation of granulation tissue. They reduce pain by restricting movement and reduce swelling. They also provide warmth and keep the under layers in place to distribute pressure evenly over the limb.

In all cases of injury it is best to cover a good length of the limb above and below the injury in the bandage. A distal limb injury will be bandaged from just below the carpus or tarsus to the distal pastern.

First layer
Wounds require a dressing material to absorb exudate, remove dead tissue and maintain asepsis. This is held in place by orthopaedic felt.
This layer is only required if there is a wound.

Second layer
A layer of cotton wool or gamgee applied so that it conforms to the limb and lies flat without ridges or lumps.
This is held in place by conforming, cohesive stretch bandages.

Third layer
This is the sealing layer and is either an adhesive, elasticated bandage like Elastoplast or a cohesive, stretch bandage like Vetrap.

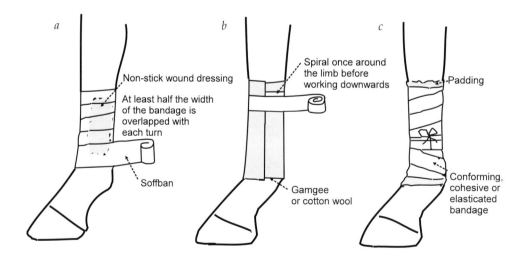

Fig.39. (a) *Bandage for a wound to the cannon.*
(b) *Applying a stable bandage over gamgee or fybegee.*
(c) *Applying a support or exercise bandage.*

Fig.40. Applying a figure-of-eight bandage to the left fore-knee.

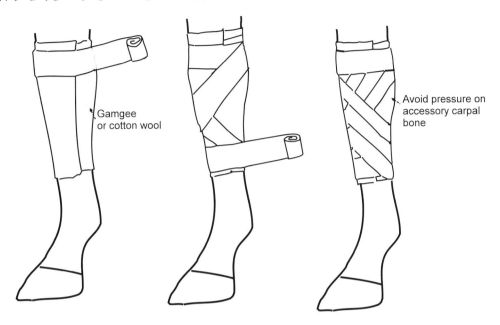

Gamgee
or cotton wool

Avoid pressure on
accessory carpal
bone

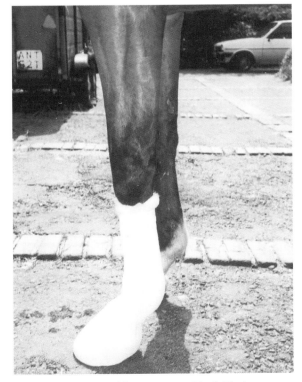

*This horse had injured her pastern and heel. The lower
limb was swollen to a point slightly below the knee. The
foot was included in the bandage.*

Bandaging limbs

Prepare all materials and ask an assistant to hold
the horse. Apply a non-adherent dressing to the
wound and bandage in place using orthopaedic
felt. The right legs are bandaged in a clockwise
direction and the left legs in an anti-clockwise
direction. This pulls the flexor tendons to the
inside of the limb. Each turn of the bandage
overlaps the previous turn by half its width.
Even pressure should be used so that the bandage is snug to the limb. A piece of gamgee or
cotton wool is wrapped around the limb with
the overlap on the outside and pointing backwards. A cohesive, conforming stretch bandage
is used to hold the padding in place. The
bandage is unwrapped and pulled to half its
stretch as it is applied round the limb.
Depending on the length of the bandage it
may be possible   to spiral down the leg and
back up to the top of the dressing. Do not
stretch the last 10 cm of a cohesive bandage,
just press it flat against the last layer of
bandage so that it will stick properly. The
bandage should not overlap the padding at
the top and bottom of the bandage. An
adhesive elasticated bandage can be applied to

give extra support and protection to the injury. Do not attach adhesive bandages to the horse's skin or hair if the bandage is to be removed each day. Injuries to the fetlock or pastern should be bandaged from the hoof to just below the knee or hock.

Adhesive bandages can be attached to the hoof wall to prevent bedding material getting inside the bandage. Bandages should be comfortable, not too tight and should not fall down.

If the bandage is too tight there will be swelling above and below it. The leg will be painful to touch when the bandage is removed. Tight bandages can result in skin sloughs and areas of white hair (acquired marks). The horse may chew the bandage if there is any discomfort.

Bandages may be protected with boots or stable bandages. Support bandages may be applied to the non-affected limbs if the horse is lame and reluctant to move.

Bandaging the knee

The knee is a difficult site to bandage as gravity is against you. The top of the limb is wider than the bottom so the bandage tends to slip down the leg. The knee is constantly bending which moves the bandage. The bony prominences of the knee should not be covered with a tight bandage as it is easy to cause pressure sores on the skin over the accessory carpal bone and the medial distal radius. The bandage is unwrapped in a figure-of-eight to avoid the bony prominences. When the bandaging is complete the outer layer can be incised over the pressure points to relieve any tension caused by traction on the padding. A lower limb support bandage with padding and a stable bandage is applied, this prevents filling of the distal limb and also prevents the carpal bandage slipping down.

Bandaging the hock

The hock is bandaged in the usual three or two layer method avoiding pressure on the point of the hock. A figure-of-eight method is used which allows the horse to bend the hock without causing pressure on the point of the hock. A distal limb stable bandage is applied for the same reason as the knee.

Alternatives to bandages for knees and hocks are:

* Tubular stockinette
* Lycra stockings with zip fastenings
* Neoprene shaped support boots with adjustable velcro fastenings

These are all available in various sizes.

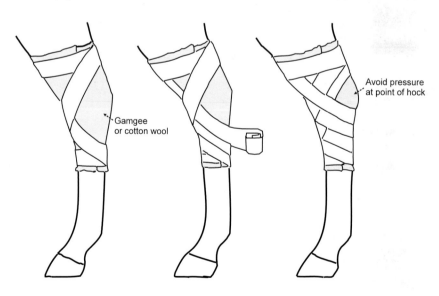

Fig.41. Bandage technique for the left hind hock; the bandage is unwrapped in an anticlockwise direction.

Tubular stockinette is cut to the required length. A small plastic bag is placed over the foot so the stocking will stay clean and be easier to slip over the foot. The stocking is rolled into a doughnut and pulled over the foot. It is taken up the limb above the area to be bandaged and rolled down to hold a dressing in place. The horse's hair should be laid flat.

The lower end of the stocking can be rolled up to clean the wound or replace the dressing. The upper end of the stocking may be secured with Elastoplast. A stable bandage is used on the lower limb.

Bandaging the foot

The foot may be enclosed in a bandage to protect the sole, the wall and injuries to the heels and coronary band. Bandages last longer if the foot is unshod. Horseshoes cut through the bandage if the horse is walking on a hard surface. Disposable nappies conform well to the foot and are easier to secure than a square of gamgee or cotton wool. A stretch, cohesive bandage anchored around the pastern and covering the foot in a figure-of-eight is applied over the nappy. This may be covered by Elastoplast or

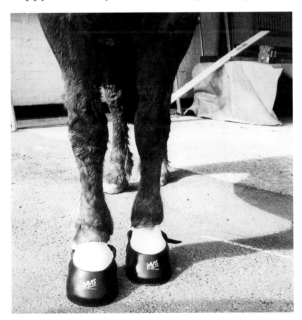

Barrier boots help protect foot dressings

waterpoof tape or a barrier boot. The foot tends to sweat if kept inside plastic bags or rubber boots and the bandages will be damp. It is important to have a high standard of stable hygiene to prevent the bandages being contaminated with faeces and urine. The bed should be thick and clean.

Poulticing the foot

Poulticing infected wounds was a popular practice and many products were used, e.g. bran and epsom salts, kaolin, magnesium sulphate paste. Today the only area poulticed is the sole of the foot and usually with the commercially prepared poultice.

Animalintex consists of a thick padding impregnated with bassorin and boric acid. The padding has a polythene backing. The poultice is cut to the required size and placed polythene side upmost in a dish of hot water. It is squeezed almost dry and the padding side placed against the cleansed foot, with a pad of gamgee or wool over it. This is covered in a foot bandage or a sock to hold the padding in place. The poultice remains warm for a short time and may improve the blood supply to that area. The polythene backing retains the heat and keeps the moisture in the padding. The poultice is supposed to draw any infection out of a hole or defect in the hoof capsule, it also softens the hoof horn and may make paring the hoof easier. The poultice is replaced at twelve hour intervals until it has had the desired effect. Overuse of poultices creates a wet, smelly foot.

Tubbing the foot

Hot tubbing is a useful method to improve the circulation to the foot and encourage abscesses to burst. The foot is cleaned and scrubbed to remove gross contamination. The horse is held by an assistant and the affected foot is lifted. The shallow bowl or bucket is positioned where you are going to place the foot. As the foot is put down the assistant picks up the opposite front leg to prevent the horse stepping out of the container. If a hind foot is being treated the front

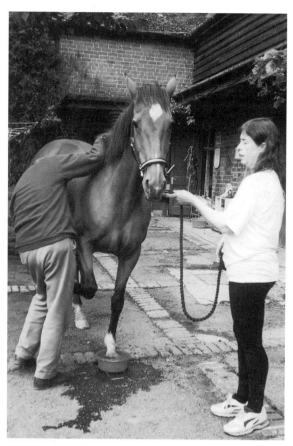

Tubbing the foot

multiple layers of cotton wool compressed by conforming bandages. It can be applied as a half or full limb bandage.

It is used to stabilise limb fractures, to restrict soft tissue damage, control limb oedema and to support wounds.

To construct an RJB four to eight rolls of cotton wool, eight to fifteen conforming bandages plus six rolls of adhesive bandage are required. Splints may be incorporated into the bandage to give more support and rigidity. This is especially useful when moving fracture patients. Not all fractures are untreatable but many become so due to incorrect first aid and damage during travelling and movement of the horse.

Applying an RJB

Wounds are cleaned and covered in a non-adherent sterile dressing held in place by orthopaedic felt. Cotton wool is applied snugly around the leg from the foot to the knee or hock for a half

limb on the same side should be lifted. A hand is placed on the front of the knee or cannon bone to keep the foot in the bowl. Warm water is slowly added to the bowl until the hoof is submerged, more water may be added as the water cools. Sometimes the water is added to the container before the horse's foot is placed in it, but it is often kicked over or spilled before the horse is positioned. Tubbing the foot may be repeated several times during the day. The limb is dried carefully between sessions. This method is cheap and easy and avoids using so many expensive bandages.

The Robert Jones bandage

A Robert Jones bandage (RJB) is constructed with many layers and uses a large amount of dressing material. It is strong and rigid due to the

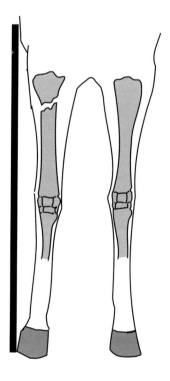

Fig.42. A lateral splint from the ground to the shoulder is used to stabilise a fracture of the radius.

132

Fig.43. The foreleg divided into four regions for Robert Jones bandaging and splinting.

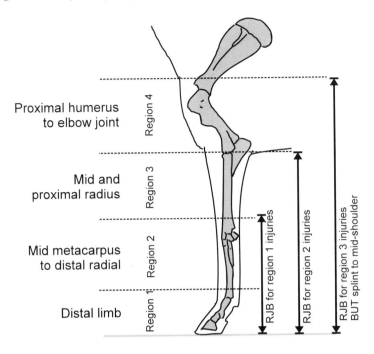

Proximal humerus
to elbow joint — Region 4

Mid and
proximal radius — Region 3

Mid metacarpus
to distal radial — Region 2

Distal limb — Region 1

RJB for region 1 injuries

RJB for region 2 injuries

RJB for region 3 injuries
BUT splint to mid-shoulder

limb or to the elbow or stifle for the full limb. Each layer should be 2 to 3 cm thick. Conforming bandages are used to compress the cotton wool using firm pressure so that the bandaged limb is a uniform thickness. This means that more wool is placed around the narrower areas of the leg, e.g. the pastern. A second cotton wool layer of 2 or 3 cm is wrapped around the limb and compressed with conforming bandages. This is repeated for at least three layers. Each layer should be evened out with half width wool on any narrow places. When all the layers have been applied the entire bandage is wrapped in elastic adhesive bandage maintaining an even pressure throughout. The finished RJB should look like a cylinder.

Splints are added to support fractures or where the suspensory apparatus is damaged and when a full limb RJB has been applied. Splints may be wooden or plastic guttering. The ends of the splints should be covered in padding to prevent them traumatising the skin. Wooden splints should be approximately 53 and 84 cm (21 and 33 in) long by $2\frac{1}{2} \times 5$ cm (1×2 in) depending on

the size of the horse and the area to be splinted. Guttering should be used in a double layer. The splints are attached to the RJB by heavy duty tape.

The fore and hindlimb may be divided into four regions which require different splinting techniques.

REGION 1

Injuries from the distal cannon to the foot require an RJB from the ground surface of the hoof wall to the knee or hock. The bones should be aligned before applying the splint to the front of the limb. The foreleg is held off the ground by an assistant holding it by the forearm so that the dorsal surfaces of the distal limb bones are aligned. The hindlimb is held above the hock to align the distal bones.

REGION 2

Injuries between the distal radius and the mid-cannon in the forelimb require an RJB from the ground to the elbow, with splints on the outside and back surface of the bandage.

133

Fig.44. The hindleg divided into four regions for Robert Jones bandaging and splinting.

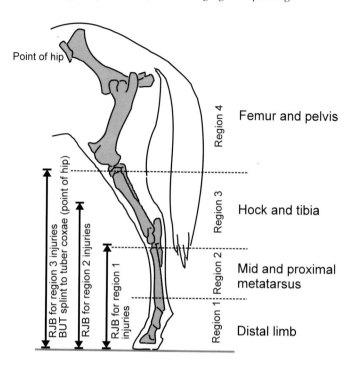

Injuries between the top and mid-section of the hind cannon require a full limb RJB with splints to the height of the hock on the outside and back of the limb.

REGION 3
Injuries to the radius require a full limb RJB with splints on the lateral side of the limb from ground to mid-shoulder. Injuries to the tibia or hock should have a full limb RJB with a splint from the ground to the hip on the lateral side of the limb.

REGION 4
Fractures to the ulna, humerus and scapula cannot be splinted. If the knee is fixed with a splint over padding to the back of the limb from the fetlock to the elbow the horse will move more easily.

Hindlimb fractures to region 4 cannot be splinted. Horses with heavily splinted and bandaged limbs may move awkwardly or panic, so the utmost care must be taken when moving them to prevent injury to the handlers.

TRANSPORTING INJURED EQUINES

The legal situation

There are a number of rules relating to the transport of injured and sick animals in the Welfare of Animals During Transport Order 1992 that apply to equines:

* No animal may be transported in a manner that causes, or is likely to cause it injury or unnecessary suffering.
* No person shall cause or allow the transport of an animal that is unfit to travel because it is diseased, infirm, ill, injured, newborn or given birth within the last 48 hours or likely to give birth in transit except under veterinary guidance.
* Only a veterinary surgeon is qualified to decide if an equine can be transported and it can only be moved to the nearest hospital which has the expertise, equipment and personnel needed to treat it. It can only be moved in the presence of and under the supervision of the vet.

Type of vehicle

Injured horses are transported in specially designed horse ambulances or in a standard horse box or horse trailer.

* Horse ambulances.
  These are mandatory on racecourses and available at many competition venues. They are supplied with experienced drivers and horse handlers. If competitors insisted on this facility at all shows with a duty equine veterinary surgeon on site, the treatment and movement of injured animals would improve.
  Trailer ambulances should be towed by a four wheel drive vehicle. They must have low loading front and rear ramps with a shallow slope. The internal partitions must be well padded and easily moved. There should be a drag mat and a winch for moving recumbent or unconscious animals. A belly sling is used to support animals that are likely to go down or are unsteady on their feet. The person travelling with the patient should be able to reach all sides of the animal with ease. There should be good internal lighting.
  Obviously ambulances must be well maintained with good suspension to give a smooth ride. They should be well ventilated with plenty of headroom inside and in the doorways. The handler should be able to communicate with the driver during the journey.
* Regular horse box and trailer.
  Ordinary transport vehicles may be used to travel the injured horse providing the ramps are low and gently sloping and there is adequate space inside with narrow partitions for the horse to lean against. The space between partitions may be reduced with mattresses or duvet covers filled with straw tied to the partition. Bales of straw may be used under the horse instead of a belly band. The floor of the vehicle should be checked to make sure that it will support the horse with extra weight on the sound limb, if not, it should be reinforced with thick plywood. The partitions must be easy to move for unloading and if the horse falls down in transit. Before loading the horse it is important to consider where it is to be unloaded and whether the ramps can be positioned to unload at the correct side. Do not load an animal into a trailer if it cannot be unloaded at the end of the journey!

The veterinary surgeon will examine the horse and apply bandages and splints and administer analgesics etc. before it is moved. The trailer should be positioned near the horse on level, smooth ground if possible. The material on the ramp and floor should be non-slip like shavings, sand or rubber mats. Ideally the horse should travel with the injured limb to the rear of the vehicle, this is only possible if there are forward and rear ramps to allow easy unloading. The horse should be held on a bridle and allowed to walk a few steps on the flat to adjust to the splints and RJB. Well supported horses can walk quite well on three legs if moved quietly and carefully.

A sensible, calm person should travel with the horse. The horse must be allowed to use its head and neck to balance itself during transit. The bar in front of and behind the horse should be padded to restrict movement and allow the horse to lean against it. The driver must be considerate and take the route with the least bends, hills and traffic lights etc. A long journey is not ideal as the horse will become exhausted. There is a list of hospitals, with the facilities needed, that are willing to take emergency cases, see page 150. They should be informed in advance that the patient is en route and the estimated time of arrival. The veterinary surgeon who has been treating the horse should send written details of the treatment to date and speak to the hospital duty vet.

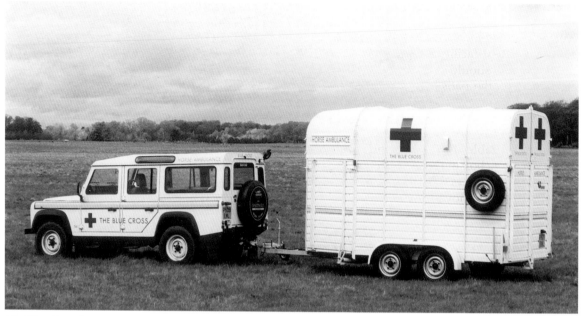

The Blue Cross horse ambulance (The Blue Cross)

The interior of the ambulance is fitted with adjustable supports and slings (The Blue Cross)

Nursing Sick Horses

General considerations

Horses may be nursed on the owners' premises or in a hospital facility. Stables used to hospitalise horses should be the correct size to accommodate the patients. The floor and walls should be easy to clean. The ideal is roughened concrete floors with sealed rubber mats and cemented walls painted in water resistant paint. The stable fittings should be easily removable. The box must be well ventilated and light with wide doors that open outwards, or be on runners and move sideways. The ceiling beams must be able to support equipment to sling a horse and be the correct height. There should be easy access to pasture or a menage, as well as for vehicles to load and unload horses. The bedding material used must suit the particular patient. Disposal of stable waste must be arranged.

Isolation box

A separate stable is needed as an isolation facility for horses with infectious or contagious diseases, e.g. viral or bacterial respiratory diseases; bowel diseases like Salmonella and rotavirus; fungal skin disease, e.g. ringworm.

Ideally the isolation area should be at least 35 m and downwind from other animal housing and have separate drains. It should be situated well away from the main buildings and thoroughfares. The isolation box should have its own feed and bedding store, and equipment for mucking out. At the box entrance a disinfectant foot bath and washing facilities for the nurse are needed. The nurse should be provided with rubber footwear, waterproof, washable outer clothing and plastic disposable gloves. One person should tend to the sick horse. They should change all their clothing and shower before going near any other horses.

All waste feed and bedding material should be burned if possible. The area should be cleaned twice a day and disinfected after the patient has recovered.

All the bedding material is removed from the box before it is steam cleaned and disinfected. The area outside the box must also be disinfected.

FAM, an iodophor disinfectant and detergent steriliser is highly effective against all bacteria and most viruses. It is active in the presence of organic material and is biodegradable and relatively non-irritant and non-toxic.

Nursing patients with respiratory disease

The patient should be kept warm in a well ventilated stable. Thermatex rugs and stable bandages may be used.

Discharges from the nose and eyes may be removed with damp cotton wool, and a smear of Vaseline placed under the eyes and on the nose to prevent further discharge from sticking to the skin. The used cotton wool is placed in a polythene bag for disposal. Fresh, clean water should be easily available and replaced several times each day. Horses with sore throats and mouth ulcers may prefer lukewarm water.

The feed should be moist and nutritious; a forage based diet with soaked sugar beet is ideal. Small, frequent meals with grated carrots, apples and hand pulled grass can be offered.

The horse should have its own water buckets and feed mangers. These should be frequently cleaned to remove nasal discharges which will contaminate them.

The hay must be dust-free and soaked for five to thirty minutes before feeding from a floor container to encourage postural drainage. Soaking the hay washes out some of the dust and swells the mould and fungal spores so they are not inhaled as they are stuck to the hay.

Horses who have contact with spores when they have a viral respiratory infection, which damages the cells lining the tract, may later develop allergic respiratory disease, e.g. COPD. Inappetent horses can be encouraged to eat if they have their heads steamed with eucalyptus or friars balsam vapours before they are fed. These aromatic oils are placed in a steamer or a bucket on cotton wool and boiling water added. The horse inhales the steam through a mask or by holding the bucket under its nose. Take care not to scald the horse!

The horse should be kept quiet and mucking out should be done with as little movement of bedding as possible to prevent airborne dust particles. Dust free white shavings or paper bedding on top of rubber mats are the best beddings. Dust extracted straw is available prepacked in bags.

Deep litter beds should be avoided as the ammonia in urine is an irritant to the respiratory tract.

The nurse should monitor progress and keep a daily record of TPR, faeces, urine and the amount the horse is eating and drinking. The medicine should be administered as advised by the vet. Medication may be given twice daily (bid) that is every 12 hours or three times daily (tid) every eight hours or four times daily (qid), every six hours. Some medicines are administered as aerosols using a nebuliser system with a face mask so the drug is inhaled into the lungs. Probiotics may be fed after antibiotic therapy.

When the patient is recovering it will accept more grooming and handling. It may be grazed in hand away from other horses or walked out to improve its mental well being. It takes four to six weeks for the respiratory tract to heal after a viral infection and during this time the horse should be convalescing.

Nursing a horse with a painful eye

Eye infections and injuries are painful and the horse may rapidly become head shy. It should be placed in a darkened box and contact with dust and flies should be avoided. Hay should be soaked and fed in a floor container, and the horse may be allowed to graze at night.

Usually a nasolacrimal catheter is fitted to administer medicaments to the eye in the acute stage of the disease. The catheter is placed into the nasal ostium in the nose and threaded up the duct. It is either sutured or glued to the external nostril and the horse's forehead and neck. It is threaded over the poll onto the opposite side of the neck to the painful eye. A head and neck cover can be worn to prevent the catheter being caught on stable fittings.

The horse should be held by an assistant standing on the horse's good side. The nurse can remove the cap on the catheter, attach the syringe to the catheter and flush solutions into the eye. The cap is cleaned and replaced. The horse may also need systemic analgesics and antibiotics.

Eye ointments are easier to apply if they are warm. Discharges are wiped away with cotton wool damped in warm boiled water. The nurse should wash her hands and wear surgical gloves. The lower eyelid is pulled away from the eyeball. The cap is removed from the tube and the hand holding the tube is rested against the horse's cheek to prevent accidentally stabbing the eye if the horse moves. The tube is held parallel to the eyeball and the ointment squeezed into the everted lid. The nozzle should be cleaned and the cap replaced. Opened tubes should be thrown away after a month. Each patient should have their own tube labelled with their name.

Nursing the colic case

All colic cases should be fitted with a padded headcollar and a pollguard. The bedding should be inedible and banked to prevent the horse becoming cast. All removable stable fittings should be taken out of the stable. The horse should not be allowed food or water unless directed by the vet. The patient should be carefully monitored without putting anyone at risk. A written record of all observations should be made and may be used by the vet to assess if the case is surgical:

* assessment of pain, both the degree and length of bouts of pain.
* heart-rate increases and continually high rates are important.
* strength of the pulse; a decrease indicates shock.

* mucous membrane and capillary refill used to monitor shock and toxaemia.
* muscle tremors usually a serious sign.
* temperature and respiratory rate.
* skin pinch to monitor dehydration.
* depression is usually a serious sign.
* gut sounds, reduction or lack of sounds in all quadrants is significant.
* passing faeces, gas and urine. The amount, colour and consistency are noted.
* digital pulses may be present in toxic animals.

The same parameters will be monitored in cases recovering from medical colics. Food and water will be given as instructed by the vet.

Surgical colics will be hospitalised after surgery and receive intensive post operative care by trained nursing staff and the veterinary team. There can be a variety of post-operative complications in these toxic and shocked patients.

When the horse has recovered to the point of eating small mashes and grass the owner may be involved with the aftercare. This involves grooming and frequent walks to encourage the horse. The owner can also monitor the physical progress and the improvement of the animal's mental attitude at this stage.

Owners often assist with the nursing of grass sickness cases. The horse's demeanour improves when visited by familiar persons and this stimulation will help to keep the horse interested. These horses may be fed by hand to encourage them to eat. The feed must be easy to swallow and nutritious especially high in protein and energy, e.g. Baileys no. 1 (high energy mash) and Alfa A (high protein forage). Succulents like freshly pulled grass, grated carrot and apples are eaten by some animals. It is a case of trying different foods to see which the horse will accept. Soaked sugar beet pulp can be used to damp grain and make it easier to swallow. Some animals prefer warm feed and lukewarm water. The appetite may vary from day to day. Frequent small feeds should be offered.

The horse should be taken for short walks and allowed to graze in hand. This will stimulate gut motility and the animal's interest. The horse may have a low body temperature and should be rugged. Thermatex rugs are the rug of choice as they are warm and allow sweat to evaporate. The horse will need to be groomed twice a day to prevent the coat becoming scurfy and sticky. The nostrils and eyes should be bathed to remove discharges and the area smeared with Vaseline. Steaming the head will encourage clearance of the nasal passages.

With good nursing about 40% of chronic grass sickness cases recover.

Nursing the recumbent horse

Horses may be recumbent for many reasons:

1 Paralysis. This may involve all four legs (quadriplegic) hindlegs (paraplegic) or both front and hindlegs on the same side (hemiplegic). This is due to loss of motor neurone function
2 Paresis or ataxia, i.e. a muscle weakness and incoordination
3 Prolonged recovery from anaesthesia
4 Acute infection, e.g. equine herpes infection, tetanus
5 Injuries, e.g. fracture of a limb or pelvis
6 Laminitis/acute founder/sinkers
7 Exertional myopathy
8 Unconsciousness/heart attack/stroke
9 Arthritis
10 Generalised debility/emaciation.

Owners may have to assist in nursing recumbent animals that have acute infections, injuries or laminitis. Recumbent animals are unable to get up and may not be able to move themselves onto their brisket (sternal recumbency). They will not be able to keep themselves clean or easily move towards food or water. They should be managed in a stable whenever possible. The stable must be large enough to allow the nurse and vet to work around the horse and turn the horse without risk of injury to themselves. A stable which has a high ceiling and strong beams to support a hoist is ideal.

The best bedding material is white dust-free shavings. The bed should be 45 cm (18 in) thick with deep banks. This will not move under the horse like straw and paper. Sandbags and cushions can be used to support the horse on its brisket so that it can eat and drink.

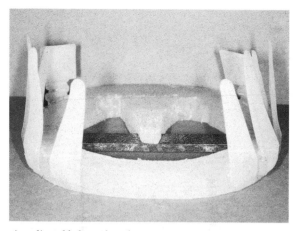

An adjustable heart bar shoe (R. A. Eustace)

Faeces and urine should be removed from the bed as soon as it is passed. Some animals will need a urinary catheter if they are incontinent or unable to pass urine.

The diet must be compatible with the patient's illness and avoid constipation. Sloppy feeds containing soaked sugar beet shreds and a nutritious high fibre diet, e.g. Alfa A or HiFi often form the bulk of the feed. The feed bucket/water bucket should be shallow with no handles. The horse may be hand fed and water offered every couple of hours when the horse is turned over. The horse's tail can be bandaged and plaited to keep it clean. The dock should be washed and dried each day.

Leg bandages will protect the limbs from rubs and a rug will protect the body. A padded head-collar and poll guard will protect the head. These should be removed twice daily and the animal massaged and groomed.

The eyes and nostrils tend to become caked in the bedding material and should be frequently cleaned. A large sheet or Vet bed can be placed under the head and neck to prevent the bedding material getting into the eyes and nostrils.

The bony prominences should be checked for bed sores (decubital sores), the areas most likely to be affected are: the point of the hip, elbow and shoulder; lateral and medial aspect of the knee, hock and fetlocks; bony ridge above the eye.

These sores must be cleaned, creamed and covered to prevent the bedding sticking to them.

The horse will be monitored in the normal way with all findings recorded and medication administered as directed by the vet. Laminitic animals will need their feet carefully checked twice daily and adjustments made to the grub-screw in the glue on adjustable heart bar shoes.

Nursing the fracture/acutely lame patient

Horses that are acutely lame need similar nursing to recumbent animals as they too will not be able to move easily.

Animals that have plaster casts/fracture surgery will require careful nursing. Bandages and casts must be checked for signs of rubs, pain or swelling. The cast must be inspected for cracks or areas of weakness. Signs of discomfort, unpleasant odour or discolouration of the cast points to a problem and it should be investigated. Signs of an increase in pain or depression should be closely monitored and the veterinary surgeon alerted to any change.

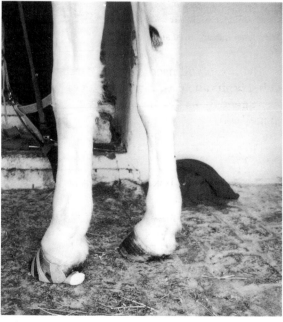

A frog support made from a roll of bandage taped to the frog

Exercise on a prepared surface

The horse will need support bandages on the other limbs and possibly frog supports. It should be rugged up as it will not be moving about. (See page 140.)

Box rest

Horses that are box rested need their body-weight and condition score checked each week to avoid wide fluctuations in body-weight. The diet should include good quality forage with a vitamin and mineral supplement.

The bedding should be kept clean to avoid respiratory and foot problems. The horse should have its feet picked out twice daily and trimmed regularly by the farrier.

Most horses adapt well to confinement in the stable while they are on box rest. The owner often does not, and is tempted to take the horse out, damaging all the surgery and veterinary treatment! As the horse recovers it will be placed on a strict exercise regime with walking in hand for set periods of time each day. Massage and physiotherapy will prevent muscle wastage and keep the horse's body toned.

The horse may be exercised in hand on a prepared surface before ridden exercise commences. Swimming and treadmill exercise may be part of the rehabilitation and fittening programme. Physiotherapy is used after injuries to enhance the body's natural repair mechanisms and restore normal function to the injured tissues.

Chartered physiotherapists working with animals should have post graduate training with veterinary surgeons and be members of the Association of Chartered Physiotherapists in Animal Therapy (ACPAT).

They are bound by a code of professional con-

Cold therapy

duct agreed by the RCVS and the CSP. They have to work within the confines of the Veterinary Act and under the guidance of the veterinary surgeon who has diagnosed the condition that is being treated.

Physiotherapists work with animals in the rehabilitation stage of their recovery as well as the healing stage.

Therapeutic machines are used during the healing stage of injury. These act at cellular level to enhance the natural healing ability of the body. They include electrical and mechanical stimulation. These therapies often reduce swelling and give pain relief. Incorrect use of these machines can be very harmful and they should only be used on horses by members of ACPAT.

1 Magnetic field therapy, e.g. pulsing electromagnetic fields.
2. Faradic treatment, e.g. electro- muscle stimulation.
3 Therapeutic ultrasound.
4 Low level laser treatment.
5 Electrostimulation, e.g. transcutaneous electrical nerve stimulation (TENS).
6 Massage.
7 Acupuncture, e.g. heat and electrical stimulation of acupuncture points are often used in physiotherapy.
8 Heat therapy, e.g. heat lamps and solarium; hot pads and hot poulticing; hot fomentations and hot tubbing.
9 Cold therapy, e.g. cold hosing, tubbing in ice water, cool packs, cold bandages (Bonner bandages).

EUTHANASIA

Euthanasia is defined as a quiet and gentle death. Euthanasia or humane destruction is rarely discussed by horse owners yet frequently they are asked to make difficult decisions at a time of great emotion and stress. It is easier if they have considered the subject and planned ahead so that they can cope in a rational manner should they have to make a quick decision. It is an advantage to be aware of all the options available in case of an emergency when immediate euthanasia is required on humane grounds to prevent unnecessary suffering. The vet is the best person to advise on humane destruction. The welfare of the animal is their first responsibility.

In an emergency situation when the horse cannot be transported a veterinary surgeon, a knackerman or a hunt kennelman will destroy the animal on site.

In a non-emergency situation the owner has to decide whether the horse should be 'put down' at home or away.

This situation is common for elderly, infirm animals and those with chronic disease or deteriorating conditions and a poor quality of life. If the animal is insured the insurance company should be informed and may request a post mortem report. These animals may well be destroyed at home in their own familiar surroundings. This is important for any companion animals who will be less stressed if they are allowed to see the body of their companion. They appear to accept death far more easily than seeing the live horse disappearing into a lorry.

If the horse is destroyed on the home premises there must be access for collection and removal of the body unless it is to be buried. Neighbours should be informed so they are not shocked or upset.

Horses that are fit to travel may be taken to the local hunt kennels or a licensed horse slaughterhouse. The transport may need to be arranged.

The horse may be destroyed by a veterinary surgeon, knackerman, hunt kennelman, or a licensed horse slaughterman.

The owner or their agent may be asked to sign a form giving their permission for the horse to be euthanased.

Whatever method is used, it should be painless and not distress the animal. There should be a rapid loss of consciousness followed by cardiac and respiratory arrest and loss of brain function. The methods used are either:

1. Lethal injection

A lethal injection of Somulose is given into a vein by the vet. The animal may be sedated first and then a catheter is placed into the jugular vein to receive the lethal overdose. The horse should gently collapse to the ground unconscious within thirty seconds and be dead within three minutes. Occasionally there is slight muscle tremor and gasping prior to death. The only disadvantage with this method is disposal of the body, which the vet will advise on. The vet will be responsible for the safety of the handler and decide where to position the horse to perform the injection. The animal's welfare should always come first.

2. Shooting

Any of the above mentioned may shoot the horse using a captive bolt pistol or bell gun. The muzzle of the gun is placed against the animals forehead and fired. The horse falls to the ground immediately. There is usually bleeding from the bullet hole and the nose and paddling movements of the legs. This method is distressing to watch and can be risky for the handler as the horse falls instantly.

Knackermen will destroy horses on the owner's premises or their own and remove the body. They are licensed and listed with the local Authority. They charge more for collecting injected carcases.

Hunt kennelmen have a firearms licence and will destroy horses on their premises or the owner's. They do not accept or collect injected carcases.

Licensed horse slaughtermen shoot horses at the slaughterhouse. The horse must be fit to travel and an appointment has to be made with the slaughterhouse. The carcase is inspected and if passed, a payment will be made according to the carcase weight.

Disposal of the body will depend on local facilities and what method was used to destroy the horse.

The cost of disposal will also vary according to the method chosen.

Cremation

Cremation is available for horses and ponies although it is expensive and the carcase may have to be transported a considerable distance. The Licensed Animal Slaughterers' and Salvage Association (LASSA) provide a nationwide service through their members. Ashes are returned in a casket to the owner.

Incineration

This will be cheaper than cremation but no ashes are returned. Costs vary according to the size of the animal and collection charges.

Burial

The local Environmental Health Department and the National Rivers Authority will advise on the suitability of the burial site. The Ministry of Agriculture, Fisheries and Food (MAFF) limit burial to specific sites away from water courses and drains. The depth of the pit is also specified. The pit has to be dug and machinery available to move the horse's body.

PART FOUR

APPENDICES

NORMAL BLOOD PARAMETERS

HAEMATOLOGY		
Parameter	Normal range	Unit
Red Cell Count 10^12/L	7.8–11	
Haemoglobin	13–17	g/dl
Packed Cell Volume	0.34–0.46	l/l
White Count	5–12	10^9/L
Neutrophils	2.5–7.5	10^9/L
Lymphocytes	1.5–4.0	10^9/L
Monocytes	<0.5	10^9/L
Eosinophils	<0.5	10^9/L

BIOCHEMISTRY		
Parameter	Normal range	Unit
Total Protein	50–70	g/l
Albumin	25–41	g/l
Globulin	19–36	g/l
Fibrinogen	1–4	g/l
Urea	3.3–7.4	mmol/l
Creatinine	20–177	umol/l
ALT (SGPT)	5–50	IU/L
Alk Phos (ALP)	50–270	IU/L
Gamma GT (GGT)	10–45	IU/L
T. Bilirubin	9–50	umol/l
Bile Acid (fasting)	<10	umol/l
Glucose	3.3–5.8	mmol/l
AST (SGOT)	100–370	IU/L
CK (CPK)	20–225	IU/L
LDH (LD-L)	80–650	IU/L
Sodium	132–146	mmol/l
Potassium	3.3–5.4	mmol/l
Chloride	89–108	mmol/l
Calcium	2.5–3.6	mmol/l
I. Phosphorous	0.9–1.8	mmol/l
Magnesium	0.6–1.0	mmol/l
Cholesterol	2.0–3.6	mmol/l

GLOSSARY OF VETERINARY TERMS

Abdominocentesis The withdrawal of fluid from the abdominal cavity through a needle. Sample used for laboratory tests, especially in colic cases.

Abortion The loss of a foetus under 300 days' gestation.

Abrasion A superficial injury to the skin surface. *See wounds.*

Abscess A cavity containing dead cells, bacteria and inflammatory fluid, i.e. pus. Can occur anywhere in the body. The commonest site is the foot.

Acupuncture A traditional oriental form of healing using fine needles to stimulate specific points or meridians.

Acute The nature of a disease with a sudden, severe onset and a short duration.

Adhesions Fibrous attachments between structures as a result of injury.

Adjuvant A substance added to vaccines to improve their efficacy.

Aerobe A micro-organism that grows in the presence of oxygen.

Afterbirth The foetal membranes that surround the foal in the uterus, which should be expelled within two hours of foaling.

Allergy A hypersensitive reaction to contact with an allergen, e.g. rash or weals due to a local reaction, or inhaled allergens causing constriction of the airways in COPD.

Alopecia Loss of hair.

Anaemia A condition where there is a reduction in the number of red blood cells or the size of the cells, or a reduction in haemoglobin. This may be caused by an increase in blood loss or cell breakdown, or a decrease in new cell formation.

Anaerobe A micro-organism that lives and grows in the absence of oxygen.

Anaesthetic Either general, where lack of consciousness prevents pain, or local, where the anaesthetic is injected into the skin or around sensory nerves to abolish pain in a localised area.

Analgesia Pain relief. Analgesics are substances that give pain relief, e.g. phenylbutazone.

Aneurysm A bulging of the wall of an artery causing a weakness, e.g. damage to the mesenteric artery in the gut by migrating large redworm larvae.

Anorexia Total lack of appetite.

Anoxia Absence of oxygen.

Antacid A medicine used to correct gut acidity.

Anthelmintic Substances used to treat worm infestation.

Antibiotic Substances that kill (bacteriocidal) or prevent the growth of bacteria (bacteriostatic).

Antibody A part of the immune system that combines with specific antigens to protect the animal against disease.

Antigen A foreign substance to which the body reacts by producing antibodies.

Anti-inflammatory A substance that reduces inflammation.

Antipyretic A substance that reduces body temperature.

Antiseptic A substance that inhibits the growth of micro-organisms and therefore prevents tissue damage.

Antiserum Serum that contains antibodies against specific disease antigens.

Antispasmodic Substances that control overactive gut motility.

Artery Blood vessel that takes oxygen enriched blood from the heart to the rest of the body tissues.

Arthritis Inflammation of a joint which may involve any of the structures around the joint.

Ascarid Intestinal roundworm, seen in horses under two years of age.

Ascites Excessive amounts of abdominal fluid caused by a variety of diseases.

Asepsis Free from sepsis, infective material and bacteria.

Aspiration pneumonia Lung infection caused by inhaling fluid or food into the lungs. May also be caused by drenching with medicines.

Ataxia Inco-ordination of limbs.

Atrophy Wasting or decrease in size of tissues, often due to lack of use.

Auscultate Listen to body sounds, e.g. heart, lungs and guts.

Azoturia. *See exertional myopathy*, equine rhabdomyolysis syndrome.

Bacillus A rod-shaped bacterium, e.g. anthrax, E. coli, tetanus.

Back racking Manually removing faeces from the rectum.

Bacteria Single-celled organisms classified by their shape, size, and reaction to stains and production of spores.

Bilateral Affecting both sides.

Bile Fluid secreted by the liver and passed via the bile duct into the small intestine where it aids fat digestion.

Biopsy A small sample of tissue removed for analysis in the laboratory.

Blepharospasm Spasm of the eyelid muscles in eye disease.

Bog spavin Distension of the tibiotarsal joint (hock) with an excess of synovial fluid.

Bolus   A portion of food which has been chewed, mixed with saliva and swallowed.

Borborygmus   The sound of food, gas and liquids as they are moved along the alimentary tract by peristalsis.

Bot   A fly that lays eggs on the horse's coat, which develop into larvae and pupae in the stomach.

Botulism   A fatal paralysing disease caused by toxins from Clostridium botulinum. Seen in equines fed on contaminated big-bale silage.

Bowed tendon   Swollen flexor tendons due to inflammation of the tendon and the tendon sheaths.

Bradycardia   Slow heart-rate.

Bracken poisoning   Bracken contains an enzyme that destroys thiamine and causes inco-ordination, staggering and muscle tremors. It is also carcinogenic and should be removed from horse pasture and destroyed.

Broad-spectrum   Having a wide range of activity especially antibiotics that affect a variety of bacteria.

Broken wind   Layman's term used to describe emphysema or COPD.

Bruise   Bleeding under the skin or sole caused by trauma.

Bursitis   Inflammation of a bursal sac, e.g. point of the elbow or hock.

Cachexia   Wasting disease or malnutrition.

Callus   The formation of new bone at the site of injury e.g. fracture. Palpable as a hard swelling.

Capillaries   Small blood-vessels that form a network between the arterioles and venules. They allow the exchange of gases, nutrients and waste products between the blood and the tissues through their thin walls.

Castration   An operation to remove the testes performed under general or local anaesthesia.

Catheter   A flexible plastic or nylon tube used to administer fluid to and drain fluid from a part of the body, e.g. lacrimal catheter, urinary catheter.

Cellulitis   Inflammation and swelling of the subcutaneous tissue due to infection or injury.

Chiropractic   Treatment by manipulation of the spine.

Cirrhosis   Fibrosis of damaged liver tissue. Seen in ragwort poisoning.

Colostrum   A thick milk produced by the mammary glands at foaling containing maternal derived antibodies to protect the foal.

Coprophagia   Eating faeces. Seen in adult animals deprived of an adequate diet. Normal behaviour in young foals.

Congenital deformities   Those existing at birth, e.g. cleft palate, club foot, over and under shot jaw.

Contagious   A disease that is spread from one animal to another.

Contraindicated   Drugs that are not advised to be used in certain patients or in conjunction with other medicines. Usually listed on all data sheets.

Crepitus   Noise made by fractured ends of bones rubbing together.

Cryosurgery   Cold therapy, e.g. liquid nitrogen used to freeze tumour tissue.

Culture   Growth of cells on a medium in an incubator at the laboratory, e.g. bacteria and fungi.

Cyanosis   Bluish tinge to the mucous membranes caused by lack of oxygen seen in severe respiratory and heart disease.

Cystitis   Inflammation of the urinary bladder.

Cytology   Examination of cells.

Debride   Removal of dead and dying tissue, usually by surgery.

Dehydration   Condition caused by loss of body water.

Dermatitis   Inflammation of the skin.

Desmitis   Inflammation of ligament.

Diagnose   To identify a disease or condition.

Disinfectant   Substance used to kill bacteria on inanimate objects, not to be used on living tissue.

Dysphagia   Difficulty in swallowing.

Ectoparasites   Parasites that live on the body surface, e.g. ticks, lice, mites.

Electrolytes   Salts found in body fluids necessary for various functions, e.g. conducting nerve impulses and muscle contraction.

Embolism   A blood clot or foreign material that blocks a blood-vessel.

Endoparasites   Parasites found inside the body, e.g. lungworm, redworm.

Endorphins   Chemicals released from the brain that relieve pain and produce a sense of well-being.

Endoscope   A surgical instrument used to visualise internal organs by fibre optics inside a thin, flexible tube.

Epistaxis   Nose bleed.

Exudate   A mixture of inflammatory cells and fluid that have leaked from blood vessels into tissue or onto the surface of tissues.

Fascia   Sheets of fibrous tissue found between muscle layers.

Febrile   High temperature or fever.

Fluke   A parasite of the liver found in sheep, cattle and equines.

Fungicide   A substance used to kill fungi.

Gelding   A castrated male horse.

Gingivitis   Inflammation of the gums.

Glossitis   Inflammation of the tongue.

Gonitis   Inflammation of the stifle joint.

Haematology   The study of blood cells.

Haemoglobin   The oxygen carrying pigment of red blood cells that contain iron.

Haemostasis   The stopping of haemorrhage.

Hepatitis   Inflammation of the liver.

Hereditary   Genetically passed on to the next generation, as in hereditary diseases, e.g. Immunodeficiency disease in Arab foals, umbilical hernias.

Hernia   A condition where an organ or tissue protrudes through a break in the enclosing muscular wall. May be hereditary or a result of injury.

Histology   The study of the structure of tissues.

Hormone   A chemical produced by a specific gland in the body that regulates the activity of target tissue.

Hygroma   The swelling of a bursa with an excess of synovial fluid due to trauma, e.g. seen on the carpus.

Hyperlipaemia   A serious, often fatal condition where the body fat is mobilised into the blood. Common in small ponies and donkeys on starvation diets.

Hypersensitivity   The overreaction of the body to a foreign substance.

Icterus   Yellow discolouration of the skin, mucous membranes and organs, i.e. jaundice.

Ileus   Lack of intestinal movement (peristalsis).

Immunity   Resistance to infection. May be natural or acquired.

Incubation   The time between contact with a disease and exhibiting the clinical signs of that disease.

Infection   A condition caused by micro-organisms.

Infra-red thermography   A technique used to detect areas of injury/inflammation by mapping temperature differences in the tissues due to the alteration in blood flow and cell activity.

Insecticide   A substance that kills insects.

Intussusception   The telescoping of a piece of intestine into the adjoining segment causing a blockage of the gut lumen. This requires surgical intervention.

Ischaemia   Lack of blood supply to an area resulting in cell death.

Jugular refill test   A indicator of the status of the circulatory system. The jugular vein is emptied by thumb pressure down the jugular groove and the time taken to refill while pressure is maintained is measured in seconds.

Keratitis   Inflammation of the cornea of the eye.

Knee   The carpus joint of the horse.

Lateral   On the outside cf. *medial* on the inside.

Lavage   Flush out with fluid.

Lymphangitis   Inflammation of the lymphatic vessels and lymph nodes.

Lysis   Destruction of cells.

Malnutrition   Incorrect feeding or diet.

Metabolism   Chemical activity in cells which provides energy for bodily functions.

Metastasis   Spread of neoplasms within the body from one part to another, usually via the blood or lymphatic system.

Mucopurulent   A mixture of mucus and pus.

Mucous membrane   The lining epithelial cells of all hollow organs, e.g. digestive, urogenital and respiratory system.

Myopathy   Muscle disease.

Myositis   Inflammation of muscle.

Necrosis   Death of cells by disease.

Neoplasm   An abnormal growth or tumour.

Neurectomy   Surgically cutting a nerve.

Obesity   Excessively overweight, a serious welfare problem in western society.

Oedema   Accumulation of fluid in the tissues outside the cells, e.g. filled legs, ventral oedema, ascites.

Ossify   To develop into bone.

Osteitis   Inflammation of bone.

Pathogen   A micro-organism that causes disease.

Peristalsis   Muscular contractions that propel food along the digestive tract.

Polydipsia   Excessive thirst and drinking.

Polyuria   Passing excessive volumes of urine.

Prophylaxis   Preventive treatment, e.g. vaccines.

Pruritus   Itching and scratching.

Pyrexia   High temperatures or fever.

Quarantine   Isolation to prevent spread of disease.

Quidding   Dropping chewed food from the mouth.

Radiograph   An X-ray plate or film.

Rhinitis   Inflammation of the nasal mucosa.

Rig   A male horse with an undescended testicle in the abdomen or inguinal canal.

Roaring   An abnormal inspiratory noise.

Sedative   A substance that acts on the central nervous system and reduces the level of awareness.

Septicaemia   Presence of pathogens and their toxins in the blood.

Sequestrum   A fragment of bone that has lost its blood supply – caused by injury or infection. Requires surgical intervention.

Sinusitis   Inflammation of the sinuses.

Subcutaneous   Under the skin.

Tranquilliser   A substance that has a calming effect without producing sedation.

Topical   A local area, as in topical application of cream.

Urticaria   An allergic skin reaction.

Vice   Stereotypical behaviour, e.g. crib biting, weaving.

SUGGESTED FURTHER READING

B.H.S. Welfare leaflets on health care/general management.

B.H.S. Road Safety Leaflet.

Colour Atlas of Diseases and Disorders of the Horse. Knottenbelt and Pascoe: Mosby Wolfe. ISBN 0 7234 1 702 4.

Current Therapy in Equine Medicine. 4th edn. Robinson: W.B. Saunders.

Equine Injury, Therapy and Rehabilitation. 2nd edn. Bromily: Blackwell Science.

Explaining Laminitis and its prevention. (1992) Robert A. Eustace: E.F.S. equine series ISBN 0 95189 740 3.

Farewell, making the right decision. Published by Humane Slaughter Association. ISBN 1 87156 106 X.

Feeding and Watering. Teresa Hollands: Crowood Press ISBN 1 85223 809 7

Horse Owner's Guide to Lameness. Stashak: Williams and Wilkinson Publication. ISBN 0 68307 985 9.

Poisonous Plants in Britain and their effects on Animals and Man. (1984) M.R. Cooper and A.W. Johnson: MAFF London Ref Book 161.

Veterinary Notes for Horse Owners, Revised. (1996) Peter Rossdale: Ebury Press. ISBN 0 09171 511 3.

USEFUL ADDRESSES

Association of Chartered Physiotherapists in Animal
　Therapy
Moorland House
Salters Lane
Winchester
Hants
SO22 5JP

Tel 01962 863801

British Association of Homeopathic Veterinary
　Surgeons
Chinham House
Stanford in the Vale
Nr Faringdon
Oxfordshire
SN7 8NQ

Tel 01367 710324

British Equine Veterinary Association
Administration Secretary
5 Findlay Street
London
SW6 6HE

Tel 0171 610 6080

British Horse Society
Stoneleigh Deer Park
Kenilworth
Warwickshire
CV8 2XZ

Tel 01926 707700

Farriers' Registration Council
Sefton House
Adam Court
Newark Road
Peterborough
PE1 5PP

Tel 01733 319911

Laminitis Clinic
Mead House Farm
Dauntsey
Chippenham
Wiltshire
SN15 4JA

Tel 01249 890784

Licensed Animal Slaughterers' and Salvage
　Association (LASSA)
Birch House
Birch Vale
Stockport
Cheshire
SK12 5DH

Tel 01663 744154

Ministry of Agriculture, Fisheries and Food (MAFF)
Hook Rise South
Tolworth
Surbiton
Surrey
KT6 7DX

Tel 0181 3304411

Royal College of Veterinary Surgeons
Belgravia House
62–64 Horse Ferry Road
London SW1P 2AF

Tel 0171 222 2001

Society of Master Saddlers
Kettles Farm
Mickfield
Stowmarket
Suffolk

Tel 01499 711642

INDEX

The Land Rover Experience

A user's guide to four-wheel driving

Second edition – October 1994

Tom Sheppard

Published by

This book deals with post-1986 model Land Rovers, Defenders, Discoverys and Range Rovers where details of controls and transmission are concerned and incorporates operational details relating to the significant changes made for 1995 Model Year. The vast majority of the book's advice and philosophy, however, may be applied to all Land Rover operations with appropriate discretion.

Published by Land Rover and distributed by Unipart to Land Rover dealerships.
Book trade: sold through WHSmith, distribution through Vine House Distribution.
Project conceived and directed at Land Rover by Roger Crathorne .
Written, designed and produced for Land Rover by Tom Sheppard, MBE, ARPS.
Illustration artwork by Mike Lister of Plum Advertising, London and Tom Sheppard.
© Tom Sheppard 1994
Reprinted 1996

Photography
Land Rover: pp 4 up lt, 15 up lt, 22 lwr lt, 31 lwr lt, 36, 43 rt, 46, lwr lt on pp 57, 58, 71, 78; pp 86, 87, 89, 119, 142 lwr, 143. Drury Lane Studio Meriden: pp 3, 11, 20, 124, 134, 136. Tarmac Construction Ltd: p 10. Mike Hallett: p 101 rt. Superwinch: p 103 lt, lwr rt. Jardine PR: p 142 top.
All remaining photography: Tom Sheppard.

Acknowledgments
The author would like to express grateful thanks for their interest, help, and enormous patience with this and the First Edition to:
David Bowyer, Bradley Doublelock (Philip Hanson), Commercial Body Fittings (Mick Bowling), Dubai Equestrian Centre (Dervilla Campbell), Fortune Promoseven (Donal Kilalea, Jihad el Sibai), Fresh Tracks (Daniel Collins), Ib Kidde-Hansen, Michelin Tyres (Terry Khokhar, Alan Baxter), Paul O'Connor, Geoff Renner, Tom Robson, Superwinch (Terry Mason), Dariush Zandi.
And within Land Rover: Chris Batiste, Ron Brown, Tony Bourne, John Carter, Roger Crathorne, Bob Dillon, Neil Dodswell, Dave Drummond, Steve Earnshaw, David Fulker, Alison Grose, Mike Gould, Kate Higton, Colin Hill, Chris Hoyle, Roger Hughes, Phil Jones, Tony Northway, Adam Ormandy, Colin Parkes, Kieth Parsons, David Saunders, Chris Scaife, Graham Silvers, Harry Turnbull, Russell Turnham, Tim Vass de Zomba, Dick Woodhouse.
The pre-distillation analysis for Section 4.1 (On-road towing) was particularly demanding and special thanks go to Brian Bevan (The Motor Industry Research Association and IMechE paper C132/83), Professor Robin Sharp (Cranfield University), and Malcolm Burgess (Land Rover) for their help and patience.

The Land Rover Experience

Contents

...continued

The Land Rover Experience

...continued

The Land Rover Experience

...continued

The Land Rover Experience

Introduction

First-timers and fleet-users. This book is aimed at first-time four-wheel drivers and fleet users alike – a wide brief we hope is met by the headings and signposting within the book.

Aim. The aim of the techniques outlined in this book is to realise the fullest potential of your Land Rover product, to make your driving as safe and relaxed as possible, to ensure that in difficult conditions you get stuck as infrequently as possible, to ensure you hazard your vehicle as little as possible and that you damage it not at all – criteria equally important for private and commercial users. For this reason safety is emphasised throughout.

Book layout. Open the book at any page and scan along the top of the left and right hand pages. You will see the Section number, the Section subject and, on the right, the Sub-section number and title – for example, 'Section 5, Operations – recovery, 5.4. Winching'. The Sub-section numbering sequence – 5.1, 5.2, etc is a constant reminder of which section you are in. Cross referencing is by Section and Sub- section, not page numbers.

Headings, summaries, access. Each Sub-section (4.1, 4.2, etc) is divided into two or more parts each with a heading; every paragraph has a heading too and side-notes give a further summary. This way you can go straight to what you want, using the summary for reminders.

Short term use. Use this book like a tiny encyclopaedia. Use the index, glossary, contents pages (and contents summary on the rear fly-leaf), section headings and side-notes. Cross-referencing and a degree of repetition in the book will enable you to do this quickly.

Long term use. You will not carry all of this book in your head. Reading it, you will absorb the principles needed to become a sensitive and (therefore) proficient off-road driver. You will not only get to know the strengths and limitations of your vehicle but you will learn how to read the ground and apply the variations of technique you will encounter. Soon it will be instinctive; you will have written your own book.

Manual and automatic transmission. Many off-road commercial operators tend to favour manual transmissions, often for reasons of initial cost and commonality with earlier fleet vehicles. Because manual transmissions require more detailed description, the emphasis in this book should not be interpreted as favouring that technology. Automatic transmission has considerable advantages and, used on- or off-road, is very operator-friendly.

Additive experience. Many readers will already have experience in off-road operation and have developed their own techniques of doing things. We found, in the preparation of this book, that such inputs are always valuable and often apparently conflicting methods did not in fact conflict at all – they were just suited to subtly different sets of conditions. Experience was nearly always additive rather than reflecting opposite techniques; given common aims of safety and care of the vehicle the best course was usually self-evident.

Glossary, index, technical data. Some terms and usages may be new to you and a glossary (Section 10.1) explains many as well as giving some insight into how things work. The technical data section shows current vehicle specifications which inevitably vary world-wide; space does not permit them all to be shown. Those given are for the UK.

Foreword

Fragile earth – care for the environment

Philosophy

On/off-road vehicles are here to stay. Industry, civil engineering, the emergency services, the overseas relief agencies, agriculture and the defence Services would be severely handicapped and in some cases totally incapacitated without them. In many overseas regions such vehicles are often the only means of maintaining point-to-point land communications and transport.

And in the developed countries they have, in addition, found a niche in the automotive marketplace among those warming to their capabilities as the most practical of family hold-alls and maids of all work – the kind of vehicle that can tow a canoe-trailer to a mountain lake or do the school run and return with four children, a wet dog, a lawn mower and four sacks of compost picked up en route. As a bonus, these vehicles are also enormous fun to drive.

But their very popularity and versatility confers on us, as operators, users, and owners, a special responsibility towards the environment in which we live and they operate. The engineers and legisla-

road enthusiasts have increased the potential for damage to vegetation, soil, water, wildlife and the solitude afforded by these areas.

We feel sure that all users of Land Rover products will wish to familiarise themselves with environmental principles.

'Torque gently' conveys both an exhortation to drive with a gentle right foot on the throttle (or brake) – as well as the implied suggestion also to 'talk gently' and not indulge in inappropriately 'macho' antics in our powerful machines.

Following the dual meaning will preserve both our vehicles and our environment for the future enjoyment of ourselves and others. Few, if any – in their heart of hearts – could disagree with such a philosophy.

...continued

tors continue their work in the pursuit of clean air; the latest diesels and catalyst-equipped petrol engines minimise atmospheric pollution.

We must also be certain not lastingly to damage the ground we drive on when off-road – especially vulnerable when wet. In so far as many of them will be new to the capabilities of their vehicles, recreational users must be especially aware of their responsibilities. There are currently many miles of off-highway road open to the public around the world. In recent years ever-growing numbers of off-

The freedom of the open countryside is made accessible through the capability of off-road vehicles. Take care of the countryside wherever you are. Where access is limited, close gates you have opened.

The Land Rover Experience

Practicalities

And few – applying little more than common sense and good manners – would not come up with the following list of practical points to remember when operating away from tarmac roads:

People and wildlife

• Allow wildlife priority over your own progress.

• Domestic animals too, especially horses and ponies, may be unused to the presence of vehicles in remote areas. Accommodate their nervousness; switch off and wait if necessary.

• Sheep that have strayed onto a track often run ahead of a vehicle rather than leaving the roadway. Be patient. Stop and let them disperse or pull over to let them by.

• Gamebirds and other wildlife often soak up the warmth of tarmac by sitting in the middle of country lanes or other clearings. Your vehicle may panic them into running across your path rather than away from you. Be prepared for this – and for the last minute appearance of a second or third bird from the hedgerow.

• Animals are often dazzled by headlights and may be unable to get away from the danger. Be aware of this; drive with extra care on unfenced lanes or open tracks. And that really does mean driving slowly.

• Be especially courteous and considerate towards walkers or riders – especially in remote areas. Like it or not, you have an ambassadorial role to play and inevitably, arriving in a comfortable off-road vehicle whilst others are progressing 'the hard way', you will, to a degree, be perceived in the idle villain's role!

• Always respect the privacy of other people; not always easy to assess, but many go to remote areas to savour the peace and solitude.

Access

• It is essential to be *certain* of your right of access to tracks and wild areas.

• A road marked on a map does not automatically confer a right of way. If in any doubt at all, ask – or refer to a highly detailed map such as one of the UK 1:25,000 series.

• Access rights to land for vehicles varies from country to country. Make yourself aware of the appropriate regulations for the country in which you are driving. Developed, highly populated or densely legislated countries usually have complex regulations. See Section 7 for an overview of UK access rights.

• Observe the Country Code – an encapsulation of common sense – whatever country you are in. Close gates you have opened.

Erosion

Four-wheel drive vehicles can contribute enormously to erosion when carelessly used off-road. Guidelines to min-

*If they can do it......
The example set – at
enormous monetary
cost – by local plan-
ning authorities and
civil engineers is all
too often overlooked
or taken for granted.
Before (above left)
and after (lower left)
shows the care taken
to landscape, replant
and minimise envi-
ronmental damage
even when a major
civil engineering pro-
ject such as the A55
Conway Crossing
tunnel in Wales is
involved. Enjoyment
of a 4x4's off-road
capabilities need not
be – must not be –
incompatible with
care for the environ-
ment.*

imise possible damage:

• New ruts form rain channels which cause erosion – especially where surface vegetation such as grass has been scraped away by spinning wheels.

• So keep off soft ground if possible – sinkage causes ruts.

• Do not spin your wheels on grass.

• Where a track exists, stick to it. Your wheel tracks away from it can tempt others to do the same and a another swathe of land can be spoiled.

• Travelling over open meadows with two or more vehicles, do not follow in each others' tracks. This will reduce the risk of forming ruts.

• Be doubly cautious when using mud tyres. Ideally they should be used only when deep mud is envisaged; they can quickly damage other ground.

• Use designated areas for training.

Litter

• Never leave litter under *any* circumstances.

• Take back what you brought with you.

Polishing your halo

Observing all the recommendations above will seem impossibly onerous the first time you read them. The second time you read them you will see just how much common-sense and simple courtesy is involved. The third time (and this may be a little later), you will start realising that that is what you actually *do* and will feel good about it.

Caring for the environment is far more important than the current fashion it may seem. We all share humankind's newly realised responsibility. Enjoy your driving!

The Land Rover Experience

Section 1

The ingredients

1.1. Why four-wheel drive

Halving the load

Terminology. It is worth an initial thought about what four-wheel drive or 4x4 really does do. Incidentally, '4x4', spoken as 'four-by-four' means there are four wheels, of which four are driven by the engine. So a normal car, be it front wheel drive or rear wheel drive, is a 4x2 'four-by-two' – four wheels in total, of which the car is driven by two. Some types of truck are referred to as a 6x4 – six (wheels driven) by four.

What it does – and doesn't do. A 4x4 does not double the power on the road; it takes the power you do have and spreads it between four wheels instead of only two. If a vehicle needs a certain amount of push (tractive effort or traction) to make it go at a given speed or traverse a certain type of terrain, a 4x4, by having twice as many driven wheels as a 4x2, will actually halve the tractive load on a given piece of ground and thus greatly reduce the chance of slipping, skidding or spinning wheels. Four-wheel drive is thus a considerable benefit to effective operation and to safety. If 4x4 is now combined with large wheels and large amounts of wheel movement on supple, well damped springs, the ingredients of an effective off-road vehicle, capable of operating on rough uneven ground, are starting to take shape.

Doubling the effect

Maintaining traction. Thus if conditions are such that an ordinary 4x2 car driving only one pair of wheels could spin those wheels and lose traction, a 4x4 will actually be twice as effective in using the power of the engine to maintain traction.

More from four. The diagrams sum up what we have been discussing. All over the world there are bits of ground – oily tarmac, icy roads, glazed snow, wet grassy fields – that will not support the tractive effort needed under certain conditions when power is put through one pair of wheels. Put that power through two axles – four wheels – thus halving the traction required of each wheel, and your 4x4 is likely to get you through – securely and under complete control.

'4x4' equals four-by-four equals four-wheel drive.

4x4 spreads power between four wheels, reducing risk of slip.

Where 4x2s slip a 4x4, demanding less of the ground, will grip.

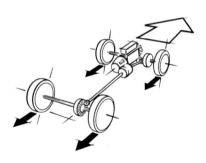

Ground thrust   Direction of travel

4x2 – all the power on two wheels. High ground stress. Wheels may slip or spin.

4x4 – same power spread between four wheels. Half the ground stress. Double the traction.

Traction from the wheel at each corner of the vehicle is the overriding advantage of four-wheel drive on roads. Off-road it is even more important.

Even 4x4s have limits. Of course conditions may be so bad or the traction required so high that even a 4x4 spins its wheels or needs lower gears. These occasions are addressed later in the book but in general four-wheel drive enhances safety and effectiveness on and off road at all times. As we shall see, if you are driving any of the current Land Rover range and are therefore in four-wheel drive all the time then you are at a further advantage – always ready for the unexpected rather than having to assess the conditions and then select 4x4 with a separate control lever as is the case in some vehicles.

4x4 enhances security. Unlike many makes, Land Rover vehicles are in 4x4 all the time.

The Land Rover Experience

1.2. Traction – 4x4 and low range

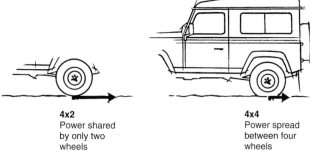

Push with float; here we are looking at push. Rear axle of 4x2 vehicle (left) is asking twice as much shear strength from the ground as the 4x4 (right). Ground stress is further reduced by big wheels and low tyre pressures – permissible under certain conditions (see Section 8.2). Less ground stress equals less chance of slip and thus more traction.

4x2
Power shared by only two wheels

4x4
Power spread between four wheels

Traction is combination of four driving wheels, low gearing and lack of sinkage.

Big footprint equals low ground stress equals more traction.

Big wheels also give smooth ride, maximum ground clearance.

Ingredients of traction
Pushing backwards and downwards. Traction tends to be thought of as pull – farm tractors pulling wagons. In fact it is push – the bottom of the wheel pushing against the surface of the ground to move a vehicle forward under varying conditions. In perfect conditions of infinite grip one-wheel drive would suffice but where roads can get wet and slippery and where no-road conditions are muddy, four-wheel drive means three wheels can still push if one gets on a slippery patch.

Push with float. Away from the perfect conditions of one-wheel drive, the real world where 4x4 is necessary is often soft as well. Spreading the weight over a bigger 'footprint' helps prevent sinkage. Big wheels have a bigger ground footprint than small ones and this footprint can be enlarged still further in emergency conditions by letting tyres down a little. (There are important speed and safety implications to this – see Section 8.2) In addition, big wheels give a smoother ride over rough ground.

Ground clearance. Big wheels also ensure greater ground clearance over obstacles. Land Rover vehicles' beam axles keep this ground clearance constant – unlike an independently sprung front

end on other vehicles – and keep the tyres' tread always flat on the ground. The diagram below shows how.

Grip and gradient – enemies of traction. If poor grip can be overcome by driving four wheels instead of one or two and also benefit from bigger wheels, the other enemy of traction is gradient – uneven surfaces, steep hills (or heavy loads up not-so-steep hills). The extra traction you need for this comes from additional low gears – the other half of the traction equation.

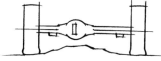

Independently sprung axle (top) loses ground clearance on one-wheel bump. Land Rover's beam axle (below) less liable to lose traction through grounding. Tyres stay flat on ground.

Extra gears

Lower gearing. Extra low gears are just what are available on most 4x4s (but not all in the same gearbox). The transfer box on a 4x4 got its name because it is what transfers power from the normal gearbox to the rear axle *and* front axle thus making it a 4x4. But this extra transfer gearbox is also a two-speed affair with a high ratio and a low ratio.

Doubling the number of gears. The two-speed transfer box is a simple solution. It is 'downstream' of the main gearbox and by selecting low ratio it gears-down *all* the gears in the normal gearbox. In 'high' the gears are unaffected. So your Land Rover has a transfer box to effect the four-wheel drive function and additionally to provide what amounts to a complete set of very low gears so that five-speed box in effect becomes a 10-speed box. Making a single gearbox with ten forward speeds which could be successively selected would result in an expensive, heavy and complicated item.

Low ratio for heavy jobs. The 'low box' is selected for specific heavy duty tasks using a separate lever as we shall see (Sections 2.1 and 2.2).

All the tricks at once. A Discovery displays the attributes of an off-road 4x4 in a common combination – the gradability (ability to climb steep obstacles) afforded by the low transfer gears, the facility of providing drive to each wheel, the extreme wheel movement – see also Section 3.3 – and the benefits of the one-piece beam-axle.

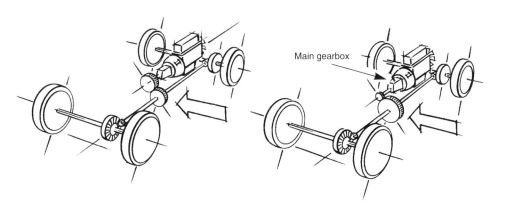

Main gearbox

Traction is power without slip. Big tyres and 4x4 minimise slip; a low ratio transfer box gives the 'power'.

Concept of transfer box in 1:1 high ratio (left) and low ratio (right) which gears-down the final drive to give more 'power' at the wheels. Note that the main gearbox is 'up-stream' – ie between the engine and the transfer gearbox.

The Land Rover Experience

1.3. Permanent four-wheel drive

Why centre differential

Selectable 4x4. On some 4x4s the four-wheel drive function is itself selectable. Normal driving is done in two-wheel drive – as a 4x2 – and the driver has to decide when conditions require 4x4. In such vehicles the front and rear axles, which in fact revolve at slightly different speeds, are usually locked together when 4x4 is selected without any ability to accommodate the front/rear speed difference. The result is transmission 'wind-up' or tyre-scrub – most usually a combination of both; such vehicles can thus only be driven in 4x4 when off-road where the small speed differences can be accommodated by slight wheel slip; they should not be driven on a hard road with four-wheel drive selected.

Permanent 4x4 is better on and off road than 4x2 with selectable 4x4.

Permanent 4x4. Since 1983/84 all Land Rover products have been designed with 'permanent 4x4' – the four-wheel drive function is engaged all the time and the front axle, as well as the rear, is driven. Two-wheel drive is not available. But as we shall see, there need be no wind-up or tyre scrub with your Land Rover vehicle.

Improved security, performance. Land Rover, pioneers of the first 'full-time' 4x4, the Range Rover, believe that the extra security and traction performance that result from permanent 4x4 is well worth the extra engineering involved. Such an arrangement also reduces driver workload and makes security and optimum performance an inherent feature of the vehicle rather than being dependent on driver use of a particular feature as in vehicles with selectable 4x4. With permanent 4x4 you are always ready for the unexpected.

Centre differential permits slight front/rear axle speed differences due to turns etc.

Centre diff – the need. Extra engineering? In the same way as the wheel on

Concept of the centre bevel-type differential that divides engine power between front and rear prop shafts.

the outside of a turn travels farther than the wheel on the inside (photo opposite), so the front and rear wheels of a vehicle travel slightly different distances too – again due to the different tracks they follow in bends. So a 4x4 vehicle with permanent four-wheel drive needs a differential arrangement *between the front and rear axle drives* to accommodate the slight front/rear rotational differences – in the same way as there has been a differential between left and right wheels on the drive axle of just about every car since the turn of the last century.

Land Rover vehicles have one. All Land Rover vehicles made since their adoption of permanent four-wheel drive have a centre differential between the front and rear propeller shafts to even-out the drive torque between front and rear axles, preclude transmission wind-up and prevent tyre scrub.

Illustration right shows different track – and distance travelled – by front and rear wheels in a turn. Without a centre differential a permanent-4x4 vehicle would encounter tyre scrub, wheel slip or transmission wind-up. Need for _locking_ centre diff is shown in picture above; a Discovery with centre differential deliberately (and incorrectly) left unlocked in demanding off-road conditions. Grip is markedly different front and rear, due to loose soil and weight transference to the rear; this allows front wheels to spin while rear wheels do not rotate.

Why lockable

Centre diff lock. Current Land Rover products not only have full-time four-wheel drive and a centre differential but that differential is lockable to enhance traction in difficult situations. It will couple automatically on Range Rovers (See Section 10.1, Glossary, Viscous coupling).

Why. The reason for making the centre diff lockable – ie the differential action is temporarily put on hold – is that traction conditions are often different front and rear. For example on a very steep slippery slope weight transference to the back axle may off-load the front wheels enough to let them lose grip and spin. Or there may be occasions when the front wheels are on a grippy rock and the rear wheels are on slippery mud. In these conditions locking the centre differential effectively locks the front prop shaft to the rear prop shaft and precludes lost traction through wheel-spin on either axle – see Section 2.3.

Where poor grip may permit excessive front/rear axle speed differences, centre differential is locked.

The Land Rover Experience

19

The Land Rover Experience

Enhanced traction

2.1. Traction controls

Small lever beside main gear lever controls engagement of high or low ratio transfer gears, the concept of which is shown in the diagram at Section 1.2. Defender left, Discovery above; Range Rover automatic facing page (note thumb-button selector release).

Land Rover products have full-time 4x4 plus two-speed transfer box plus centre diff that may be locked.

Transfer lever

Traction aids – how and when. As a 'full-time' (permanent) 4x4, a Land Rover vehicle already gives you enhanced traction compared to vehicles driven by one axle only or compared to those with selectable or 'part-time' four-wheel drive. But as we have seen, your Land Rover has additional aids further to enhance its traction – a two-speed transfer gearbox and a lockable centre differential. This section is about how to select these functions and when to use them.

The 'little gear lever'. The small lever aft of the gear lever on Defender and ahead of it on other models is called the transfer gear lever since it controls the two-speed transfer gearbox – see diagram at Section 1.2 to refresh your memory on what the transfer gearbox does. You may hear the lever referred to also as the 'hi-lo' lever or the 'range-change'. If your vehicle has a transfer lever its function is the same on vehicles with manual and automatic gearboxes and is to select high

Transfer lever controls low/high ratio when moved fore and aft; shift only when stationary or under 5 mph. (See Section 2.4.)

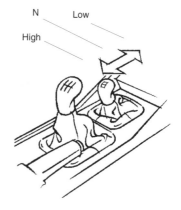

Drawing shows range change concept for all these vehicles. Lever should normally only be moved when vehicle is stationary or moving slower than 5 mph. See Section 2.4 for when and how low range should be used.

range – normal on-road gears – when pulled fully aft, or low range (sometimes referred to as 'low ratio') when pushed fully forward. Normally these selections should be made only when the vehicle is stationary or when moving at less than walking pace (below 8 kph – 5 mph) though there may be occasions (see Section 6.1, 6.2.) when you may wish to (and can) go from low to high range at higher speed.

The new Range Rover. The 1995 model-year Range Rover (as distinct from the classic 1993 version) uses a different system for controlling the transfer gearbox in both manual and automatic transmission variants. In both vehicles the range change is effected electrically and the transfer lever has been eliminated; the manual gearbox vehicle has a fascia-mounted button to select low and high range while the automatic gearbox vehicle has an 'H-gate' transmission selector which combines both gearbox and range change command functions in the same lever. This is dealt with more fully on the next two pages and in Section 2.3.

Low range. Section 2.4 gives detail on when and how the low transfer gears should be used.

Centre differential lock. Centre diff lock is manually controlled by lateral movement of the transfer lever on Defender and Discovery (automatic diff lock on both models of Range Rover) and its use is covered in Section 2.5.

New Range Rover has electric range change – see next spread and Section 2.3.

...continued

The Land Rover Experience

2.1. Traction controls – contd

Electric range change

Same function, plus logic gates. On the New Range Rover the range change is effected electrically by pressing a button on the fascia in the case of the manual-gearbox model, or by use of the gear selector lever in the auto-transmission vehicle. In both cases a simple 2-parameter logic gate is employed:

Electric range change eliminates need for transfer lever. Operates by button with manual gearbox; through gear selector lever on auto.

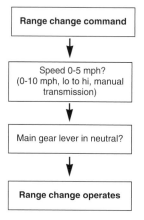

```
┌─────────────────────────────────┐
│     Range change command        │
└─────────────────────────────────┘
              ↓
┌─────────────────────────────────┐
│       Speed 0-5 mph?            │
│  (0-10 mph, lo to hi, manual    │
│         transmission)           │
└─────────────────────────────────┘
              ↓
┌─────────────────────────────────┐
│   Main gear lever in neutral?   │
└─────────────────────────────────┘
              ↓
┌─────────────────────────────────┐
│     Range change operates       │
└─────────────────────────────────┘
```

Manual gearbox version – indications. The fascia button has a built-in light (LED) that works in conjunction with the instrument-pack Message Centre as shown in the table below to show the status with a reminder of why the change may not have taken place. Electric range change with auto transmission is covered in Section 2.3; when and how to use low range is at Section 2.4.

Both versions have speed and neutral logic gates. Message Centre and lights confirm status

Electric range change – indicators, **manual gearbox** version		
What you do	*Range change light (LED)*	*Message Centre indications*
Press once for 'LOW'	Steady ON - you are in low	'LOW', then 'L' prefix. eg 'L3' means low box 3rd
Press again for 'HIGH'	Steady OFF - you are in high	'HIGH', then no further indication except gear
	Flash briefly – shows one or other 'gate' criteria not met, ie	
	a. Speed above 5 mph	a. 'SLOW DOWN' shows for 4 sec
	b. Main lever not in neutral	b. 'SELECT NEUTRAL' shows for 4 sec

Electric range change button on fascia of manual-transmission versions of New Range Rovers (left). Note there is no normally selectable 'N' position in the transfer box on this vehicle. This can only be obtained (for dead-engine towing) by inserting a 5 amp fuse in position 11 in the under-seat fusebox.

Really steep slopes (right) call for all the traction controls – low transfer gears , centre diff lock, and a readiness to use the parking brake. As diagram shows (below), handbrake operates on propeller shaft so should not be used when vehicle is moving. Stopped on extreme slopes,vehicle should also be in gear with diff lock engaged.

Electronic traction control, handbrake

Electronic traction control – (ETC). ETC is an *automatic* feature available on all current ABS-equipped Range Rovers which inhibits wheel-spin by applying pulsed brake to a spinning rear wheel and thus enhances traction on ice, snow or in severe off-road conditions. Like ABS, it is especially effective in maintaining control when one side of the vehicle is on a more slippery surface than the other. A dashboard light indicates, purely for information purposes, when it is operating; there are no driver controls. A further note appears at Section 10.1, Glossary.

Handbrake – only when stationary. As it is adjacent to the transfer gear lever it is worth mentioning the handbrake at this point although it is not strictly speaking a traction control. The handbrake on Land Rover products acts on a drum on the rear propeller shaft immediately aft of the gearbox and as such it is extremely powerful. The handbrake should be regarded as a *parking brake only*. Use of this handbrake when the vehicle is moving at all will cause severe juddering

shock loads and wind-up to the transmission. For this reason, except in emergencies, the handbrake should never be applied *until the vehicle is stationary*. **WARNING. Under no circumstances should you attempt to use it for trying to do 'hand-brake turns'.**

CAUTION. Handbrake is a transmission brake; do not apply while the vehicle is moving. Use as parking brake only (except in emergency).

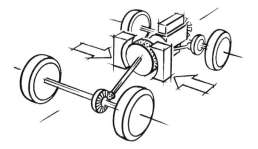

Concept of handbrake shown, with drum on rear propshaft immediately aft of transfer gearbox . When centre diff-lock is engaged handbrake effectively works on both prop shafts as they are then locked together.

2.2. Automatic transmission

Basic knowledge

Standard procedure. Adherence to Driver's Manual techniques will ensure competent, non-damaging performance from a vehicle equipped with automatic transmission off-road in high or low ratio. The tolerance and smoothness of an auto transmission, indeed, will often permit operation in high ratio where off-road conditions are not unusually demanding. Standard operating procedure can be summed up briefly:

1. The automatic gearbox is a ZF four-speed unit with automatic lock-up on 4th ratio above a certain speed to minimise torque converter slippage.

2. 'D' *enables* (ie permits the use of) all four forward ratios. **'3'** enables the lower three – ie it will use 1st, 2nd and 3rd but not change above 3rd. Similarly **'2'** enables 1st and 2nd only and **'1'** enables 1st-only. (The above and Items 3-5 below refer to high range mode with the H-gate auto selection arrangements on the new 1994/5 Range Rover; see Section 2.3.)

3. Select **'N'** on the main gear selector before making a transfer box selection. If it will not immediately engage, apply the brakes, engage **'D'** briefly, go back to **'N'** and try again. See Section 6.2 for low transfer to high box on the move on Discovery and old Range Rover.

4. If you are stationary for any length of time, engine running, select **'P'** or **'N'** rather than let the vehicle idle 'in-gear' which will unnecessarily heat up the transmission fluid.

5. If you are in **'P'** or **'N'** apply the footbrake before selecting a forward or reverse ratio to avoid creep.

6. Remember there is no 'gate' between **'D'(or '4')** and **'3'** (ie the catch does not have to be released) so for a sudden acceleration requirement and to force a very rapid change-down all you have to do is 'slap' the selector lever back into the '3' position. This will give you quicker response than a 'kick-down'.

Because of certain operating differences, the H-gate auto transmission on the New Range Rover is dealt with in detail at Section 2.3 but the basics above are valid. You will find it useful, however, to absorb the operating philosophy outlined here first.

Controlling the automatics

Automatic transmission off-road. Though traditionally most off-road operations are carried out by vehicles with manual transmission, this is no more than a statistical fact rather than validating any preferences. That there is considerable advantage in the use of automatic transmission off-road is attested by the fact that major power and other military users specify it in their general service vehicles.

Advantages and disadvantages. Whilst the most obvious advantage of auto transmission is that of ease of operation for the driver – important for the military or public utilities user whose mind will be on other things as well as driving – there are also significant benefits in terms of vehicle durability and protection from driver mis-use and transmission shock loads. Off-road performance can itself be enhanced by an automatic's quick seamless changes of gear in 'lift-off' situations – see opposite. The only disadvantages are higher initial cost and increased brake wear though, as already indicated, major professional users with cost-effectiveness in mind compare this with the higher maintenance and repair costs of mis-used manual vehicles and still opt for automatic.

Operating philosophies – knowledge still needed. A Discovery or any Range Rover with auto transmission can be operated on a minimum-knowledge basis by, say, a fleet or pool operator with dis-

Automatics for off-road use have considerable functional advantages – endorsed by major military users.

Automatics off-road can be operated in two ways – minimum knowledge or advanced.

Auto transmission is an elegant, least-stress way of dealing with on-the-limits terrain. Knowing how to get the best from it is well worth the trouble.

Changing to low range (where selection is by manual lever), select 'N' on main selector before moving transfer lever. Perusal of overall gear ratios on auto (Section 9), explains why an automatic needs low range 1st for adequate down-slope retardation. For 'up and over' (right) use low range '3' for climb but slip into '1' for descent. For slippery 'forest floor' (above) low 3rd is best (see below) – with diff locked manually on Discovery.

parate drivers of differing experience; for these or the inexperienced a basic knowledge will suffice. On the other hand refinement of operating effectiveness and vehicle capability will result if time is taken to learn to get the best from the system – see Sections 6.2, and 6.3.

Gradability vs engine braking. In comparison to a manual transmission, you will find an auto has surprising gradability in high range but, particularly off-road, engine braking is inherently poor even in low range. You will need to engage '1' low range to obtain satisfactory engine braking on a descent. Note that if speed is too high this will not engage, even though it has been selected – see next paragraph.

Steep up and down. A steep climb followed by a steep descent sums this situation up well. Whilst you will probably be able to climb well enough in high

range on 'D', you will need low range '1' for the descent. To save doing a range change at the top of the incline the technique should thus be to engage low range before the obstacle, select '3' (see below why), make the ascent and, at the top, with forward speed at a minimum, pull the main selector back to '1' in order to get maximum retardation for the descent. If you are over the summit and select '1' with the speed too high, it will not engage; you will stay in 2nd or 3rd with little or no engine braking – see Section 6.4. for emergency procedure.

'Lift-off' elimination of wheel-spin. The reason for selecting '3' before a slippery ascent or other potential wheel-spin situation is that as soon as the wheels begin to spin the auto sensors will recognise the reduced torque and change up; this will tend to eliminate wheel-spin as soon as it occurs – in just the same way as you would lift off the throttle with a manual transmission to quench wheel-spin near the top of a steep loose slope. Selecting '3' rather than 'D' ensures change-up is not too high.

Muddy, 'forest floor' situations. The same applies for 'forest floor' slippery mud situations. Even though the main ratio actually in use may be 1st or 2nd, having the selector in '3' ensures that, as soon as wheel-spin and its reduced torque is sensed, the gearbox will change up to 3rd to eliminate spin.

The main off-road control you will use with auto is aimed at improving down-slope retardation.

Auto will change up to low-box 3rd on a loose slope better than you could on a manual. Use the facility and save wheel-spin.

2.3. H-gate automatic transmission

On New Range Rover selector lever has separate plane of movement for HI and LO; picture shows low range quadrant illuminated with 'Manual' mode selected – see text opposite below. Note there is no normally selectable 'N' position in the transfer box on this vehicle. TRANSFER NEUTRAL can only be obtained (for dead-engine towing) by inserting a 5 amp fuse in position 11 in the under-seat fusebox.

H-gate provides two-plane operating quadrant for selector lever – HI plane nearest driver, LO plane farthest away.

HI an LO·quadrants are separately illuminated according to which transfer range is active. Use in conjunction with Message Centre messages.

Normal operation

The H-gate. In 'Normal' mode (see Mode switch, next column) the H-gate automatic transmission *functions* in exactly the same way as the unit controlled by selector lever and transfer lever. The difference is only the manner of control – an H-shaped operating gate with the selector lever able to move along either side of the H to give high range in the plane nearest the driver and low range in the plane farthest from the driver.

Transfer neutral. The 'crossover' from one plane to the other is at the **'N'** point of each operating quadrant; at the centre of that crossover line is the Neutral position for the transfer gearbox, not normally selectable – see caption above.

High range. Operate the selector lever in the plane nearest the driver to use high range gears. All the basics mentioned in the previous section (Section 2.2) in high range apply equally well to the H-gate transmission.

Low range. Operate the selector lever in the plane farthest from the driver to use low range gears. In low range, operation is also the same as standard automatics though there are, as a reminder about

climbing a steep slope in '3' and descending in '1', small pictograms in the 3 and 1 quadrant positions to indicate respectively steep ascent and steep descent.

Indicator lights

Indicators and Message Centre. As with the manual version of the New Range Rover, a combination of steady or flashing indicator lights and readouts on the instrument binnacle Message Centre give you information about the status of a range change. As before, in general a steady light means a completed range change whilst a flashing light shows a process is still under way.

H-gate lights. The illumination under each side of the H-gate selector quadrants is used as a 'Active range' and 'Target range' indicator. When high is selected (active), the quadrant nearest the driver is illuminated; when low range is selected, the quadrant farthest from the driver is illuminated. Following the philosophy that flashing means things are still going on, moving the selector lever across the bar of the H from high to low range will result in the high range quadrant lights remaining on and the low range (the target range) lights will flash until the range change is actually complete. When that happens, the 'low' quadrant light will remain on and the 'high' light will extinguish. LO to HI is a similar sequence.

Message Centre information. As with the manual gearbox version of the new Range Rover, the instrument binnacle Message Centre will show the transfer gear range you are in, eg going into low you will first get 'LOW', then an 'L' prefix to the gear number.

Mode switch

'Normal' vs 'Sport' or 'Manual'. The Mode switch, located beside the H-gate, may be pressed to turn normal high range

Electric range change logic sequence

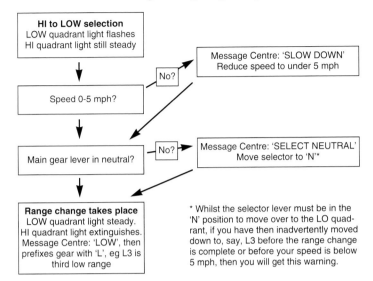

HI to LOW selection
LOW quadrant light flashes
HI quadrant light still steady

↓

Speed 0-5 mph? —No?→ Message Centre: 'SLOW DOWN'
Reduce speed to under 5 mph

↓

Main gear lever in neutral? —No?→ Message Centre: 'SELECT NEUTRAL'
Move selector to 'N'*

↓

Range change takes place
LOW quadrant light steady.
HI quadrant light extinguishes.
Message Centre: 'LOW', then
prefixes gear with 'L', eg L3 is
third low range

* Whilst the selector lever must be in the 'N' position to move over to the LO quadrant, if you have then inadvertently moved down to, say, L3 before the range change is complete or before your speed is below 5 mph, then you will get this warning.

Electric range change will only change transfer ratios if speed is less than 5 mph and main gear selector is in neutral.

into 'Sport' and low range into 'Manual'.

'Sport' mode – high range. Pressing the Mode switch in high range gives 'Sport' mode which moves gear change points within the automatic gearbox higher up the engine rpm range thus achieving a more sporty acceleration profile without having to resort to kick-down or use of the selector to hold a given gear (though these facilities are still available).

'Manual' mode - low range. Pressing the same mode button when you are currently in 'Normal' low range turns the low range auto transmission virtually into a manual gearbox. Thus to select **'3'** when stationary in low range 'Manual' is effectively to start off in third gear and hold it until you select another gear. As will be seen in Section 3.2, 'Gentle right foot', there are times when off-road surface conditions are so slippery that you want the gentlest possible pull-away to avoid wheel-spin. Low range 'Manual' enables you to judge the best gear for these conditions and select it. In fact the gearbox does not actually start in third when low

range '3' Manual mode is selected since this would lead to excessive slip and temperature rise in the transmission fluid; however, it spends a very short time indeed in 1st and 2nd before going to (and holding) the gear you have selected.

Message Centre information. As with the manual gearbox version, the Message Centre will give an indication of the gear, the range and the mode selected. Thus low range third in manual mode will show as LM3.

Range change logic criteria

Speed and neutral – as before. The same logic will prevail as with the manual gearbox version with electric range change; that is, speed must be below 5 mph and the main gear selector must be in neutral before a change will occur. *Both* criteria have to be met before the range change will take place. The diagram above gives a visual summary of what happens in the case of a HIGH to LOW change; similar criteria and warnings apply in LOW to HIGH.

Press MODE switch and NORMAL HI becomes SPORT; NORMAL LO becomes MANUAL.

LO MANUAL effectively turns low range into a clutchless manual gearbox.

2.4. Low range – when and how

'Power' and 'control'

Low range for *power*. As we have seen, selecting low ratio on the transfer box is not just another gear but affects *all* the gears in the main gear box (including reverse), gearing them down by nearly 2:1. The obvious uses of the low range are thus occasions when you want a great deal of 'power' or tractive effort – towing a car out of a ditch, ascending a very steep slope, getting out of deep mud or sand, pulling a fallen tree trunk out of the way.

Low range for *control*. Less immediately obvious uses for the low ratio include the provision of control rather than high tractive effort. Examples of this might be steadying the vehicle on a very steep descent without use of the brakes or, classically, allowing the vehicle to crawl over rocks slowly, steadily, without jarring – and with your foot off the clutch pedal and without use of the brakes. Low box, first gear excels in this kind of exercise and can often be used with minimal

throttle opening or even at idling revs.

Low 1st – too low? Low range first, because of its enormous 'power' capability, is often too low for slippery surface conditions and it is easy for you to spin the wheels inadvertently through the application of more torque than the ground can take. It should be used when grip is very good, when momentum is not required and when there is little danger of spinning the wheels – mainly when considerable tractive effort is needed. Its particular application is in affording engine braking down very steep slopes (see Section 4.5, 'Descending steep slopes'.)

What to start off in

Low 2nd – rule-of-thumb. Second is a good rule-of-thumb starting-off gear for most low ratio situations – muddy conditions, steep slopes and the like even with a heavy trailer. Because tractive effort available is then more closely matched to what the ground will take, there is less risk of wheel spin and the lost traction that results. As indicated on the previous page, with automatic transmission select '3'; this can sometimes also be the solution with manual transmission where conditions demand the delicate touch.

Low 3rd, 4th, 5th – versatility. Third, fourth and fifth gears in the low range are good 'getting about' gears with manual transmission ('D' or '4' in auto) for the better parts of derelict mountain or desert tracks, for getting across the field, for forest tracks that are a bit tight for high range. They bring out the vehicle's versatility and the ease with which it traverses cross-country terrain; you can make a respectable speed in fifth or 'D', yet change all the way down to second when the going gets more difficult (see Section 4.2, 'Driving on tracks').

Low ratio gears the vehicle down by nearly 2:1 and provides enormous tractive effort.

Low range 1st gear provides superb control for slow, steady crossing of obstacles such as rocks and for brake-less descents; too low for inclines.

For most situations, start in 2nd. Use 3rd, 4th, 5th are for 'getting around' on rough ground.

Saharan boulders epitomise the 'control' case where low range 1st gear gives steady rock-crawling capability. 1st gear start is sometimes appropriate to heavy towing but higher gears provide general off-road flexibility (left). Avoid temptation to 'use clutch as another gear'.

Driver still the key. We shall see in the ensuing sections specific examples of what gears to use. And also that there is more to maintaining traction than just selecting a low gear; driver sensitivity is half the battle – see Section 3.2, 'Gentle right foot'. (Also Section 6.1, 'High/low range overlap'.)

Automatic transmission. As in high range, automatic transmission will start the vehicle in first gear and change up as far as it is permitted by the position of the gear selector lever – all the way up to 4th gear if it is in 'D', up to 3rd if the lever is at '3', no higher than 2nd if the lever is at

'2', and it will hold 1st for steep descents if the lever is moved back to '1'. You thus have total control – see also Section 2.2 and 6.2, all on the subject of automatic transmission. Section 2.3 deals with the specific features of 'Manual' mode low range automatic (H-gate) transmission on the New Range Rover.

Driver sensitivity – a gentle right foot – is still the main key.

The Land Rover Experience

2.5. Centre differential lock

When to use diff lock

Poor traction overcome. As we have seen, the centre differential may be locked as required or, on Range Rovers, will lock automatically when this action is needed. The reason for the provision of the locking facility on the centre differential which separates the front and rear propeller shafts is that there are a number of poor-traction situations when such a lock will enhance the vehicle's performance. See also Section 1.3, 'Permanent four-wheel drive'.

Range Rover's centre diff lock is automatic – actuated by viscous coupling (see glossary Section 10.1.).

Spinning wheels. Many will be familiar with the single spinning wheel of a conventional car on an icy road. This is the result of the drive wheels being on surfaces of different grip characteristics – one wheel on ice with the other on dry road. It is possible for the same situation – fore and aft – to arise in a 4x4; front axle on firm, grippy concrete while the rear axle is in mud – an extreme example but the principle applies to a greater or lesser extent in nearly all off-road situations.

On Discovery and Defender, select centre diff lock when there is any risk of losing grip.

When to use diff lock. A simple rule-of-thumb is to use diff lock when you use the low range transfer gears on any loose or slippery surface. Use of low range generally means that you are on difficult or uneven ground and wanting a high tractive effort. Such ground usually has uneven traction characteristics as well as an uneven surface and you will be needing all the traction (grip) you can get. Locking the centre differential will preclude loss of traction resulting from potential front/rear differences in grip.

High range diff lock? It is possible to engage diff lock in high range too. When, if ever, is this desirable? It will be useful to engage diff lock in high range when

Be sure to de-select diff lock when on a firm, level, non-slippery surface.

Diagram shows movement of transfer lever to select diff lock. Inset shows warning light – not present on Range Rovers which have automatic diff lock. Poor-traction low-box off-road conditions such as loose sand are invariably more effectively tackled with diff lock.

driving on potentially difficult surfaces such as wet grass, mud, loose or packed snow, or loose sand on tracks or in open desert.

When to de-select diff lock. It is important to de-select diff lock when on any hard grippy surface such as tarmac or concrete (wet or dry) whether you are in high or low range. The 'DIFF LOCK' warning light will illuminate when the diff is locked and should be a reminder to you. If you do not de-select on grippy surfaces the steering will feel stiff, there will be excessive tyre wear through scuffing and there will be transmission wind-up putting excessive strain on the transmission which may make it hard to use the transfer gearbox lever to disengage low ratio.

Diff lock indicator light

To select diff lock, ease the throttle, dip the clutch, move transfer lever to left; move to right to de-select. (Discovery and Defender only – Range Rover has automatic diff lock.)

Controls and indicators

How to select and de-select diff lock.
On any Land Rover model where diff lock selection is not automatic the transfer lever can move side-to-side as well as fore and aft; move the transfer lever to the left to select diff lock – whether you are in high or low range. Make it a habit to briefly ease the throttle and dip the clutch as you do this – in case there is a transitory speed difference between front and rear axles at the moment when you select the inter-axle lock. Move the lever to the right to de-select diff lock; when the diff lock disengages the warning light will extinguish.

Diff lock indicator light actuation.
The 'DIFF LOCK' indicator will come on when the diff lock is actually engaged –

not just when you move the lever to select it. Similarly it will only extinguish when the diff lock is actually disengaged. If the light is reluctant to go out after de-selecting diff lock some transmission 'wind-up' may be present. Reversing a few metres, then going forward will usually disengage diff lock , extinguishing the light.

Range Rover – automatic diff lock.
All current Range Rovers have viscous coupling unit (VCU) centre diff 'lock' actuation for which no manual selection or indicator light is required. A viscous coupling (see Glossary, Section 10.1.) sits across the two halves of the centre differential and when relative motion between the front and rear propeller shafts is sensed, the coupling becomes extremely stiff, effectively locking the differential.

Diff lock light comes on only when diff lock actually engaged.

The Land Rover Experience

Section 3

Preliminaries

3.1. Mind-set

Smooth operation, making the vehicle flow over the ground – right – rather than jolt, is an indication of the required mechanical sympathy. Work your vehicle well (left) but take the drama out of your driving.

Mechanical sympathy

Be smooth and gentle with your vehicle. Using the power is not the same as being brutal.

Aim smooth. All machinery responds well to being treated with mechanical sympathy – even a vehicle with a reputation for ruggedness such as the Land Rover. There is more to this than just following maintenance schedules and keeping the oil topped up; that is vital but is not the whole user-interface picture. Smooth driving operation is the aim.

Be kind. Using the very considerable capabilities of your Land Rover product need not preclude your being kind to it. It is a very tolerant vehicle but clunks in the transmission, prolonged wheel-spinning, misuse of the clutch and harsh treatment of any of the controls, engine or suspension should be avoided. Specifically:

Avoid transmission clonks; let the clutch grip fully when it has to. Kill wheel-spin quickly.

1. Transmission controls. (Gear lever and transfer box lever.) Moderate force and moderate speed is the best way to use these levers – firm and gentle. If it is difficult to engage low range, leave the transfer lever where it is, dip the clutch, engage first gear and let the clutch up slightly to reposition the gear wheels. Keep the clutch down and try again.

Similarly, difficulty engaging first or reverse (or noise in doing so) may be eased by dipping the clutch, quickly engaging a higher gear (say, third) and then trying again.

2. Riding the clutch. Don't slip the clutch or 'use it as another gear'. Don't 'ride' the clutch either; by this is meant resting your foot on the pedal with slight pressure so as to be able quickly to disengage it. It is natural enough for a properly cautious or inexperienced driver negotiating a difficult piece of terrain to want to be able to use clutch and brake with the minimum delay but riding the clutch – in effect reducing the pressure of the clutch springs – will encourage clutch slip and cause premature wear. Have the clutch fully engaged and your foot clear of the pedal whenever possible.

3. Wheel-spin .... As we shall see in more detail, wheel-spin is lost traction and *prolonged* wheel-spin will scoop earth from under the wheels worsening the situation. It is not good for the transmission either. A fast spinning wheel suddenly getting grip can cause shock loading on

the transmission and the possibility of transmission damage.

3a .... but.. There *are* circumstances – certain types of mud with the best mud tyres – when controlled, short-period wheel-spin will permit the tyre to cut through to drier ground and obtain traction where none existed before. The same approach in sand would be disastrous. So you must become wheel-spin-aware, know how your tyre tread is faring and, as we shall see, make judgements.

Pride – learn when to back off

Minimise the drama. Probably the most golden of the rules governing difficult off-road driving is to admit defeat early and reverse out. Good off-road driving is achieved with the minimum of drama. Huge water splashes, spinning wheels and flying clods of earth are rarely necessary. Even the best drivers perpetrate these fireworks occasionally if they have misjudged the terrain – and usually feel a little sheepish afterwards.

Back off, try again. Often such drama stems from fear of failure and then trying too hard. You will learn from this book, and with practice, that part of the learning process is acquiring the procedures for initially getting it wrong – typically the failed hill scenario (Section 4.4). You will learn that getting it wrong first time usually does not matter; you will learn to relax. When a very steep slippery climb stops your vehicle and the wheels begin to spin, back off at once; try again, possibly with a little more speed and in a higher gear. Holding the vehicle with uncontrolled wheel-spin will cause excessive damage to the ground, will usually worsen the vehicle's chances of making it up the slope and, in some cases, will cause a vehicle to slew sideways-on to the slope and possibly tip.

Wheel-spin alert! The same goes for stretches of deep mud or sand – though the two are quite different. If you do not make it through the patch first time and there is any *sustained* and ineffective wheel-spin, stop before you bog deeper, reverse out and try again using a different route or different tactics. Do not be too proud to admit that you got it wrong.

If it isn't going to go, reverse out while you can and try again.

Getting through second time is better than having to be towed out on the first.

3.2. Gentle right foot

Climbing slopes like this requires a very sensitive foot on the throttle. Paradoxically you may find you need to ease off the throttle at the steepest part – where risk of wheel-spin is greatest.

Wheel-spin, traction control

Reading the ground. You will have seen that effective use of the low range and realising the extraordinary potential of your vehicle depends a lot on a driver's appreciation of how much traction the ground itself will take without allowing *inappropriate* wheel-spin.

Ease off the throttle before you get sustained wheel-spin.

Excessive throttle. As with a car on ice, too much throttle will 'over-torque' the driving wheels and make them spin. With such low gearing in the low ratio gears, the same thing can happen with your Land Rover in slippery conditions. Drivers will quickly develop a delicate throttle foot and learn when the conditions are putting the vehicle on the verge of wheel-spin.

Spinning wheels dig. Spinning wheels represent loss of traction, often a loss of directional control as well and can also result in ground being scooped by the spinning tyres from under the wheel and the vehicle becoming stuck. In some cases (Section 4.7) this scooping will get through slippery mud onto drier ground – but not always. Alertness is the key-word. So there are many good reasons for acquiring a sensitive throttle foot and not choosing too low a gear. Both will avoid wheel-spin and help to maintain traction.

Wheel-spin and brake lock-up: two versions of the same thing – a discontinuity of rolling contact.

Electronic traction control, ETC. As already introduced in Section 2.1 under 'Traction controls', ETC, when fitted, will monitor, and inhibit, inadvertent wheel spin and considerably assist in maintaining traction under limiting conditions.

Slide, cadence braking, ABS

Excessive brake. Wheel-spin represents a discontinuity of rolling contact with the ground – the ground and the periphery of the wheel are not in stationary contact with one another. Exactly the same situation arises in the case of excessive braking on slippery ground. One or more wheels lock up and slide over the ground resulting in a discontinuity of rolling contact – the periphery of the wheel and the ground are not going the same speed. In one case the wheel is slipping past the stationary ground; in the other the ground is (relatively) slipping past the stationary wheel.

Cadence braking – same foot, same cure. And again the same cures may be

Continuous rolling contact. Using throttle or brake, avoid spin or slip. Think of your wheels and the ground as a rack and pinion like this.

Engine braking's progressive and controllable retardation is best for slopes like these (right) – and almost every other one too. But learn cadence braking for the times when you have got it wrong (above).

used. Lifting your right foot off the throttle will stop wheel-spin and lifting your right foot off the brake will stop wheel slide or skidding. In the case of braking, though, you applied the brakes because you wanted to stop. So re-apply them more gently and, best of all, employ 'cadence braking' technique – repeated jabbing of the brake pedal, quite gently, as fast as you can so that the wheel never gets a chance to lock. Though it takes will-power to take your foot off the brakes to do this when you are trying to slow down, cadence braking is remarkably effective.

ABS – automated finesse. It is thus no surprise to find out that the advanced anti-lock brakes (ABS) fitted to Land Rover vehicles operate on exactly the same principle. They employ a very fast

form of cadence braking to obtain the maximum retardation on the most difficult surfaces, *on or off road*, without locking up any of the wheels – you will hear and feel the brake relay working. So in the case of a vehicle fitted with this feature you will get maximum available braking and retain directional control – *for given ground conditions* . Beware, however; ABS will not reverse the laws of physics.

Engine braking – elegant, gentle. Engine braking, of course, is a very controlled and gentle way to achieve retardation as we shall see in the sections to follow. But even that should not be regarded as an infallible solution to every problem, especially when it is very slippery; you can still finish up with sliding wheels – see Section 6.4.

Wheel slide? Back off the brakes and re-apply with repeated gentle jabs.

Engine braking is best for steep down-slopes.

3.3. Geometric limitations

Clearance angles

Appreciating clearance. Common to negotiating all types of obstacle off-road is an appreciation of under-body clearance angles, clearance under the chassis and axle differentials and the amount by which the axles can articulate (move up on the near side and down on the off side – and vice versa – see next spread).

Ground clearances, under-chassis angles. It is soon obvious how well all Land Rover products perform cross country but a few moments to study the accompanying diagram will help to refine your judgement on the kind of thing that can and cannot be done without touching bodywork or chassis on the ground. Under-axle clearance is relevant to the size of a single isolated rock on the track between the wheels that can be driven over without fouling but under-belly clearance relates to the (bigger) size of ridge undulations that can be crossed.

Be aware of under-axle clearance – and how it differs from belly clearance.

Ramp angle – belly clearance. The angle measured from the chassis at the centre of the wheelbase down to the periphery of front and rear wheels is the ramp breakover angle, usually called the ramp angle. Its significance is self evident since it governs whether or not you will 'belly' the vehicle on a hump. Such a hump taken without thought of the ramp angle can result in getting bellied with the wheels grappling for traction and the vehicle's weight taken directly on the chassis on the top of the hump – see photos at Section 5.1.

Low-set towing hitch can cause tail to dig in on steep ascents or crossing ditches.

Air suspension. A Range Rover fitted with electronic air suspension (EAS – see Glossary, Section 10.1) has the facility, with 'High profile' selected, to increase ride height by 40 mm over standard and, in the process, further improve ramp angle.

Axle clearance. Under-axle clearance is a more obvious limitation. Whilst a Land Rover vehicle running out of axle clearance on soft going will sometimes plough out its own path, do not get into the habit of doing things this way. Deep ruts, rocks submerged in soft mud or encountering hard or rocky going will cause the vehicle to come to a sudden damaging stop when the axle differential housing hits the obstacle.

Approach and departure angles. Approach angles are large on all Land

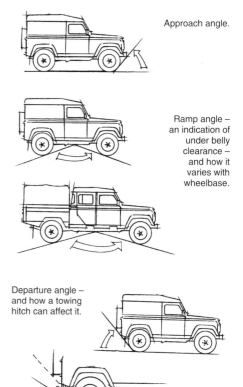

Approach angle.

Ramp angle – an indication of under belly clearance – and how it varies with wheelbase.

Departure angle – and how a towing hitch can affect it.

Under-axle clearance (top) – about 19-23 cm (about 7.5-8.5 in) – is less than under belly clearance. See Section 9 for exact model dimensions.

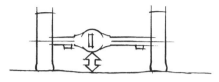

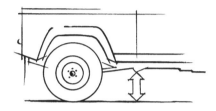

Try and develop an awareness, off-road, of where parts of the vehicle may touch the ground; the tow hitch (above) is the most commonly forgotten. Under-axle and under-belly clearances (diagrams) need remembering too.

Rover models but remember that tail overhang and departure angle is the one that will catch you out going up a very steep slope. Regarding the common problem of 'hitting the tail', the departure angle – already less than the approach angle – is further reduced when a low-set towing hitch is fitted and it is not uncommon for an inattentive driver to dig the tow hitch into the ground while going forward up a very steep incline and then find that he cannot reverse back because the tow hitch prevents him doing so.

Big wheels, short wheelbase. The biggest wheels and the shortest wheelbase will give best under-chassis clearance angles – a Defender 90 on 7.50 x 16 tyres takes the prize; its short rear overhang also yields the best departure angle. Details of all clearances and geometric limitations for all models and variants are shown at Section 9.

Long wheelbase and tail overhang call for more caution on rough ground.

The significance of – left to right – approach angle, departure angle and ramp angle.

...continued

The Land Rover Experience

3.3. Geometric limitations – contd

The short wheelbase Defender 90 has a smaller turning circle than a 130.

A short wheelbase vehicle will be more agile than one with a long wheelbase.

Axle articulation permits the ultimate 'twisty ground' performance; keeps wheels on ground and producing traction.

Manoeuvrability

Axle movement. We have already seen that articulation is the amount by which one axle can move – left wheel up, right wheel down or vice versa – in relation to the chassis and its fellow axle. Clearly it represents the degree to which your vehicle can keep its wheels on the ground on undulating 'twisty' terrain and thus retain traction under difficult conditions. All Land Rover products have very good articulation due to having coil springs and large wheel travel. But for a given amount of articulation – say a 40 cm lift under one front wheel before the other front wheel begins to lift – a shorter wheelbase actually represents a greater 'twisty ground' capability than a long wheelbase. So do not expect your Defender 130, although it has about the same axle articulation as a Defender 90 (assuming full wheel movement), to be able to traverse equally tortuous ground without lifting a wheel. See 'longitudinal articulation angle', Glossary, Section 10.1 and suspension movement figures on the tech data pages in Section 9.

Manoeuvrability, lateral lean. As the diagram shows, the shorter the wheelbase the tighter the turning circle. The angle to which the vehicle can lean laterally without tipping is very similar on all models with standard bodywork. As covered in Section 4.6, 'Traversing slopes', this is a static figure and should not be relied on when driving. Local bumpiness and the effect of even minor steering corrections make a considerable difference and a limit of half the figures shown is recommended.

Wading depth. Maximum wading depth (see also Section 4.10, 'Wading') is quoted as 0.5 metre but for special cir-

Land Rover products' long wheel travel gives exceptional articulation, ensuring optimum off-road performance.

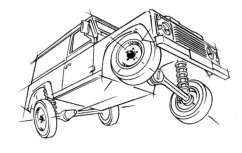

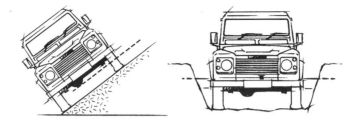

Land Rover do not quote exact lateral lean limits; exercise extreme caution at all times. See also Section 4.6. Do not wade without fitting wading plugs – see Section 4.10.

If you are close to the limits, get out and take a closer look – see next spread.

cumstances using diesel engines and a raised air intake this can be increased.

Inspection first. When close to any of the above limitations a preliminary survey on foot is what is required, preferably with someone to marshal you through or round the obstacle. Whilst all Land Rover products are tough and capable off-road vehicles, it is pointless to risk underbody damage or getting stuck for the want of properly surveying the obstacle first. This is fully dealt with in the next spread.

Photos show uses of articulation (left) in crossing ditch – see Section 4.3. Note gentle bow-wave when wading – see Section 4.10.. Side slopes always feel worse than they are – but don't press your luck!

3.4. Look before you leap

On-foot survey

Inspect before you drive. It is invariably beneficial to do an on-foot survey of difficult obstacles before committing the vehicle. The aim of the survey is to pick the best route and ensure there are no previously unnoticed hazards such as rocks to foul the axles, deep ruts hidden in undergrowth or the lie of firm ground under snow. A reconnaissance also gives you the chance to test the firmness of visible ground – soft mud or the strength of the sand crust on a dune.

Prod before you drive. An on-foot recce is especially important when fording streams and rivers where there is no established safe path. Nor will it be easy since you will have to establish not only the firmness of the river bed but also its evenness. Dropping into an underwater rock hole or suddenly descending to a depth that will drown the engine will require fundamental and major recovery procedures. Water deeper than about 35 cm demands that wading plugs be fitted to the clutch housing and cam-belt drive housing. (See 'Wading', Section 4.10.)

Always worth it. An on-foot survey will delay you and is usually mucky or wet. It is, however, far preferable to damaging the Land Rover or finding you have a major recovery problem on your hands.

Always make an on-foot inspection of difficult obstacles.

Use an external marshaller to direct you where clearances are tight.

Marshalling

External guidance – marshalling. If you are not alone, an invaluable adjunct to negotiating difficult ground with small clearances is to have your passenger marshal you through from outside the vehicle. Only someone outside the vehicle can properly see all four wheels and where they are going – and see the exact clearances under the axle casings (see photos Section 4.9).

Overall view, take it steady. A marshaller should stand 5 to 15 metres ahead of the vehicle – facing it – where all the wheels can easily be seen. Guidance by the marshaller should be given unam-

On-foot inspection especially important in rivers where hazards are hidden.

On-foot pre-inspection establishes feasibility. Then marshaller can see all four wheels, gives precision guidance and can avoid tyre damage on rocks.

biguously and entirely by hand and arm signals rather than by voice. At the risk of stating the obvious, be sure there is just one marshaller who is in total charge and make a conscious effort to take things one step at a time. Situations in which marshalling is required frequently spawn two or three people all shouting half-heard directions at one time; the general tension often generates a feeling that something decisive and effective must be done, immediately...! The calm and measured approach is to be preferred!

Marshaller in control. Obey the marshaller completely. Try not to take your eyes off him or her to make your own judgements on a situation you cannot assess as comprehensively as someone outside the vehicle. Stop if you are not happy but once moving, the marshaller is in control.

One marshaller only in control. Directions by signs, not voice.

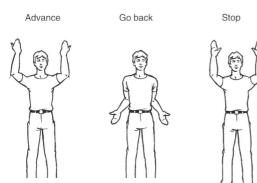

| Advance | Go back | Stop | Steer in this direction | Steer in this direction |

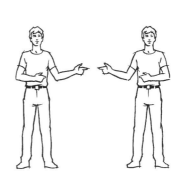

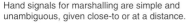

Hand signals for marshalling are simple and unambiguous, given close-to or at a distance.

Section 4

Operating techniques

4.1. Towing – on-road

Preliminaries – the theory

Theory matters? There will be many who, faced with pulling *that* trailer (no choice) with *this* vehicle (no choice) are of a mind to doubt the value of theory and just get on with it. An understandable view from a busy operator but airline pilots, similarly limited in choice of type or design of the aircraft they fly, do benefit a great deal – and safety is immeasurably enhanced – by knowing what is going on aerodynamically. There is much folklore and many rules of thumb associated with towing and it is helpful and refreshing to know that what goes on really is quantifiable now and every parameter may be taken into account – from the spring rates of the towing vehicle (tug) to the types of bushes fitted to the suspension.

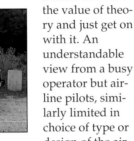

When trailer weight exceeds around 75% of tug weight, the laws of physics dictate you are entering a critical zone for stability. Be aware of the theory of trailer dynamics and know what is going on.

However hard-nosed and down to earth the job, knowing the theory will make operations safer.

Famine and feast. Land Rover's Design Analysis computer could produce enough information and study of variables to fill a book on this subject alone. The object of this section, in just eight pages, is to steer a middle course between the information famine of preceding years and the feast of data now available. The good news, for readers braced for another 'breakthrough' and overturning of received wisdom, is that virtually all the rules of thumb are valid. Knowing why, though – and their limitations – is absorbing and there are enough surprises to make it worthwhile reading further.

Trailer dynamics

Stability. Overriding priority will be given by all operators examining this subject to the question of stability and safety and brief treatment will be given therefore to:

- Straight line stability.
- Oscillation or weave.
- Steady turn stability.

Straight line stability. Consider a towing vehicle (tug) of infinite mass – the implication being that the towing pin moves in an undeviating straight line, uninfluenced by the trailer. The trailer behind it will tow straight for the same reason a dart or aircraft flies straight; as soon as the trailer deviates due to a gust or random side-load, the tyres will then be at an angle to the direction of motion

With imaginary non-deviating tug, trailer displacement gives rise to tyre slip angle which in turn generates restoring side-force to put trailer back on course in single or decaying series of swings. If trailer can influence tug (diagram opposite, far right) complex swings can be self-sustaining.

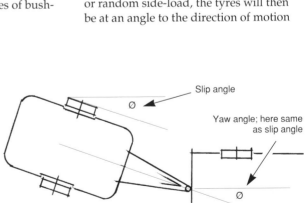

Slip angle

Yaw angle; here same as slip angle

Ø

Ø

'Non deviating' tug

and as a result a side-force will be generated by the tyres to push the trailer back in line behind the tug.

As the trailer approaches zero slip angle the side force also reduces until, when it is in line again, the side force has disappeared. Fairly obvious stuff but it is important to consider this – the concept of slip angle and tyre side force – before going on.

Oscillation, weave
Concept of decaying or
increasing oscillation. Few who have seen TV pictures of caravans 'mysteriously' turning over on motorways will need a definition of weave, yaw or snaking. However, distinguish between decaying (convergent) and increasing (divergent) oscillation; the difference between what is mildly alarming and peters out and the ever-increasing swing that can result in an accident. Take an ordinary school ruler (the type with a hole in one end) and let it swing on a pencil held in your hand – diagrams below.

The middle diagram (the hand remains perfectly still) corresponds exactly to the tug of infinite mass mentioned opposite where the tug continues undisturbed on a perfectly straight course. The swing of the ruler gradually decays to nothing. The third diagram corresponds

Right – an illustration not designed to scare but inserted (from a complete computer sequence) only to indicate that the result of a given combination of parameters and driving techniques can be predicted as a matter of routine. (50 mph, 2000 kg trailer, CG aft of axle, severe avoidance manoeuvre, .22 g braking.) How to avoid it in absence of precise data is less easily predicted; knowledge of general theory, care and caution are best ingredients. Diagrams below – dynamics of tug/trailer interface with decaying or increasing oscillation can be analogous to swinging a school ruler on a pencil. See text.

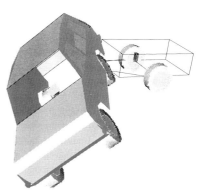

to a tug that can move. As you know, moving your hand in a particular way can make the ruler swing with increasing amplitude. In moving your hand (holding the pencil pivot) to make the ruler swing you are instinctively introducing an appropriate frequency and phasing of your movement to make the ruler swing as wide as possible. Try analysing *exactly* what you are doing and you will see how difficult it is to pinpoint the phase lead and frequency you are introducing. This is mentioned because although the computer, when given the tug/trailer dynamics to sort out, can apply the equations of motion and all the myriad modifying influences with tireless brilliance and accuracy, it reflects the number of variables and how critical they are when the overall stability result is considered.

Exact prediction of dynamics is possible.

But the myriad criteria and their varying influence make it impractical to attempt in every case.

Displace ruler

Static hand, decaying swing

Moving hand, increasing swing

...continued

4.1. Towing – on-road – contd

Whiplash effect. Let us therefore resort once more to an analogy, again using the school ruler. This time hold it in a horizontal plane, with your thumb and forefinger over the hole. Flick your wrist left and right and you will see as you do so that the ruler trails, moves and then over-shoots the action of your wrist – what may be termed a whiplash effect. Get the combination of thumb-grip (damping) and wrist-speed wrong and nothing much happens; get it 'right' and a perfect 'whiplash' takes place; again you will note there is a particular combination of parameters that 'excite' the system and these are related to the weight of ruler, speed of motion, etc.

The parallels between these three 'ruler cases' and a tug and trailer –

- The decaying oscillation
- The increasing oscillation due to hand movement and
- The 'whiplash' effect – closely related to the above.

– will be seen at once. With the ruler/pendulum the restoring 'side-force' is provided by gravity and inertia where in the case of the trailer the side force is provided by the tyres.

Applying the analogy. It is clear so far that lateral motion of the *tug* – at given phase differences and amplitudes – is a fundamental influencing factor in the generation, sustaining and 'amplification' of lateral oscillation. Because it will affect what we can do about it, it is worth now probing just a little deeper into the actual situation with a tug and trailer.

We have considered the ruler (trailer) swinging about the pivot point (tow hitch) for convenience because that is what actually happens. But we must now grasp the fact that a trailer (or any other 'body'), given a turning motion, will *naturally* want to rotate about its own centre of gravity (CG). Spin a Coke bottle on the kitchen table and it will spin about its CG. If you constrain one end while it is revolving (trailer nose hitched to a tow-hook) it will turn about that point but is still trying to rotate about is own CG so will exert a reactive lateral force on the hitch.

Look now at where, in a typical tug/trailer combination, the tug and trailer CGs are located and how this affects the influence of trailer on tug – diagrams opposite (upper)

In a swing, a forward trailer CG tends to reduce yaw angle Ø; in effect reducing the angle between the tug and trailer. This situation therefore permits the oscillation to decay. This gives a result like the middle diagram (no hand movement) on the previous spread. The *aft* CG, on the other hand tends to increase Ø, tending therefore, to encourage an increasing swing. Most readers will already know that a forward CG is best for trailers. When we look to the next sub-section, however, we will find that CG should not be *too* far forward

Steady-state cornering
Extreme forward trailer CG. Where you might perhaps have felt that the further forward the trailer CG the better would be its stability, the *destabilising* effect of the trailer on the tug actually increases with forward movement of trailer CG in fast bends. The computer confirms that moving the CG even 30 cm ahead of the axle in an accelerating steady turn can, in certain circumstances, cause breakaway of the tug towards the centre of the circle and subsequent roll-over. The lower diagram opposite makes clear what

Forward trailer CG benefits stability in weaves but too far forward will exacerbate problems in sharp turn manoeuvres.

Aim for trailer CG 10-20 cm ahead of axle. Knowing the length of your draw bar the equivalent nose load can be calculated. See Note in diagram, next spread.

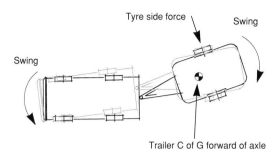

Tyre side force · Swing · Swing · Trailer C of G forward of axle

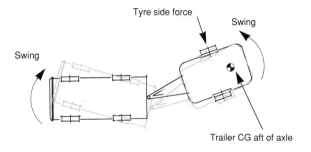

Assume trailer displaced to right, so tyre side-force is from right. Tyre side-force tends to turn trailer <u>about its own CG</u>, imparting motion to tail of tug that is stabilising (forward CG – left) or desta-bilising (aft CG – below)

Tyre side force · Swing · Swing · Trailer CG aft of axle

is happening. Although it is tyre side force acting about the trailer CG, you may find it easier to think of it as 'centrifugal force' on the mass represented by the CG; either way, the trailer CG, being far forward, tends strongly to push the nose of the trailer (and tail of the tug) towards the outside of the circle. There comes a time when the rear tyres of the tug can no longer hold on and the tail of the tug breaks away and the trailer, in hot pursuit, can provoke a rollover.

The compromise

Moderation in all things. In concept, therefore, we have a conflict. The weave damping case demands a forward CG and the steady-state turn is sensitive to a too-far forward CG. Whilst *all stability problems are more critical with a high trailer weight*, your particular combination of variables and cornering methods will dictate your choice of CG position. On most of the initial computer runs a CG about 10-20 cm ahead of the axle gave the best margin for stability. There are also, as

we shall see, other factors that favour limiting the forward CG position such as keeping a moderate trailer nose load on the tug's towing hitch.

Evening–up the (side) loads. Clearly to minimise the effect of the trailer on the tug (where a trailer of comparative weight to the tug is used), we must aim to spread the cornering forces evenly between all the wheels involved. In an *ideal* world: same load, same tyres, same tyre pressures on all axles. The world is not ideal so we must instead be sure of the following:

- Do not overload the rear axle of the tug.
- Tyre pressures appropriate to axle load; if in doubt err high.
- Trailer CG forward but not too far.

High trailer weight makes things worse – everything! Drive with extra care.

Fast or tightening steady turn with far-forward CG on heavy trailer can eventually cause tug rear tyres to give up, permitting tail end to slide to outside of turn due to excess 'centrifugal force'. Long tug rear overhang makes things worse as trailer has more leverage.

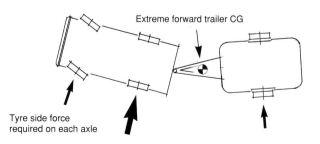

Extreme forward trailer CG

Tyre side force required on each axle

...continued

4.1. Towing – on-road – contd

Practicalities

Safety first. No apology is made for the over-used cliché nor for the accent so far in this section on stability and safe operation. Provided the dozens of relevant parameters are known, the behavioural characteristics of any tug/trailer combination can be predicted but in the real world they are not known and awareness of the principles of what is going on is doubly important. In many parts of the world, and here the UK is included, legislation for trailer operational safety is skeletal and flimsy. Though complex, it extends to little more than construction and basic use and no regulations cover regular testing or functional checks to what are, in many cases, infrequently-used vehicles. Apart from catch-all 'roadworthy condition' regulations, no periodic tests for brake function etc are laid down.

Your responsibility. It thus behoves the user more than ever to ensure that trailers are in first-rate condition. Readers of this book will in many cases be those using heavy trailers up to and exceeding the weight of the towing vehicle. Be aware that, even using a Land Rover tug product, *once you are past a trailer weight of around 75% of the weight of the towing vehi-*

cle the simple laws of physics dictate you are entering a critical zone in regard to stability, steering and braking; unrelenting care in operation is your responsibility.

General towing considerations. The diagram opposite encapsulates all the criteria relevant to optimum load and stability in a trailer and should be studied care-

Surprisingly, trailer operation is under-legislated with no periodic or age-related tests.

Intermittently-used vehicles such as trailers are prone to rusting-up or jamming of brakes. Don't let it happen to you.

Heavy trailers are potentially dangerous. Loading, operating and driving requires unrelenting care.

From top: RTC9565 3500 kg limit ball – also with twin rear towing shackles. Combination 3500 kg tow ball/jaw RTC8159 with variable height hitch – essential for twin-axle trailers (see Item 6, opposite). Four-bolt-fixing hitch cleared for 3500 kg on ball, 5000 kg on pin. Bottom 'NATO' pintle.

Manufacturer's approved maximum gross trailer weight (subject to local regulations)						
Trailer/braking	On/off road	Defender with 2.5D kg	Defender, any other engine kg	Discovery kg	Range Rover kg	New Range Rover kg
1. Unbraked trailer	On road Off road	750 500	750 500*	750 500†	750 750	750 500
2. Trailer with overrun brakes	On road Off road	3500 1000	3500 1000	3500** 1000†	3500 1000	3500 1000
3. 4-wheel trailer with coupled brakes (see above).	On road Off road	3500 1000	4000 1000	4000† 1000†	4000 1000	3500 1000
* 750 kg for 110 with self-levelled suspension.			**Discovery Mpi 2750 kg		†Not Discovery Mpi	

The Land Rover Experience

General towing considerations

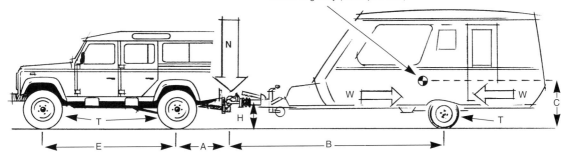

Centre of gravity (trailer plus load)

Go slowly through the variables:
1. A:E – minimise the ratio (small A, big E) when considering a towing vehicle.
2. A:B – minimise the ratio (small A, big B) when considering a trailer.
3. C:B – C not to exceed 40% of B, so keep CG low.
    C not to exceed 95% of trailer track (small C, wide track).
4. E:B – Small E, big B makes for easier reversing.
5. T – Tyre pressures – hard: use GVW settings (Sec 8.2) unless off road (Sec 6.4).
6. H – Same for trailer and towing vehicle. Specially important with twin-axle trailer.
7. **N** – Trailer nose weight. More nose weight equals more anti-weave stability but less cornering stability (lower diagram, previous spread and Note in Trouble Shooting table next spread) – 7% of trailer gross weight is a guide, BUT:
    1. Do not exceed limits of ball hitch or coupling head – usually 100–150 kg.
    2. Remove twice this amount from towing vehicle payload – ie if N = 75 kg, take 150 kg off listed max payload of vehicle when working out how much else you can carry in towing vehicle.
8. W – For a given nose weight, concentrate load close to trailer axle to reduce moment of inertia.

Note. CG position. To calculate CG position you need to know trailer gross weight (weighbridge), axle-to-hitch distance (drawbar length) and nose weight (bathroom scales or weighbridge). Then:
CG position (in cm, ahead of trailer axle) = Nose load in kg times drawbar length in cm divided by the trailer gross weight in kg.

fully in relation first to your particular requirements and then to the trailer/tug combination you have. Nose load is critically important to towing stability when setting up a given trailer.

Braking and weight. Braking method and capacity are especially important. Design and regulatory limitations applicable to all Land Rover products are shown opposite. Above 3500 kg trailer gross weight coupled brakes are mandatory but will be beneficial below this for their sensitivity. Single or twin line air or vacuum brakes with various reservoirs may be fitted. Fitment of such systems requires specialist knowledge and workmanship and should only be carried out by Special Vehicles department at Land Rover or their designated agents.

Tow hitch, coupling head strength. Remember that the widely used 50 mm ball hitch is limited to a 3500 kg trailer gross weight. Above this use one of the hitches shown opposite. Nose load must normally not exceed 150 kg.

Rear axle load. The effect of trailer download on the rear axle of the tug has already been shown to be very relevant to stability – some but not too much is required. The download on the towing hitch is also like having additional payload far aft of the centre of the vehicle load bed – check the diagram at Sec 8.1 (3rd spread) and you will see that 250 kg carried on the tailgate actually increases the rear axle load by 341 kg. The same applies to trailer nose load; see Note 2 under 'N' (Item 7) in diagram above.

Trailer nose load is critical to stability. Be sure too that you are within the strength limits of the tow hitch.

Nose-load is tug payload. Take double the nose-load off your residual tug payload.

...continued

The Land Rover Experience

4.1. Towing – on-road – contd

Where vehicles are in continuous heavy-duty industrial use it is especially important that tow hitches and brakes systems chosen are appropriate to the maximum loads towed and that fleet use is properly monitored. Front-mounted hitch can be invaluable for precise manoeuvring and positioning.

than unbraked. That said, *any* braking situation will exacerbate a marginal stability or safety problem. Keep this always in your mind together with the need to avoid braking except when the trailer and tug are in line. These considerations should lead to a conscious and consistent effort to drive with as much space between you the vehicle ahead as possible so that you are never called upon to brake suddenly or fiercely. Often your cargo (horses, say) will dictate this anyway.

Reversing. Reversing with a trailer is a well known difficulty for drivers not used to it. In general, trailers which are long relative to the wheelbase of the towing vehicle (such as articulated trucks) are easier to reverse than those that are short. Those that are shorter than the wheelbase of the tug are all but impossible to reverse any distance. As with all aspects of operating your Land Rover, do not be afraid to admit you have got it wrong. If a trailer is that short, it will also be light and uncoupling to manoeuvre it by hand will save the difficulty of reversing it.

Auto-reverse brakes. Overrun trailer brakes work on the principle that a braking tug will cause the trailer to push against the hitch and in doing so apply its own brakes. Reversing such a trailer would ordinarily therefore cause the trailer brakes to come on and you must get out of the vehicle to apply an inhibiting catch before and after doing so.

As soon as you are moving, check braking response and behaviour.

Braking aggravates any potential stability problem. Always keep maximum space between yourself and vehicle ahead.

Keep tug and trailer in line for braking. Always use a braked trailer if you can; it will be more stable.

Driving with a trailer

Always check brakes. Although light, unbraked trailers will seem not to affect the vehicle very much it is wise to check overall braking action as soon as possible after starting off. Trailers with overrun brakes – especially if they have not been used for some time – can suffer from grabby, non-progressive brakes due to rusty brake drums and a test on a clear piece of road is essential before setting off with a newly loaded trailer. Whilst coupled brakes should be more progressive, a test is still wise since the trailer may not be proportionally braked and still exert some residual push on the towing vehicle during braking.

Braking, general. Whatever the regulations, braked trailers are more stable

Gross trailer weights above 3500 kgs demand a ring-hitch and coupled brakes – a special vehicle modification. Top and centre (left) show electrically driven compressor unit and associated couplings for air brakes (as opposed to vacuum brakes) – a Land Rover Special Vehicles fit; lower shot shows heavyweight turn-table trailer which is stable but brings its own reversing problems.

Currently, all new trailers with overrun brakes have an auto-reverse fitment that senses the difference between overrun and reversing and no driver action is required. Be sure you are aware of which brake type you have.

Excessive braking. Harsh braking when towing causes the trailer to increase down load on the towing vehicle

hitch (hence need for centre of gravity constraints, diagram previous spread). This produces a rotating moment about the rear axle and a resulting off-loading of the vehicle front wheels which can, in slippery conditions, produce front wheel lock-up. This will not happen with ABS brakes and the risk can be reduced by use of cadence braking (Sec 3.2).

Electrics. Lights, brake lights and direction indicators should be checked with the trailer and electrics connected.

Towing off-road – see Section 6.4.

Does your trailer have auto-reverse brakes? Or must you operate a catch before and after reversing?

The knack of reversing is easier with a long trailer than a short one.

Towing – trouble-shooting guide	
Symptom	*Things to do*
1. Weaving	Move trailer CG forward, reduce trailer weight, reduce moment of inertia (concentrate weight closer to axle), increase trailer and tug tyre pressures, fit a hitch yaw damper, increase trailer drawbar length, reduce speed.
2. 'Oversteer' cornering (tendency to 'tuck-in' when cornering)	Move trailer CG further *aft*, reduce speed, increase tug rear tyre pressures. small reduction in tug front tyre pressures, reduce trailer weight, increase trailer drawbar length.

Note. You will see that, from the point of view of trailer CG position, the two conditions above are (literally) 'swings and roundabouts': improve the weave (swing) stability by moving the trailer CG forward and you are in danger of encountering divergent oversteer on sharp/fast bends (such as roundabouts). Tendency to weave will in some cases be due to an inherent conditions (in relation to your load) you can do nothing about – such as tug rear overhang, for instance. You may be compelled here to move trailer CG further forward than you would wish in order to quench tendency to weave. In these circumstances it may be the right decision so long as you ensure your cornering speeds are reduced.

4.2. Driving on tracks

Deep ruts with slippery sides can mask normal steering feedback. You can be unaware your wheels are not pointing straight ahead and when grip is available, vehicle suddenly veers. See also Glossary, Section 10.1, 'Steering feel'.

Existing wheel tracks

Driving – smooth, calm. When a rough track is encountered your driving technique should aim to have the vehicle flow smoothly over it rather than jolt and jar. All current Land Rover products are coil or air sprung front and rear with progressive dampers so this will be easier basically to achieve than on most other makes of off-road vehicle. The application of the mechanical sympathy mentioned in Section 3.1 will do much to foster an appropriately smooth driving technique for these conditions. Taking a calm and unhurried approach will also help.

Aim to flow smoothly over rough terrain – don't let the vehicle jolt and jar.

High gears, low range. As mentioned before (Section 2.4, 'Low range – when and how') the high gears in the low range are often very useful on rough tracks. Such tracks usually have short, difficult sections for which the steady control of the low range will be required without constant use of the brake and clutch pedals. Thus taking a track in, say, top gear low ratio will allow the driver to make a good pace yet change right down to 2nd or even 1st when the ultimate low speed control and torque is required – without the need to change transfer gear range. (High range, of course, is often quite adequate for track driving; to get a clear picture of the overlap between high and low range gears, see Section 6.1, 'High/low range overlap'.)

High gears in the low box very useful for rough tracks.

Railway line effect. Driving along a deeply rutted track where the ruts are cut into slippery ground can be like driving along railway lines; turning the steering wheel left or right does not have any effect since the tyres will not grip on the steep slippery sides of the ruts. The dan-

Let self-centring castor-action periodically align your wheels in deep ruts.

ger of this situation is that you can be driving along with some steering lock applied (which the vehicle is not responding to) and not know it. When the vehicle reaches level ground or a patch where traction permits it to respond to the steering lock applied, the vehicle will suddenly veer off the track with possibly dangerous consequences.

Wheels straight ahead? Since this condition is not met every day it is doubly important to have the possibility in the back of your mind that the prevailing conditions may be of this type when you are in ruts. The way to preclude the occurrence is to monitor the self-centring of the steering; periodically reduce your grip on the steering wheel by keeping just a frictional grip with the palms of your

Typical rough tracks have moderately fast sections (above) for which 5th low ratio may be ideal. Low ratio enables you to change down to a cautious 2nd for the really rough bits (left).

hands, letting it regain, through castor action (see Glossary, Section 10.1), the straight ahead position. Also a visual check from the driver's window will establish which way the wheels are pointing. When using the window in this way beware of branches of shrubs or trees flicking in your face.

Existing wheel tracks – traction. If there are already wheel tracks along the unsurfaced road you are travelling, this can affect the traction of your vehicle – for better or for worse. On wet or muddy tracks or in snow it is best to follow in the tracks of a previous vehicle since, in gen-

eral terms, that vehicle will probably have cut through to the drier ground beneath and this will offer your vehicle more traction. See also Section 4.4, 'Climbing steep slopes', and Section 4.7, 'Soft ground' .

Desert and bush. On sandy tracks in desert or bush or on routes over desert plains avoid the tracks of previous vehicles since they will have broken the thin crust that normally forms on wind blown sand. Beneath this crust is soft sand offering less flotation; often this is badly churned which will make flotation and traction even worse. See 'Sand', Section 4.8.

Beware driving with non-gripping steering lock on.

Drive in previous wheel-tracks in mud and snow, but not in soft sand.

...continued

4.2. Driving on tracks – contd

Fast relatively smooth tracks are one of the delights of 'off-road' driving but you should always be on your guard against sudden deterioration and the reduced braking the loose surface causes. Muddy tracks call for a delicate right foot.

Deep ruts, gullies

Under-axle clearance. Rough tracks will sometimes deteriorate into deep V-shaped gullies due to water erosion or extra deep ruts caused by the passage of trucks with big wheels. Keeping in such ruts will lead to grounding the chassis or axle case of your vehicle and anticipation is needed to take appropriate advance action. As the diagram shows, you should aim to get out of the ruts early so as to straddle the gully. Care will be necessary to avoid steering up one or other of the

Be on the lookout for ruts that have become gullies. They will run you out of under-axle clearance.

gully walls which could lead to the vehicle being trapped with its side against the gully.

Steering feel. As indicated in the previous spread, because of the depth or slipperiness of the rut or gully, you may well lose the natural feel of the steering and find it hard to know exactly which way your wheels are pointing. For this reason and to ensure front and back wheels are surveyed all the time when driving over gullies, use a marshaller ahead of the vehicle giving you precise directions. If

Rain or flood erosion can cause deep ruts to become gullies and there is the danger of the vehicle slipping down one side. Careful guidance by a marshaller who can see all wheels is the only way to negotiate this kind of obstacle.

Do not stay in badly eroded ruts (1). Get out of ruts and (2) straddle the gully. Vehicle must be carefully guided in gully to sit evenly across it. If necessary, cut steps with a shovel to give tyres a positive footing and use a marshaller.

1.

2.

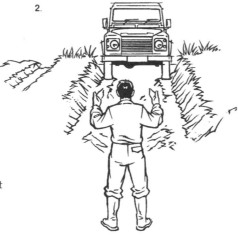

You will lose steering feel driving gully sides. Get guidance and/or look out of the window.

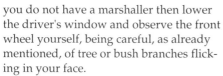

you do not have a marshaller then lower the driver's window and observe the front wheel yourself, being careful, as already mentioned, of tree or bush branches flicking in your face.

The Land Rover Experience

4.3. Ridges and ditches

'Landscaping' – digging under the hung-up wheels – will lower the vehicle so that all four wheels are in contact with the ground and traction is regained.

Diagonal wheel-spin is the main hazard. Know your vehicle's articulation limits.

Diagonal suspension

Ridge – a mirror-image ditch. Ridges and ditches can be encountered both on tracks and across open country. Though one is a mirror image of the other, ridges and ditches can introduce the same problems for the vehicle – grounding the chassis or hanging diagonally-opposite wheels in the air and losing traction by reaching the limits of articulation. The method of crossing these obstacles will require judgement according to their size since the recommended method of crossing a small ridge will lead to trouble if it is applied to a big (or abrupt) one.

Methods of crossing ridges and ditches vary according to the size of the obstacle.

Size determines technique
Potential hazards. The diagram shows the potential hazards and the best *general* advice is to take ridges and ditches diagonally with as much momentum as you judge to be prudent. If that seems like the ultimate escape clause, remember that some obstacles are better taken at right angles (if you can) to avoid risk of diagonal hang-up; others are best taken diagonally (if you can) to avoid jarring or hitting the tail as you exit – check the table below. Consider these obstacles in three sizes:

1. Small ridges and ditches. These may be taken at right angles within the limits dictated by vehicle underbelly clearance and rear overhang (departure angle). However this does mean that the respective front and rear axles will hit the obstacle square-on and probably impart an undesirable jolt. By taking the obstacles diagonally the vehicle will flow over the obstacle with a rolling motion but without any shock loading. Indeed if, when driving quickly over a plain you encounter a shallow ditch which you had not seen earlier, alter direction immediately to take it diagonally.

2. Medium sized ridges and ditches. These may be classified as those that will give problems of underbelly or departure angle clearance and therefore cannot be taken at right angles. With these ones you thus have no option but to take them diagonally. The technique outlined above should be used.

3. Tall ridges and deep ditches. On-foot inspection and the assistance of a marshaller will almost certainly be neces-

Diagonal approach is always best – but beware severe ridges and ditches.

Ridges and ditches: diagonal approach vs right angles		
Approach	*Advantage*	*Disadvantage*
Right angles	Precludes diagonal hang-up	May jolt, belly vehicle or hit tail
Diagonal	Avoids jarring	May cause diagonal hang-up

Photographs show close-to-limits artic-ulation as vehicles cross ridges and ditches. 'Hanging' wheels have little load in this situation so could spin if provoked. Aim for optimum balance of momentum and throttle.

sary. These are obstacles that definitely cannot be taken at right angles and also, if taken slowly diagonally, will result in diagonally-opposite wheels lifting to allow wheel spin and loss of traction. In these cases you have two options:

a. *Provided the going is smooth enough* take the obstacle diagonally but fast enough for momentum to carry the vehicle past the momentary lifting of corner wheels.

b. *Provided it is permitted,* 'landscape' the ground with a shovel to remove the top of the ridge or edge of the ditch that will cause grounding of the chassis or tail

end or suspension of the wheels and then proceed as at 1 above.

Learning gently. As with so many skills it takes longer to write and read this advice than to apply it. You will quickly learn to judge which situation you are in. So long as you do not jolt the vehicle badly or ground the chassis it does not matter if you do not get this right first time – at least on small and medium obstacles. As ever, do not be afraid to take it gently at first or admit you got it wrong; back off and try again – no damage has been done. (See also 'Self recovery', Section 5.1.)

Judgement required: speed and diagonal approach can help. Digging under hung-up wheels may be needed.

The Land Rover Experience

4.4. Climbing steep slopes

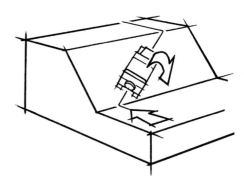

Grip, gradient, momentum

Grip and gradient. The twin problems with steep slopes – gradient and grip – usually reduce themselves to one in most cases with a Land Rover since all Land Rover products have the power and appropriate gearing to climb a continuous slope of nearly 1-in-1 or 45° if the grip is there. Grip is far more likely to be the limiting factor and we have seen in Section 3.2, 'Gentle right foot', how use of the right gear (not necessarily the lowest one) allied to a sensitive right foot can eliminate the wheel-spin that can result from insufficient grip. Climbing steep slopes is the classic application of sensing grip and being gentle with the throttle – and, see below, admitting defeat early in cases of wheel spin. Don't floor the throttle when you get wheel-spin in the vain hope of getting up the slope; the vehicle could slide sideways off course and may tip – see diagram, right.

Grip invariably the limiting factor on steep slopes. The right gear (usually 2nd or 3rd low) and a sensitive throttle foot is the answer.

Go straight at the slope. Whilst a walker would take diagonal tacks up a steep hill to reduce the gradient, you should take the fall line direct in a vehicle, ie take the slope at right angles, head-on. This is to ensure the vehicle is laterally level – your walker can stand up straight when traversing a steep hill; a vehicle leans over (see 'Traversing slopes', Section 4.6) and is in danger of tipping down the slope in extreme cases.

Momentum, traction, throttle control. Commonsense steep slopes need no more than commonsense tactics: if it is reasonably smooth and not excessively steep take a bit of a run at it in the right gear and do not over-torque the wheels to provoke wheel spin. Select the right gear before the slope and stay in it; only an automatic will do a smooth enough

Keep at right angles to the slope – going up or when reversing back down – see next spread.

Going up a slope at right angles to the lip of the ridge is safe; a diagonal approach can provoke a roll-over down the slope. The risk is made worse by any wheel-spin.

change if one is needed. But on really difficult slopes, as ever, an on-foot survey will help. Such slopes are unlikely to be smooth and tramping out the chosen route to locate any local bumps, tree stumps or rabbit holes that might cause a wheel to lift will be useful.

Extra grip – from the steering wheel. If the track is rutted – and this can apply on level ground too – limiting grip can be enhanced by moving the steering wheel from side to side (11 o'clock to 1 o'clock) and cause the tyre sidewalls to contribute grip.

Higher gear – with lift-off. Unless you are tackling an unusual and excep-

Classic example (above) of a 2nd gear low range slope needing a bit of momentum at the bottom and a readiness to lift off the throttle towards the top. One of the rare 1st gear low range slopes (left) where grip permits full use of vehicle's ultimate climbing ability.

tional climb such as 40° on rough dry concrete, 1st gear low box will be too low and will provoke wheel-spin. Most 'normal severe' climbs will be best tackled in 2nd gear low box, or, if there is any amount of run-up available, 3rd. Use the most run-up momentum you can, having established the ground is smooth enough to permit it, since the more you can utilise this, the less will be the demand for grip from the ground actually on the slope. As you near the top of the slope your momentum may be running out and the vehicle will become more reliant on grip and traction. This is the point (quite near to the top) where the wheels are most likely to start slipping or spinning – and it is thus, paradoxically, the point where you may find that lifting off the throttle helps put that final bit of power on the ground without spinning the wheels.

Automatic applications. The equivalent of lift-off to de-stress the ground where traction is marginal will occur on an auto transmission vehicle if 3rd is selected before a steep climb. The gearbox will change to 3rd as the throttle is lifted and reduce the risk of wheel-spin. Note that the new (1994/95) Range Rover automatic used in low range 'Manual' mode will behave like a manual gearbox – see Section 2.3.

Be prepared to lift off near the top to preclude wheel-spin.

...continued

The Land Rover Experience

4.4. Climbing steep slopes – contd

Nothing to fear getting it wrong even on slopes like this (left). But remember to keep both hands on the steering wheel and back STRAIGHT down the hill.

2. Forward motion ceases, engine stalled – gradient problem.

Using the following procedures you will come back down the hill with both hands on the steering wheel (important, that), feet off the pedals – ie not on clutch, or footbrake but covering the throttle. Engine braking controls your speed of descent and no frantic use of gear lever or handbrake is needed. (Procedure for manual transmission shown; Auto procedure is shown in brackets)

Failed climb, engine running. If you have failed the climb through loss of grip and wheel-spin:

1. Clutch pedal down, hold the vehicle firmly on the footbrake, engine idling. (**Auto:** allow engine revs to die, brake, engage **'R'** low box, gently release brake, jump to step 4.)

2. Engage reverse gear low range.

3. With *both hands* on the steering wheel and leading with the clutch, release the clutch and footbrake. The vehicle (engine still idling) will start back down the slope fully controlled by engine braking. At this stage your feet can be off all three pedals – ie you are in reverse, clutch fully engaged and engine idling. Remember that *in reverse, steering castor action is also reversed and there is a tendency for the steering wheel to 'run-away' to full lock if you do not hold it firmly.*

4. Keeping both hands on the steering wheel, go straight back down, at right angles to the slope, to less steep ground.

5. Note. The admit-defeat-early credo is very important in a traction failure on a hill – ie with spinning wheels. If you do

Just as you would always go up a slope at right angles to the maximum gradient, do the same coming back down.

Remember that in reverse, steering castor action is also reversed. Grip the wheel firmly to prevent 'runaway'.

Engage reverse with the engine dead. Then foot off clutch, touch the starter.

Failed climb, recovery

First-time scare. If you are losing grip on a steep climb don't boot the throttle and accentuate the wheel-spin; de-clutch and apply the footbrake. Your first failure on a very steep climb – nose of the vehicle pointing at the sky, brake leg trembling, maybe a dead engine and a plan view of the world in your rear view mirror – can be mildly scaring; it can sometimes also be mechanically traumatic for the vehicle if a driver tries to bluff it out or attempt impossibly quick sequences of control selections during the 'recovery' descent.

Slowing the adrenaline. Observing – and practising – the following procedures makes a fail-and try-again climb so matter-of fact that both driver and vehicle have a far easier time. Knowing this means you do not cane the vehicle unnecessarily hard in a white-knuckle attempt to get up first time. Climbs can fail with or without a dead engine:

1. Forward motion ceases, engine running, wheels spinning – grip problem.

not quit the moment it is clear you are not going to make it, it is very likely the vehicle, wheels spinning on a slippery surface, will slew sideways-on to the slope and there is a risk of it capsizing down the hill. Even if it does not do this, the spinning wheels – usually one front wheel with its diagonally opposite back wheel – will scoop depressions in the ground to make your next attempt more difficult.

Failed climb, stalled engine. If you have failed the climb and stalled the engine in the process (see also diagram sequence right):

1. Engine is dead. Hold the vehicle on the footbrake, clutch position immaterial. (**Auto:** go to step 5.)

2. Engage reverse gear low range and remove left foot from clutch.

3. With both hands on the steering wheel, slowly lessen the pressure on the footbrake until your foot is off it. The vehicle is now held by the engine.

4. The vehicle may begin to move backwards on its own and in so doing 'bump'-start the engine. In which case let it continue, under full control of engine braking, keeping both hands firmly on the steering wheel.

5. If the engine has not started under gravity, take one hand off the wheel to operate the starter motor briefly – with the vehicle still in reverse gear and clutch fully engaged. This will invariably kick the engine into life and you are, as in 4. above, slowly descending back down the slope in full control, in gear, clutch fully engaged, left foot on the floor, both hands on steering wheel to resist any steering 'run-away', right foot hovering over throttle. (**Auto:** foot still on brake, select **'N'** or **'P'**, start engine, engage **'R'**, both hands on wheel, slowly release footbrake.)

6. Just as you would climb the slope at right angles to the gradient, make sure you go straight back down the slope – still at right angles to the gradient. When you reach less steep ground, use the controls in the normal way.

Dead-engine failed-climb – so straight-forward and calm it is worth shutting off the engine to use this procedure even if it has not stalled. Stalling engine puts very high stresses on it. Feet off all the pedals (but throttle-ready), touch starter.

1, 2.

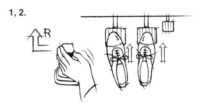

These procedures take far longer to read about than to do. They are really very simple. Practice on gentle slopes, then steeper ones.

3, 4.

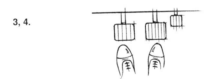

5.

Aim after a failed climb is to come straight back down the slope, both hands on the wheel, feet off pedals.

Recovery sequence, stalled engine – list, adjacent column. 1, 2. Clutch, footbrake, into reverse. 3, 4. Feet off all pedals – but throttle foot ready. 5. Touch the starter briefly; both hands on steering wheel. 6. Preferably reverse back on mirrors.

4.5. Descending steep slopes

Stop 2m from the edge (engine off, 1st gear, handbrake) and inspect on foot. Plan to use engine braking.

Gear to use
Remove the drama. Land Rover vehicles' extraordinary agility may make your first really steep descent an intimidating experience. A 45° down-slope itself is unusual enough but to this angle you add the fact that you are looking even further downward over the bonnet; the result can seem vertical, especially when you are hanging forward in your seat harness. But this is an experience that you will very quickly get used to – usually after just one steep descent. As with climbs, the aim is to take the drama out of the situation and utilise the vehicle's facility for keeping you in control.

The view over the nose comes only when you are committed to the slope; so recce on foot first. At the point of commitment you can often only see sky or the far side of the dip.

Get out and look. A 45° slope is extreme but there are many lesser slopes that can still seem very steep and, as with the climb, an on-foot inspection is advisable to ensure that your planned route is safe. This is doubly important since when you come to the edge of a steep descent you can sometimes see nothing over the nose of the vehicle except the other side of the dip; only when you are actually pointing down the slope can you see the ground immediately in front of you. (For this reason, among others, stop the vehicle for the on-foot inspection at least two metres before the edge of the slope – engine off, in gear, handbrake on. This will give you time, when you do start the descent, to get the vehicle fully in gear and with your foot off the clutch for the descent.)

Use 1st gear, low range, foot off the throttle to brake you down 99% of all steep slopes – see Section 6.4 for the other 1%.

Gear – rule of thumb, 1st gear low range. Using 1st gear low range will in nearly every case result in a perfectly controlled, feet-off-all-pedals descent. Actual retardation will depend on whether you have a diesel or petrol engine, whether or not it has a manual transmission and the condition of the slope but the rule is a good one and a safe one. It is important to

Retardation will will be greater with diesels and manual transmissions.

remember that due to their higher gearing and the way they function, *automatic transmission offers poorer engine braking* down steep slopes

The rationale. Your aim is to obtain maximum retardation without resorting to the brakes which despite the sensitivity and feel of the disc brakes on Land Rover vehicles, can result in wheel locking and sliding. As always your aim is to preclude any possibility of discontinuity of rolling contact (see Section 3.2, 'Gentle right foot') – ie no wheel-spinning or, more likely in this case, sliding.

Ready for throttle. If the ground is too slippery to provide the grip for the retardation of the throttle-off engine and you begin to slide, be ready to use the accelerator to help the wheels 'catch up' with the vehicle and eliminate any wheel slide.

Ready for exceptions. There may be occasions – typically long descents of loose ground or extremely slippery clay,

The ideal descent is with both feet on the floor and the engine doing the braking. Be ready to use throttle if the retardation is too strong and the wheels begin to slide.

steep initially – where low range 2nd gear will be better in order to preclude an initial sliding-wheel glissade. One or two exceptions are covered at Section 6.4. Some descents – see photo Section 6.4 – will actually demand 3rd low range and considerable throttle to prevent nosing-in on a soft surface. As before, it is best to select the gear for the whole descent and stay in it.

Brakes

Brakes? Never... An easy generalisation - and for good reasons – is to counsel against ever using brakes on a steep slippery descent. Braking on wet, muddy or loose-surface slopes – even with the excellent sensitivity of the Land Rover's discs – can easily cause one or more wheels to lock and the loss of directional control in the resulting slide could be dangerous. The use of engine braking down steep slopes makes, in general, for a very safe, controlled way of keeping the vehicle from gaining speed and there is no danger of overheating the brakes. Often you are able to take both feet off the pedals and rest them flat on the floor while the vehicle trundles gently down the slope with the engine idling.

But... But there are times when engine braking is not the infallible solution (see Section 6.4) and the sensitive use of brakes or, preferably, cadence braking as described in Section 3.2 can help. If your Range Rover or Discovery is fitted with ABS brakes - Land Rover's Wabco systems is one of the few that can cope on- and off-road – then brakes may be used on a slippery down-slope. There is a very good case, however, for getting into the habit of using engine braking first.

Rule of thumb – 1st low and do not use the brakes. But... see Section 3.2 for cadence braking and ABS is magic in reserve. Accelerate if necessary.

4.6. Traversing slopes

A static rig-test tip angle is around 40° but the dynamics of real driving make this dangerous to approach. Escape manoeuvre (below) applies if you feel you are getting close to tipping.

Assessing the ground

Side slopes are different. From the last two sections – 'Climbing steep slopes' and 'Descending steep slopes' – the doctrine of always taking such obstacles at right angles to the slopes implies that traversing a slope is dangerous. And so it can be when the angle of gradient is severe. There will be times, however, when, on less severe slopes, you do need to traverse the slope laterally. Like your first steep climb and descent, your first traverse will be unnerving. Unlike climbs and descents, however, you will not quickly get used to it. And that is a good thing since the consequences of getting it wrong on a traverse are a great deal more serious than getting it wrong on a climb or descent.

Trust your instincts. There appears to be a built-in safety feature of human perception that makes a traverse feel a lot more dangerous than it is. Your vehicle will actually tilt to quite high angles on perfectly smooth ground without rolling over but to the driver, a traverse along a slope even one third of the maximum per-

Side-slopes don't feel right. Trust your unease and treat them with great caution.

As ever, inspect on foot looking for bumps or hollows that can affect vehicle's lateral stance.

missible can feel alarming. Follow your instinct and do not traverse slopes that feel dangerous. As ever, carry out an on-foot reconnaissance first:

1. Slippery surface. Assess the surface to be sure it is not so slippery that the vehicle will slide sideways down the slope.

2. Bumps and dips. Look out for dips that the down-hill wheels may encounter and bumps that the up-hill wheels may roll over – rabbit holes and sawn-off tree stumps in particular. Both will increase

The on-foot inspection is especially important. Look for bumps or dips that affect lateral lean. Every inch of ground irregularity makes approximately 1° difference to lateral lean – a 4" bump equals 4°. Digging away the hillside ahead of the up-slope wheels can lower the actual tilt angle. Lateral slopes that are also slippery (right) demand special caution.

the tilt of the vehicle and increase the risk of it tipping over.

3. Secure load. Any load in the back of your vehicle should be secure and as low as possible. Be particularly wary of roof-rack loads. Passengers should sit on the up-hill side – or dismount.

4. Marshalling. If there are any doubts about the effect of the terrain or if there are obstacles to avoid, then use a marshaller (see Section 3.4) to see you forward and make sure he or she keeps an eye on all four wheels.

Escape manoeuvre

Be ready. Steer down the hill if the vehicle slips or seems too close to the maximum tip angle. As with normal steep descents, the nearer you can get the vehicle pointing directly down the slope the less the danger of lateral tipping. If you feel the machine getting laterally unstable turn down the hill quickly and give a little burst of throttle. The centrifugal force of the quick turn, further enhanced by the blip of throttle, will help keep the vehicle upright.

'Escape' by steering down the hill, with a touch of throttle.

The Land Rover Experience

4.7. Weak ground

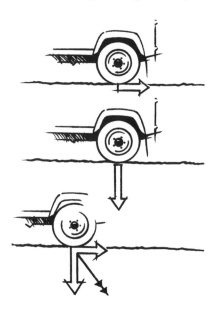

'Green lanes' are classic examples of low vertical and low horizontal ground strength combined – a mixture of the soft and slippery. If a vehicle is used continuously on unstable ground, snow-chains can be useful traction aid.

A 4x4 under power generates, on the ground, horizontal thrust (top) and vertical thrust (centre) to produce a resultant diagonal (bottom). Decreasing weight or tyre pressure (weight per unit area) and exercising care with throttle and brakes reduces both components of ground stress.

Ground stress – horizontal, vertical
Reading the ground. Soft ground is weak ground – vertically and laterally as well. The vertical context is well known – the tendency for a vehicle to sink in it – and the lateral connotations mean it will not take much thrust (or braking) from wheels without degenerating into slippery wheel-spin (or slide); the gentle right foot on brakes and throttle (Section 3.2) comes into its own. Read the surface and adjust your throttle foot accordingly: getting the traction where you can, backing off where you can afford to do so in order not to lose the traction you do have – and occasionally (on the right tyres) applying a carefully judged burst of wheel-spin to get through slime onto drier grippy ground; reading the ground.

Soft ground is weak laterally as well as vertically – so it's that gentle right foot again.

'Fifth-wheel' traction. On the limits in rutted ground, turning the steering wheel from side to side, 11 o'clock to 1 o'clock, is effective in getting that little extra traction from the tyre sidewalls – especially with bold-tread mud tyres.

Lock the centre diff, read the ground, judge what it will take without spinning the wheels.

Horizontal load – throttle, brakes. The most immediate control you have when encountering weak ground is from within the vehicle. You should be in four wheel drive – which you are in all current Land Rover products – and the centre differential should be locked so as to preclude the possibility of one axle spinning any faster than the other. No hard and

Examples of ground that is vertically weak (soft, left), horizontally weak (slippery, below left) and close to the limit on both (right).

fast rule can be laid down as to the 'best' action then to take. Some situations will demand you accelerate on the good going to take you through the soft and slippery patch using momentum, others will demand you slow down to take it gently because it is uneven or of extended length. The only invariable rule is to heighten your awareness of the risk of wheel-spin and to take appropriate action with the controls. Choose the highest gear you judge will get you through without either wheel-spin or over-stressing the engine – this will often be 2nd or 3rd low range. As for brakes, remember they stress the ground in the same way as driving torque at the wheels and insensitivity will result in sliding.

Low range 2nd or 3rd will usually be the gears for soft ground.

...continued

The Land Rover Experience

4.7. Weak ground – contd

Tyres and tyre pressures

Tyres. Section 8.2 deals with tyres in more detail but the subject is inseparable from weak ground operation so some coverage is given here. Differentiating between vertical and horizontal weakness in soft ground is important. As already mentioned, some weak ground needs cutting into to get to the firmer ground beneath: an aggressive, probably quite narrow, very open tyre tread for mud – mud is slippery, fairly shallow and thus horizontally weak. Other types of soft ground need the 'soft-shoe' approach – more tyre width to give flotation on bog or peat or moorland where the surface is fragile and damage has to be minimised; this ground is notable for being vertically weak. Sand is a special case (Section 4.8) but is also classifiable as vertically weak and thus needing maximum flotation; for special reasons it also requires a very mild and particular tread pattern. As Section 8.2 makes clear, tyres can only be 'best' in one set of conditions and 'compromise' or all-purpose tyres are exactly that – a compromise. Nor is it true, as you see above, that the fattest tyres are the 'best'.

Vertical load – per square inch. Once you have your chosen tyres and are on your 'chosen' terrain, vertical load per unit area – the tyre pressures, rather than total vertical load – is what you will have easiest control of. You may not think tyre pressures would make much difference since the total weight of the vehicle will usually remain the same, sitting on the same four tyres. But bear in mind that 'emergency flotation' pressures (Section 8.2) can be two thirds of road pressures or less. This means the tyre footprint size increases (see diagrams Section 8.2) and the weight of the vehicle is spread over a correspondingly larger area so that – as in recognising the benefits of 4x4 which spreads the thrust over four instead of two wheels – you are asking less of the ground that is already having difficulty in supporting the vehicle's weight.

Reduced tyre pressures – when and how much. Reduce pressures only when

Weak-ground tyres for 'cutting' and 'floating'. Michelin XCL (left), class-leader in mud/clay – open, bold, self-cleaning tread but noisy, L-rated (75 mph max, see Section 8.2) and less than ideal on road. High flotation version (265/75 x 16) of Goodrich Mud-Terrain (right) is S-rated, quieter and grippier on-road but tread pattern (even on narrower variants – 235/85 and 225/75) not as ultimately effective as XCL on mud/clay, No one tyre can be good at everything.

Horizontally weak (slippery – left) and vertically weak (soft – below) ground need appropriate tyres and techniques. Note (left) how narrow a good mud tyre really is – here being used with controlled wheel-spin to cut through to better traction. Flotation (below) absolutely on the limits; left tyre has broken crust, right tyre just holding on. See next Section.

needed – then re-inflate (see Section 4.9, 'Rock, stones, corrugations'). The golden rule is not to run with low tyre pressures without reducing your speed. With inappropriately low tyre pressures the steering and handling of the vehicle will be adversely affected. Moreover, if you don't slow down serious overheating of the tyre will occur which could lead to tyre damage and loss of control of the vehicle. Tyre pressures for particular conditions will vary according to the vehicle, the axle load and the manufacturer of the tyres. Typical axle loads and off-road tyre pressures for Land Rover vehicles are given in Section 8.2, 'Tyres'. Rule-of-thumb guidance figures are shown below:

1. Tracks and poor roads – 80% of road pressures, maximum speed 65 kph (40 mph).

2. Emergency flotation pressures – about 60% of road pressures, maximum speed 20 kph (12 mph).

Vertical load – reducing the total. It is commonsense that reducing the overall load will give the vehicle a better chance in soft going also enabling reduction in tyre pressures to be used. In practical terms few users will be able to dispose of payload to suit the going but the principle is worth remembering for the case of recovering a bogged vehicle - see Section 5.1, 'Self-Recovery'.

Previous wheel tracks. As already mentioned (Section 4.2, 'Driving on tracks'), if the weak ground is wet or muddy, it will usually pay to follow the wheel tracks of a previous vehicle since that vehicle will have cut through to firmer ground and you will be able to take advantage of that. If the weak ground is sandy see next section.

Tyres MUST be re-inflated before exceeding the low pressure speed limits.

Choice of tyres is important for frequent soft-ground operation – see Section 8.2.

The Land Rover Experience

4.8. Sand

Innocuous-looking sebkha (above) can be extremely treacherous. Tracks (far right) can be difficult when previously traversed by large trucks; there is then a case for getting onto untrodden sand – rarely quite as firm as this example (near right).

There are many types and conditions of sand – all with characteristic bearing strengths.

When a track starts getting difficult try high range with diff lock or low range 4th or 5th with diff lock.

If the going has been churned up, break out of the track onto unbroken sand. It will be stronger.

Initial rules

Different types. Wet sand, damp sand and a dozen types and conditions of dry sand each lead to different expectations of vertical and horizontal strength (flotation and surface shear strength) as well as behaving differently as far as compaction strength is concerned. Each thus demands different driving techniques. Avoiding wheel-spin, a golden rule of most off-road driving, is nowhere more important than in sand. All, where there is doubt, demand on-foot inspection and 'stamping out' to ascertain firmness and, when close to the limits, the vehicle will have a far better chance if tyre pressures are reduced – see diagrams and tyre pressure/speed limit tables Section 8.2, 'Tyres'.

Initial rule-of-thumb. Initial guide rules are therefore in order if you are to get through the sand rather than trying to learn all the different varieties of problem at once.

1. Dry sand. If you are running out of traction or flotation, keep off previously churned or broken sand. Make your own new tracks.

2. Damp sand. Follow previous tracks which will have compacted the sand and made it firmer.

3. Wet sand. Keep off altogether. It can contain areas of 'floating' sand, or quicksand – bottomless with virtually no vertical strength.

4. Sebkha (salt flat). Very dangerous – unpredictably soft and bottomless. If a well-used track goes over a sebkha it will have compacted the surface (seemingly from beneath) into a smooth, relatively strong route. Do not stray off the hardened track by even a tyre's width.

Sand types - the detail

Dry sand. Being an aggregate of small grains and large grains, nature's wind-blown sand, helped by night dews and diurnal heating and contracting, forms a surface crust which has more strength than the sand beneath; it is stronger in the cool of the morning than in the heat of the day. Use these characteristics to your advantage and be very careful not to break through into the soft sand beneath; think of the analogy of driving on a pie crust.

1. Sandy tracks. Sandy tracks, by reason of the previous passage of vehicles, have no pie crust. Difficulty is likely where there has been a lot of previous truck traffic. Three things will happen here – the ruts will get deeper, the depth of churned sand will increase and the width between the ruts will increase. This is simply a function of the size of the previous vehicles – their wheel diameter and the width of their axles. As ever, be ready to admit defeat early – before getting into real trouble – and steer out of the track

onto virgin ground if you can. The higher gears – 3rd, 4th and 5th – in the low range (centre diff locked) will probably be best for tracks of this kind. The advantage of being in low range is that it will enable you to accelerate through suddenly worsening conditions without the risk of being unable to restart, having stopped to change from high to low box. For this reason do not stop except on firm going – or if you do have to stop be gentle with the brakes. As the going gets heavier and more demanding you will find you have to be firm with the throttle and use a lot of the torque at your disposal; this is different from the technique used on virgin sand.

2. Virgin sand. Some desert sand is remarkably firm and strong. But if you are close to the limits of flotation when on virgin, unbroken sand in the open desert (or once out of the ruts on the track) you have to be more delicate with the throttle in order not to break the crust of clean sand supporting you. The same goes for the brakes and steering. On some dune surfaces there is a good case for letting the vehicle come to a rolling stop without brakes at all. Similarly, when stopping your vehicle on sand remember that restarting when facing up a slope is almost impossible and you should therefore stop on level ground, or, if possible, with the vehicle facing downhill.

Previously unbroken sand, particularly, has a 'pie crust' that can be surprisingly strong. But be careful with throttle and brakes.

...continued

The Land Rover Experience

4.8. Sand – contd

*Dune formations
will have firm areas
dependent on posi-
tion relative to crest,
valley and wind
direction.*

Sand types , dry sand – contd

3. Sand dunes. Small, closely packed
dunes (randomly oriented, up to four
metres high) are better driven round
rather than attempting to drive over
them. When dunes are that small the sand
is invariably loose and weak. Dunes larger than 4–5 metres are usually sufficiently
spaced-out to permit driving between
them and taking advantage of the firm
areas. The variation of flotation over a
dune structure is soon learned – the hard
way. Whilst no two dune chains are the
same, the diagram shows the general
principles of where to expect the firm bits.
Avoid the sand-falls completely. No vehicle will ever get up one but most are so
soft that the vehicle will sink and lose
steering-way even trying to descend one –
but see photo at Section 6.4. Also in this
context, see Section 10.1, 'Glossary',
Caster angle and Steering feel.

4. Fesh-fesh. Fesh-fesh is a thin crust
of fine gravel or sand over powder-fine
dust with very little surface strength.
Maximum flotation and instant application of power will be required to avoid
getting stuck.

*All sand has
increased bearing
strength if cold,
dewy or rained-on.*

*Salt flat is inherently
dangerous. Except
on established tracks,
keep off.*

In general, going is firmer where the up-wind
side of the dunes meet the valley floor.

Damp sand. Sand that is damp – such
as it might be after a rain shower or even
morning dew – just makes driving easier.
The water binds it together, strengthens
it, gives more flotation and on tracks actually makes it compact to yield considerably more strength than the dry, churned-
up sand had before the rain.

Wet sand. It becomes a matter of
judgement and definition to say when
damp sand gets to be wet sand. Beach
sand will frequently behave as dry, cut-
up, churned sand where it is dry and
become considerably firmer where it is
washed by the tide – though this is not an
invariable rule. The warning sounded
earlier refers to really wet sand of the
kind encountered where a river or stream
meets the sea and where a kind of 'floating' sand is encountered. This is akin to a
quicksand where motion by the person or
vehicle on it just causes further sinkage.

Sebkha (salt flat). Sometimes also
marked on maps as 'chott', a sebkha
forms where lakes used to be and consists
of a crust of dried salt-mud covering soft,
bottomless salt-mud underneath. The
crust is of variable and unpredictable
strength but appears to have the curious
characteristic of consolidating from
underneath when progressively heavier
vehicles run over it. Thus a track over a
sebkha usually consists of wheel marks
indented probably no more than a few
centimetres into the surface – implying
that the surrounding ground is firm. Yet
as the stern warning above indicates, this
is not the case and straying off the track
even a tyre width or a metre can sometimes result in disastrous sinkage. A vehicle stuck in sebkha will quickly sink to the
chassis and sometimes go on sinking. It is
usually impossible to effect self-recovery
and even assisting vehicles should have
very long tow ropes or winches in order
that they too do not sink.

Sand tyres. As already indicated, each
kind of terrain demands its own specialist
tyre. This is particularly important in the

The classic desert tyre of all time, the Michelin XS – worn example at reduced pressure shown left – with a tread optimised to get the most traction out of all types of sand. Diagrams Section 8.2 show increase in footprint area of XS deflated to emergency soft. Certain parts of dunes can be surprisingly firm but (above left) even with the best tyres, the limits can be found.

case of sand. Even here the carefully named 'desert' tyre has to accommodate the different requirements of travel on rock and sand. In general, however, the greatest design conflict would be between a mud tyre and a sand tyre – the one requiring a bold angular tread and the sand tyre needing a far gentler, more subtle tread design. And whilst the sidewall of a desert tyre must be strong to resist rock damage it must also be flexible to accommodate the greatly reduced tyre pressures used in the worst sand condi-

tions. If contemplating desert operations, your vehicle's performance will be considerably enhanced if desert tyres are fitted. Section 8.2 shows tyre types, axle loads and tyre pressures for typical conditions. See also 'Sand tyres', Section 10.1, 'Glossary'.

Getting stuck, recovery. Self-recovery and assisted recovery is covered in this Section 5. Inevitably, sand is a little different. Just as inevitably, the recovery methods are commonsense honed with pragmatism and experience.

Fitting specialist desert tyres is particularly important in achieving optimum performance in sand.

The Land Rover Experience

4.9. Rocks, stones, corrugations

Regular operation in rocky conditions demands extra awareness of under-axle clearance and of tyre sidewall vulnerability.

Under-axle and under body clearances dictate 20–30 cm rocks as about the maximum size to drive over.

Take every precaution against grounding the vehicle on rock. As usual, use a marshaller when clearances are tight.

Risks – chassis, tyres

Rocks – 30 cm high. The sections dealing with use of the low transfer box and the methods of driving on rough tracks (Sections 2.4 and 4.2) will prepare you for the techniques best suited for driving over rocks and stone. The rough definition applicable here to 'rocks and stone' is that stones are taken to be anything from gravel up to fist-sized stones and rocks are taken to be over fist sized and up to about 20–30 cm high – the maximum permitted by the under-body and under-axle dimensions of Land Rover products.

Clearances. What you have read about clearance angles and under-axle clearances at Section 3.3, 'Geometric limitations', is doubly important in the context of driving over rocks and stones. Getting it slightly wrong on clearances when traversing mud will probably scrape earth from the obstacle and take paint off the underside of the vehicle. Making the same mistake over rocks will likely bring the vehicle to a very abrupt halt and be likely to damage components as well. Land Rover products' robustness and resistance to 'battle damage' should be regarded as accident insurance, not

When forced onto limiting rocks for short distances use a marshaller and 1st gear low range. See also photo at Section 2.4.

part of deliberate everyday driving. Take every precaution to ensure you do not run the vehicle into contact with heavy stones or rocks.

Tyres. Tyres too are potentially very vulnerable to damage on rocky ground – especially the sidewalls of radial-ply tyres – but this and overall operating costs can be reduced by attention to:

1. Inflation. Be sure the tyres are fully inflated to road pressures before traversing rocky going – even if this means re-inflation after deflating for previous soft ground.

2. Sidewall awareness. The most vulnerable parts of a tyre on rocks are the sidewalls. The best on/off-road tyres are radials but these, with their thinner, flexible sidewalls, are particularly prone to 'bacon-slicer' damage – so-called because the action of the tyre sidewall against an intrusive sharp rock. Develop 'sidewall awareness' when driving over rocks.

3. Cross-ply tyres. Where operations are almost exclusively off-road on rock or stone – such as fleet operations in quarries – the more damage-resistant qualities (at full inflation pressures) of cross-ply tyres could help keep operating costs down. It is essential, however, to consider and accommodate the following criteria:

a. Virtually all 7.50 x 16 cross-plies are 'L' speed rated (see table Section 8.2), ie limited to 125 kph (75 mph), so should not be fitted to high powered vehicles operating on-road.

b. Cross-ply tyres have higher rolling resistance so will slightly reduce fuel economy.

c. Cross-ply tyres have marginally less grip than radials so handling on-road would be affected.

Stony tracks and plains. Not all your rock/stone traverses will be over on-the-

limits boulders. Stony tracks or vast stony plains in the desert will be very much less hazardous. Well inflated tyres and an alertness for potential further hazards, however, will be important. As with corrugations (next spread) braking will be much less efficient on loose stones.

On-foot survey, marshalling. All the points mentioned so far point to the need for looking at a difficult rocky stretch or obstacle on foot and then being marshalled across by a helper. This will ensure – since the marshaller can see all eight sidewalls and the under-side of the vehicle and axles – that no damage is done.

Low range control. The relevance of low range and its ability to control the vehicle's forward motion steadily (rather than just make considerable power available) is nowhere more applicable than in traversing large rocks. First gear, low range, clutch fully-in, low engine speed will enable the vehicle to crawl steadily – without heaving, jerking or lurching – over the very worst rocky terrain.

Cross-ply tyres could lower costs in continuous rock/stone operations. BUT, note speed limitations.

Braking is far less effective on stony going.

On-the-limit rocky going demands 1st gear low range for control.

...continued

4.9. Rocks, stones, corrugations – contd

Palliative effect of the 'harmonic' speed applies *only* to transverse corrugations of the type shown opposite. Irregular obstacles like the boulders shown left can only be taken at a crawl – 1st gear low range – with the foot fully off the clutch and the centre diff lock disengaged. Steering feedback can be sharp, even with power assistance, so thumbs must be kept on and parallel to the rim of the steering wheel. With great care and the use of a marshaller, no damage should result.

Corrugations
'Harmonic' speed. A special manifestation of something between stony going and rough or unsurfaced tracks is the phenomenon of transverse corrugations across graded earth, sand or gravel tracks – regular, wave-form undulations that can stretch for tens of kilometres in front of you on remote area routes. The corrugations, also called 'washboard' in

Transverse corrugations on track demand a 'harmonic' speed to reduce the vibration on the vehicle.

America, have a peak-to-peak distance of 0.5 to 1 metre and can be as much as 20 cm deep. They are formed by the action (and harmonics) of the suspension and tyres of the track's major-user vehicles on the soil. This latter is an important point since the technique to adopt when driving over them involves using the natural harmonics of your own vehicle's suspension to minimise the apparent roughness of the ride. There will be a speed of driving – usually between about 40 and 60 kph (25–35 mph) in Land Rover products –

The 'harmonic' speed reduces body shake to just-bearable limits but still tortures unsprung components like axles.

where the effect of the corrugations *on the vehicle body* will be minimised. The italics are used as a reminder that the suspension and un-sprung parts such as the axles are undergoing a rare form of torture over such ground, even though the body and passengers may be (relatively) more comfortable.

Reduced brake effectiveness. An indication of the ordeal of the unsprung components will be clear when enduring the acceleration to these speeds and when decelerating from them. (If you still have

Range Rover travelling at 'harmonic' speed on moderate corrugations (below) reduces jarring on body though suspension still suffers. Remember dramatically reduced steering and brake effectiveness. Travel on such tracks is invariably accompanied by thick dust clouds (below left).

any doubts about what the suspension is going through, look out of the driver's window at the front axle.) It is vital to remember also that, since the wheels are virtually jumping from the crest of one corrugation to the next, they are in touch with the ground for a fraction of the time they would normally be. *Steering and particularly braking effectiveness will be dramati-*cally reduced *when going rapidly on corrugated tracks. Driving a Land Rover on a track where the corrugations were formed by, say, a four-ton truck will be especially unpleasant since the suspension harmonics of the truck will not match those of your Land Rover and there will be no 'magic speed' where the ride appears to smooth out.

Dramatic reductions in braking and steering effectiveness take place when driving on corrugated tracks.

4.10. Wading

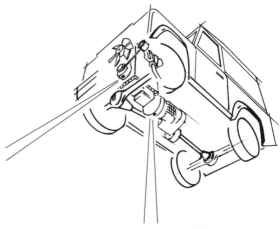

Preparations

Think ahead. Think of wading as a wet, blind and usually cold manifestation of every other type of obstacle and hazard you may come across. This is not meant as an unduly gloomy warning so much as a reminder that the same kind of potential problems can lurk beneath the water as you may see on dry land and that advance knowledge of them is no less important.

The same obstacles can lurk – unseen – under the water as on dry land. Plan, and recce, ahead.

Wading plugs. Other advance knowledge it will pay to acquire well before you get anywhere near a wading situation is the location of the vehicle's wading plugs and how to put them in. All Land Rover products are provided with drain holes in the clutch housing between the engine and gearbox and also (where such a belt is fitted) at the bottom of the camshaft belt drive housing at the front of the engine beneath the fan. These holes are a safety feature to ensure that, in the event of an oil leak in these regions, the oil can drain away and not get onto the clutch or

Always fit the wading plugs. Make the plugs, a 13 mm spanner and a groundsheet part of your standard kit.

cam drive belt. In case of deep wading, however, these holes must first be blocked off by the insertion of screw-in wading plugs. It is convenient to keep these plugs (available from Land Rover dealers) and the appropriate 13 mm (or 1/2" AF) spanner handy within the vehicle. It is important that the plugs be removed after wading – not necessarily at once but within a few days. If a vehicle is used for regular wading the plugs should be removed, checked for oil leakage and replaced every week or two. The new

Always walk the stream before committing the vehicle – above, and Section 3.4. Wading plugs (left) are fitted in clutch housing (photo opposite, right – location above and ahead of chassis cross member) and, if applicable, in the bottom of the cam drive-belt housing (opposite, left – location ahead of the sump; above, and slightly aft of front axle casing).

R380 manual gearbox leaves the factory with wading plug already fitted; it should be removed periodically to check for possible oil leakage or it may be removed and refitted only for wading as above.

Walking the course. Water obstacles, large or small, should always (as mentioned at Section 3.4, 'Look before you leap') be examined first. Rubber boots and a long stick are the extras required for an on-foot survey before committing a vehicle. Generally, stagnant water is more likely to be a hazard than a river or a stream as flowing water tends to prevent a build-up of silt. The silt in a stagnant pool or mud hollow can be several feet deep and very soft. Ensuring that the bottom of the pool or stream is firm enough along all of your proposed traverse is essential and it will inevitably take some time to do thoroughly. Markers may be necessary (such as sticks) to be sure the vehicle follows the route you have proved on foot.

Always walk through first with a stick. Better to get wet legs than have your vehicle stuck in an underwater hollow.

...continued

The Land Rover Experience

4.10. Wading – contd

The normal wading depth limit of 0.5 m runs just beneath the top of the wheel rim, just above the door shut line and about equal to exhaust height.

Limitations

Wading limitations, how to proceed. The maximum advisable wading depth for Land Rover products is 0.5 metre – about 5-6 cm (a thumb length) below the top of the wheel rim or, perhaps more memorably, 5-6 cm higher than the top of the average rubber boot. Note the implications of this – your brakes will be completely immersed in water but the radiator cooling fan will be clear and so will the exhaust pipe exit – just. Land Rover customers all over the world frequently travel through water where the depth exceeds 0.5 metres. In these conditions the following precautions are advisable:

Normal wading depth limit 0.5 m – just below the top of the wheel rim.

1. Gear and speed. Low range with a gear appropriate to the amount of power and control over rocks required. Keep enough rpm to preclude water entering the exhaust pipe if it is submerged. Speed in general should be low but fast enough to keep a small bow-wave ahead of the bumper and thus reduce the height of the water behind the bumper, so keeping water away from the fan. In practice, low range 2nd gear is usually about right.

Not too fast, not too slow – fast enough for a small constant-height bow wave. Probably 2nd low.

2. Keeping the ignition dry. If you are using a petrol engine equipped vehicle it is important to keep the ignition dry. The right bow-wave will help. A sheet of plastic lowered in front of the radiator will stop water cascading straight through and onto the fan, reducing the chance of spray over the electrics; it will also prevent liquid mud from blocking the radiator matrix. Additionally an old coat, blanket, sack or other heavy fabric can be draped over the engine behind the fan to keep the harness dry; remember, however, this can be a fire hazard so keep it well clear of the exhaust manifold. *Do not remove the fan belt* as this will stop the water pump and damage the engine.

It is VITAL not to let water near the engine air intake – through splash or any other cause.

3. Essential – keep engine air intake clear of water. Major damage to engines can result if even small amounts of water get past the air filter and into the cylinders. Never risk this happening. Choose another route where the water depth is less. You may have seen pictures of Land Rover vehicles taking part in the Camel Trophy almost submerged in water but these vehicles will have been specially modified with raised, roof-level air intakes for the engine.

After wading. It is essential to dry your brakes after wading, especially if your vehicle has drum brakes. Whilst still in low range, drive a short distance applying the brakes lightly; this will squeegee the discs or linings dry. Remove any plastic sheeting or other engine protection used for the operation. The wading plugs need not be removed immediately if further wading is envisaged – but see previous spread about regular use. Remember the handbrake too will be wet.

Oil contamination. If you regularly undertake wading be aware of the risk of water contamination in the vehicle lubricating oil. This will manifest itself as emulsified oil, easily identified because of its milky appearance. A hot axle case or

Bow-wave – too much upper left, optimum above – produces dip aft of bumper, keeps water away from fan. Raised air intake permits deeper wading for diesels. Pre-attached tow rope useful precaution. Select air suspension on Range Rovers to high profile.

gearbox plunged into a cold stream for any time will cool suddenly, tending to suck water in through oil seals or breathers. All Land Rover vehicles now have carefully designed remote breathers (long black nylon pipes that vent the transmission casings high in the engine compartment) but periodic checks are still advisable.

Getting stuck, recovery and precautions. Covered fully under Section 5, recovery principles remain the same but are complicated by the lower part of the vehicle being under water. Anticipation is the key – such as pre-attachment of a tow rope (or pre-extension of the winch line) so that you do not have to grope with the problem under water.

Squeegee the brakes dry after wading – 20 m or so, low range, against light brake.

Pre-attach tow rope and coil it on bonnet if there is a risk of needing a tow.

4.11. Ice and snow

More traction, same brakes

4x4, 4x2 differences. Most readers of this book will have experience of driving on snow and ice in ordinary cars. Indeed many will have bought a Land Rover product partly because it will give them more reliable transport in wintry conditions. Though traction in snow is best in temperatures below -20° to -30°C and less good between -20°C and freezing point, the basic principles of being very gentle

4x4s are better than 4x2s on snow and ice for traction – but remember your braking is very similar.

ABS will give the best possible braking under the prevailing conditions – but cannot change packed snow into dry tarmac.

with both the throttle and the brakes will apply in just the same way on a 4x4 so it is well to establish first just what the differences are between the two types of vehicle:

1. Double the traction.... As we have seen, the 4x4 has double the traction. In snow and ice conditions this should be regarded not as a means of putting twice as much power on the road but as a means of putting the same power on the road spread between twice as many wheels. This asks less of the surface in terms of grip and so you are less likely to get spinning wheels.

2. ...but the same braking. What is often forgotten in the feeling of confidence that a 4x4's tractive performance in snow generates is that the method of stopping is the same as that of any normal car – four wheels on the ground, each one's rotation retarded by brakes. Indeed, 4x4s are generally a lot heavier than normal cars and have a correspondingly increased amount of kinetic energy to arrest. Beware, therefore, of letting your feeling of invincibility extend to the braking department when you are on snow or ice.

3. ABS – very good, but not magic. ABS anti-lock braking will give you *the best braking possible under the circumstances* but will not reverse the laws of physics. Land Rover's ABS system is one of the best and most versatile there is and it will eliminate the human error of locking the wheels; it will yield the maximum retardation possible from given surface conditions – as well as enormously improving directional control – but it will not turn ice into dry tarmac. The surface conditions are still the limiting factor.

Gentle right foot – again

Driving technique. The driving techniques employed for snow and ice are generally similar to those used for mud or wet grass.

1. High gear. Select the highest gear possible for the conditions. ('D' in Auto.)

2. Diff lock. Engage the centre differential lock (if manually selected) – and disengage it as soon as non-icy ground is reached.

3. Throttle, brake, steering. Use minimum throttle opening when driving away and accelerating, even if electronic traction control (ETC) is fitted; avoid violent movements of the steering wheel. Drive slowly and brake with great caution to avoid locking the wheels. Cadence braking will help (see Sections 3.2 and Glossary at Section 10.1).

....contd

The same principles apply as for slippery slopes – highest gear possible, gentle and sensitive use of brakes, throttle and steering.

When you have to get through – or even when it would just be convenient – a good 4x4 is only half the battle; the other half is a sensitive driver.

4.11. Ice and snow – contd

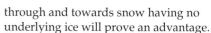

Gentle right foot – contd
What lies beneath. As with sand, there are, of course, a dozen combinations of criteria affecting snow and ice – mainly concerned with what lies beneath the present surface of the snow. These will extend or reduce the limits of traction of your vehicle; they cannot be quantified in any book but acquire new relevance in the light of a large-wheeled 4x4:

What lies under the snow? If you are the first out, it will just be road.

1. First on the road? If, as if often the case, you and your Land Rover are first on the road after the first snow on untreated roads, this is the best traction you will get in snow. Bold and/or sharp treaded M+S tyres will cut through the soft snow either to the ground beneath or will make the first compressed snow 'rails' for you to travel on. These are as grippy as they will ever be. Conditions get worse from now on.

Snowfall on top of compressed snow will be very slippery. A classic case for diff lock in high box.

2. Second or later? When others have been on the roads first, their compressed tracks will make slippery going and, as you will have done many times, driving out of the previous tracks will get fractionally more traction. As before, 4x4 will give more traction but no improvement, *per se*, in braking. On long descents or hairpin bends stay in a low gear.

3. Subsequent snowfalls. Snowfall on top of previous compressed tracks which may in places have slicked-over into streaks of pure ice is another well enough known phenomenon in which a large-wheeled and heavy 4x4, delicately driven, will prove its worth in obtaining traction. Braking will be fractionally better than a car by reason of the tyre treads but only as long as it is done gently. Again, if you have no ABS, cadence braking (see Section 3.2 and Glossary) will pay dividends and the big wheels' ability to steer

As a 'first on the road' vehicle hub-high snow is no problem. Deeper than that and with small drifts, use momentum laced with discretion.

Carry a long tow-rope, shovels, gum boots to low-box others out of ditches and be on your way.

through and towards snow having no underlying ice will prove an advantage.

Auto transmission, traction control. Land Rover vehicles fitted with automatic transmission, electronic traction control (ETC) and ABS will be at an advantage in wintry conditions but these aids to gentler traction enhance the 'gentle right foot' driving philosophy; the don't replace it.

Snowdrifts. A Land Rover's big wheels, locked centre diff and appropriate tyres driven on all four wheels are ingredients for charging snowdrifts and getting through. Or they can be ingredients for getting it wrong and finishing up sitting on top of a vehicle's length of compressed snow and having to dig the snow out from under the vehicle. Do not be too ambitious with what you attempt to barge through. Anything above hub depth is starting to get marginal for sustained travel; individual small drifts deeper than this can often be successfully tackled. As ever, the low box, probably in 2nd or 3rd (with diff lock), will be the appropriate weapon.

Helping yourself and others. Other traffic and those inappropriately equipped having got into trouble will all too frequently be the cause, in winter conditions, of your not getting through to your destination despite your having, without them, the capability to do so. To free them and yourself from delays, carrying a long tow rope, shovels, gumboots, gloves and some kind of under-wheel

Off-road snow demands careful sounding – on foot with a stick. On road, with the right tyres, hub-high snow will present little difficulty. On front wheels use only Land Rover approved snow chains.

traction aid (Section 5.1, 'Self-recovery') will help reduce everyone's problems. Pulling a car from a ditch with this equipment and careful use of the low range and throttle takes only minutes – see Section 5.2, 'Recovery – towing out'.

Tyres and tyre pressures. As mentioned already, each type of terrain has an optimum tyre type and whilst your Land Rover can cover a wide variety of terrain, a single set of tyres for such a spread will limit your capability in one or more medium. In general, a mud or M+S (mud and snow) kind of tyre – they will have quite a bold, sharp-edged tread – will be best for use in snow. Use normal road tyre pressures. Details: Section 8.2 – 'Tyres'.

Snow chains. If you do not have a full set of four snow chains fit the first pair to the front wheels since this will give you grip as well as steering in slippery conditions. To some extent it will also prepare a path for the back wheels. Since a 4x4 has four driven wheels a second set of chains will be beneficial. If using front snow

chains off road there is a danger, with certain types of chain, that full axle articulation and full steering lock at the same time could enable the chains to damage the front brake pipes. A new type of chain, more easy to attach, is now available as an approved Land Rover accessory which obviates this danger (Land Rover part numbers RTC9590 for 7.50 x 16 tyres and RTC9589 for 205 x 16 and 6.50 x 16 tyres). Check with your dealer 235/70 x 16 tyres. Also Section 5.1, 'Self-recovery'.

Snow off-road. As there is not a smooth potentially slippery surface beneath it, snow off-road is easier to cope with than snow on tarmac carriageways. A moment's thought, however, highlights the dangers of minor drifting of the snow covering potentially destructive obstacles such as small rock outcrops or gullies on hillsides. The situation is similar to fording streams in that the dangers are hidden; the solution is the same – an on-foot inspection and prodding with a stick in doubtful areas.

Tyres with bold sharp tread patterns are best. Fit only the latest Land Rover approved snow chains.

Off-road snow is generally easier - but probe for hidden obstacles like rocks or ditches.

Section 5

Recovery

5.1. Self-recovery

Traction aids

The calm approach. Having got 'stuck', self-recovery is the art of remedying the situation without the need to call upon outside assistance. The brutal truth is that in most cases getting stuck is a function of driver error – misreading the ground or the obstacle, or not accurately knowing the limitations of your vehicle. Whilst we all try our best with these things and all gradually get better, equally certain is the fact that we all occasionally make mistakes. Admitting this is at least half the battle for it enables you to go about the remedial action in the right spirit – philosophically cheerful acceptance of a minor challenge rather than agitation, embarrassment, bluster or the suspicion that life has just dealt you the ultimate humiliation!

Knowing the problems. It helps to know what problems may be ahead. The categories in which you may find yourself stuck are shown below. Knowing this helps you see the problems coming and avoid them.

Wheels spinning – two causes.. A given amount of power plus a combination of not enough grip and not enough weight on a wheel can cause it to spin. In these circumstances ETC (Electronic Traction Control – see Section 10.1, Glossary), if fitted, will brake the spinning rear wheel automatically. Without ETC, in the case of not enough weight on the wheel (the axle may be at an angle to the chassis and the lower wheel is spinning) see under Articulation on the next spread. If grip is the problem in a static re-start case, first try a higher gear and a very gentle throttle.

More grip. If that fails, inserting some gripping medium between the wheel and the ground is the solution – stones, brush-

Everyone gets bogged occasionally. Do not take it as a personal slight!

If you've missed the chance to reverse out, admit it, smile and go on to the next stage ....

...the next stage is digging and the use of something to put under the wheels.

wood, mats, baulks of timber or items designed especially for the purpose: sand ladders, metal planking and recovery channels. Beware (see sub para 2 below) of anything that can flick up beneath the vehicle and cause damage.

1. Sand ladders can of course be used in any medium – sand, mud, snow – and are specially made aluminium ladders about 1.5 metres long, 35 cm wide and with rungs about 15 cm apart (gripping edges outermost). They are thrust under the front – or rear – of the wheels (if necessary scooping out earth or sand to get them farther in) and the vehicle will find grip on the ladders and haul itself out. If necessary, the ladders are moved round to the front (or rear) of the vehicle a second, third or fourth time to provide further traction in the direction of travel. Sand ladders of the right type – side members 6-7 cm deep – can be used for minor bridging of ditches.

2. Steel planking (PSP – the perforated lengths of interlocking steel planking originally made for WW2 bush airfields) is used in the same way as sand ladders. PSP is heavier and more difficult to use than aluminium sand ladders; it is too flexible to be used for bridging (and can bend upward to snag the underside of the vehicle) but is excellent for laying over logs or branches to provide a vehicle trackway. Despite the contradiction in terms, PSP is sometimes available in aluminium.

3. Recovery channels. These combine the best aspects of sand ladders with a third of the bulk. They are in effect a pair of purpose-built aluminium alloy grip panels 1.5 metres by 35 cm, each cut into three equal lengths and joined with nylon rope – large photo opposite. The articulation afforded by the rope links makes them easier to push in front of the wheels without – as is the case with ladders or PSP – the danger of the remainder of the unit fouling the vehicle chassis. Best of all, when you have finished with them, the

The same principles apply to use of traction aids in mud or dry sand. Use them before the situation gets too bad and dig sufficient space for them to work first time.

three sections can be folded up, bagged and stowed within the vehicle. (At present these items are only made and available from Barong, F.92370 Chaville, France.)

Flotation – sinking in soft ground. Although technically there is a difference between a lack of traction and a lack of flotation, in practice the two usually strike together and a joint solution – use of

reduced tyre pressures (see Section 8.2, 'Tyres') and/or load spreaders such as sand ladders etc mentioned above – will be the answer. If no load spreaders are carried, branches or brushwood should be used. If sinkage is considerable so that the vehicle is hung up (see next page) digging to remove the obstacle or jacking to permit the channels to be put under the wheels will be necessary.

Use shovels early to save a wheel-spinning bogging getting worse. Invest an extra few minutes' digging and get out first time.

Always dig away in front of a wheel before inserting the sand tracks. This helps ensure first-time extraction.

...continued

The Land Rover Experience

5.1. Self-recovery – contd

Use a marshaller to prevent this. Digging the ground away from under a vehicle hung-up on the chassis provides good motivation for not letting it happen again.

Digging, recovery tools

Under-vehicle obstacles – hung-up on ridges or rocks. Least forgivable of driver-inflicted situations (especially if you have a passenger with you who could have got out and marshalled you over the obstacle), getting the chassis hung up on ridges or rocks is also potentially the most damaging. The price will be paid, however, since the only way out of this predicament unless you have a high-lift bumper jack (see 'Recovery tools' below and diagram/photo opposite), is actually to dig the obstacle away from under the vehicle with a shovel. It will be difficult using the shovel at full arm's length under the vehicle and in addition the vehicle will be tending initially to collapse down onto the shovel as it is used. Knowing what is involved and having the patience to do it slowly but surely will unfailingly get you out of this situation. If it is immovable rock and you are hung up with the centre of the chassis on it the situation is more serious but jacking front or rear to put packing under the wheels will achieve a recovery just as reliably.

Articulation – diagonal wheels in the air. As we have seen (Section 4.3, 'Ridges and ditches') it is possible to get a vehicle immobilised by misjudging the amount of axle articulation involved in crossing a ridge or ditch diagonally. (An axle is on full articulation when one wheel is pushed up into the wheel arch as far as it will go and the other wheel is hanging down as far as it will go.) A very common manifestation is 'the diagonal tightrope' in which, say, the rear offside wheel and front nearside wheel are both on full bump and the complementary wheels are hanging down – with the axle differentials permitting the hanging-down wheels to spin when you apply power (see photos Sec 4.3). This situation will stop you

but has a very straightforward solution – either pack up beneath the spinning wheels or dig away beneath the full bump wheels. It is difficult to get earth packed in tightly enough under the hanging wheels (though inserting a sand ladder, levering up and packing with rocks can work) so almost invariably digging under the hung-up wheels is the solution. As with the case above, the vehicle is trying to collapse on your shovel as you dig but, again, patience will invariably win the day.

Recovery tools. If you are planning a journey in which off-roading and the risk of getting stuck exists (see also Sec 7.4), the following equipment is worth taking:

Rubber boots, gloves, overalls.

Electric tyre pump for re-inflation of tyres.

Two shovels (pointed blades, not square ends like spades).

Two tow ropes (totalling 25 metres) and appropriate end fittings.

Articulated sand channels or sand ladders – see previous page.

Hi-lift jack – if appropriate to the vehicle (see below).

Wood block about 30 x 20 x 5 cm to prevent jack sinkage.

Avoid under belly hang-up on ridges and rocks – can be damaging. Recovery awkward, time consuming.

Exceeding articulation limits is a common way of becoming immobilised. Dig under the 'high' wheels or pack under the 'low' ones.

For planned off-roading, carry a full self-recovery kit.

Hi-lift jack is a valuable recovery tool but must be used with strict adherence to safety instructions – including use of diff lock. Bottle-jack with shovel and timber baulks can be used in similar fashion on wheel or hub. Use wood 'cushion' on alloy wheel rims.

Hi-lift jack can be used to raise a vehicle out of deep ruts and 'lateral pole-vault' it onto easier ground.

Hi-lift jack. As the sketch shows, the hi-lift jack is a mechanical bumper jack capable of a lift of a metre or more. A Defender, for instance, that has been run into deep ruts and is unable to get out could have the front end physically lifted out of the ruts and, by then pushing the jack over sideways, could be 'pole-vaulted' onto more suitable ground. Equally, the front end could also be lifted to insert ladders or branches under the wheels. Hi-lift jacks are very effective in operation – one can also be converted into a hand winch – but are very heavy and awkward

to carry; additionally, as bumper jacks they require the square section of the Defender bumper and are not suitable to use on a Range Rover or Discovery – unless special bumper modifications are done. If you have an operating spectrum in which a hi-lift jack would be a useful recovery tool, it would be worth making modifications to enable it to be carried in a rack and used on appropriate sockets on the vehicle.

Hi-lift jack – safety. Pay special attention to safety when using a hi-lift jack. As a 'mono-pod' it is inherently unstable and hand-brake, diff-lock and wheel chocks should be used to prevent the vehicle rolling forward or back. *Do not leave the jack unless the operating handle is in the vertical position.*

Winch. Unless required for operating in particular conditions, a winch is expensive and heavy to have as a 'just-in-case' recovery aid. When trying to co-ordinate it with power from driven wheels it is slow in operation, but provided there is something to winch onto – it can work wonders in certain self-recovery situations. See Section 5.4.

Hi-lift jack versatile, effective, needs care in use – plus brake, diff-lock, chocks.

5.2. Towing-out

Ropes and attachments
Second-vehicle safety; long ropes.

Take a second vehicle for safety and to assist recovery if you are going off-roading.

Where conditions are likely to be close to the limits of your Land Rover's capabilities, you are strongly advised not to go off-roading without a second vehicle. As this and the next spread will show, the potential for recovery where one vehicle is able to help another is a considerable improvement on the situation of a solo vehicle trying self-recovery. Firstly, always use a long towing rope – better still a combination of two that make up a long rope. That way the towing vehicle will not be in the same bog or soft sand that has stopped the first one. As with any rope, do not let it tangle round axles.

Use – and prepare – a long tow rope. If you have no towing hitch, use BOTH lashing eyes and a bridle.

Tow rope attachment – vehicle. Tow rope attachment to the towing vehicle should naturally be at the towing hitch if one is fitted. This uses the longitudinal chassis members and the rear cross member to provide a load-spreading attachment point. At the front and rear of all Land Rover vehicles, beneath the chassis, lashing points are fitted (two front and two rear), principally for securing vehicles on trailers. If a tow hitch is not fitted these can be used (as pairs, not singly) for towing. Better still, and designed to cope with far higher loads, extra-strong lashing/towing rings (Land Rover part no RRC3237) can be fitted in lieu of the normal lashing rings at the same chassis points (lower left photo opposite).

Preparation of tow ropes should include U-bolts and shackle pins.

Bridle and two attachment points.
The standard lashing points are designed for loads less than maximum towing loads but can be used for normal recovery towing (not snatch towing – see next section) if *both* eyes are used with a long bridle – a rope attached to both lashing eyes and joined to the main tow rope two or

NEVER loop tow rope round the rear axle of a Land Rover vehicle – it could damage the brake pipes.

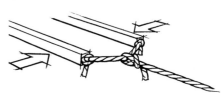

Attached at mid point, tow rope will bend a weak bumper, drawing chassis members together. Move rope close to bumper attachment points.

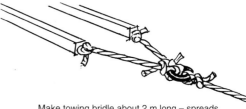

Too short a towing bridle will have same effect – also putting extreme strain on bridle rope.

Make towing bridle about 2 m long – spreads load without any 'pinching' component.

three metres away of the vehicle. (Do not make this bridle less than two metres in length and do make it of a rope to each lashing ring rather than a single loop through both rings. This way you will minimise rope tension and also eliminate any tendency to draw the chassis members together – see diagram.) Never put a tow rope round a bumper since this will lead to the rope being cut by the bumper's sharp edge. Nor should a rope be put

U-bolt and pin is reliable, repeatable way of attaching ropes (top). Standard tow hitch cleared for 3500 kg (upper right). If not fitted, use long bridle on lashing eyes or RRC3237 shackles (above and right).

round an axle since this involves the virtual certainty of damaging brake pipes.

Tow rope ends. Ensuring that your tow ropes have properly prepared ends is a very worthwhile precaution. Few things can add so effectively to the problems of having to extract a bogged vehicle than finding that tow ropes have to be knotted round tow points and then need a marlin spike in order to undo the knot afterwards. Spliced-in metal eyes and the use

of U-bolts and shackle pins on properly prepared ropes makes the exercise extremely simple and quick. If you do not have a tow hitch at both ends of the vehicle, prepare a suitable length of rope with U-bolts at each end to pick up on the chassis lashing eyes and act as a two metre bridle onto which the main tow-rope can be attached. The main tow rope should be similarly prepared for your particular vehicle.

Ideally don't use bumpers for towing; most bumpers cut tow ropes. In emergency pad with sacking, move rope close to attachment bolts.

...continued

The Land Rover Experience

5.2. Towing-out – contd

Co-ordinated recovery

Meaning, procedure. A co-ordinated recovery is one in which the power and traction of both vehicles – even though one of them, being stuck, has a limited capability – are used together at the moment when the tow is undertaken. This is a commonsense point but all too often, in the stress of a vehicle becoming bogged, the point is forgotten and spinning wheels and slack, then jerking tow-ropes become the ingredients of minor confusion. A helpful sequence aide-memoir for a normal assisted recovery would be as follows:

1. Marshaller, co-ordinator. Ingredients of a co-ordinated recovery: one stuck vehicle, one recovery (towing) vehicle, appropriate – long – tow ropes, two drivers and a third person to act as marshaller and co-ordinator.

2. Take your time. If the stuck vehicle is hung up on an obstacle invest ten minutes spade work to ensure the first extraction attempt is the one that works. Even if there is no digging, still take your time.

3. Backwards best? Towing out backwards is sometimes a more reliable option. At least the stuck vehicle has wheel tracks leading to its present position. In this case, with the vehicles back-to-back during recovery, a second marshaller standing in 'front' of the stuck vehicle is useful to keep that driver in the picture by relaying the hand signals of the principal marshaller ahead of the tug. As with reversing back down a hill (Section 4.4), the driver of the stuck vehicle should keep both hands on the steering wheel to preclude steering 'runaway' in reverse.

4. Towing vehicle clear. Position the towing vehicle so that it is well clear of the conditions that bogged the first vehicle (a long rope is almost invariably more use than a short one for this reason), attach the rope to both vehicles, position the third person so that both drivers can easily see him and have him marshal the tug forward until the rope is tight.

5. Visual signals, simultaneous clutches. Decide on the gear to be used – not necessarily 1st low range; 2nd could well be better – have both vehicles start engines, engage gear and wait for the signal from the marshaller for both drivers to engage the clutch. As with all marshalling, (Section 3.4 'Marshalling') this should be a visual not a spoken signal: a raised arm to instruct both drivers to be ready and in gear, raised arm describing small circles to instruct them to rev the engines, then drop the raised arm to instruct them to engage the clutches.

6. Marshaller in control. The marshaller should move backwards as the vehicles move towards him, still controlling the operation and being ready to give an immediate STOP signal if he sees any problems. He is the only one who can properly judge how the recovery is going. He too can judge when it is done; he can signal the lead vehicle to stop and the now mobile towed one to come forward slightly to slacken off the rope before disconnecting.

Safety – the danger of breaking ropes. A tow rope breaking whilst under

Use a long tow rope and a marshaller to control the operation. Take your time.

Marshaller should use only visual signals, not voice, to co-ordinate both vehicles' power.

WARNING. When tow starts, NO-ONE should be anywhere near the tow rope.

If stuck vehicle is heavy or badly mired a tandem-tow, carefully co-ordinated, will usually achieve first-time results.

A third-man marshaller is invaluable (right) to ensure clutches of both vehicles are engaged at the same time. A fourth, 'relay', marshaller (left) is useful in a reverse tow.

strain can be lethal or inflict serious injury. No bystanders or crew should be allowed near a tow rope during the actual tow. Four to five metres is usually a safe distance but the danger area varies with the length of rope and the techniques used – see next spread, 'Snatch towing'. A breaking rope recoils with whiplash violence. Adequately strong tow ropes are essential as well as rigidly enforced safety procedures in their use.

Pull required. As a guide, the pull required to move a vehicle (as a proportion of its total weight – ie including payload) assuming level ground, is given below:

Hard metalled road – about 5% of total vehicle weight.

Grass – about 15%.

Hard wet sand, gravel, soft wet sand – about 15-20%.

Sand – soft, dry, loose – about 25-30%

Shallow mud – about 33%.

Bog, marsh, clinging clay – about 50%.

Rule-of-thumb. It makes sense that the rope to keep in the back of your Land Rover is the worst-case rope – the one for marsh/bog/clay. Allowing a safety margin to account for unseen damage to the rope and other exigencies it should have a quoted breaking strain about equal to the laden weight of your vehicle. For example, a 14 mm 3-strand polypropylene rope has a breaking strain – when new and undamaged – of 2.79 tonnes (quoted breaking strains are governed by British Standards in the UK) which would be an appropriate minimum for all except a laden Defender 110 or 130. For details of laden weights of all Land Rover products see Section 9, 'Technical Data'.

Use a tow rope with a breaking strain about equal to the weight of the vehicle.

WARNING. Breaking tow ropes can be lethal. Regularly inspect for damage. Keep bystanders away.

5.3. Snatch towing

WARNING. Snatch towing can involve very high forces and is a potentially dangerous procedure. Use only the fixtures and ropes of the kind specified below with methods to ensure loads in the rope and towing fixtures do not exceed 3.4 tonnes – a figure allowing essential safety factors. Ropes, towing fixtures and their attachment areas on the vehicles must be in sound mechanical condition without rust or physical damage. Only the procedure outlined on these pages can be recommended; use it only for vehicle recovery, not on static objects such as tree stumps.

Small, strictly limited, amount of momentum can help recover stuck vehicle.

Vital criteria

Using 'stretch' energy and momentum. Stretching an elastic rope is a means of storing energy. Using vehicle acceleration and then momentum – two different entities here – to effect that stretch is a means of achieving a higher towing pull to recover a bogged-down vehicle than would be achieved by traction alone. The momentum (or more accurately the Kinetic Energy or KE) is stored in the rope and added to the vehicle's tractive effort.

Two types of force. Total pull on the rope derives from:

1. Traction. Traction between the ground and the wheels of the towing vehicle - theoretical maximum around 1.73 tonnes on dry concrete (Defender 90, Tdi, 205 x 16 tyres, 2nd gear low ratio).

2. Kinetic energy. Any KE the towing vehicle has at the time the rope goes taut.

The concept of operation outlined here is that *the sum of 1. and 2. above must never exceed 3.4 tonnes.* If traction is good, KE must be limited; if the towing vehicle is on mud, KE can be allowed to rise to keep the sum at 3.4 tonnes.

Why 3.4 tonnes? This is the factored maximum load, in snatch towing conditions, to be applied to a pair 'JATE rings' part no RRC3237 (see below).

NEVER exceed permitted 'step-back'. Table shows examples. Towing attachments MUST be in first class condition.

Special ropes only. ONLY nylon ropes or straps specifically designed for this procedure should be used – with the manufacturer's recommendations. Snatch towing with chain, steel or other inextensible rope will result in major structural damage to both vehicles involved due to shock loading.

Inherent danger. The potential dangers of snatch towing cannot be over-emphasised. Although widely practiced on an ad hoc basis, few operators are aware of just how high are the forces involved. Some currently practiced procedures incur tensions in excess of 13 tonnes – enough to tear out towing attachments with explosive force and lethal potential – see photo opposite. This, not rope breakage, is the main hazard.

Essential criteria. Consider:
Specification of rope used.
Weight of towing vehicle.
Speed of towing vehicle.
Strength of towing attachments.

Note that the weight of the vehicle being towed is immaterial. Whatever is stuck may be stuck fast – whatever its weight – so the rope and procedure has to cope with an 'immovable' load.

Twin rope attachment points. Use a bridle on both vehicles plus safety lanyards (from the eye of the rope) attached respectively to the front and rear trailer hitches – see photo. The safety lanyard will restrain any hardware coming lose.

Attachment points. These should only be military specification Land Rover towing shackles ('JATE rings': part number RRC3237) – on both vehicles.

Rope specification. Use only ropes developed specifically for snatch or kinetic energy recovery. The table below refers to a one-off test on a rope of the following specification:

Identification: Yellow colour (polyurethane coating) with marker yarn.

Construction: 24 mm diameter, multi-plait nylon.

<u>Ultimate</u> *breaking strain* : 12 tonnes.

Length: 8 metres with formed, sheathed end eyes and 20 mm safety lanyards.

Attachment bridles: 6 metre yellow 18 tonne roundslings supplied.

Weight and speed of towing vehicle. The particular rope above would be suitable for all Land Rover products from an unladen Defender 90 (1645 kg) to a laden Defender 130 acting as towing vehicle but speed at the point of snatch – here catered for by the amount of 'step-back' from the taut rope condition – must be lower for the heavier vehicle.

Procedure – keep people clear

1. Attach ropes and safety lanyards as above. Drive towing vehicle (tug) slowly forward until rope is taut. As with normal towing, keep people clear of rope.

2. 'Step back'. Reverse tug an appropriate distance to avoid exceeding 3.4 tonnes load – see examples below.

3. Using (only) 2nd gear, low range, accelerate hard to extract stuck vehicle.

4. If stuck vehicle does not move, do not exceed a rope stretch beyond normal length (on the rope specified here) of 22% - about two paces on the ground with this rope. This stretch represents 3.4 tonnes pull – a useful cross-check.

Life of the rope, storage, care. A nylon KE rope has a finite fatigue life depending on the load to which it is subjected. It must be kept clean, free from grit and sand or other sources of abrasion and must not be stored in direct sunlight. Store dry, in a breathable canvas bag.

ONLY specifically designed snatch-tow ropes should be used for this purpose - using manufacturer's load criteria. These ropes are not widely available. Do not be tempted to improvise.

Keep nylon snatch-tow ropes clean, dry, out of sunlight. They have a fatigue life dependent on load.

Maximum 'step-back' from taut 8 metre rope (specified above) to not exceed 3.4 tonnes pull			
Assumes 2nd gear, low ratio, strong acceleration			
Vehicle type and load	Dry concrete	Dry grass	Wet grass/mud
1. Defender 90, unladen	<u>Zero</u> step-back. Rope sags 100 mm*	1.5 metres	2 metres
2. Defender 130, laden	Do not attempt. Will cause overload	1.8 metres	2.3 metres

Note: The tension achieved in the rope is extremely sensitive to the amount of 'step-back' combined with the type of traction surface you are operating on. It is essential that the safety limits inherent with the 3.4 tonne maximum pull are not infringed. Interpolate between values shown above both for vehicle weight and traction conditions.
* Only unladen Defender 90 (ie low mass vehicle) suited to dry concrete, strong acceleration case with this rope.

5.4. Winching

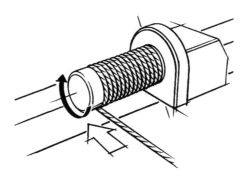

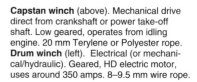

Capstan winch (above). Mechanical drive direct from crankshaft or power take-off shaft. Low geared, operates from idling engine. 20 mm Terylene or Polyester rope.
Drum winch (left). Electrical (or mechanical/hydraulic). Geared, HD electric motor, uses around 350 amps. 8–9.5 mm wire rope.

Concepts, winch types

Weighty decision; safety vital. The subject of winching cannot be covered fully in this section but a broad overview can be provided which will enable you to make your choice and get a feel for some of the principles of operation. Winching is comprehensively covered in a Land Rover Directory publication, 'Winching in Safety'. You are advised to read this book in detail before purchasing or operating a winch. Give careful thought to the implications of a winch before buying – it is more than an add-on accessory. In general winches are expensive and heavy, sometimes requiring special front springs for the vehicle. Depending on the type of winch, mechanical and electrical additions will have to made to the vehicle – power-take-off shaft drives, hydraulic pumps or fitment of an up-rated alternator or second battery where an electric winch is involved – further increasing weight. Winches require special care in operation since enormous mechanical forces are involved; children, animals – and under-informed adults – should be kept well away, and that includes spectators in the vicinity of cables under tension.

Slow operation. Winches are slow - but immensely powerful and capable of precise control in most cases. This will be what you want a winch for: there are many applications for this low speed alone – the slow controlled pull of a boat from the water or of heavy tree trunks. But for recovering other vehicles you will find many occasions are better catered for by towing with a rope (see Section 5.2); using a winch to recover a stuck vehicle makes it hard to coordinate the slow speed of the winch with power from the stuck vehicle's own engine (though this 'drive and winch' technique can be beneficial provided care is taken not to over-run the cable when traction does become available.) On the other hand, extreme boggings where a towed extraction can be difficult can be handled with ease by a winch and if your business includes recovering passenger cars from ditches or the like, the slow speed and precise controllability of a winch will be exactly what you need.

Approved winches. You are most strongly advised to consult your Land Rover supplier when buying a winch and to buy only winches supplied through Land Rover Parts. These will have been

Be sure a winch is what you need before fitting one.

Electric drum winches not well suited to continuous use. Capstan or mechanical drum winches best for continuous heavy duty work.

Fit only Land Rover approved winches and installations.

approved for your vehicle and the accessories kit will have been specifically engineered for it with safety in mind and so as not to overload the vehicle. Winches may be ordered factory-fitted. Additionally there will be a small Handbook of Winching Techniques issued with the winch which will summarise how to prepare and operate the unit. The following few pages cannot deal with the subject comprehensively.

Winch types. There are two generic classifications of winch:

1. *Drum winches* comprise a drum rotating about a horizontal axis parallel to the bumper and use 8–9.5 mm wire rope stored on, and spooled onto, the drum. They can be driven electrically or there can be mechanical or hydraulic drive for continuous heavy duty operation.

2. *Capstan winches* consist of a bollard – like a giant cotton reel – rotating about a vertical axis. Such winches do not store any rope; they function by moving appropriate ropes – usually 20 mm Terylene/polyester or polypropylene – which have been wound two or three times round the bollard and tensioned on the out-feed side. Capstan winches are mechanically or hydraulically driven and are suitable for continuous heavy duty work.

Pros and cons. Relative advantages and disadvantages of the different types and drive methods are dealt with in the table on the next spread.

Know your proposed needs for a winch, study the concepts on this page plus the tables on the next spread. Then go firm on what you will buy.

Capstan winch (above) powers rope – of any length – looped round capstan. 10000 lb Superwinch E10 (above right) is among most powerful electrically powered winches and designed for intermittent heavy duty use; stores cable on drum. Mechanical H14 (right) is designed for continuous heavy duty work.

Of prime concern is whether your work is intermittent – 'casual' – or continuous heavy duty winching. See next spread.

...continued

5.4. Winching – contd

heat is generated and very high charge rates from the alternator are required. A mechanically driven capstan or drum winch is an altogether more relaxed concept which operates directly from the engine at tick-over; it can thus be used all day without mechanical stress.

Be aware of the different generic types of winch and the very broad spectrum of applications.

Casual or heavy duty. Winching can be 'casual' – towing a boat out of the water or the occasional use for self recovery – or 'heavy duty' which implies regular *continuous* use, usually for professional purposes such as logging or cable laying. Electric winches are not normally suitable for continuous heavy duty use; very high amperages are involved, considerable

Assess your requirement. Assess your needs very carefully and accept the fact that installation of a heavy duty winch will be necessary for where use is continuous and that such an installation will be heavy and relatively expensive since either mechanical shafting from a power take-off (PTO) or else installation of a PTO-mounted hydraulic pump will be required.

Table 1. Winch types and general characteristics			
Type	*Applications*	*For*	*Against*
Electric drum	Intermittent light, medium or heavy duty use according to specification.	Low cost, simple installation, relatively low weight 54-87 kg. Wide range from light to medium/heavy duty. Easy to use. Minimal maintenance. Wire stored on drum.	Electric motor will overheat if used for long periods. Very high amperage draw from battery necessitates high engine rpm and alternator output to recharge. Installation may need second battery.
Hydraulic drum	Continuous heavy duty industrial use.	Can operate for long continuous periods of industrial use with engine at low output or tick-over. Automatic rpm control. Vehicle has capability for other hydraulic tools/applications.	High initial cost for winch and PTO hydraulic pump installation. Needs specialised maintenance for precision components. Engine must be running. Heavy – up to around 115 kg.
Mechanical drum	Continuous heavy duty industrial use.	Can operate for long continuous periods of industrial use with engine at low output or tick-over.	High initial cost for PTO gear and drive shafts to winch position. Two-man operation – one controls engine, one controls winch. Engine must be running. Heavy – up to around 112 kg.
Mechanical or hydraulic capstan	Continuous heavy duty industrial use.	Can operate for long continuous periods of industrial use with engine at low output or tick-over. Constant pulling power due to rope being constant distance from drum axis all the time. Easy to operate. No limit to length of rope used. Around 63 kg.	High cost plus specialist maintenance if hydraulic drive. No room for mechanical drive on current Tdi Defender. Rope not contained on winch. Engine must be running.

Span of applications is so wide that a winch ideal for one kind of usage can be quite unsuitable for another.

Table 2. Data on some Land Rover approved winch types (Superwinch)						
Type	Name	Max line pull	Gearbox type	Brake type	Free spool	Elec/hydraulic power requirements
Electric drum	1. X6 2. X9 3. Husky 4. E10	6000 lb 9000 lb 8500 lb 10000 lb	Planetary Planetary Worm/wheel Planetary	Dynamic In drum Irreversible Disc, wet	Lever Lever Lever Plunger	12v, 390 amps 12v, 435 amps 12v, 360 amps 12v, 360 amps
Hydraulic drum	1. H8 2. H14W	8000 lb 8000 lb	Planetary Worm/wheel	Disc, wet Irreversible	Plunger Plunger	32 litre pump, 2500 psi 32 litre pump, 2500 psi
Mechanical drum	1. H14W	8000 lb	Worm/wheel	Irreversible	Plunger	Power take-off shafts
Mechanical or hydraulic capstan		4000 lb	Worm/wheel	Irreversible	N/A	Power take-off shafts or PTO hydraulic pump

Terminology
1. Gearbox type. This is an indication of the kind of reduction gear used in the winch. Worm and wheel can be arranged (and is here) to be irreversible hence there is no need for a brake.
2. Free-spool. Free spooling is the process of disengaging the winch in order to reel out the cable to the item being winched. 'Lever' or 'plunger' indicates the method of activating winch cable release.
3. Brake. Braking is provided for the mid-pull power failure case. Knowledge of brake principle is needed. 'Dynamic' brake is only the running of the winch motor in high-geared reverse as a generator so is a retarder rather than a stop brake. (X6CD has centre drum brake.) Drum and disc brakes activate automatically via one-way clutch in the event of power being lost in mid pull. Worm and wheel gearing is itself irreversible so runaway after power failure is just not possible.

In considering choice of winch, relate your proposed work to existence/type of brake, power requirements and amount of use at a given session.

...continued

Discovery with Superwinch X6 winch in a low-profile fitting. Protrusions under driving lights indicate 'crush cans' fitted from '95 model year; these establish set deformation rate in collision for air-bag deployment. Only approved and compatible winch fitments should be used on these vehicles.

Air bag equipped vehicles. In choosing your winch it is essential to remember that ONLY Land Rover approved winches are fitted to vehicles fitted with air bags. Being front-mounted, the mountings of these winches will have been engineered to exhibit the correct crush-rates compatible with the triggering devices for the air bag Secondary Restrain System (SRS).

The Land Rover Experience

5.4. Winching – contd

• **D-shackles** – see Section 5.2. For winching, where line pulls will be higher than for normal vehicle-to-vehicle tow-outs, stronger D-shackles will be needed. A 3/4-inch pin diameter is a good guide.

• **Tree strap.** Usually available from the winch manufacturer, an 8-foot by 4-inch tree strap should be acquired to put round trees to protect them from bark damage that would occur when using a tree as a winching anchor with a bare cable. Always use a tree strap – and as low as possible on the tree.

• **Split pulley block**. Where direction of pull is likely to be off vehicle axis or where a double-line pull is needed (or possible) to increase the line pull, a pulley block (see photo) will be needed – see diagrams next spread.

• **Ground anchors.** Where high line pulls are envisaged, possibly on slippery ground, a pair of ground anchors will be necessary to prevent forward movement of the vehicle during the pull. The right ones will be heavy and cumbersome and take up space and payload in the vehicle.

• **Back-anchor rope.** Where ground anchors are not available or where additional security is required, winching vehicle can be anchored with rope and tree strap to a tree behind it.

• **Gloves.** Steel cables can have small broken strands along their length; use thick winching gloves to protect your hands. Do not let a steel winch cable slip through your hands even when using gloves. Always pay it in or out hand-over hand. The same gloves will be useful for the handling of capstan winch ropes too.

The extent of your proposed winching activity will dictate how much of the above you need – it will vary from very little if you are going only to pull a boat out of the water once per week end to virtually the whole kit if you are going to be a recovery marshal on an off-road trial or are carrying out logging operations in a forest area. It will all figure in and be part of your eventual choice of winch.

Protect living things – trees, by using a strap; people by observing safety rules and keeping clear of ropes and cables.

Unless self-recovering, anchor winch vehicle with ground anchors or ropes to other trees.

Always use thick leather gloves when handling winch cables.

Techniques overview
Accessories. Paradoxically, it is wise to consider the accessories you will need before going firm on your choice of winch since you must envisage the entire operating regime and method of use before you have a clear picture of what is involved. Number of operating crew is a fundamental first consideration since if you are always going to be solo then a mechanical drum winch will not be suitable. Length of cable is a consideration. Most drum winches are supplied with 30 metres (100 feet) of cable and, whilst this can be attached to extensions, there may be times when a continuous long pull is required and thus a capstan winch would be the best equipment. If this is the case then thought must be given to storage of the rope – which will be bulky and must be kept in good condition – within the vehicle. For any winch you are going to need some or all of the following additional ancillary equipment:

Slope and line pull. Knowledge of your required line pull in various conditions is necessary as the final consideration before choosing a winch.

1. Level ground. For recovering vehicles – or any wheeled object with reasonably large wheels – the pull required to move it varies according to the surface on which it is standing. The pull, as an approximate proportion of its weight, is:

Hard road – 5%
Grass – 15%
Hard/soft wet sand, gravel – 15-20%
Soft dry sand – 25-30%
Shallow mud – 33%
Bog, marsh, clay – 50%.

Thus if the vehicle to be winched is a part-laden Discovery with a total weight of 2300 kg (5060 lb), the line pull to get it out of shallow mud will be just under 1700 lb.

2. Sloping ground. If the ground you are winching up is sloping you must *add* an increment to account for this. This is very simply calculated as the slope in degrees, divided by 60, times the total load of the vehicle being towed. Thus going up a 15° slope with the Discovery above would add 15/60 = 1/4 of its 5060 lb total weight to the line pull. So in this example we have:

Terrain component = 1700 lb
Slope – 1/4 of 5060 = 1265 lb
So total pull needed is 2965 lb.

Note that the slope component is surprisingly high – and this is assuming an even slope. In real life, of course, ground is uneven and a small local obstacle like a boulder or a tree root can put the immediate local slope up to 30 or 40°. Note also that it is the heaviest ground, eg clay, that is likely to get you stuck and in this case the terrain component goes up to 2530 lb and the whole total to 3795 lb.

Simple approximations enable required pull to be calculated.

Margins. Comfortable margins and, probably even more important, a knowledge of how the winch works and whether your usage is to be intermittent or continuous should then be applied in establishing your choice of equipment. Electric winches being hard-working, high revving, hot-running devices that also require the vehicle engine to be running fast are obviously less suited to continuous work than, say a capstan winch running at engine idle speed. Their relative lightness and cheapness, however, would win the day where the occasional winching of a boat or caravan is concerned.

Pulley is invaluable 'carry always' accessory to double or direct pull.

Ground anchors (opposite) prevent winching vehicle sliding forward when hauling heavy loads (diagram next page). Winch cable looped through split pulley block (right) and back to vehicle bumper doubles effective pull of winch – 8500 lb Husky shown in this mode above (see diagram next spread). Pulley can also be used for indirect pull – photo next page.

...continued

The Land Rover Experience

5.4. Winching – contd

Winching is a potentially dangerous procedure. But the danger can be eliminated by care and operator knowledge.

Safety first. Whilst a clichéd paragraph heading like this will not always do its job, the reminder is nonetheless very necessary since winching is laden with the possibility of accidents if real care is not taken. The good news, however, is that you, as operator, are in charge and there is seldom if ever any rush. Rest

Photo shows indirect pull electrical winching with cable through pulley block – see facing page. Although itself winch-equipped, stuck vehicle (left) is being winched up slippery slope by recovery vehicle (right). Note use of strap to preclude damage to tree bark and that the winching vehicle is square-on to the direction of initial pull.

Always use thick leather gloves when handling winch cables.

assured that thinking ahead, thinking things through, keeping people away from tow ropes and winch ropes, observing the few rules outlined here and *reading the instruction book thoroughly* WILL result in safe winching.

Breaking cables. Breaking cables and ropes are extremely hazardous. Never step over a cable under tension and ensure no-one is close to it when winching is in progress. Wire cables as used on drum winches flail laterally when they break so are particularly dangerous.

Control cable safety. Be particularly careful that electrical winch control cables are kept well clear of the winch wire. Caught up in the winch, a short circuit could make the winch unstoppable without disconnecting the control wire.

Directing – or doubling – the pull. Unlike the bulk and weight of ground anchors, split pulley blocks (previous

Pulley doubles winch maximum 'power' for moving obstacles

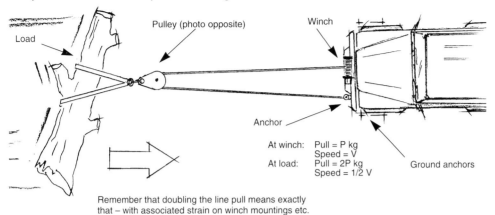

At winch: Pull = P kg
          Speed = V
At load: Pull = 2P kg
          Speed = 1/2 V

Remember that doubling the line pull means exactly
that – with associated strain on winch mountings etc.
Never try shifting the immovable with a double pulley.

*Pulley is invaluable
'carry always' acces-
sory to double or
direct pull.*

Pulley reduces line strain in self-recovery

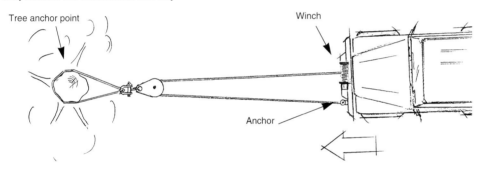

spread) are light and small and worth
carrying at all times with extra straps and
ropes. Be sure its rating is compatible
with your winch. They are invaluable as a
means of producing an indirect pull (facing photo) and for producing a given pull
with half the strain on the winch at half
speed.

**Maintenance, care of cables and
ropes.** Drum winch cables should spool
onto the drum evenly and will do so if the
pull is at the correct angle. If there are
signs of it not doing so, stop the winching, pay out the cable and spool back onto
the drum guiding it by (gloved) hands.
Inspect and clean cables and ropes regularly; excessive mud will get into the

strands or fibres and cause damage.
Extend the cable to full length and check
in detail for damage. Check gearbox oil
levels and for the presence of hydraulic
leaks regularly.

**Towing attachments – vehicle recov-
ery.** As with towed and snatch recovery,
the towing attachments on vehicles being
recovered must be sound and purpose-
built. Attach cables using D-shackles
tightened and then backed-off half a turn.
NEVER attach cables to axles or steering
components.

Training and practice. Fully absorb
the winch instructions, be familiar with
the equipment and take time to train and
practice before real-life use.

*Practice to gain com-
plete familiarity with
your equipment
before using it on real
situations.*

The Land Rover Experience

Section 6

Advanced driving

6.1. High/low range overlap

Each bar represents the speed you can do in that gear between max torque (about 1800 rpm) and max power (about 4000 rpm). Diagram drawn for Tdi diesel engine but values for other Land Rover engines are reasonably similar. Optimum change point for low box to high on the move is clear.

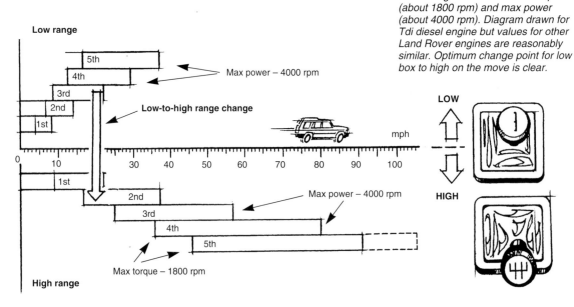

Speeds in the gears

High/low range overlap – your choice. You will see if you study the gear ratios data – and the diagram above – that there is some overlap between low range and high range – for example 4th gear low is roughly equivalent to 2nd gear high so that a given piece of ground could be covered equally well in either. You will frequently find, however, that being in low range rather than the high will give you the ability to tackle sudden track deteriorations such as road washouts or obstacles, without having to carry out a range change. (See also 'Low range – when and how', Section 2.4.)

Low to high change – when you need it. As already shown there are times when it is very useful to be able to start your Land Rover in low range and, once you are moving, continue in high. Typical examples of this are towing a heavy trailer on hard roads (Section 4.1), towing a trailer off-road (Section 6.4) or just starting the vehicle in marginal trac-

tion conditions such as soft sand or mud where it would be risky, once moving, to stop in order to re-select high range.

On-the-move range change - manual Low/high change – what gear, what speed. We have seen there is an overlap between low range and high range so a change across from low to high from 3rd, 4th or 5th could be useful – and is possible on vehicles having a lever range change (ie, not electric range change). In practice it is best to get the vehicle properly moving – say 20-25 mph – before doing a range change; that way, momentum will keep you going when you execute the change. The diagram also shows that the speed/rpm band between max torque and max power nicely suits a 3rd low to 2nd high change. Naturally before contemplating a change from low range to high you should also be sure that conditions are suitable for sustained travel in high range since to change back again you will have to stop.

Low range is not just extra-low gearing. It overlaps high range to let you choose best overall gearbox span.

Changing from low to high on the move – without clunks – is well worth learning.

3rd low to 2nd high on the move – procedure. As the diagram opposite shows, 3rd low is roughly equivalent to 2nd high in terms of road and engine speed. Given the max torque and max power rpm vs speed in the two gears, the range change will have to be made fairly briskly but need not be hurried.

1. Start off in 1st or 2nd low range, accelerate through the gears until you are doing 20-25 mph in 3rd gear, low range.

2. With the main gear lever still in 3rd, double-de-clutch the transfer lever towards you from low to high range, ie depress the clutch and move the transfer lever into neutral; clutch up. (Note, this will need a short, sharp action with a definite halt at the mid-point of the lever's range of movement.) Clutch down again and transfer lever all the way into HIGH .

3. With clutch still depressed, main gear lever 3rd into 2nd gear – towards you again, and across. As the engine was losing rpm whilst you moved the transfer lever, you will find you will need a blip of throttle to raise engine revs to the right level for 2nd gear, high range at 20 mph. Continue in high 2nd on up through the gears. Retain or de-select centre diff-lock as required (Defender and Discovery).

Electric range change. Low to high mobile range change on manual transmission new Range Rover is possible only up to 10 mph. At this speed in low 2nd, select gear lever neutral, press range change button; when Message Centre registers 'H', select 1st high and procede.

High to low on the move? No. This can be done under certain conditions to demonstrate driving skill but there is little practical application. Deteriorating heavy going is when you might need this change and here the time taken to execute it will be enough for the speed to have decayed to nothing. Make life easy; always change to low range when stationary, or easier still, just before the vehicle comes to a halt and with the main gear lever still in a gear.

1.
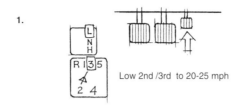
Low 2nd /3rd to 20-25 mph

Low to high – do it from 25 mph in 3rd low. Seems complex to read but is simple to do.

2.
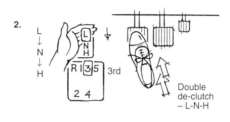
3rd

Double de-clutch – L-N-H

Practise it first on hard roads, then off-road. Momentum decay will be different.

3.
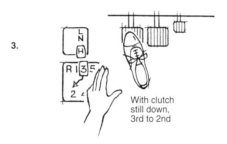
With clutch still down, 3rd to 2nd

Classic situation for low-to-high change on the move – softish sand, hard to start in but which, moving, you can take in high range. More usual example, nearer home, is trailer towing – hill starts or moving off from traffic lights.

Do not bother trying high to low on the move. Stop to make the change.

6.2. Automatic transmission

*To tow a dead-engine automatic with all four wheels on the ground, unlock steering and put **both** gear levers into 'N' – see Section 2.4 for selection of transfer neutral with electric range change. (See driver's manual for details of lifted tow and prop-shaft disconnect). Tow-starting is not possible.*

Low to high range on the move is easier to do well on an auto than on a manual.

With electric range change an electronic speed sensor prevents range change on automatics above 5 mph.

It is worth learning to obviate the excess torque converter slip that would result from a high load start in high box.

Low to high – moving (auto). As in the manual transmission case (Section 6.1) there are many occasions when it is very useful to start in low range, attain a speed and positive momentum where high range can take over – probably 20-25 mph – and then effect a change of transfer ratios without stopping. Using the procedures shown here, this is possible where range change is by manual lever. (With electric range change and automatic transmission, as explained at Section 2.3, speed sensors will prevent range change above 5 mph. In this case, and to eliminate any consequent clunk, it is arguably better to execute the change with the vehicle stationary.)

Low/high change – what gear, what speed. The diagram of speed in the gears at Section 6.1, although drawn for the Tdi engine and five-speed manual transmission, reflects a state of affairs similar to that of the four-speed ZF automatic fitted to Discovery and Range Rover. The prin-

ciple of change-over points remains the same – getting to a high part of the power curve in low range at a speed that will not decay through ground rolling resistance too much to enable transfer to a suitable gear and part of the power curve in the high range.

Low-to-high change – procedure. Since the auto transmission will take care of selecting the appropriate main gearbox ratio, it is only necessary (unlike manual Section 6.1) for the driver to attend to the moving of the transfer lever (*diagram facing page*):

1. Start off in low range with **'3'** selected. Accelerate to 3000 rpm once the gearbox has changed up to 3rd ratio.

2. When at 3000 rpm, simultaneously lift off the throttle and, as the transmission goes from drive to over-run, move the transfer lever aft into neutral.

3. When the rpm have dropped to 1500, ease the transfer lever further aft into the HIGH range position.

1.

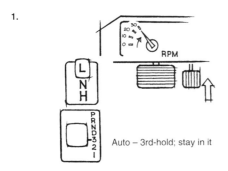

Auto – 3rd-hold; stay in it

2.

L
↓
N

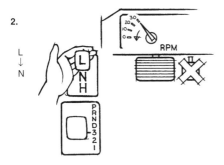

Low to high, mobile. Snick transfer lever into N – remember detent is very small so make a sharp, positive stop with your hand when moving the lever from L to N – allow revs to drop, then pull back from N into H. See text and diagram left.

Low to high range on the move – where range change is by manual lever. Diagram shows sequence corresponding to text on facing page.

3.

N
↓
H

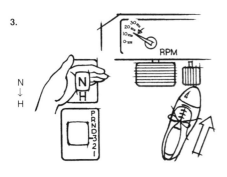

Although this is a very simple operation, it will pay to practise it on road and in undemanding conditions before using it in earnest. As with the manual transmission case, it its important to judge movement of the transfer lever into neutral properly.

High to low, moving? Sometimes.
Unlike the firm 'No' given at Section 6.1 in the manual case, following the Driver Manual procedure of changing down to low transfer on the move can be done if forward speed is at or under 8 kph (5 mph). Whilst rate of speed decay in worsening conditions will be the same as in the manual case, the auto transmission's ability to re-select the main gear ratio virtually instantaneously will make this a practical manipulation in cases where speed decay is not too rapid:

1. Slow to 8 kph (5 mph) in HIGH.
2. Lift off accelerator, move main selector to 'N' and transfer lever to LOW.
3. Re-select 'D' and drive on.

Unlike manual transmission, high to low with auto can be a useful technique in certain cases.

The Land Rover Experience

6.3. Engine braking

Steep initial section, you find you have too low a gear; wheels are sliding.

Engine braking in general is a safe, economic way of reducing speed.

Just as excessive braking can cause wheel slide, so can excessive engine braking – 1st gear low range on a very steep, long, slippery slope.

Be ready to use the accelerator – and keep cadence braking in the back of your mind all the time.

Slippery slopes
Engine braking recommended...but. Read this section after reading Section 4.5. Engine braking is the safe way to reduce speed. On long hills use engine braking to keep your speed from building up because that way you are not overheating the brakes – important, since even today's disc brakes can suffer from a degree of 'fade' (reduced efficiency) when they get very hot. All this is a well accepted part of our armoury of safe driving techniques.

Sensitive, delicate braking. But think first of a two-wheel drive car on an icy road. Engine braking derives retardation through one pair of wheels on the driven axle whilst sensitive and delicate use of the foot brake uses all four. The same retardation spread between four wheels instead of two reduces the risk of wheel locking. The relevance of this example is to make the point that there is a place for sensitive and delicate braking in many situations in which we have 'learned' to leave the brakes alone. ABS and cadence braking (see Section 3.2, 'Gentle right foot') are especially relevant here.

Beware sliding wheels. In the case of a 4x4 the situation is improved since both engine braking and slowing with the brakes is achieved using all four wheels. But just as excessive use of the brakes can cause lock-up and discontinuity of rolling contact between the wheels and the ground, so excessive engine braking can cause exactly the same thing – sliding wheels. So tackling a really steep slippery slope using 1st gear low box can amount, in special circumstances, to excessive engine braking and result in wheel slide. Be ready to use the accelerator. Or it will likely be better to use a higher gear such as 2nd – even 3rd sometimes. (See Section 4.5 and photo top right opposite.)

Emergency procedures
Discs for delicacy. The brakes on all current Land Rover models are power assisted discs, light and sensitively progressive. Delicacy of control is easy to achieve and there are some extreme down-slopes where, if you are not equipped with ABS, this delicacy combined with cadence braking (see Section 3.2) will give more controllable retardation than engine braking alone. There are two classic cases to consider:

1. Almost the right gear, brake assistance. Take the case of an initially steep, long slippery down-slope with a loose surface. You judge that 2nd low is appropriate and begin your descent. But the initial section is so steep that the vehicle gains speed faster than you anticipated. Clearly it is inadvisable to attempt to change down at this critical stage (even an automatic will not always change down to 1st in these conditions – see Section 2.2) so a gentle and intermittent use of the brake pedal – gentle cadence braking – can be used to slow the vehicle within the limits of the available grip for the initial steep part of the descent. Don't let the wheels lock; and if they do, release the brakes altogether, immediately.

2. Wrong gear, cadence braking take-over. Take the same steep, long, slippery down-slope. Starting down it in 1st gear low box may result in wheel slide because in such a low gear – even with the engine revving hard – the wheels will not be able

Add throttle. Delicate application of brake; quit at the first suspicion of lock-up.

If, in gear, wheels just cannot keep up with speed increase, de-clutch and use cadence braking. Keep front wheels pointing straight down slope.

Select a higher gear once the problem is over, boost the revs as you engage clutch and resume engine braking.

A matter of judgement (above). If it is this steep you want retardation but too low a gear when it is slippery or loose will give you slide. 2nd low, rather than 1st, would be best if it were muddy earth. In the special case of this giant sand dune you need to go higher still – 3rd or 4th low or even 1st high range – to prevent the vehicle nosing into the sand. (In this context see also Glossary 'Castor angle', and 'Steering feel', Section 10.1.) With ABS (left) the brakes are always a reliable fall-back.

to turn fast enough to maintain rolling contact with the ground. You realise too late that you have got the wrong gear so, after using all the throttle you can, you must undertake a rescue operation. De-clutch so that the wheels can regain rolling contact with the ground, then with great sensitivity carry out cadence brak-ing – *rapid gentle jabs at the brake pedal that never permit the wheels to lock* but which give you the best retardation the circum-stances allow. The Range Rover and

Discovery's ABS brakes, of course, being anti-lock will carry this operation out for you if you just keep your foot on the clutch and brake pedals; it will signal the fact that ABS is operating by the audible pulses of the brake relay. (While you have the clutch down put the gear lever into 2nd or 3rd ready for when you wish to engage the engine again.) This is a rare scenario but keep it in the back of your mind rather than slide out of control, throttle wide, in 1st.

Emergency proce-dure: really sensitive use of the brakes, releasing them the instant they lock the wheels – or cadence braking.

The Land Rover Experience

6.4. Towing off-road

High-density industrial plant trailers (right) need treating with more than expected care off-road – mainly due to inertia and limitations of trailer suspension. Treatment of horse-boxes, boats and the like is more self evident (below).

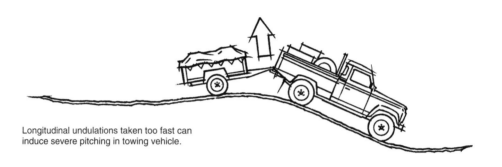

Longitudinal undulations taken too fast can induce severe pitching in towing vehicle.

Heavy trailer off-road – or light trailer driven briskly – will feed back considerable inertia loads to tug.

Potential problems

Greater trailer feedback. (Read Section 4.1, 'Towing – on-road', first, noting maximum off-road towing weights shown in the table.) Using trailers off road requires even greater anticipation and care. Feedback effect to the towing vehicle is much more noticeable than on hard road. For example, traversing undulations too fast can cause interactive responses between vehicle and trailer.

Specifically, the trailer can cause considerable pitch in the towing vehicle as it swoops into and out of a dip. This can be bad enough in extreme cases to lift the rear end of the vehicle momentarily off the ground.

Drag, push and lateral roll. Trailer drag over uneven ground and 'trailer-push' down steep slopes will be more pronounced – with braking correspondingly more difficult and liable, in extreme

cases, to provoke the trailer to try and overtake the vehicle in a form of jack-knifing. Off-road there is also a surprising susceptibility to lateral roll. Trailer suspension is seldom damped sufficiently in the laden condition compared to that of the towing vehicle, often compounded by a degree of roll-steer due to crude axle location geometry on the trailer. Lateral roll over an uneven track which the Land Rover suspension will cope with easily can result in alarming roll angles on the trailer – sometimes resulting in capsizing. (See next spread, revolving tow-hooks.)

Centre of gravity position vital. This background and the aspects of trailer dynamics covered at Section 4.1 emphasise the vital importance of low, and forward centre of gravity (giving appropriate nose-weight) when off-road towing. Take twice the nose-weight out of the available vehicle payload.

Beware especially of under-damped lateral roll of trailer on poor tracks.

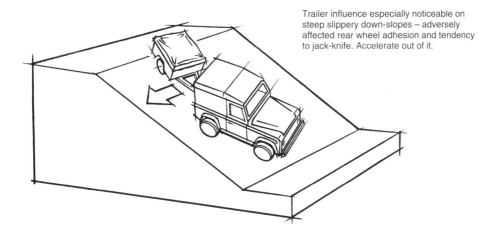

Trailer influence especially noticeable on steep slippery down-slopes – adversely affected rear wheel adhesion and tendency to jack-knife. Accelerate out of it.

... continued

6.4. Towing off-road – contd

Keep trailer payload as low as possible to permit low tyre pressures and give combination the best chance off-road.

Trailers can avoid an overload situation in expeditions – but tyres must be large and there must be manpower to man-handle the trailer when stuck.

Checks and procedures
Overload solution: provisos. For overlanding expeditions, use of a really robust trailer can be quite an elegant solution to the problem of having a payload requirement in excess of that shown as the maximum for your vehicle on its own. Spreading the load over six wheels is better than the unacceptable alternative of overloading the vehicle's four. The prolonged stress of an overland trip is perhaps an extreme case but it encapsulates the potential problems of all off-road towing so is worth examining. Four provisos should be remembered for sustained off-road trailer operation:

1. Weight. Minimise the weight of the trailer and load to give the vehicle the best working conditions off-road. An ex-military 750 kg trailer with overrun brakes, loaded to no more than 500 kg gross provides a sensible margin of strength and is in roughly the right category for a Land Rover towing vehicle.

2. Tyres. The same rationale mentioned earlier (see Section 1) about big wheels applies to trailers and is arguably even more important since the trailer wheels are following in ground already cut up by the towing vehicle. Trailer axle loads of the order indicated above will enable trailer tyre pressures to be lower (see Section 8.2) than those of the tug, enhancing flotation in the wake of the towing vehicle. Note that off-road a trailer needs the best combination of low rolling resistance and flotation (mainly the latter), not traction, so in absolute terms tyre requirements will be unique. However, in practice it is sensible to use the same wheels and tyres on the trailer as you have fitted to the towing vehicle; this is right functionally and has the additional advantage that the same spare wheel will fit trailer and towing vehicle. As noted, flotation can be optimised by the use of lower pressures.

3. Personnel. There will be times, off-road and overlanding, when the trailer has to be detached and man-handled. It will be necessary to have at least two people to do this; three or four will be better still.

4. Towing hitch. The standard 50 mm ball hitch is widely used in the UK and Europe but it should be remembered it is suitable for a maximum gross trailer weight of 1000 kg off-road on all Land

Rover products. The European specification ball hitch (Part no RTC9565) is stronger than the standard UK item. Note also the ratings of the 2-bolt and 4-bolt Land Rover Parts combined ball/pin hitches shown at Section 4.1. Because of problems of trailer lateral stability in extreme off-road conditions as noted on the previous spread, be sure your trailer has an EC-standard hitch that can rotate at the trailer since a tipped trailer would not then affect the towing vehicle.

Low range start. As with heavy trailers on hard roads (see Section 4.1) there will be many occasions off-road when it will make for a smoother start to move off in low range 2nd gear, continue up the low ratio gears and change into high range on the move using the techniques outlined in Sections 6.1 and 6.2 . For off-road towing, low range is sometimes the better choice to stay in.

Pay meticulous attention to condition of towing hitch, bolts and attachment areas.

Classic demonstration (below) of the benefits of trailer tyres being larger than those of towing vehicle and thus able to run on lower pressures; better flotation, less drag. Beware, however, since low trailer tyre pressures can cause weaving at speed. Fore and aft motion of loose fitting towing eye over long off-road distance caused considerable wear (left).

Starting in low range with an on-the-move change to high ratio is particularly useful with trailers off-road.

The Land Rover Experience

Section 7

Expedition basics

7.1. The call of the wild

Freeing the spirit

The pace of everyday life often constrains us to under-utilise what we have – be it our own skills, the potential of our hobbies or the potential of our four-wheel drive vehicle. Our early plans, made at the time of purchase, may not have been realised and we may be left with a gnawing urge to utilise more of the latent capability of our 4x4, to use it for some of the more adventurous projects for which we bought it. With a machine of such potential in your possession it would perhaps be the more unusual *not* to want to stretch its operating envelope. Without any doubt at all, there is little to compare with the feeling of being in the world's wilder places with a well-equipped and well trained expedition savouring the space, the beauty, the feeling of being self-sufficient.

Whilst this Section is inevitably aimed, primarily, at private recreational use it is hoped that it will also be of interest to commercial operators, perhaps in tourist-related or leisure pursuits, where operation of a vehicle in complete safety away from its home territory may form part of a package or proposal.

Basics only. Note, right from the start, however, that the whole of Section 7 is entitled 'Expedition basics' and it claims to be no more than that. An 'expedition' can be a half-day trip to the hills or a major three-month overseas project. They will have in common the importance of infallible preparation – an examination of all the 'what-if?' situations – but there will be in the major projects less margin for error and the need for very precise logistic control. This Section is an introduction to the subject and aims to help you prepare to broaden your enjoyment of your Land Rover product in relatively short trips. More demanding projects including the planning of overseas expeditions that may include a scientific project are covered in the book EXPEDITIONS, shortly to be published by Land Rover. The book also contains considerable extra detail on vehicle preparation, modifications, navigation, photography and emergency procedures.

'Expeditions' – be it half a day in the hills or a major overseas project – hugely enhance enjoyment of your vehicle. But you have just stepped into careful-planning territory.

Day trip or major expedition?

We are not all able to respond unquestioningly to the call of the wild since time, cost and other responsibilities will influence where we are able to go. What is certain, however, is the importance of how we tackle what we propose to do, however 'big' or 'small' it may be. As has been observed about that most unforgiving of all environments, the Sahara desert, you can die pinned under a capsized motorcycle behind a knoll a kilometre from the track just as easily as if you did the same thing 500 kilometres farther out in the desert. A sombre example that nevertheless makes the point admirably regarding the differences between everyday on-road operations where the swish of passing traffic is your assurance of some help, and being a few miles up a mountain track with what is becoming more than a minor problem on your hands.

Although a gentle progression up the scale of challenge is the natural way to do things, the importance of taking things a step at a time cannot too strongly be emphasised. Going hand in hand with this – importantly and almost inevitably – will be the growth in your confidence. Confidence begets early recognition of, thus avoidance of and measured response to problems. Confidence (well-founded confidence, not over-confidence or cockiness) further begets the ability, comfortably, to say 'no' and turn back before getting into trouble.

Savour but beware the feeling of amazement and invincibility you may

Safely operated, a 4x4 epitomises – and realises – the need to seek the earth's wild places.

have experienced on your first competent off-road demonstration of your (or your dealer's) Land Rover. The feeling of unstoppability is very strong but, as has been emphasised throughout this book, all vehicles, even Land Rovers, have their limitations and in a *competent* demonstration you will have been shown what *can* be done, not what happens when you get it wrong.

So, assuming you are just making a start, the answer to the 'day-trip-or-major-expedition' question is clearly 'day-trip' – and then only after planning and training. If you are already thinking that actually it was release you were after and not another career development project, be of good cheer; the training and practice is great fun – putting into practice what you have read in the other Sections of this book. And during training there is someone to help when you get into trouble; there is also a hot shower to go home to afterwards.

Planning

The aim. Paradoxically, despite the emphasis on planning, it will not be easy to plan in a 'capability vacuum'. In other words, until you know a little of what you individually can do with your vehicle it will be hard to make a realistic plan for an expedition. It is likely, however, that

Take your projects a step at a time. Confidence and competence will then build on a sound foundation.

...continued

7.1. The call of the wild – contd

Fundamental navigation is about maps, headings, distances – wherever you are. GPS devices (opposite) give pin-point fixes in desert, mountain, plain.

To establish an aim, know first what you and your vehicle can do – train; see Section 7.2.

you may want to explore some unsurfaced tracks you have seen on the map as part of a week-end break you may be taking in the mountains. The aim can be as general as this for the time being.

Maps, research. Small, 'white-roads' trailing off into areas of close contours or wide-open space on the map, together with a ford or two and linking up with another 'white' or 'yellow' road away from all the traffic can have an irresistible appeal. It is worth, at this stage, re-reading the Foreword to this book to remind yourself that ownership of a 4x4 brings considerable responsibilities in regard to environmental care, the obligation to set an example and acceptance of the often complex matter of rights of access. This latter will be different in every country and must be individually checked. The rising general population of 4x4 vehicles has regrettably brought with it a small element of irresponsible users and a corresponding tightening of access rules.

Be certain about rights of land access for off-road vehicles – an increasingly sensitive subject in developed countries.

Awareness of these rules is therefore essential. Quoting a summary of the UK will give an idea of what to expect in 'developed' countries – countries with relatively high populations and a legislature steeped in historical evolution. The UK situation is at once knocked slightly off-balance by the fact that a new system of classification in *being* introduced and is not yet reflected on all maps. The maps to use are the excellent 1:50,000 Ordnance Survey Land Ranger maps, backed, where possible, by the 1:25,000 series. On these maps there are:

• Public footpaths – vehicles not allowed.

• Public bridleways – vehicles not allowed.

• RUPPs (Road Used as a Public Path) – being re-categorised on most maps as BOATs (see below) and in many *but not all* cases, implies that vehicles may be used on them. Local Authorities do have an obligation under the Wildlife and Countryside Act 1981 to reclassify all RUPPs as byway, bridleway or footpath (see below, The Definitive Map).

• BOATs (Byway Open to All Traffic) – this is what it sounds like, vehicles are permitted.

• UCRs (Unclassified County Roads) – these are minor roads or lanes, many with a sealed surface, others comprising only rough stone. These may be driven by vehicles.

Some confusion may be added to complexity by the fact that, to quote the Foreword, the indication of a road on a map does not automatically confer a right of way. Worth the trouble, and in any more ambitious expedition essential, is a visit to the County Council offices where may be inspected the Definitive Map which will indicate the current legal access status of every road in the County. Since all of this is aimed at keeping within

the law and not upsetting people on whose property you may find you have inadvertently trespassed, asking permission from the local landowner, if you can ascertain who it is, will always be a safe alternative. Other local people will also usually know the status of tracks and interesting trails. A catch-all and usually temporary TRO (Traffic Regulation Order) can, however, be issued at the discretion of the Highway Authority on given routes in relation to given types of vehicles (to cover the case, for example, of local over-use causing damage – a reasonable enough concept despite the further confusion factor).

Navigation. It goes without saying that close attention must be paid to map-reading and navigation in order that you may, at any time, be able to pin-point your position on the map and know where the next track-junction or other waypoint may be. Accept that this will take time and that you will probably have to stop the vehicle frequently to check it all out. Heading-and-distance navigation will seldom be appropriate to back-lanes trips in countries such as the United Kingdom but it is a principle that must always be in the back of your mind.

Ascertaining compass heading in a vehicle is almost a contradiction in terms since the internal magnetic field is strong, variable and virtually uncorrectable for a normally mounted magnetic compass. Use the compass outside the vehicle and about five metres away from it.

GPS navigation. If your long-term aims include a demanding overseas trip and you have already obtained a GPS (Global Positioning System) navigator – which may be hand-held for use on the hills or vehicle-installed – then you will have satellite-derived speed, heading and position (accurate to 100 metres) at the touch of a button. Such equipment, especially after the labours and uncertainties of manual navigation in bad weather, is a boon and a minor miracle. With costs driven steadily downward by competition, most units can be removed from the vehicle installation, a vehicle position way-point registered and the GPS taken with you when walking on the hills; in the event of sudden bad weather overtaking you, the unit can give you a bearing and distance back to the vehicle from your current position.

Second vehicle, safety message. Two vehicles driven in sensibly-spaced convoy is a wise precaution on most routes off-road. If one vehicle gets stuck in mud the other will be able to tow it free, or go for help if mechanical damage has occurred through sliding off the track. It is well appreciated, however, that the whole point of some trips will be to 'get away' in a single vehicle and it behoves you for such excursions to pick routes which you know will be safe and from which, even in bad weather, you will be confident to walk for help should the occasion arise. Training trips (see next spread) with schools organising safaris will give you a feel for the conditions and safety requirements. As with some hill-walking and mountain routes on foot, it is wise, wherever possible, to inform someone of your route and expected return time.

As with expedition projects, develop your navigation skills a step at a time. Map, compass, distance travelled, cross bearings.

Take a second vehicle for safety unless you are certain about a particular route.

7.2. Training for the trip

Before planning your own expedition, establish and hone your driving skills – first with professional tuition such as The Land Rover Experience, then with an off-road site day-pass, then within the safety of group safaris.

Learn the full spectrum of your vehicle's and your own capabilities before planning a trip.

Developing the skills. 'Training for the trip' may initially sound a forbidding concept when many 'expeditions' are no more than recreational excursions. But you would not go rock climbing without knowing how to do it and having the equipment and you would not go canoeing without being instructed on how to control the canoe and observe the correct safety precautions. To do any of these things without proper preparation would be foolhardy; and that applies to vehicle-based expeditions as well.

Off-road training. Use one of the many off-road driving schools to become familiar with your vehicle away from tarmac and in the low-range transfer gears. If you have read this book you will have the enormous advantage of having absorbed the theory – and the written-down practice – but it is essential that you try it yourself and become completely comfortable with your own and your vehicle's behaviour in demanding conditions before going out on an expedition, however 'small'. If you are in the UK and within range, clearly the best starting point is Land Rover's own LAND ROVER EXPERIENCE driving school at Solihull. You will not find that is enough on its own; you cannot become an expert in a single day. Taking on board their message, however, will be a very significant first step.

Practice on your own. You will have experienced the dynamics of off-road driving and the significance of the gentle right foot but you will need a lot more practice and for this you should go to a local school for consolidating tuition and, most important of all, a day-pass access to their off-road site which will enable you to 'play' in your own time and practice the techniques you have been taught. Take your time, read this book, know and analyse what you are doing. Being on a driving school site you will do so in the knowledge that should you get stuck, help will be on hand to tow you free. Such sites, additionally, are designated for off-road practice and you will not have the worry of seeking special permission for where you go. A considerable number of such schools advertise in the off-road magazines; go for the ones that emphasise thorough briefing and care for the vehicle. Do not be rushed into precipi-

tate driving methods; you are paying the bill and it is your vehicle.

Safari. A number of schools also organise 'safaris' lasting one to three days in which a small group of owner-driven-vehicles is led along pre-chosen routes which incorporate a variety of demanding driving conditions – and usually some exhilarating scenery. The experience is enjoyable in itself and valuable in a hundred ways for learning driving techniques. Choose a safari school that operates under similar terrain conditions to those you wish to travel later.

Fitness. Your off-road driver training and the physical effort required to push, jack, lay sand channels or dig out a stuck vehicle will be a reminder that your own fitness is no less important than that of your vehicle. In a perfect world your training will have conferred such skill and judgement that you never get your vehicle into a condition warranting the undignified description of 'being stuck'. Few will need reminding of the world's imperfections and from the fitness point of view it is wise to be prepared...!

Initial impressions of your vehicle's off-road performance will be dazzling; but learn the demarcation between what it can and cannot do.

After tuition, consolidate your abilities and confidence with practice on your own – with help at hand if required.

7.3. Vehicle preparation

Schedule service must be right up to date. But re-familiarise yourself with routine owner maintenance tasks. Jacking the rear is a long reach; groundsheet, overalls, wood block help.

Initial preparation will be mundane – simple things like knowing the driver's manual, jacking (and reading this book!)

What preparation? Rest assured that buying a Land Rover product will enable you to drive the vehicle from the showroom and turn in a best-in-class off-road performance without further preparation. Having said that, your attention will have been drawn already, in this book, to the fine-tuning that may be appropriate to given sets of conditions. Tyres in particular (where the point has already been made that particular tyres perform best in one set of conditions only), weights, wading plugs, loading, recovery equipment, towing hooks, underslung fog lights and spoilers are some of the items that spring to mind. And of course you must ensure that your vehicle has been properly maintained to Land Rover servicing schedules and is thus on the top line mechanically.

Vehicle knowledge. Your training sessions should have refreshed your knowledge of the traction enhancement facilities such as low range and the

Tyres, their fitness for the job you have in mind, condition, and pressure are fundamental to defining your expedition capability.

applicability for your vehicle of centre differential lock or viscous coupling, ABS brakes, Electronic Traction Control and the extra under-belly clearance available where Electronic Air Suspension has been specified. You should know and apply, for the tyres you have *and the weight of the vehicle as you will operate it*, the correct road pressures; be aware of what pressures you can reduce to for tracks (max speed 40 mph) and in the event of encountering exceptionally soft conditions (not above 12 mph).

Jacking. Tyre reliability these days is such that few of us get experience in fitting the spare wheel; an off-road expedition may result in sidewall damage and a flat if you are not sufficiently vigilant – see Section 3.4, Marshalling. Check the handbook procedures; practice choc-ing the wheels, positioning and operating the jack (take the main tightness off the wheel nuts with the wheel still in contact with the ground). You will find it quite a stretch positioning the jack under the rear axle; keep a set of overalls in the car for this job. Be sure you can undo and properly tighten the wheel nuts. If you have to jack on soft ground you will need a small wood baulk as a load spreader – about 45-50 mm thick and the size of this book; keep it in the vehicle. A second jack and wood block is useful where the ground is really soft and you may have to jack up a stage at a time.

Tyres. As indicated above, tyres can only be optimised for one set of conditions; other conditions, for those tyres, will involve a degree of performance compromise. Study the detail on tyre types, axle loads and pressures in Section 8.2. You will probably find your vehicle fitted with road-oriented or M+S tyres when you buy it and you would probably be wise to adjust the demands of your first expedition to be within the still considerable capabilities of these tyres before going to the expense of buying others. In temperate zones such as Europe you will find the main compromise with these tyres is reduced performance in mud/clay mixtures; this should not strike alarm since all Land Rover off-road press demonstration vehicles are fitted with these production-line tyres. Nevertheless where the best performance in mud is required, the Michelin XCL will provide it. (Be aware that only Defender will accommodate 7.50 x 16 tyres without modification. Range Rover and Discovery will take 7.00 x 16 with minor modifications at your dealer's discretion.) Remember that one aspect of a mud tyre's effectiveness derives from a carefully judged width – or narrowness – that enables it, together with an equally deliberate tread design, to cut through slippery upper layers of soft mud and into the grippier ground beneath. Thus the extra-wide after-market tyres frequently seen on recreational vehicles will usually yield poorer traction on wet grass and mud than will standard items; certainly they will be less effective than the mud tyres mentioned above. If fitting non-standard tyres outside those listed in Section 8.2 do check the Load Index and Speed Symbol (especially the latter) also listed in that section.

Ground clearance. Depending on type, specification and fitments to your vehicle, there may be alterations you wish to make to enhance ground clearance. For example, many Range Rover models are equipped with a front spoiler as standard and this may be removed (together with the associated driving lights) to improve approach angle and clearance at the front of the vehicle. If side steps have been specified on Discovery these too can be removed if you envisage there being a problem with lateral under belly clearance. Tow hooks too, especially those with an extra low mounting, can be temporarily removed if (see Section 3.3) you will need extra departure angle for tackling steep up-slopes. In extreme conditions where the rear wheels run up

Wide tyres, per se, are not always 'best'. These Goodrich Mud-Terrains shine where a combination of flotation and traction is needed (peat, marsh) but are outperformed on pure mud by Michelin XCL. Match to conditions.

against obstacles aft, mud flaps can get torn off by being trapped between the rear wheel and the obstacle. If this is a risk, the mud-flap can be rolled up on itself and tied in this position with cord or a small strap until resuming travel on road.

Tie-downs, internal stowage. As mentioned in Section 8.1, there is much to recommend the fitting of tie-downs in your vehicle if it is to operate over rough ground. Used in conjunction with modular containers such as lidded plastic storage boxes of the kind available in DIY stores, equipment such as wet-weather gear, camping equipment, recovery items, spare jack, and refreshments can be strapped-down so that they do not slide around the vehicle on uneven tracks or off-road. Some form of secure mounting will be essential for really heavy items such as a high-lift jack or even a spare hydraulic jack and shovels. This is part of the basic philosophy of eliminating loose articles so that not only does equipment avoid damage but the vehicle itself, as a result, is free from rattles and other internal noise. You will find that vehicles in this condition, tight and rattle-free, are driven better and more sympathetically than those full of nerve-jangling equipment avalanches.

Think ground clearance. Does spoiler or tow-hook have to be removed to enhance approach and departure angle?

Plan, containerise and secure the load. Read that bit again!

7.4 Equipment

A second vehicle and a long tow rope are two of the most comforting items of equipment to take when venturing far from the beaten track. An inadvertent bogging of a single vehicle need be no more than a brief incident when a safety vehicle is with you.

Simple problems can develop into emergencies when no help is at hand. Don't be self-conscious about taking sensible safety measures.

Influencing criteria. Television news bulletins continually remind us of how easily a short recreational excursion can turn into a life-threatening drama. Common to many of these news items is how simple were the precautions that could have avoided trouble. Occasionally, this is proven when someone, well prepared, has survived cheerfully by building a snow-hole or taking appropriate action that has enabled them to ride out the storm or assist rescue teams to find them when things have gone wrong. European weather systems, especially in the regions attractive to outdoor or adventurous people are notorious for their changeability and the suddenness with which conditions can become threat-

ening. Some of the 'what-if' questions that must be asked in deciding what equipment to take on an expedition are:

• **Weather.** If the weather turns from to-day's fine sunny conditions to 'snow-on-high-ground' or a downpour, am I appropriately equipped?

• **Track condition.** Can I self-recover a vehicle brought to a wheel-spinning halt in mud?

• **Off-road.** If my vehicle bellies-out on a bank can I recover it?

• **Overnighting.** If my recovery problems take so long that we are overtaken by darkness or sudden bad weather, have we food and warmth enough to overnight in the vehicle and resume operations in the morning?

• **Going for help.** If I get myself into such deep trouble off-road that I am unable to recover, how far is it to help and can I walk it with the equipment I have?

• **Emergency equipment.** Do I have any means of attracting attention?

(These are questions that will also influence your taking along a second vehicle)

Protective clothing

Plan for the worst. Usually you will be protecting against cold and wet. On any expedition, even a short drive on mountain tracks, you will not wish to – and certainly not be able to – remain in the vehicle with the heater on all the time. Assume, as a matter of course and whatever the weather at the start of your trip, that it will rain, get cold and blow a gale. Assume also that you will find it necessary to wade up to your knees in mud or water and/or walk a number of kilometres on rough ground. Equip yourself with appropriate clothing and add overalls and a groundsheet to lie on when you have to insert wading plugs or change a wheel. If you have not got recent (or any) experience of hill walking or similar outdoor pursuits, consult one of the many

Gumboots (note grip tread), light walking boots, extra socks, keep feet dry, warm and effective. Typical layers over day clothes: Helly Hansen fibrepile inner, Goretex trousers and outer (note drawstrings at waist and hem, hood with drawstring). Woolly hat, scarf and, shown here, thin motorcycle gloves.

outdoor centres or camping gear shops for advice on the latest clothing. Some (for example Field and Trek in the UK) issue comprehensive catalogues containing invaluable advice on the pros and cons of different equipment. Standards of design and materials technology have never been higher – Goretex breathable water/windproof membrane and Thinsulate insulation being two developments that have made considerable impact on the design and effectiveness of outdoor clothing. Do your own study, adopt the layering principle – several layers of garments rather than a single very thick/warm one. The following will act as a guide:

• **Footwear.** Take two sets, knee-length rubber boots and hill-walking boots, each to be used with an extra pair of thick socks over your normal-wear socks. (You would not wish to walk far in gumboots nor carry out a reconnaissance wade-through of a stream in walking boots.) Keep them in a boot-bag or plastic sack to keep the inside of the vehicle clean.

• **Outer layer.** Fabric and Goretex overtrousers, roomy-fit hooded anorak of similar material with draw-cords at hood, waist and hem (preferable to waxed cotton which holds dirt, spoils seats, cannot be machine-washed, does not breath and needs regular re-proofing). Woolly hat or

Most common cause of problems is climatic – too cold or too hot. Be properly equipped.

Breakdown or bad bogging will involve prolonged work or walking outside the vehicle. Assume the worst weather and plan for it.

...continued

7.4 Equipment – contd

Don't let your enjoyment of scenery like this be marred by the consequences of cutting down on proper safety equipment. The same philosophy applies in 'green and pleasant lands' as in harsher climates elsewhere.

The satisfaction of being properly clad against the elements is complementary to that of being the master of difficult terrain in a 4x4.

similar to prevent heat-loss from the head. Two pairs of gloves – thin leather for driving, another set for mucky outside work.

•**Inner layers.** As experience demands. Fibre-pile jackets such as Helly-Hansen are excellent for warmth and wicking of perspiration; use as an either/or (or additional to) a Thinsulate zip-in liner to your anorak. Often a boiler-suit or overalls of generous cut can make a very practical inner layer over your day clothes when not wearing the wind/water proof out layers.

• **Other.** Groundsheet, as mentioned above.

• **Emergency.** Take a sleeping bag for emergency use in case you are overtaken by night or storm when stuck. It seems to be a rule of nature that all serious boggings take place just as the sun is going down.

• **Vehicle heater.** Remember, if you run the engine to keep the vehicle heater effective in snow, to be sure the exhaust pipe is clear of drifting snow that could prevent escape of poisonous exhaust fumes.

Recovery gear

Causes. Getting stuck with a greater or lesser degree of permanence will the be result of a temporary mis-match of your driving skills, assessment of the ground, capability of the vehicle and what the ground is actually like. More direct and specific causes will be:

- Soft ground.
- Slippery ground.
- Some manifestation of articulation limit.

Commonly a combination of all three is what will halt you. Note the exclusion of gradient as a cause of getting stuck. A vehicle capable of a nearly one-in-one climb on dry concrete is unlikely to be halted by any sensible gradient.

What to take, what to do. Getting close to the specifics like this will again emphasise the value of a second vehicle in the convoy. Re-read Section 5 and take:

- Two shovels (pointed ends, not spades); fold-away type will do.
- Long tow-rope, 7-tonne breaking strain minimum, not less than 25 metres long, with soft spliced-in eyes and U-bolt shackles.
- Standard hydraulic axle jack as supplied, wood baulk load spreader as above, plus second jack and baulk.
- Aluminium sand ladder. PSP or Barong grip/load spreaders.

Goretex bivvy-bag and light sleeping bag (above) for emergencies. Below a selection of recovery gear – winch (with tree straps), load spreaders, <u>long</u> tow rope, shovels, fire extinguisher (cooking stoves?) and first aid kit.

Sound recovery gear need not be complex. Shovels, long tow ropes with shackles, jacks and load spreaders – re-read Section 5.

Section 8

Pressing down, pushing up

8.1. Loading

Capacity – weight and bulk

Never overload. This is probably the prime rule in operating any vehicle and, despite their reputation for strength, it applies to Land Rover products as well. Every engineered object has strength criteria to which it is designed – with margins that are adequate or generous according to design philosophy. To overload is to eat into strength and durability margins and, in the case of cargo in vehicles, will adversely affect handling and performance as well. Payloads for your particular vehicle appear in the Technical Data section – Section 9.1-9.6.

Margins of durability, strength, handling and braking will be eroded if you overload.

Minimise off-road weights. For a given duty load choose a vehicle specification which will comfortably cope with the weight involved rather than be on the limits. Do not exceed specification payload and gross vehicle weights (GVW).

Load density – weight vs bulk. A cubic foot of lead vs a cubic foot of compressed straw is an analogy of weight vs bulk that would immediately catch our attention. But in the rough and tumble of day to day fleet operation with loads of less obvious density variation it can be forgotten. This is particularly the case with high density loads where the availability of space can often obscure the fact that the payload limit has been reached. Operators should be especially alert to this and – following pages – pay attention to load distribution as well.

Bulk capacity – biggest single slide-in box (15 mm finger clearance sides/top)

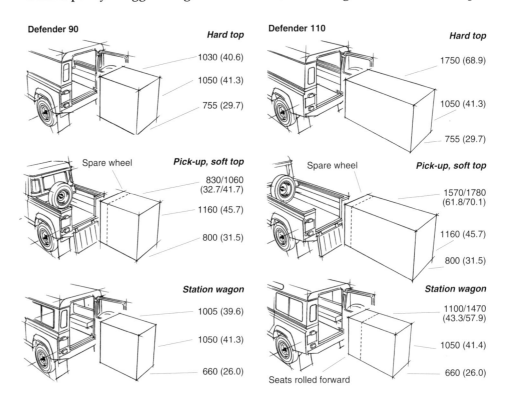

Defender 90

Hard top
- 1030 (40.6)
- 1050 (41.3)
- 755 (29.7)

Spare wheel — *Pick-up, soft top*
- 830/1060 (32.7/41.7)
- 1160 (45.7)
- 800 (31.5)

Station wagon
- 1005 (39.6)
- 1050 (41.3)
- 660 (26.0)

Defender 110

Hard top
- 1750 (68.9)
- 1050 (41.3)
- 755 (29.7)

Spare wheel *Pick-up, soft top*
- 1570/1780 (61.8/70.1)
- 1160 (45.7)
- 800 (31.5)

Station wagon
- 1100/1470 (43.3/57.9)
- 1050 (41.4)
- 660 (26.0)

Seats rolled forward

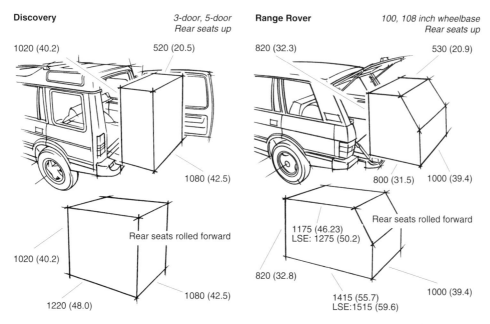

Discovery   *3-door, 5-door*
Rear seats up

1020 (40.2)   520 (20.5)

1080 (42.5)

1020 (40.2)   Rear seats rolled forward

1220 (48.0)   1080 (42.5)

Range Rover   *100, 108 inch wheelbase*
Rear seats up

820 (32.3)   530 (20.9)

800 (31.5)   1000 (39.4)

1175 (46.23)
LSE: 1275 (50.2)   Rear seats rolled forward

820 (32.8)

1415 (55.7)
LSE:1515 (59.6)   1000 (39.4)

Exact length depends on position of front seats

Defender 110/130 Hi Cap

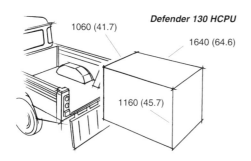

Defender 110 HCPU

1060 (41.7)

1980 (78.0)

1160 (45.7)

Defender 130 HCPU

1060 (41.7)

1640 (64.6)

1160 (45.7)

New Range Rover

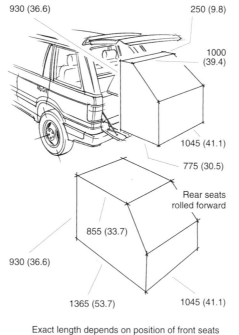

930 (36.6)   250 (9.8)

1000 (39.4)

1045 (41.1)

775 (30.5)

Rear seats rolled forward

855 (33.7)

930 (36.6)

1365 (53.7)   1045 (41.1)

Exact length depends on position of front seats

Remember load density. Just because there is room in the vehicle does not mean you have the spare payload.

...continued

The Land Rover Experience

8.1. Loading – contd

Generic payload span*	
Defender 90	654–923 kg
Defender 110	1020–1245 kg
Defender 130	1400 kg +
Discovery	667–830 kg
Range Rover	400-440 kg

*Depending on engine, body type, suspension and transmission. See Section 9 for precise payloads for your vehicle.

Typical unit weights	
205 litre (45 Imp gal) barrel, empty	20 kg
205 litre barrel full of petrol, kerosene	185 kg
" " diesel, lube oil	200 kg
" " water	225 kg
20 litre (4.5 Imp gal) steel jerry can, empty	4 kg
20 litre steel jerry can full of petrol, kerosene	20 kg
" " diesel, lube oil	22 kg
" " water	24 kg

Tables show payload span of Land Rover product range and can be used with unit weights and diagrams opposite to get a feel for bulk/weight of typical standard-unit loads. Oil drums can be rolled into Hi Cap through its wider tailgate (below, left); they will fit, lying down, between standard Defender wheelboxes but cannot be rolled through tailgate (lower right).

Standard 205 litre (45 Imp gal) barrel, jerry can
mm, (inches)

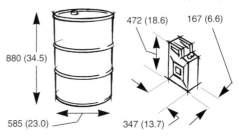

880 (34.5)

585 (23.0)

472 (18.6)   167 (6.6)

347 (13.7)

Bulk and weight – common loads compared

Defender 90/110 – standard pick-ups

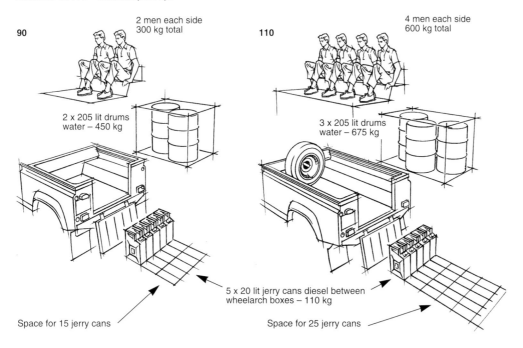

90

2 men each side
300 kg total

110

4 men each side
600 kg total

2 x 205 lit drums
water – 450 kg

3 x 205 lit drums
water – 675 kg

5 x 20 lit jerry cans diesel between
wheelarch boxes – 110 kg

Space for 15 jerry cans

Space for 25 jerry cans

Defender 110/130 – High Capacity pick-ups

110 HCPU: 5 x 205 lit drums diesel – 1000 kg
5 x 205 lit drums water weigh 1125 kg
(*NB Space available for 6 drums but max
payload is 1087 kg*)

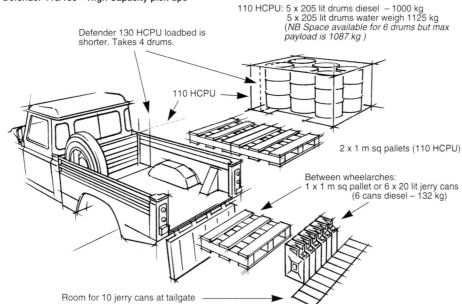

Defender 130 HCPU loadbed is
shorter. Takes 4 drums.

110 HCPU

2 x 1 m sq pallets (110 HCPU)

Between wheelarches:
1 x 1 m sq pallet or 6 x 20 lit jerry cans
(6 cans diesel – 132 kg)

Room for 10 jerry cans at tailgate

...continued

The Land Rover Experience

8.1. Loading – contd

Excessive roof rack load – above – increases risk of tipping. (NB Camel Trophy vehicles have internal roll-cages which increase roof strength.) Photographs below show Land Rover Parts approved roof racks – ideal for bulky, relatively light, items such as surf-boards, skis or ladders. Maximum recommended roof load is 75 kg (50 kg for Discovery). Internally stowed and lashed loads (see next spread) are preferable to roof racks like that above.

Weight distribution would be better termed weight concentration. Concentrate it low down and at the front of the load bed.

In on-the-limit flotation conditions 50/50 front/rear axle loads is best. Keep main load ahead of rear axle.

Avoid roof rack or anything that will increase vehicle's moment of inertia. If you really do need one, put only light loads on it.

Weight distribution

Normal weight distribution. As the axle load table at Section 8.2 shows, all Land Rover products are designed to take a greater load on their springs and axles at the rear when fully laden because that is the inevitable nature of the easy-access bonneted design.

Low down, 50/50 fore and aft. However, a degree of control over weight distribution lies with the operator. From a handling and flotation point of view in the most demanding conditions, the near-er a vehicle can get to a 50/50 fore and aft axle load condition the better it will be. Except with the lightest loads, even front/rear distribution will not be possi-ble but *keeping the main load ahead of the rear axle* and as low down as possible will enhance both handling and flotation.

Distribution within the load. Thus even within a given load which may get close to your vehicle's maximum GVW it is sensible to place high density items at the front of the load bed and as close to the floor as possible. A vehicle bogging in soft sand or in mud will all too often be seen to sink at the rear first due to less than ideal weight distribution; evening-out the fore and aft load will help.

Check weights for best tyre pres-sures. Users regularly operating in limit-ing flotation conditions at less than maxi-mum payload where rear axle load is low, can benefit from a calculated assessment of how low rear tyre pressures can go. Where standard loads or load kits are involved it would pay, as suggested at

Section 8.2, to have a vehicle weighed front and rear to determine what axle loads really are.

Roof racks, external bolt-ons. A nat-ural corollary of this attention to weight distribution is the elimination, where pos-sible, of roof racks or other external bolt-on paraphernalia. These items increase a vehicle's moment of inertia in pitch and roll and can be a safety hazard when mis-

Variation of axle load with load position – 250 kg load

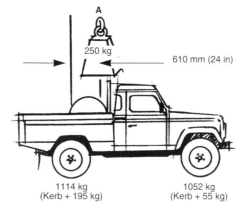

250 kg

610 mm (24 in)

1114 kg
(Kerb + 195 kg)

1052 kg
(Kerb + 55 kg)

Defender 110 HCPU Tdi at kerb weight

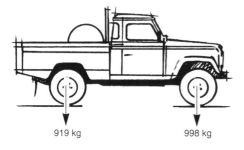

919 kg

998 kg

B

250 kg

1016 mm (40 in)

1260 kg
(Kerb + 341 kg)

907 kg
(Kerb − 91 kg)

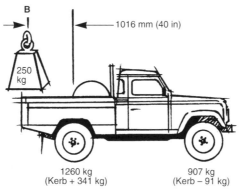

NB. *Danger of exceeding axle weights.*
A 638 kg load positioned aft at B would increase rear axle load to the top limit of 1850 kg. Front axle load in this case would be 250 kg lighter than at kerb weight.

CAUTION. Poorly distributed load – too far aft – can result in rear axle load being exceeded.

used. Many expedition Land Rover vehicles have been grossly overloaded on the roof rack – and some, unsurprisingly, have paid the price by tipping. There are many operators, however, for whom a roof rack is essential and in these cases remember that the maximum roof load recommended for a Defender and Range Rover is 75 kg (50 kg for Discovery). This is enough to accommodate light bulky

items such as ladders, small-section timber, canoes and the like.

Effect of trailers. Remember that a trailer, with its appropriate trailer preponderance (see Section 4.1 and 6.4), will, for a given actual nose load, exert a disproportionately high download on the rear axle because the tow hitch is well aft of the axle line. This is another reason for keeping cargo forward.

Count trailer nose-weight as payload and remember its effect on vehicle dynamics – see Sections 4.1, 6.4.

...continued

8.1. Loading – contd

Lashing cleats – military vehicle shown above – may be fitted to any Land Rover. Part number is RRC 3588/3674 plus locknuts. Older, non-plated version (left) from 1-tonne, is 395104. Typical suitable lashing straps are shown above – 1-inch and 1.5-inch webbing with over-centre tensioners.

Rattle-free load carriers get driven well; lash the load.

Securing the load
Eliminating rattles, good driving. A rattling, sliding load jars the nerves as much as it does the vehicle and those who have experienced both will attest the beneficial effects of a well-secured load (and the resultant reduction of noise) on their driving ability and general composure. Noisy, rattling vehicles tend to be driven without consideration and the converse is true – a quiet, rattle-free vehicle is driven smoothly and with mechanical sympathy.

The pay-off for this in multi-vehicle fleet operations and also in overland expeditions is notable in terms of reducing the stress the vehicle undergoes in difficult conditions.

Tie-downs. In general, loads may be stabilised by using rope in the cleats around the periphery of the Defender pick-up cargo area. The ease with which the cargo area of virtually any Land

Load lashing in practice: nowhere is it more important than on overland expeditions of the kind shown here using the Land Rover military One Tonne. Though expedition routine makes load lashing second nature, it need not be a chore in give-and-take fleet operation if thought is given to placing of cleats and provision of the right kind of straps.

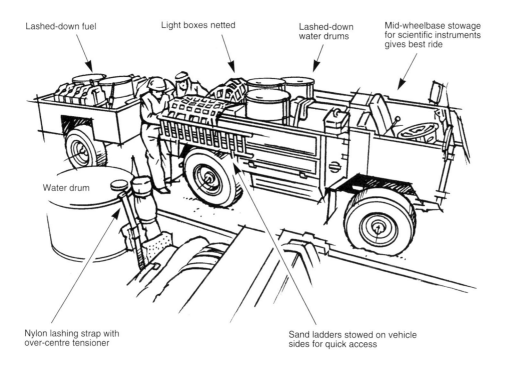

Lashed-down fuel

Light boxes netted

Lashed-down water drums

Mid-wheelbase stowage for scientific instruments gives best ride

Water drum

Nylon lashing strap with over-centre tensioner

Sand ladders stowed on vehicle sides for quick access

Rover product can be customised with tie-downs makes the securing of planned loads a very straightforward business. Robust-gauge aluminium alloy panels permit tie-down cleats to be bolted into position without the risk of corrosion causing subsequent damage; position them astride strengtheners where possible. Military versions of Defenders have usually got these cleats in position already but the same parts (RRC 3588/3674) may be obtained from Land Rover dealerships for tailored installations. Use lashing straps with hooks and non-slip tighteners.

Cargo nets. A simple, unfussy way to secure a mixed load, particularly of 'soft' items, is to use a cargo net over a small tarpaulin and roped to the hood-canvas cleats.

Install internal lashing cleats to suit your most-used cargo format and use built-for-purpose lashing straps.

The Land Rover Experience

8.2. Tyres

Tyres function optimally – ie at their very best – in only one set of conditions. Operators can maximise effectiveness – including COST-effectiveness – by careful choice of tyre type, tread type, pressures and driving technique. 'Africa-S' shown here is limited-production specialist tyre.

Specialist tyres exist for every use. The converse of that is that for any variation in vehicle use all tyres are a compromise.

Tyre types, axle loads
What this Section does. This Section:
• Gives an overview of generic tyre types, with for and against information – Table 1.
• Shows how, with a knowledge of axle loads and payload, to arrive at an optimum tyre pressure for your particular job using any tyre for which you have data. Tables 2 and 3.
• Gives 'ready-made' data for a wide range of approved OE tyres – Tables 4-10.

Tyre types – specialisation vs compromise. For optimum traction there is a specialist tyre for just about every type of terrain. The converse, of course, is also true: whatever tyres you have fitted will have disadvantages on ground other than that for which they were designed. This is a simple fact of life – and the laws of physics – and any attempt to produce a multi-purpose, compromise tyre results in exactly that; a compromise. So, for example, a good mud tyre will be noisy, have a reduced tread life and be not very grippy on wet tarmac in comparison with a road-optimised tyre which in turn would have poor traction in muddy conditions. Road oriented and even M+S tyres (see table opposite) will usually have an S or T speed rating (113 or 118 mph max) whereas a good mud tyre, with its heavier build will probably be L – 75 mph max (see tables at end of this Section).

Major-use compromise. In very general terms, most 4x4s spend more time on public roads with tarmac surfaces than they do off-road, however important or challenging their off road forays may be. All Land Rover products are supplied with original equipment (OE) tyres appropriate to the needs of these average model users since, in the same general terms, it is sensible to use tyres that retain the hard-road grip required for steering and braking. It is ultimately for you, as operator, to decide in which direction you wish to optimise your tyre performance. The information that follows gives a guide to the strengths and weaknesses of each specialist-use tyre type.

Table 1 – Tyre types and characteristics

Road oriented	Optimised for tarmac. Close tread, relatively smooth with sipes ('knife cuts')	**For:** Long life, quiet, smooth running, best braking. **Against:** Close tread susceptible to filling in mud, reducing traction.	
M+S tyre	M+S = Mud and Snow. Bolder tread version of road tyre. Quite a close, small bold tread. Sometimes provision for studs also.	**For:** As above but slightly less so. Good grip in snow and on grass. **Against:** Better in snow than mud. Close tread susceptible to filling in mud, reducing traction. (Note: Tread too bold to perform well on sand.)	
Mud tyre	Bold, open tread pattern, sharp right-angle edges. The best are quite narrow, have 'swept-back', self-cleaning tread pattern (illustration) designed for particular direction of rotation.	**For:** Very good in all types of mud and clay. **Against:** Grip on wet tarmac slightly impaired. 'Heel and toe' wear on tread blocks shortens life. Noisy. Limited speed rating. See also discussion at Section 4.7. (Note: The worst possible tyre for dry sand.)	
Multi purpose	Combination of mud tyre and road tyre build – usually a zig-zag centre band with bold transverse edge lugs. Wide variation in off-road performance among brands. Non-directional.	**For:** A good compromise for frequent on/off road use, eg farming. **Against:** Grip on wet tarmac slightly impaired on some multi-purpose tyres. Wears faster than road tyre, slightly noisy. See also discussion at Section 4.7. (Note: Poor on dry sand.)	
Sand tyres	Subtly shaped tread with shouldered blocks to compress sand in 'cups' (enhancing flotation and traction) rather than cut through it. Circumferentially grooved tyres look good but are ineffective in sand.	**For:** Very good for extracting last gramme of traction from sand. Robust enough for all desert terrain. **Against:** Poorer grip on wet tarmac must be allowed for. Some 'heel and toe' wear on tread blocks, some noise. Watch sidewalls on rock. (Note: Good flotation but poor performance in mud.)	
Tyres for rock	There are no tyres made specially for rock – by rock is meant any rough surface of large or small angular rocks or stones. The key to traversing rock lies with the driver – see Section 4.9. Clearly a robust tyre is best, in most cases a radial with a reinforced tread – but see below. The M+S, mud and multi-purpose types listed above would do well though the mud and multi-purpose tyres would have greater tread thickness. See below for special conditions applicable to sustained off-road operations in rocky conditions without on-road use*.		

*Cross-ply tyres. Where operations are almost exclusively off-road on rock or stone – such as fleet operations in quarries – the more damage-resistant qualities (at full inflation pressures) of cross-ply tyres could help keep operating costs down. It is essential, however, to consider and accommodate the following criteria:

a. Virtually all 7.50 x 16 cross-plies are – see table last page of this Section – 'L' speed rated, ie limited to 120 kph(75 mph), so should not be fitted to high powered vehicles operating on-road.

b. Cross-ply tyres have higher rolling resistance so will marginally reduce fuel economy.

c. Cross-plies have marginally less grip than radials on-road so handling affected.

Tyre designers have an impossible task trying to cater for all uses. Learn as much as you can about tyres and you will enormously enhance their effectiveness.

Land Rover OE (original equipment) tyres cover most operations. This Section guides you through choice, loads and pressures where you have special needs or re-supply problems....

.... and will in any case foster the requisite tyre-awareness!

... continued

The Land Rover Experience

8.2. Tyres – contd

Tyre pressures and axle loads are interdependent – both affect sidewall deflection, a critical criterion.

Tables 4-9 give you pressures for Land Rover OE tyres at GVW and kerb weight on- and off-road. For other tyres follow the Table 3 example.

Tyre pressures – relevance of axle loads. Tyres give their optimum performance – the best combination of grip, handling response, operating temperature (important for structural reasons) and a degree of shock absorption – when their elements (tread, beads and sidewalls) are optimally disposed to one another. The main criterion in determining this is sidewall deflection and this is established by the load on the tyre and its internal pressure. There is thus a theoretically optimum tyre pressure for every change in axle load or payload within the vehicle; this is why front and rear tyre pressures are different. In practice (and to ensure you do not spend your whole life changing tyre pressures) there is some latitude and usually two sets (ie front and rear) of pressures are quoted for vehicles – one for the unladen and one for the fully laden condition. These, of course, are based on individual front and rear axle loads – the weight each axle carries. Because they will be of use in determining the pressures to be used with specialist tyres – ie any not shown on the following pages – a table of axle loads for all Land Rover vehicles is given on the facing page.

Vehicle type Maximum weights GVW and maximum individual axle loads. See notes 1 and 2. GVW/front/rear max	Body type and/or manual/auto	Axle loads at kerb weight – 2.5 petrol engine Front/rear Kg	Axle loads at kerb weight – V8 petrol engine Front/rear Kg	Axle loads at kerb weight – 2.5D or VM engine Front/rear Kg	Axle loads at kerb weight – Tdi engine Front/rear Kg
Defender 90 Std: 2400/1200/1380 Hi-load suspension: 2550/1200/1500	Soft top Pick up Hard top Station wagon	922/714 919/717 916/767 911/790	908/719 905/722 902/770 897/793	946/710 943/722 940/763 935/786	971/724 967/727 960/786 959/834
Defender 110 Levelled suspension: 2950/1200/1750 Unlevelled susp'n: 3050/1200/1850	Soft top Pick up Hi cap pick up Hard top Station wagon County	941/864 940/875 938/915 938/902 924/1019 935/1044	941/865 939/876 937/916 937/903 935/1009 935/1045	972/856 972/867 970/907 970/897 955/1014 966/1039	1004/868 1000/880 998/919 994/919 982/1036 993/1061
Defender 130 3500/1500/2200	Crew cab HCPU	-	1027/985	-	1070/1016
Discovery V8: 2720/1100/1650 Tdi: 2720/1200/1650	3 dr manual 3 dr auto 5 dr manual 5 dr auto	- - - -	921/998 921/998 921/1065 921/1065	- - - -	991/1017 - 1006/1047 -
Range Rover 3.9 V8: 2510/1100/1510 Tdi Diesel: 2510/1200/1510 4.2 LSE: 2620/1200/1620	2 dr manual 2 dr auto 4 dr manual 4 dr auto LSE	- - - - -	952/968 979/972 964/922 980/1020 1070/1080	1027/1004 - 1039/1027 - -	1024/1028 - 1024/1028 - -
New Range Rover All versions: 2780/1320/1840	manual auto	4.0 V8 1171/1081 1176/1086	4.6 V8 1171/1081 1176/1086	2.5 diesel 1187/1072 -	

Table 2 – Actual axle loads, Land Rover product range – front and rear

If you want the best tyre performance or want to save the time wasted in recovery in your fleet, check axle loads and tyre pressures.

NOTE 1: Gross vehicle weight (GVW), ie weight fully laden, is the maximum weight for which the suspension was designed so is constant for a given vehicle type. Only where the suspension itself has an alternative specification, as in the Defender 90 and Defender 110, or where heavier diesel engines are fitted, are different GVWs or GVW axle loads shown.

NOTE 2: Because it is not always easy to get weight distribution front/rear precisely correct, individual axles may be loaded to the 'max' figures shown so long as the *overall* GVW is not exceeded. Note that in most cases the sum of the front and rear 'max' figures would exceed the GVW so do not load both axles to max. The Defender 110 has max and actual axle loads at GVW that are the same.

NOTE 3: Kerb weight (sometimes 'EEC kerb'), is defined as unladen weight plus full fuel plus a 75 kg driver.

NOTE 4 – Using the figures. *Example:*

Defender 90
Std: 2400/1200/1380

This means the Defender with standard suspension (ie not fitted with the hi-load heavy duty springs) has a maximum loaded weight of 2400 kg. *Individual* axles can take a max of up to 1200 kg at front, 1380 kg at rear – but not at the same time (since 1200 +1380 = 2580 which would exceed the 2400 kg GVW maximum for standard suspension.)

NOTE 5 – Using the figures. *Example:*

Defender 90. Station wagon, Tdi engine, axle loads at kerb weight: 959/834

This means an *empty* Tdi Defender 90 Station Wagon has axle loads of 959 kg front and 834 kg rear. If you aim to carry a 300 kg payload in the rear (assume exactly over the rear axle), the rear axle load will be 1134 kg. So 959/1134 are the figures you would enter into the tyre pressures table on the next page.

... continued

The Land Rover Experience

8.2. Tyres – contd

*Load and speed
determine
optimum/least tyre
pressure for best
traction; hence the
procedure outlined
here.*

Do axle loads really matter? In a word, yes. The reason you are reading this section at all is that you want the best flotation and performance from your tyres under specific conditions; clearly you do not want this if it will hazard your vehicles' safety or durability or damage your tyres. Applying the correct axle loads (accurate to 100 kg will do) to tyre data from a manufacturer will enable you to select a pressure that will yield best flotation and performance without compromising safety and durability. The span of the figures is considerable; an unladen Defender 90 rear axle carries only 38% of the load that the rear axle of a laden Defender 110 does. That matters. The above table can be used to interpolate axle loads – between unladen and fully laden – for your particular type of operations. For precise further details contact the tyre manufacturer but they will need the axle loads given above. Axle load is greatly (and surprisingly) affected by load distribution – diagrams Section 8.1.

If you are using non-OE tyres , the manufacturer/dealer should have a table like Table 3. Don't take no for an answer.

Table 3 – Pressures (on/off-road) vs wheel load, speed – example 7.50 x 16 Michelin XS													
Axle load	Wheel load	On-road tyre pressures – bar										Off-road pressures – bar	
												Track	Sand/ mud
					Speed km/hr								
kg	kg	120	110	100	90	80	65	50	40	30	20	65 kph	20 kph
2000	1000	3.75	3.8	3.8	3.5	3.4	3.4	3.4	3.3	3.3	3.1	3.1	1.7
1880	940	3.5	3.4	3.3	3.2	3.2	3.1	3.1	3.1	3.0	2.8	2.5	1.2
1800	900	3.3	3.2	3.1	3.0	3.0	3.0	3.0	2.9	2.8.	2.7	2.4	1.2
1600	800	2.8	2.7	2.7	2.6	2.6	2.6	2.5	2.5	2.4	2.3	2.1	1.0
1400	700	2.4	2.3	2.3	2.2	2.2	2.2	2.1	2.1	2.1	2.0	1.7	0.8
1200	600	2.0	1.9	1.9	1.8	1.8	1.8	1.8	1.8	1.7	1.6	1.4	0.6
1000	500	1.6	1.5	1.5	1.4	1.4	1.4	1.4	1.4	1.3	1.3	1.1	0.6
800	400	1.2	1.1	1.1	1.1	1.0	1.0	1.0	1.0	1.0	0.9	0.8	0.6

NOTE – Using the figures. *Example:* Take the Tdi Defender 90 Station Wagon on the previous page (Note 5) with front/rear axle loads of 959 and 1134 kg.
• *On-road.* Reading from the axle load column above, for a 120 kph road speed (interpolating or using next highest pressure), the vehicle should run at 1.6 bar front and 2.0 bar rear <u>minimum.</u>
• *Off-road.* Similarly the off-road figures that may be used, where you want the lowest pressures for reasons of flotation or ride, are 1.1 bar front and 1.4 bar rear *on tracks* at a *<u>speed not exceeding 65 kph.</u>*. If you got bogged in soft sand, the emergency soft would be 0.6 bar front and rear at *<u>at a speed not over 20 kph (12 mph).</u>* (NB Here, for handling reasons, 0.6 bar not recommended; see Tables 4 and 10.)

Overall picture. Having chosen your tyre type from Table 1, and ascertained your axle load from Table 2 you would apply it to a manufacturer's data sheet like Table 3 above to get the operating pressures on and off-road. (Note incidentally that 65 kph on-road demands a higher pressure than 65 kph off-road due to heat dissipation problems). The next two spreads give you ready-access information for Land Rover approved OE tyres.

Don't be put off by the figures and tables. It is a lot simpler than it looks!

Optimum pressures

Tyre pressures – three conditions. To get the best out of your tyres and vehicle on:

- roads
- on tracks and poor roads and
- emergency flotation conditions

you need three sets of tyre pressures. As we have seen (Sections 4.7, 4.8, and in the adjacent diagram) lowering tyre pressures increases the size of the tyre 'footprint' and thus lowers the unit pressure on the ground. The ground is thus less stressed and will yield better traction and flotation, so assisting a vehicle in traversing difficult terrain or in self-recovery if it is stuck. But we have also seen that a tyre has an optimum operating pressure. This assumes given criteria of handling response and maximum speed.

Limit the speed when deflated. It follows, therefore, that if we reduce the tyre pressures we must also accept different handling characteristics and, for structural and safety reasons, also limit the maximum speed when at reduced pressures. The tables that follow list (at kerb weight and at maximum permitted laden weight – GVW), firstly, normal road pressures which assume best handling and unlimited speed; secondly, 'tracks and poor road' pressures which might be applicable to tracks with more difficult off-road diversions; and finally 'emergency flotation' is listed where the terrain requires the absolute maximum flotation and traction. This latter would be applicable to terrain at the limits of your vehicle's off-road capabilities or for self-recovery from a bogged situation; such use *must be followed by re-inflation to appropriate road or tracks pressures*.

Preliminary note: For reasons of simplicity of operation, Land Rover handbooks quote a single set of front/rear tyre pressures (shown underlined in the tables here) catering for all conditions up to maximum load on hard roads. However, where flotation, traction and/or comfort are important, operators should follow the lower pressure recommendations in the tables on the next spread. (Note that these pressures assume 'normal' ambient temperatures – about 15°C ±10°. Tyre pressure should always be checked 'cold', ie after the vehicle has been standing for an hour or more; never 'bleed' pressure from a warmed-up tyre. If ambient temperatures are high – around 30–45°C – increase all inflation pressures shown by 10% – eg 2.0 bar would be 2.2.)

Tyre footprint of Michelin XS at (left to right) road pressures, track pressure and emergency flotation pressure. Percentage increases in area are considerable.

Details count - even when you are having a difficult time. Always use tyre valve caps and replace them - without dirt and grit on the inside – when deflating and re-inflating tyres.

... continued

The Land Rover Experience

8.2. Tyres – contd

Different tyre pressures for different conditions. ESSENTIAL to keep within speed and load limitations and reinflate tyres when back on easier ground.

Tyre no	Tyre name and size	Load index / speed symbol (See end of Section)	Vehicle weight	Hard-road pressures (to max speed) Front / rear	Tracks and poor roads. 40 mph max Front / rear	Off-road emergency flotation. 12 mph max Front / rear
Table 4 – Defender 90 – tyre pressure in bars (bars to psi – see table end of Section)						
1.	Michelin 205 R 16 X M+S	99Q	Kerb	1.9 / 2.1	1.6 / 1.9	1.2 / 1.2
			GVW	1.9 / 2.4	1.7 / 2.1	1.2 / 1.4
2.	Michelin 7.50 R 16 X 4x4	108N	Kerb	1.8 / 2.0	1.4 / 1.6	1.1 / 1.2
	Michelin 7.50 R 16 X-CL *	112L	GVW	1.9 / 2.9	1.5 / 2.2	1.1 / 1.7
	Michelin 7.50 R 16 XS *	108N				
	Michelin 7.50 R 16 XZL *	108N				
3.	Goodyear 7.50 R 16 G90	116N	Kerb	1.8 / 2.0	1.4 /1.6	1.1 / 1.2
			GVW	1.9 / 2.9	1.5 / 2.2	1.1 / 1.7
4.	Goodrich 265/75R16 Mud Terrain	120Q	Kerb	1.7 / 1.9	1.4 / 1.4	0.8 / 0.8
and....	Goodrich 265/75R16 All Terrain	120Q	GVW	1.9 / 2.4	1.4 / 1.6	1.0 / 1.4
NB Can also be used with **Defender 110 and 130** (heavy duty wheel) to give softer footprint. Check with dealer.						
Table 5 - Defender 110 – tyre pressure in bars (bars to psi – see table end of Section)						
1.	Michelin 7.50 R16 X 4x4	108N	Kerb	1.8 / 2.0	1.4 / 1.6	1.1 / 1.2
	Michelin 7.50 R16 X-CL *	112L	GVW	1.9 / 3.3	1.5 / 2.5	1.1 / 2.0
	Michelin 7.50 R16 XS *	108N				
	Michelin 7.50 R16 X ZY	112L				
	Michelin 7.50 R16 XZL *	108N				
2.	Avon Rangemaster 7.50 R16	108/106N	Kerb	1.8 / 2.1	1.6 / 1.6	1.1 / 1.1
			GVW	1.9 / 3.3	1.8 / 2.1	1.1 / 1.8
3.	Goodyear 7.50 R 16 G90	108N	Kerb	1.8 /2.1	1.4 /1.6	1.1 / 1.2
			GVW	1.9 /3.3	1.5 / 2.5	1.1 / 2.0
Table 6 – Defender 130 – tyre pressure in bars (bars to psi – see table end of Section)						
1.	Michelin 7.50 R16 XZY	112L	Kerb	1.9 / 2.1	1.6 / 1.6	1.2 / 1.3
	Michelin 7.50 R16 X-CL *	112L	GVW	3.0 / 4.5	2.4 / 3.6	1.8 / 2.8
	Michelin 7.50 R16 XS *	108N				
	Michelin 750 R16 X ZL *	108N				
2.	Goodyear 7.50 R 16 G90	108N	Kerb	1.9 / 2.1	1.6 / 1.6	1.2 / 1.3
			GVW	3.0 / 4.5	2.4 / 3.6	1.8 / 2.8
Table 7 – Discovery – tyre pressure in bars (bars to psi – see table end of Section)						
1.	Michelin 205 R 16 XM+S 244 TL	104T	Kerb	1.9 / 2.2	1.6 / 2.0	1.2 / 1.2
			GVW	1.9 / 2.6	1.6 / 2.3	1.2 / 1.4
2.	Michelin 235/70 R 16 4x4 TL	105H	Kerb	1.8 / 2.0	1.6 / 1.8	1.2 / 1.2
			GVW	1.8 / 2.3	1.6 / 2.0	1.2 / 1.4
3.	Pirelli Akros 205 R 16	104S	Kerb	1.6 / 1.8	1.3 / 1.4	1.1 / 1.2
			GVW	1.9 / 2.6	1.6 / 2.2	1.4 / 1.9
4. .	Goodyear Wrangler 205 R 16	104T	Kerb	1.9 / 2.2	1.6 / 2.0	1.2 / 1.2
			GVW	1.9 /2.6	1.6 / 2.3	1.2 / 1.4

Tyre no	Tyre name and size	Load index/ speed symbol (see end of Section)	Vehicle weight	Hard road pressures (to max speed) Front/rear	Tracks and poor roads 40 mph max Front/rear	Off-road emergency flotation 12 mph max Front/rear
Discovery (contd)						
5.	Goodyear Eagle GT+4 235/70R16 105H		Kerb GVW	1.8 / 2.0 <u>1.8 / 2.3</u>	1.6 / 1.8 1.6 / 2.0	1.2 / 1.2 1.4 / 1.4
Table 8 – Range Rover – tyre pressure in bars (bars to psi – see table end of Section)						
1.	Michelin 205 R 16 XM+S 244 TL	104T	Kerb GVW	1.9 / 2.1 <u>1.9 / 2.4</u>	1.6 / 1.9 1.6 / 2.1	1.2 / 1.2 1.2 / 1.4
2.	Goodyear Wrangler 205 R16	104T	Kerb GVW	1.9 / 2.1 <u>1.9 / 2.4</u>	1.6 / 1.9 1.6 / 2.1	1.2 / 1.2 1.2/ 1.4
Table 9 – New Range Rover – tyre pressure in bars (bars to psi – see table end of Section)						
1. and....	Michelin 235/70 R 16 4x4 TL Pirelli Scorpion II 235/70 R 16	105H 105H	Kerb GVW	1.9 / 2.2 <u>1.9 / 2.6</u>	1.6 / 2.0 1.6 / 2.3	1.2 / 1.2 1.2 / 1.4
2. and....	Michelin 255/65 R 16 4x4 TL Pirelli Scorpion II 255/65 R 16	109H 109H	Kerb GVW	1.9 / 2.2 <u>1.9 / 2.6</u>	1.6 / 2.0 1.6 / 2.3	1.2 / 1.2 1.2 / 1.4

NOTE – Table 10

Off-road tyres. Although low speeds are involved, Land Rover have imposed the lower limits of tyre pressures in Tables 4-9 for handling reasons and to reduce the possibility of dislodging a tyre. Certain of Michelin's off-road tyres – **indicated * above** – are, however, cleared by Michelin structurally and operationally to function at and benefit from exceptionally low pressures – down to 0.60 bar (9 psi) – where the absolute limit of flotation must be combined with the tyres' other unique features. Michelin stipulate only that 'track' and 'emergency flotation' speed limits (as above) are observed and that, in sand, tubes should be used in case sand gets between bead and seat. These tyres will perform magnificently but you must still treat them with care; beware of damaging sidewalls, beware of extreme lateral stress that could roll them off the rims. Observe the speed limits scrupulously, re-inflate when clear. Pressures, listed against axle load, for the various tyres are shown right. You may ascertain the likely axle load for your vehicle by consulting Table 2 on the second spread of this Section.

Table 10 – Michelin off-road tyres			
Tyre type/size	Axle load kg	Tracks 40 mph max	Sand/mud 12 mph max
7.00 R16 XCL	1000 1400 1600 1800	1.20 1.90 2.30 2.70	0.60 1.00 1.20 1.40
7.00 R16 XZL	1200 1400 1600 1800	1.30 1.50 1.80 2.70	0.60 0.80 0.90 1.30
7.50 R16 XCL	1000 1400 1600 1800 2240	1.10 1.80 2.20 2.50 3.30	0.90 0.90 1.10 1.30 1.80
7.50 R16 XS	1200 1600 1800 2000	1.30 1.90 2.20 2.60	0.60 0.90 1.10 1.30
7.50 R16 XZL (Also known as '4x4 O/R')	1200 1400 1600 1800 2240	1.40 1.80 2.20 2.50 3.30	0.70 0.90 1.10 1.30 1.80

... continued

The Land Rover Experience

8.2. Tyres – contd

Tyre pressures – speed warning. It is important to emphasise the speed limitations at reduced pressures shown in the columns on the previous spread. Never exceed the speed limits shown there. Driving too fast on under-inflated tyres will cause structural damage to your tyres through over-heating and possible delamination of the carcass; it will usually produce unacceptable handling and the possibility of rolling the tyres off the rims on corners. Be sure always to *be equipped with an accurate tyre pressure gauge and a re-inflation pump* if you are going off-roading.

WARNING.
A repeated warning about NEVER exceeding the speed and load limitations on tyres at reduced pressures.

Make it easy if you can. Re-inflation by muscle power is very hard work taking four tyres from emergency low to track pressures – especially in hot climates. Where there is a repeated heavy duty working requirement for re-inflation, using a line from the air brakes compressor (where fitted, see Section 4.1) or from a unit such as the ARB (opposite, top) fitted to one vehicle amongst a team may be more suitable. The ARB is actually designed for a locking axle differential but can inflate tyres as well. 12 volt electric pumps are probably best solution (opposite).

Pressure gauges, re-inflation. It has often been shown that concern for and care of tyres can be set at naught by that weakest of weak links the tyre pressure gauge. The pen-type gauge is often inaccurate and some dial gauges are not necessarily an improvement. Others, however, are good but should still be checked against one or more air hoses at service stations. In the UK such hoses and gauges have to be checked by law and can usually be relied upon. Once you have your accurate, proven tyre gauge, keep it in a dust-proof plastic bag in the vehicle at all

Obtain – and take care of – a good and accurate tyre pressure gauge.

Pen-type tyre gauges are better than no gauge but are not always accurate. Regularly checked against a calibrated source they are cheap and effective. Not all dial gauges are an improvement. Those shown are good.

tubed tyre, the same thing would not be possible with a tubeless tyre. A note, however, about alloy wheels which are designed with an internal AH (asymmetric hump) rim profile to enhance bead retention at very low pressures; these wheels are not recommended for use with tubes since low pressure flexing of the tyre can cause chafing of the tubes on the internal rim humps.

Small cheap electric pumps are surprisingly effective but get hot. It is worth having two – one cooling while the other is pumping. If using an electric pump be sure it cannot 'inhale' dust.

times. Re-inflation of the tyres after pressure reduction for-off road work is best done by an electric pump carried with you. Again you should be circumspect about the standard of unit you buy. Tyres fitted to Land Rover vehicles need a lot of air compared to car tyres so get a pump that is large, robust and can stand up to long periods of use without overheating.

Tubeless tyres. When severe off-road conditions are likely it is in most cases sensible, for two reasons, to fit tubes in your tyres. Firstly, encountering extreme conditions of roughness when inflation has been reduced to emergency soft could conceivably cause unseating of a tubeless tyre from the rim and thus cause total loss of pressure. Secondly, severe off-road conditions are often associated with operations away from full service facilities. Whilst changing or repairing a tyre by hand in the field is possible with a

Tubed tyres are best for remote-region off-roading as repair or replacement can be done by hand using low volume air supply. However, do not fit tubes to rims designed for tubeless tyres.

12 v electric tyre pumps are effective for in-the-field re-inflation.

... continued

The Land Rover Experience

8.2. Tyres – contd

Data on load and speed ratings, tyre construction and build are inscribed on the sidewall – see diagram opposite for full data and tables below for de-coding load index and speed symbol. Thus the Michelin X M+S 244 in the photographs, having a 99T load/speed rating is cleared to a maximum load per tyre of 775 kg up to 118 mph (at appropriate pressures).

If you have to buy an unfamiliar tyre, everything you need to know about it will be written on the sidewall. If it isn't, don't buy it.

Tyre nomenclature. A considerable amount of information is inscribed on the sidewall (and tread) of tyres, all of which is relevant to its specification – despite the assurances of those who would try to sell you tyres that are 'the same' as the one you specifically seek. The principal dimensions of a tyre are its width (not the depth between tread and bead) and the wheel diameter to which it is fitted. Thus a '7.50 x 16' is a tyre designed for a 16 inch diameter wheel and having a normal inflated width – ie the external maximum width of the inflated, unladen tyre – of 7.50 inches; it is not necessarily the width of the tread itself. This width data can also be shown in millimetres (still allied to a rim size in inches) as in the 205 x 16. Other criteria, some of which are shown in the diagram opposite, are:

Manufacturer's generic name such as 'X'
Manufacturer's type number or name, eg XCL, Rangemaster, Wrangler
Metric width in mm, eg 205, 235
Aspect ratio (cross section height:width ratio percentage)
         - follows metric width when shown (would be 235/70).
'R' for radial
Overall tyre diameter (usually given in the US)
Load index/speed symbol – see tables opposite
Maximum load and pressure – in lb and psi in addition to load index (US requirement)
Sidewall and tread construction – plies and material, eg steel, rayon (US requirement)
Ply rating – (equivalent) sidewall plies in a crossply tyre
Wear indicators
Country of manufacture
Direction of rotation – sometimes shown
ECE and US Dept of Transport type approval mark

Tyre sidewall markings

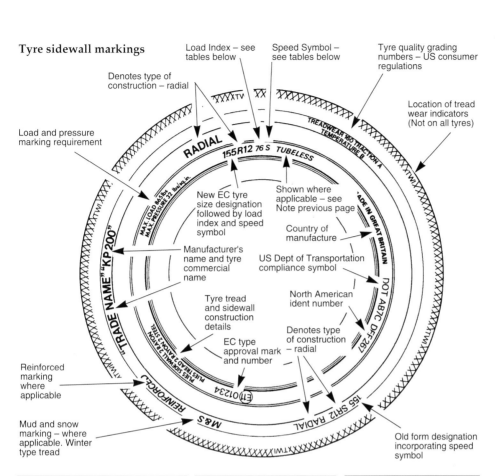

Tyre Load Index			
(NB Max load <u>per-tyre</u> at full road pressures at speed shown by accompanying speed symbol)			
Index	kg	Index	kg
97	730	111	1090
98	750	112	1120
99	775	113	1150
100	800	114	1180
101	825	115	1215
102	850	116	1250
103	875	117	1285
104	900	118	1320
105	925	119	1360
106	950	120	1400
107	975	121	1450
108	1000	122	1500
109	1030	123	1550
110	1060	124	1600

Tyre Speed Symbol		
(NB Max speed at full road pressures at per-tyre load shown by load index)		
Symbol	kph	mph
J	100	62
K	110	68
L	120	75
M	130	81
N	140	87
P	150	95
Q	160	100
R	170	105
S	180	113
T	190	118
U	200	125
H	210	130
V	240	150
VR	210/240	130/150

Tyre pressures – bars to (nearest whole) psi			
Bars	psi	Bars	psi
1.1	16	2.7	39
1.2	17	2.8	41
1.3	19	2.9	42
1.4	20	3.0	44
1.5	22	3.1	45
1.6	23	3.2	46
1.7	25	3.3	48
1.8	26	3.4	49
1.9	27	3.5	51
2.0	29	3.6	52
2.1	30		
2.2	32	4.3	62
2.3	33	4.4	64
2.4	35	4.5	65
2.5	36	4.6	67
2.6	38	4.7	68

Using the figures:
A load/speed index of 108N defines outer-limits ultimate capability: max load of 1000 kg <u>per tyre</u> ; max speed 87 mph. Having selected your tyre, then apply tyre pressures according to actual loads and speeds in tables 1-10.

Most good mud tyres and crossplies (heavy tread) have an L-rating – 75 mph maximum.

Section 9

Technical data

The Land Rover Experience

9.1. Technical data – Defender 90

Weights

Model	90 Soft Top				90 Pick-Up				90 Hard Top				90 County Station Wagon			
Engine	2.5P	3.5P	2.5D	2.5Tdi	2.5P	3.5P	2.5D	2.5Tdi	2.5P	3.5P	2.5D	2.5Tdi	2.5P	3.5P	2.5D	2.5Tdi
Gross vehicle weight kg	Standard suspension: 2400															
Kerb weight kg	1652	1643	1672	1686	1652	1643	1681	1686	1699	1688	1719	1733	1717	1706	1737	1751
Payload kg	748	757	728	714	748	757	719	714	701	712	681	667	683	694	663	649
Gross vehicle weight kg	High load suspension: 2550															
Kerb weight kg	1659	1646	1675	1689	1655	1646	1684	1689	1703	1692	1723	1737	1721	1710	1741	1755
Payload kg	891	904	875	861	895	904	866	861	847	858	827	813	829	840	809	795
Seating capacity	2 – 7				2 – 7				2 – 7				6 – 7			

Defender 90 comes in four body options, each with four engine options, standard or high load suspension, manual or power assisted steering, two tyre-size options.

Exterior dimensions – mm (ins)

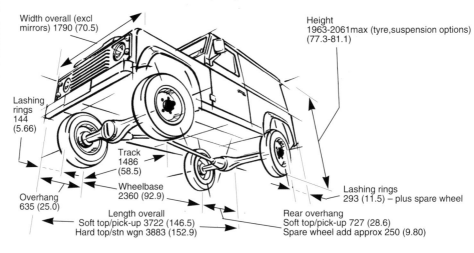

Width overall (excl mirrors) 1790 (70.5)

Height 1963-2061 max (tyre, suspension options) (77.3-81.1)

Lashing rings 144 (5.66)

Track 1486 (58.5)

Wheelbase 2360 (92.9)

Overhang 635 (25.0)

Length overall
Soft top/pick-up 3722 (146.5)
Hard top/stn wgn 3883 (152.9)

Rear overhang
Soft top/pick-up 727 (28.6)
Spare wheel add approx 250 (9.80)

Lashing rings 293 (11.5) – plus spare wheel

Wheelbase is 92.9 inches – the '90' name is wheelbase rounded to nearest 10 inches.

Interior dimensions – mm (ins)

See also Section 8.1– biggest slide-in box

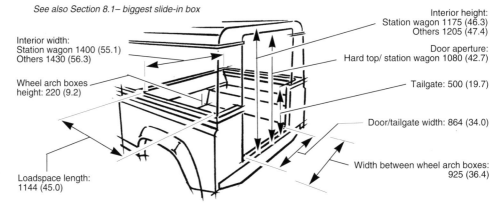

Interior height:
Station wagon 1175 (46.3)
Others 1205 (47.4)

Interior width:
Station wagon 1400 (55.1)
Others 1430 (56.3)

Door aperture:
Hard top/ station wagon 1080 (42.7)

Wheel arch boxes height: 220 (9.2)

Tailgate: 500 (19.7)

Door/tailgate width: 864 (34.0)

Width between wheel arch boxes: 925 (36.4)

Loadspace length: 1144 (45.0)

Length of load space times interior width gives load area of 1.63 sq metres.

Geometric limitations

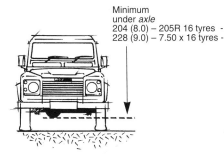

Minimum under *axle*
204 (8.0) – 205R 16 tyres -
228 (9.0) – 7.50 x 16 tyres -

Min mid-chassis under *belly* – unladen
290 (11.4) approx
314 (12.4) approx

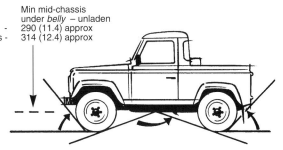

Tyres	Approach angle	Ramp angle (Kerb wt)	Departure angle
205R 16	48°	150°	49°
7.50 x 16	51°	146°	52°

Normal wading depth 500 (19.7). See Sec 4.10 re wading plugs

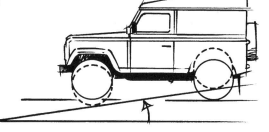

Max payloads of 649-904 kg give cargo 90s best power to weight ratio of the Defenders; best articulation of product range gives best off-road potential.

Longitudinal articulation angle: 7.51° (see Glossary)
Wheel movement at GVW, bump stops 50% compressed:
Front: 166 (6.5) up, 125 (4.9) down, total 291 (11.5)
Rear: 186 (7.3) up, 148.(5.8) down, total 334 (13.1)

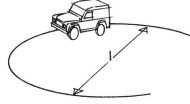

Minimum kerb-kerb turning circle:
205R 16 tyres 11.7 m (38.4 ft)
7.50 x 16 tyres 12.3 m (40.4 ft)

Castor angle (kerb) 3°±0.5°
Swivel pin inclination 7°±0.5°
Ground offset 63.0 mm
Front wheel toe-out 0.60-1.80 mm
Turns, lock to lock. 4.0
Wheels. 5.50F x 16 in steel. 6.00JK x 16 styled, optional.
Tyres. See Section 8.2..

Beam axles and coil springs front and rear. Disc brakes front, and rear, servo assisted. Power assisted steering standard. (UK)

CHASSIS
Type. Box section, ladder construction. 2mm (14 swg) steel.
Paint treatment. Zinc phosphate, cathodic electro coat followed by waxing in rear cross member.

SUSPENSION
Standard suspension. Long travel single-rate coil springs, double acting hydraulic dampers. High-load rear springs (2550 kg GVW) are dual-rate

Front. Beam axle located by radius arms and Panhard rod.
Rear. Beam axle located by trailing links and central A-frame.
High load suspension. As above but with dual rate coil springs on the rear axle.

STEERING
Type. Power assisted, worm and roller (Adwest Varamatic).
Ratio (straight ahead).
Straight ahead – 19.1:1
On lock – 14.2:1
Camber angle (kerb wt) 0°

BRAKES
Type. Vacuum servo-assisted. 1-1 split dual-circuit hydraulic. Solid disc brakes front and rear.
Handbrake (parking brake). Drum type. Single drum operating on transfer box rear output shaft. Handbrake not for use while vehicle in motion. Cab warning light.

...continued

9.1. Tech data – Defender 90 – contd

ENGINE – PETROL V8
Type. V8-cylinder, aluminium construction with 5-bearing crankshaft and self-adjusting hydraulic tappets.
Bore. 88.9 mm (3.50 in)
Stroke. 71.12 mm (2.80 in)
Displacement. 3528 cc (215 in^3)
Compression ratio. 8.13:1
Max power. 134 bhp @ 5000 rpm (100 kw) 80/1269/EEC
Max torque. 187.0 lbf ft @ 2500 rpm (253 Nm).
(US spec: Fuel injected 3.9V8)

ENGINE – DIESEL Tdi
Type. 300 Tdi, 4 cylinder in-line, intercooled and turbo-charged high speed direct injection diesel. Cast iron with aluminium cylinder head. Rigidly-mounted auxiliaries with serpentine multi-ribbed belt and dynamic spring tensioner.
Bore. 90.47 mm (3.56 in)
Stroke. 97.00 mm (3.82 in)
Displacement. 2495 cc (152 cu in)
Compression ratio. 19.5:1
Max power. 111.3 bhp @ 4000 rpm (83 kw) 80/1269/EEC
Max torque. 195 lbf ft @ 1800 rpm (265 Nm).
Turbo-charger model. Garrett T25 BCI 15
Turbo operating pressure. 0.8-1.01 bar (0.81-1.05 kgf/cm^2, 11.6-14.9 lbf/in^2) @ 2500 rpm.

ENGINE – DIESEL N/A
(N/A = normally aspirated, ie not turbo-charged)
Type. 4 cylinder in-line. Cast iron block and cylinder head, 5 bearing crankshaft.
Bore. 90.47 mm (3.56 in)
Stroke. 97.00 mm (3.82 in)
Displacement. 2495 cc (152 cu in)
Compression ratio. 21:1
Max power. 67 bhp @ 4000 rpm (50 kw) 80/1269/EEC
Max torque. 114 lbf ft @ 1800 rpm (155 Nm)

ENGINE – PETROL 4 CYL
Type. 4 cylinder in-line, cast iron block and cylinder head, 5 bearing crankshaft.
Bore. 90.47 mm (3.56 in)
Stroke. 97.00 mm (3.82 in)
Displacement. 2495 cc (152 in^3)
Compression ratio. 8:1
Max power. 83 bhp @ 4000 rpm (62 kw) 80/1269/EEC
Max torque. 133 lbf ft @ 2000 rpm (181 Nm).

FUEL SYSTEM – PETROL V8
Carburettors. Two SU HIF44.
Fuel pump. Electrical, submerged in fuel tank.
Filters. In line.
Fuel tank construction. Mild steel, tin terne coated, seam welded. (US spec: high density polyurethane, blow moulded.)
Fuel. 91/93 RON leaded, 91/93 RON unleaded.

FUEL SYSTEM – DIESEL Tdi
Pump. Bosch R509.
Injectors: Bosch KBAL 90 P37 (2 spring).
Fuel pump. Bosch mechanical.
Fuel tank construction. Mild steel tin terne coated and seam welded.
Filters. In line filter.
Fuel. Derv class A1 or A2.

FUEL SYSTEM – DIESEL N/A
Type. Self governing DPA distributor type.
Fuel pump. Engine driven mechanical pump.
Fuel tank construction. Mild steel tin terne coated and stitch welded.
Filters. In line filter.
Fuel. Derv class A1 or A2.

FUEL SYSTEM – PET 4 CYL
Carburettor type. Weber 32/34 DM TL.
Fuel pump. Electrical, submerged in fuel tank.
Filters. In line.
Fuel tank construction. Mild steel, tin terne coated, stitch welded.
Fuel. 90 RON (2 star) leaded

90 RON unleaded.

COOLING SYSTEM
Type. Pressurised liquid with pump and mechanical fan.
Radiator
Except Tdi – copper and brass full face area type.
Tdi – copper and brass integral unit with oil cooler and aluminium intercooler.
Thermostat
Petrol 4 cyl, diesel N/A – 82°C.
V8 and diesel Tdi – 88°C.
Fan
V8 and diesel Tdi – 406 mm (16 in). Temperature sensitive viscous drive.
Petrol 4 cyl and diesel N/A – 390 mm (15.5 in), 4 blade.

ELECTRICAL SYSTEM
Battery (see also Glossary)
Petrol – 12v, 210/85/90.
Diesel and US spec petrol – 12v, 380/120/90.
Diesel N/A, cold climate – 12v, 490/170/90
Alternator
Petrol – 65 amp.
US spec petrol – 85 or 100 amp
Diesel – 65 amp.
Headlamps. 75/50 watt sealed beam units.

TRANSMISSION
Clutch
Hydraulic push, reduced-load clutch operation. Asbestos-free lining. Clutch plate diam:
V8 engine – 267 mm (10.5 in)
4-cyl engines – 235 mm (9.25 in)
(2.5P – 240 mm, 9.45 in)
Main gearbox. R380 manual gearbox: five forward speeds, one reverse. Synchromesh on all gears – triple cone 1st, 2nd and 3rd; large single cone on 4th and 5th. Synchronised constant-mesh reverse gear train. Integral oil pump with remote cooler in heavy duty derivatives.
Transfer gearbox. LT230T 2-speed reduction on main gearbox output. Front and rear drive permanently engaged via a third differential – locked mechanically by movement of the transfer lever to the left.

MAIN GEARBOX RATIOS – Defender 90, and mph per 1000 engine rpm

	Ratio	mph/1000 rpm 205 x 16 tyres		mph/1000 rpm 7.50 x 16 tyres	
		High	Low	High	Low
3.5.l V8 petrol					
5th	0.770:1	25.22	9.26	26.51	9.73
4th	1.000:1	19.42	7.13	20.41	7.49
3rd	1.397:1	13.90	5.10	14.61	5.36
2nd	2.132:1	9.11	3.34	9.57	3.51
1st	3.692:1	5.26	1.93	5.53	2.03
Rev	3.536:1	5.49	2.02	5.77	2.12
2.5 l petrol and N/A 2.5 l diesel					
5th	0.831:1	20.10	8.54	21.13	8.98
4th	1.000:1	16.71	7.10	17.56	7.45
3rd	1.507:1	11.09	4.71	11.65	4.95
2nd	2.301:1	7.26	3.09	7.63	3.24
1st	3.585:1	4.67	1.98	4.90	2.08
Rev	3.816:1	4.38	1.86	4.60	1.96
2.5.l diesel 300 Tdi					
5th	0.770:1	21.70	9.22	22.81	9.69
4th	1.000:1	16.71	7.10	17.56	7.46
3rd	1.397:1	11.96	5.08	12.57	5.34
2nd	2.132:1	7.84	3.33	8.24	3.50
1st	3.692:1	4.53	1.92	4.76	2.02
Rev	3.536:1	4.73	2.01	4.97	2.11

Defender 90 hard top

FINAL DRIVE
Axle ratios. 3.540:1
Transfer ratios

	V8	All 4-cyl engines
High	1.214:1	1.411:1
Low	3.308:1	3.320:1

Front axle. Spiral bevel crown wheel and pinion with fully enclosed constant velocity joints.
Rear axle. Spiral bevel crown wheel and pinion with fully floating shafts.

BODY
Material. All panels with the exception of the dash bulkhead are of aluminium alloy. Front wheelarches of galvanised steel.
Plating/painting. Zinc phosphate. Cathodic electrocoat, polyester surfacer. Colour coat – alkyd for solid colours.

CAPACITIES (litres, Imp gal)
Full fuel tank
54.5 lit (12 gal)
Cooling system
V8 petrol: 12.8 lit (22.5 pint)
4 cyl petrol: 10.8 lit (19 pint)

Diesel Tdi: 11.1 lit (20 pint)
Diesel N/A: 10.8 lit (19 pint)
Engine oil, including filter
V8 petrol: 5.66 lit (10 pint)
4 cyl engines: 6.85 lit
(12 pint), *300Tdi:* 6.65 lit (11.7)

Main gearbox
2.67 lit (4.7 pint)
Transfer gearbox
2.3 lit (4.0 pint)
Front differential
1.7 lit (3.0 pint)
Rear differential
1.7 lit (3.0 pint)
Swivel pin housing
0.35 lit (0.6 pint)
Power steering
2.9 lit (5.0 pint)
Windscreen washer reservoir
4.0 lit (7.0 pint), 5.5 lit (9.7 pt) if air conditioning fitted

9.2. Technical data – Defender 110
Pick-ups and soft-top

Weights

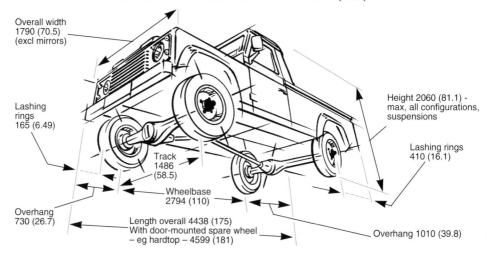

Model	110 Soft Top				110 Pick-Up				110 High Capacity Pick-Up			
Engine	2.5P	3.5P	2.5D	2.5Tdi	2.5P	3.5P	2.5D	2.5Tdi	2.5P	3.5P	2.5D	2.5Tdi
Gross vehicle weight kg	Unlevelled suspension: 3050											
Kerb weight kg	1821	1822	1844	1866	1821	1831	1855	1873	1869	1869	1893	1911
Payload kg	1229	1228	1206	1184	1229	1219	1195	1177	1181	1181	1157	1139
Gross vehicle weight kg	Levelled suspension: 2950											
Kerb weight kg	1845	1846	1868	1890	1845	1855	1879	1897	1893	1893	1917	1936
Payload kg	1105	1104	1082	1060	1105	1095	1071	1053	1057	1057	1033	1014
Seating capacity	2/3/11				2/3/11				2/3			

Exterior dimensions – *all* Defender 110 – mm (ins)

Defender 110 comes in six body options (see Sec 9.3 for full length hard-tops), each with four engine options, unlevelled or levelled suspension, manual or power assisted steering.

Overall width 1790 (70.5) (excl mirrors)

Lashing rings 165 (6.49)

Track 1486 (58.5)

Overhang 730 (26.7)

Wheelbase is exactly 110 inches.

Wheelbase 2794 (110)

Length overall 4438 (175) With door-mounted spare wheel – eg hardtop – 4599 (181)

Height 2060 (81.1) - max, all configurations, suspensions

Lashing rings 410 (16.1)

Overhang 1010 (39.8)

Interior dimensions – 110 std pick-ups, soft tops – mm (ins)

See also Section 8.1– biggest slide-in box

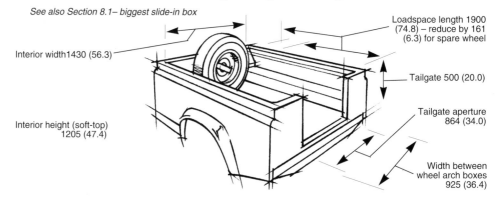

Interior width 1430 (56.3)

Interior height (soft-top) 1205 (47.4)

Length of load space times interior width gives load area of 2.72 sq metres (3.36 sq metres on Hi Cap pick-up opposite).

Loadspace length 1900 (74.8) – reduce by 161 (6.3) for spare wheel

Tailgate 500 (20.0)

Tailgate aperture 864 (34.0)

Width between wheel arch boxes 925 (36.4)

Defender 110 High Capacity Pick-Up (HCPU) is cleared for slightly higher payload (about 38 kg) than standard version but its main strength is ability to accept far bulkier loads. HCPU left, standard 110 pickup, right.

Exterior dimensions – 110 High Capacity pick-up (HCPU)– mm (ins)

Dimensions differ from 110 standard pickup only in overall length, rear overhang, rear lashing rings, height.

Defender 110's max payloads of 1014-1229 kg (see Sec 9.3 for hard-tops) are higher than 90's and give best trade-off of power-weight ratio for load capacity. Hi Cap is optimised for lower-density bulky loads.

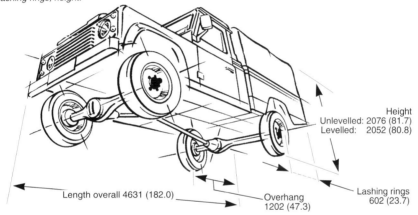

Height
Unlevelled: 2076 (81.7)
Levelled: 2052 (80.8)

Length overall 4631 (182.0)

Overhang
1202 (47.3)

Lashing rings
602 (23.7)

Loadspace – Defender 110 HCPU – mm (ins)

See also Section 8.1 – biggest slide-in box

Loadspace length 2010 (79.2) – NB
Longer than Defender 130 HCPU

Beam axles and coil springs front and rear. Disc brakes front and rear, servo assisted. Power assisted steering standard.

Interior width 1670 (65.75)

Width between
wheel arches
1090 (43.0)

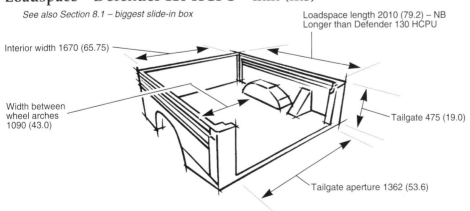

Tailgate 475 (19.0)

Tailgate aperture 1362 (53.6)

...continued

9.2. Technical data – Defender 110
Pick-ups and soft top – continued

Geometric limitations

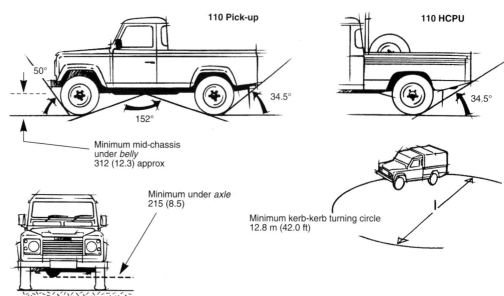

Hi Cap is designed for low-density loads, has full width tailgate, minimal intrusion of wheel arches and can accept 1-metre pallets.

110 Pick-up
50°
34.5°
152°

Minimum mid-chassis under *belly*
312 (12.3) approx

110 HCPU
34.5°

Minimum under *axle*
215 (8.5)

Minimum kerb-kerb turning circle
12.8 m (42.0 ft)

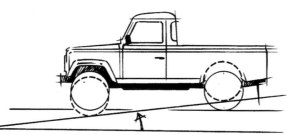

Normal wading depth 500 (19.7). See Sec 4.10 re wading plugs

Longitudinal articulation angle: 6.35° (see Glossary)
Wheel movement at GVW, bump stops 50% compressed:
Front: 166 (6.5) up, 125 (4.9) down, total 291 (11.5)
Rear: 186 (7.3) up, 148.(5.8) down, total 334 (13.1)

CHASSIS
As Defender 90 – Sec 9.1.

SUSPENSION
Type. Long travel coil spring, dual-rate front spring, single rate rear. Double-acting hydraulic dampers.
Front. Beam axle located by radius arms and Panhard rod.
Rear – unlevelled. (3050 kg GVW). Beam axle located by trailing links and central A-frame.
Rear – levelled. (2950 kg GVW). As above plus levelling unit and anti-roll bar.

STEERING
As Defender 90 – Sec 9.1
Wheels. 5.50F x 16 in steel. (Styled steel wheels from Defender 90 not suitable for 110 or 130).
Tyres. 7.50 x 16, see Sec 8.2.

BRAKES
As Defender 90 – see Sec 9.1.

ENGINES
Petrol V8, 3.5 ltr
Petrol 4 cyl, 2.5 ltr
Diesel Tdi, 2.5 ltr
Diesel N/A, 2.5 ltr
Engines as Defender 90, Sec 9.1

FUEL SYSTEMS
All fuel systems as Defender 90 according to engine type – see Sec 9.1. But see below regarding fuel tank capacity.

COOLING SYSTEMS
All cooling systems as Defender 90 according to engine type – see Sec 9.1.

ELECTRICAL SYSTEMS
All electrical systems as Defender 90 – see Sec 9.1 – except headlamps on County Station Wagon (Sec 9.3) which are halogen 60/55 w.

TRANSMISSION
Transmission system as Defender 90 – see Sec 9.1.

MAIN GEARBOX RATIOS,
mph per 1000 engine rpm

Defender 110 pick-up .. ... and HCPU (below)

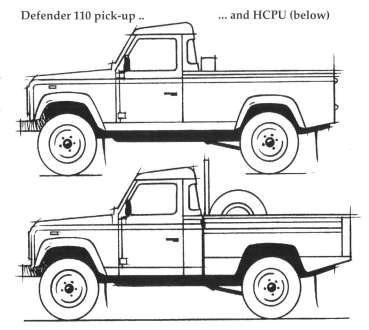

Ratio	mph/1000 rpm 7.50 x 16 tyres	
	High	Low
3.5 l V8 pet, 2.5 l 300Tdi diesel		
5th 0.770:1	22.81	9.69
4th 1.000:1	17.56	7.46
3rd 1.397:1	12.57	5.34
2nd 2.132:1	8.24	3.50
1st 3.692:1	4.76	2.02
Rev 3.536:1	4.97	2.11
2.5 l petrol and N/A 2.5 l diesel		
5th 0.831:1	18.56	8.98
4th 1.000:1	15.42	7.46
3rd 1.507:1	10.23	4.95
2nd 2.301:1	5.71	3.24
1st 3.585:1	4.30	2.08
Rev 3.816:1	4.04	1.96

FINAL DRIVE
Axle ratios. 3.540:1
Transfer ratios

	V8, Tdi	Other 4-cyl
High	1.411:1	1.607:1
Low	3.320:1	3.320

Front axle, rear axle. As Defender 90 – see Sec 9.1.

BODY
Material and finish. As Defender 90 – see Sec 9.1.

CAPACITIES (litres, Imp gal)
All capacities as Defender 90 – Sec 9.1. – except the following:
Full fuel tank
Standard rear tank 79.5 lit (17.5 gal)
Side tank option – station wagon only – 45.5 lit (10.0 gal)
Side tank option – others – 68.2 lit (15.0 gal)
Rear differential
2.26 lit (4.0 pint)

9.3. Technical data – Defender 110, 130
Full-length hard-tops, 130 HCPU and crew cab

Weights

Model	110 Hard Top				110 Station Wagon				110 County				130 Crew Cab, HCPU	
Engine	2.5P	3.5P	2.5D	2.5Tdi	2.5P	3.5P	2.5D	2.5Tdi	2.5P	3.5P	2.5D	2.5Tdi	3.5P	2.5Tdi
Gross vehicle weight kg	Unlevelled suspension: 3050												3500	3500
Kerb weight kg	1856	1856	1883	1901	1959	1960	1975	2006	1970	1971	1996	2015	2066	2133
Payload kg	1194	1194	1167	1149	1091	1090	1075	1044	1080	1079	1054	1035	1434	1367
Gross vehicle weight kg	Levelled suspension: 2950												N/A	N/A
Kerb weight kg	1880	1880	1907	1925	1983	1984	1999	2030	1986	1987	2011	2031	N/A	N/A
Payload kg	1070	1070	1043	1025	967	966	951	920	964	963	939	919	N/A	N/A
Seating capacity	2/3/11				9/10/11/12				9/10/11/12				5/6/12	

Defender 130, as a production line vehicle, comes with a 6-man crew cab and slightly shortened Hi Cap pick up back end.

Exterior dimensions – Defender 130 (see Sec 9.2 for 110) – mm (ins)

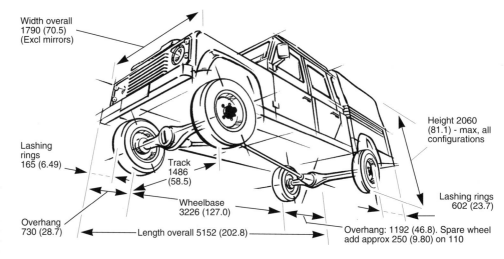

Width overall 1790 (70.5) (Excl mirrors)

Height 2060 (81.1) - max, all configurations

Lashing rings 165 (6.49)

Track 1486 (58.5)

Lashing rings 602 (23.7)

It is also available, through Land Rover Special Vehicles as a chassis-cab – 3-man 2-door or 6-man 4-door – with almost any body a customer may require. Engines are V8 or Tdi only. Wheelbase is 127 inches.

Overhang 730 (28.7)

Wheelbase 3226 (127.0)

Length overall 5152 (202.8)

Overhang: 1192 (46.8). Spare wheel add approx 250 (9.80) on 110

Loadspace – Defender 130 Crew Cab HCPU – mm (ins)

See also Section 8.1– biggest slide-in box

Interior width 1670 (65.75)

Loadspace length 1670 (65.75) – NB Less than 110 HCPU

Length of load space times interior width gives load area (in the pick up portion) of 1.82 sq metres. Modular body options shown next spread.

Width between wheel arches 1090 (43.0)

Tailgate 475 (19.0)

Tailgate aperture 1335 (52.5)

Geometric limitations Defender 130 (all 110s at Sec 9.2) – mm (ins)

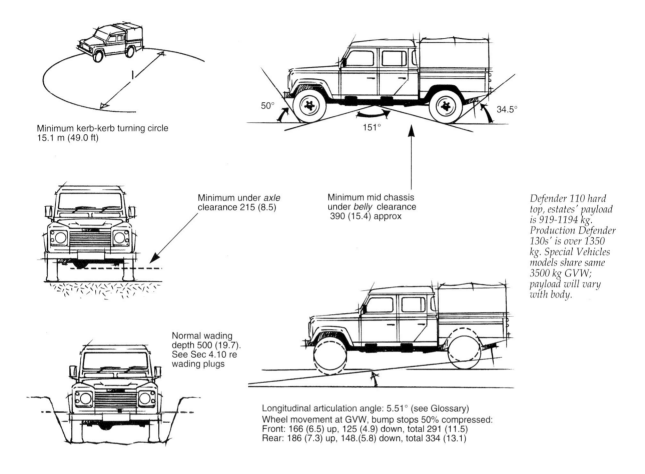

Minimum kerb-kerb turning circle
15.1 m (49.0 ft)

50°   151°   34.5°

Minimum under *axle* clearance 215 (8.5)

Minimum mid chassis under *belly* clearance 390 (15.4) approx

Normal wading depth 500 (19.7). See Sec 4.10 re wading plugs

Longitudinal articulation angle: 5.51° (see Glossary)
Wheel movement at GVW, bump stops 50% compressed:
Front: 166 (6.5) up, 125 (4.9) down, total 291 (11.5)
Rear: 186 (7.3) up, 148.(5.8) down, total 334 (13.1)

Defender 110 hard top, estates' payload is 919-1194 kg. Production Defender 130s' is over 1350 kg. Special Vehicles models share same 3500 kg GVW; payload will vary with body.

Interior dimensions – 110 hardtop (see also Sec 9.2) – mm (ins)

Dimensions similar to Defender 90 hardtop except for loadspace length

See also Section 8.1 – biggest slide-in box

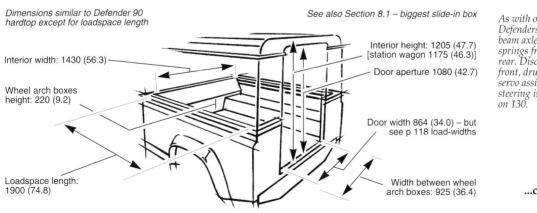

Interior width: 1430 (56.3)

Wheel arch boxes height: 220 (9.2)

Loadspace length: 1900 (74.8)

Interior height: 1205 (47.7) [station wagon 1175 (46.3)]

Door aperture 1080 (42.7)

Door width 864 (34.0) – but see p 118 load-widths

Width between wheel arch boxes: 925 (36.4)

As with other Defenders, 130 has beam axles and coil springs front and rear. Disc brakes front, drums rear, servo assisted. Power steering is standard on 130.

...continued

9.3. Technical data – Defender 110, 130
Full-length hard-tops, 130 HCPU and crew cab – continued

Land Rover Special Vehicles Quadtec modular body system for Defender 130

Quadtec 1 and 2 for 6-man crew-cab

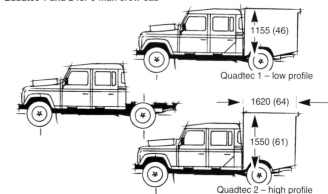

1155 (46)

Quadtec 1 – low profile

1620 (64)

1550 (61)

Quadtec 2 – high profile

Quadtec 3 and 4 for 3-man cab

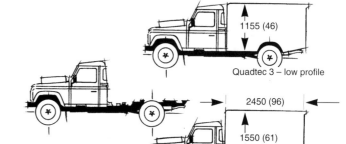

1155 (46)

Quadtec 3 – low profile

2450 (96)

1550 (61)

Quadtec 4 – high profile

NB Technical data for hard-top Defender 110 in this section is the same as for 110 pick-ups and soft top as shown in Section 9.2. Written data here mainly concerns Defender 130.

CHASSIS
As Defender 90 – see Sec 9.1.

SUSPENSION
Defender 110 – see Sec 9.2.
Defender 130 – as below:
Type. Long travel coil springs. Single rate front spring. Rear springs comprise two sets of single rate coil springs co-axially mounted each side, one within the other. Double-acting hydraulic dampers.
Front. Beam axle located by radius arms and Panhard rod.
Rear. Beam axle located by trailing links and central A-frame. Unlevelled, with anti-roll bar.

STEERING
Defender 110 – see Sec 9.2.
Defender 130:
As Defender 90 – Sec 9.1
Wheels. 6.50F x 16 in steel.
Tyres. 7.50 x 16, (130 tyres must be 12 ply rating).

BRAKES
As Defender 90 – see Sec 9.1.

ENGINES
Defender 110 – see Sec 9.2.
Defender 130:
Petrol V8, 3.5 ltr
Diesel Tdi, 2.5 ltr
Engine details as Defender 90 – see Sec 9.1.

FUEL SYSTEMS
Fuel systems as Defender 90 according to engine type – see Sec 9.1. But see below re fuel tank capacity on 130.

COOLING SYSTEMS
Cooling systems as Defender 90 according to engine type – see Sec 9.1.

CAPACITIES
As Defender 110 – see Sec 9.2.

ELECTRICAL SYSTEM
Defender 110 – see Sec 9.2.
Defender 130:
As Defender 90 – see Sec 9.1.

TRANSMISSION
As Defender 90 – see Sec 9.1.

GEAR , FINAL DRIVE RATIOS
Defender 110 – see Sec 9.2.
Defender 130:
Defender 130 is only fitted with petrol V8 or diesel Tdi engines. Overall and final drive ratios are as for Defender 110 with these engines – see Sec 9.2.

BODY
Material and finish. As Defender 90.
Defender 130: Special Vehicles bodies mainly aluminium.

Defender 110 hard top and estates (main picture) share same overall dimensions; 3-door hard top is all cargo aft of driver. 130s (lower shot) are, from left, Land Rover Special Vehicles Quadtec 4, tipper and Quadtec 1.

Defender 110 County and (below) 130 HCPU crew cab

9.4. Technical data – Discovery

Weights

Model	3 door			5 door		
Engine	3.9V8	2.5Tdi	2.0Mpi	3.9V8	2.5Tdi	2.0Mpi
Gross vehicle weight kg	All models 2720					
Kerb weight kg	1919	2008	1890	1986	2053	1925
Payload kg	801	712	830	734	667	795
Seating capacity	5 (7 if optional rear seats fitted)					

Notes:
1. Options affect kerb weight as shown:
adjust payload to keep within GVW.
　　Air conditioning　　　　　+42 kg
　　Auto transmission, V8, Tdi　-7 kg
　　Catalyst on V8 (Std on Mpi)　+7 kg

Discovery comes as a 3-door or a 5-door, each with the option of 3.9V8 or 2.0 l petrol or 2.5 l diesel engines. Auto transmission available with V8 and diesel.

Exterior dimensions mm (ins)

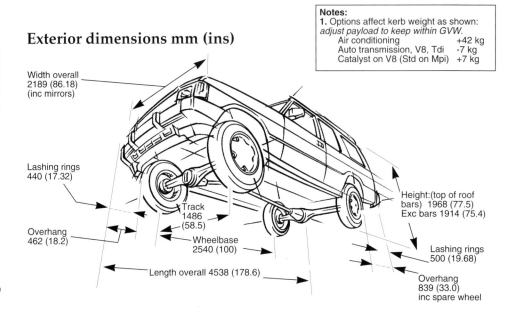

Width overall
2189 (86.18)
(inc mirrors)

Lashing rings
440 (17.32)

Overhang
462 (18.2)

Track
1486
(58.5)

Wheelbase
2540 (100)

Length overall 4538 (178.6)

Height:(top of roof bars) 1968 (77.5)
Exc bars 1914 (75.4)

Lashing rings
500 (19.68)

Overhang
839 (33.0)
inc spare wheel

Wheelbase is 100 inches.

Interior dimensions – mm (ins)

See also Section 8.1– biggest slide-in box

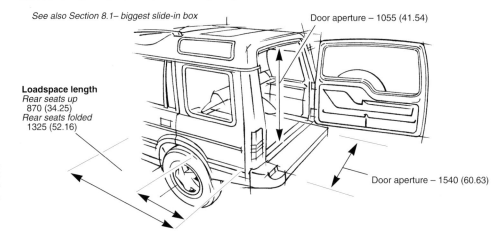

Loadspace length
Rear seats up
870 (34.25)
Rear seats folded
1325 (52.16)

Door aperture – 1055 (41.54)

Door aperture – 1540 (60.63)

Luggage capacity is 1.29 cu m (45.8 cu ft) seats up, 1.97 cu m (69.8 cu ft) seats down.

Geometric limitations

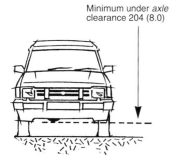

Minimum under *axle* clearance 204 (8.0)

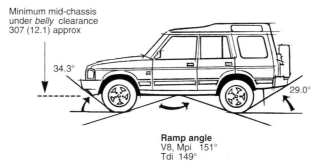

Minimum mid-chassis under *belly* clearance 307 (12.1) approx

34.3°

29.0°

Ramp angle
V8, Mpi 151°
Tdi 149°

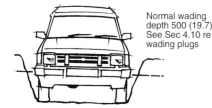

Normal wading depth 500 (19.7). See Sec 4.10 re wading plugs

Payload varies between 667 and 830 kg according to body type and engine.

Longitudinal articulation angle: 6.98° (see Glossary)
Wheel movement at GVW, bump stops 50% compressed:
Front: 166 (6.5) up, 125 (4.9) down, total 291 (11.5)
Rear: 186 (7.3) up, 148.(5.8) down, total 334 (13.1)

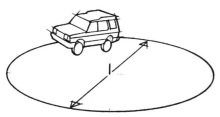

Minimum kerb-kerb turning circle
11.9 m (39.0 ft)

CHASSIS

Type. Box section, ladder construction. 2mm (14 swg) steel. 'Crush-can' energy absorbers at front bumpers.
Paint treatment. Zinc phosphate, cathodic electro coat followed by waxing in the box sections.

SUSPENSION

Type. Long travel coil spring, single rate front, dual rate rear. Double acting hydraulic dampers.
Front. Beam axle located by radius arms and Panhard rod.
Rear. Beam axle located by trailing links and central A-frame.

Levelling and control. Front and rear anti-roll bars.

STEERING

Type. Power assisted, worm and roller (Adwest Varamatic). Tilt-adjustable steering column.
Ratio, geometry.
Straight ahead – 19.3:1
On lock – 17.2:1
Camber angle (kerb wt) 0°
Castor angle (kerb) 3°±0.5°
Swivel pin inclination 7°±0.5°
Ground offset 63.0 mm
Front wheel toe-out 0.0-2.0 mm
Turns, lock to lock. 3.375.
Wheels.
7.00J x 16 in styled steel (standard, 3 door)
Alloy wheels with asymmetric

safety-hump feature to aid tyre retention at blow-out (suitable for Land Rover Parts design snowchains.):
7.00J x 16 in 5-spoke alloy (optional 3 door, standard 5 door; special style with 'Freestyle Choice' option)..
Tyres. See Section 8.2; tubeless tyres on asymmetric-hump safety alloy wheels.

BRAKES

Type. Vacuum servo-assisted. IH split dual circuit hydraulic, solid disc brakes front and rear. (Ventilated front discs, certain markets.) Asbestos-free pads on all vehicles. Optional anti-lock facility (ABS) provides electronic 4-channel anti-lock braking system usable on- and off-road.
Handbrake (parking brake). Single drum operating on transfer box rear output shaft. Handbrake not for use while vehicle in motion.

Beam axles and coil springs front and rear. Disc brakes front and rear, servo assisted; ABS optional. Power steering standard.

...continued

9.4. Technical data – Discovery – contd

ENGINE – V8i 3.9 litre, petrol
Type. V8-cylinder, aluminium construction with 5-bearing crankshaft, self-adjusting hydraulic tappets. Electronic engine management with a fuel injector for each cylinder. Rigidly-mounted auxiliaries with serpentine multi-ribbed belt and dynamic spring tensioner.
Bore. 94.0 mm (3.70 in)
Stroke. 71.1 mm (2.80 in)
Displacement. 3947 cc (241 in^3)
Low compression engine
Compression ratio. 8.13:1
Max power. 170.3 bhp @ 4750 rpm (127 kw) 80/1269/EEC.
Max torque. 220 lbf ft @ 2500 rpm (298 Nm).
High compression engine
Compression ratio. 9.35:1
Max power. 185.1 bhp @ 4750 rpm (138 kw) 80/1269/EEC.
Max torque. 235 lbf ft @ 2600 rpm (319 Nm).
High compression catalyst engine
Compression ratio. 9.35:1
Max power. 182 bhp @ 4750 rpm (135.5 kw) 80/1269/EEC.
Max torque. 230 lbf ft @ 3100 rpm (313 Nm).

ENGINE – Tdi 2.5 litre, diesel
Type. 300 Tdi, 4 cylinder in-line, intercooled and turbo-charged high speed direct injection diesel. Cast iron with aluminium cylinder head. Rigidly-mounted auxiliaries with serpentine multi-ribbed belt and dynamic spring tensioner.
Bore. 90.47 mm (3.56 in)
Stroke. 97.00 mm (3.82 in)
Displacement. 2495 cc (152 in^3)
Compression ratio. 19.5:1
Max power. 111.3 bhp @ 4000 rpm (83 kw) 80/1269/EEC .
Max torque. 195 lbf ft @ 1800 rpm (265 Nm).
Turbo-charger model. Garrett T25 BCI 15
Turbo operating pressure. 0.8-1.01 bar (0.81-1.05 kgf/cm^2, 11.6-14.9 lbf/in^2) @ 2500 rpm.

ENGINE – Mpi 2.0 litre, petrol
Type. 2.0 Mpi, 4 cylinder in-line. Iron block, aluminium head, 16 valves with self-adjusting hydraulic tappets. Twin overhead camshafts, belt driven. Distributor-less, breaker-less quad-coil electronic engine management system. Catalyst exhaust standard. Poly-V belt accessory drive.
Bore. 84.5 mm (3.33 in)
Stroke. 89.0 mm (3.50 in)
Displacement. 1994 cc (121 in^3)
Compression ratio. 10.0:1
Max power. 134 bhp @ 6000 rpm (100 kw) 80/1269/EEC.
Max torque. 140 lbf ft @ 3600 rpm (190 Nm).

FUEL SYSTEM – PETROL V8
Fuel injection type. Lucas electronic fuel injection with 14CUX-ECU.
Fuel pump. Electrical, submerged in fuel tank.
Filters. In line.
Fuel tank construction. Blow moulded plastic – high density polyurethane.
Fuel. 97 RON leaded, 95 RON unleaded.

FUEL SYSTEM – DIESEL Tdi
Injector pump. Bosch KBEL 98 PVI 870398 (2 spring).
Fuel pump. Engine driven mechanical pump.
Fuel tank construction. Blow moulded plastic – high density polyurethane.
Filters. In line filter.
Fuel. Derv class A1 or A2.

FUEL SYSTEM – PETROL Mpi
As V8 system except:
Fuel injection type. Multi-point electronic fuel injection with MEMS 1.6 fuelling and ignition ECU.
Fuel. 95 RON unleaded.

COOLING SYSTEM
Type. Pressurised liquid with pump and mechanical fan.

Radiator
V8 engine – copper and brass full face area. No oil cooler.
Tdi engine – copper and brass integral unit with oil cooler and aluminium intercooler.
Mpi engine – copper and brass full face area type. No oil cooler.
Gearbox oil cooler
V8 engine – single air blast.
Tdi and Mpi engine – none.
Thermostat. 88°C.
Fan
V8 – 432 mm (17 in).
Tdi – 406 mm (16 in). Temperature sensitive viscous drive.
Mpi – single electrically driven 290 mm (11.4 in) fan; twin units when air conditioning fitted.

ELECTRICAL SYSTEM
Battery (see also Glossary)
Petrol – 12v, 210/85/90.
Diesel – 12v, 380/120/90.
Alternator
All models – 100 amp.
Headlamps. 60/55 watt halogen bulbs.

TRANSMISSION
Manual transmission
Clutch
Hydraulic push, reduced-load clutch operation. Asbestos-free lining. Clutch plate diam:
V8 engine – 267 mm (10.5 in)
Tdi engine – 235 mm (9.25 in)
Mpi engine – 242 mm (9.35 in)

Main gearbox. R380 manual gearbox incorporating five forward speeds and one reverse. Synchromesh on all gears – triple cone 1st, 2nd and 3rd; large single cone on 4th and 5th. Synchronised constant-mesh reverse gear train. Integral oil pump with remote cooler.
Automatic transmission
Automatic gearbox. Available on V8 and Tdi engines only. ZF type 4HP22 with four forward and one reverse speed. Incorporates automatic torque converter lock-up on 4th.
Manual and auto transmission
Transfer gearbox. LT230T 2-speed reduction on main

gearbox output. Drive to front and rear propeller shafts permanently engaged via a third differential which may be locked mechanically by movement of the transfer lever to the left.

MAIN GEARBOX RATIOS, mph per 1000 engine rpm

	Ratio	mph/1000 rpm	
		High	Low
V8i manual			
5th	0.730:1	26.60	9.75
4th	1.000:1	19.50	7.12
3rd	1.397:1	14.00	5.10
2nd	2.132:1	9.07	3.34
1st	3.321:1	5.84	2.14
Rev	3.429:1	5.64	2.08
300 Tdi manual			
5th	0.770:1	25.30	9.24
4th	1.000:1	19.50	7.12
3rd	1.397:1	14.00	5.10
2nd	2.132:1	9.07	3.34
1st	3.692:1	5.24	1.93
Rev	3.429:1	5.64	2.08
Mpi manual			
5th	0.791:1	21.20	7.95
4th	1.000:1	16.80	6.30
3rd	1.396:1	12.00	4.50
2nd	2.131:1	7.90	2.96
1st	3.321:1	5.10	1.91
Rev	3.429:1	4.90	1.84
V8i and 300 Tdi automatic			
4th	0.728:1	26.80	9.79
3rd	1.000:1	19.50	7.14
2nd	1.480:1	13.20	4.82
1st	2.480:1	7.90	2.87
Rev	2.086:1	9.23	3.40

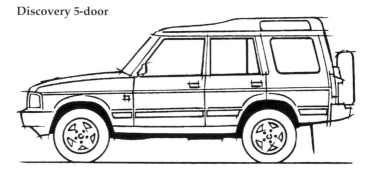

Discovery 5-door

FINAL DRIVE RATIOS
Axle ratios. 3.540:1
Transfer ratios

	All models
High	1.214:1
Low	3.308:1

Front axle. Spiral bevel crown wheel and pinion, enclosed constant velocity joints.
Rear axle. Spiral bevel crown wheel and pinion with fully floating shafts.

BODY
Construction. Steel monocoque frame with aluminium alloy body panels (roof panel steel). Side intrusion beams in front doors.
Aluminium panels. Front wings, bonnet, body sides, rear quarters, door outer panels.
Plating/painting. Zinc phosphate. Cathodic electrocoat, polyester surfacer. Colour coated either clear over metallic or alkyd solid colours.

CAPACITIES (litres, Imp gal)
Full fuel tank
88.6 lit (19.5 gal)
Usable fuel
81.7 lit (18.0 gal)
Low fuel warning
12 lit approx
Cooling system
V8 – 11.3 lit
Diesel Tdi – 11.5 lit
Mpi – 10 lit
Engine oil, including filter
V8 – 5.66 lit
Diesel Tdi – 6.75 lit
Mpi – 4.5-5.5 lit (min-max)
Main gearbox (manual)
V8 – 3.17 lit
Diesel Tdi and Mpi – 2.67 lit
Main gearbox (auto)
9.8 lit
Transfer gearbox
2.8 lit
Front differential
1.7 lit
Rear differential
1.7 lit
Swivel pin housing
0.36 lit
Power steering
2.9 lit
Windscreen washer reservoir
7.4 lit

9.5. Technical data – Range Rover

Weights

Model	4 door 100 inch		4 door LSE 108 inch
Engine	3.9 V8	2.5Tdi	4.2 V8 Auto
Gross vehicle weight kg	All 100 inch models: 2510		2620
Kerb weight kg	2070	2110	2185
	440	400	435
Seating capacity	All models 4/5 seats		
To kerb wt add 42 kg for air conditioning. Reduce payload to keep within GVW.			

Range Rover comes as a 4-door; also available in long wheelbase format. The long (108 inch) wheelbase (known as Vogue LSE or County LWB – US Spec) has a 4.2 l engine, auto transmission and air suspension as standard.

Exterior dimensions – mm (ins)

External dimensions the same for LSE except :
Wheelbase: 2743 (108)
Overall length: 4676 (184.1)

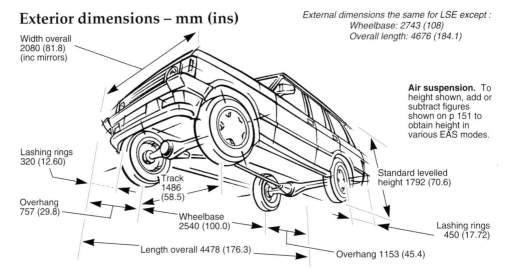

Width overall 2080 (81.8) (inc mirrors)

Air suspension. To height shown, add or subtract figures shown on p 151 to obtain height in various EAS modes.

Lashing rings 320 (12.60)

Track 1486 (58.5)

Standard levelled height 1792 (70.6)

Overhang 757 (29.8)

Wheelbase 2540 (100.0)

Lashing rings 450 (17.72)

Length overall 4478 (176.3)

Overhang 1153 (45.4)

The Vogue and Vogue SE Range Rover has a 100 inch wheelbase. It is available with a 3.9 l petrol engine or a 2.5 l Tdi diesel. Both versions available with auto transmission and air suspension.

Interior dimensions – mm (ins)

See also Section 8.1- biggest slide-in box

Loadspace length
Rear seats up
870 (34.25)
Rear seats folded
100 inch – 1445 (56.9)
LSE – 1545 (60.8)

Tailgate aperture height – 870 (34.2)

Tailgate width – 1313 (51.7))

Luggage capacity is 1.02 cu m (36.2 cu ft) seats up; with seats down it is 2.00 cu m (70.8 cu ft) on the 100 inch, 2.16 cu m (76.3 cu ft) on the 108 inch.

Geometric limitations

Minimum under *axle* 204 (8.0)

108 in wheelbase (LSE)

Minimum mid-chassis under *belly*, approx:
Air Standard 305 (12.0))
Air High profile 345 (13.6)

EAS posn (see Glossary)	Approach angle	Ramp angle	Departure angle
Standard	35°	153°	30°
High profile	37°	150°	32°
Extended	39°	147°	33°

100 in wheelbase

Minimum under *belly*:
Air suspension as LSE
Coils as 'Standard' above

Payload varies between 400 and 440 kg according to body style and engine.

EAS posn (Glossary)	Approach angle	Ramp angle	Departure angle
Standard	35°	151° (Tdi 150°)	30°
High profile	37°	147°	32°
Extended	39°	145°	33°

Normal wading depth
500 (19.7)
With EAS: 540 (21.3)
See Sec 4.10 re wading plugs.

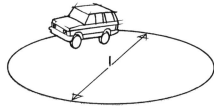

Longitudinal articulation angle (see Glossary, Section 10.1)
100 inch wheelbase: 6.98°
108 inch wheelbase: 6.47°

Wheel movement at GVW, bump stops 50% compressed:
Front: 166 (6.5) up, 125 (4.9) down, total 291 (11.5)
Rear: 186 (7.3) up, 148.(5.8) down, total 334 (13.1)

Minimum kerb-kerb turning circle
100 in wheelbase 11.9 m (39.0 ft)
108 in wheelbase (LSE) 12.9 m (41.8 ft)

CHASSIS

Type. Box section, ladder construction. 2mm (14 swg) steel. 'Crush-can' energy absorbers at front bumpers.

Paint treatment. Zinc phosphate, cathodic electro coat followed by waxing in the box sections.

SUSPENSION

Type. Long travel single rate coil springs (standard), or (optional) electronically controlled, variable-height air suspension. Double acting hydraulic dampers.

Front. Beam axle located by radius arms and Panhard rod.
Rear. Beam axle located by trailing links and central A-frame.

Levelling and control
Standard suspension
Self-energising Boge ride-levelling unit fitted to rear axle. Front and rear anti-roll bars standard on Vogue.

Air suspension (LSE, SE , option on Vogue). See Glossary - 'EAS'. Variable rate air springs. System activated by electric air compressor with pressure reservoir and modulated by an electronic control unit (ECU). Four selectable ride heights – standard, low, high and access. Auto selection of low above 50 mph (unless manually inhibited), automatic reversion to normal setting at given speeds. Automatic self levelling

Beam axles front and rear with coil springs or air suspension, both self-levelled. Disc brakes front and rear, with ABS and ETC option. Power steering standard.

...continued

9.5. Technical data – Range Rover – contd

front and rear. Ride height sensors fitted to radius arms. Front and rear anti-roll bars.

STEERING
Type. Power assisted, worm and roller (Adwest Varamatic).
Ratio.
Straight ahead – 19.3:1
On lock – 14.3:1
Camber angle (kerb wt) 0°
Castor angle (kerb) 3°±0.5°
Swivel pin inclination 7°±0.5°
Ground offset 63.0 mm
Front wheel toe-out 0.0-2.0 mm.
Turns, lock to lock. 3.375.
Wheels.
6.00JKJ x 16 in styled steel (standard model)
7.00J x 16 in alloy (Vogue, and SE).
Tyres. See Section 8.2; tubeless tyres on alloy wheels.

BRAKES
Type. Vacuum servo-assisted. IH split dual circuit hydraulic brakes, ventilated discs front, plain discs rear; asbestos-free pads.
Anti-lock brakes (ABS). Electrically driven hydraulic pump and reservoir provide power for electronic 4-channel anti-lock braking system usable on and off-road. ABS standard on Vogue SE and LSE models, optional on others.
Handbrake (parking brake). Single drum operating on transfer box rear output shaft. Handbrake not for use while vehicle in motion.

ENGINE – V8 4.2 litre
Type. V8-cylinder, aluminium construction with 5-bearing crankshaft, self-adjusting hydraulic tappets and fuel injection. Exhaust catalyst standard.
Bore. 93.98 mm (3.70 in)
Stroke. 77 mm (3.03 in)
Displacement. 4278 cc (261 in^3)
Compression ratio. 8.94:1
Max power. 200 bhp @ 4750

rpm (149 kw) 80/1269/EEC.
Max torque. 250 lbf ft @ 3250 rpm (340 Nm).

ENGINE – V8 3.9 litre
Type. V8-cylinder, aluminium construction with 5-bearing crankshaft, self-adjusting hydraulic tappets and fuel injection. Exhaust catalyst standard.
Bore. 94.0 mm (3.70 in)
Stroke. 71.1 mm (2.80 in)
Displacement. 3947 cc (241 in^3)
Compression ratio. 9.35:1
Max power. 181.6 bhp @ 4750 rpm (135.5 kw) 80/1269/EEC.
Max torque. 231.5 lbf ft @ 2600 rpm (314 Nm).

ENGINE – DIESEL Tdi
As Discovery – Sec 9.4.

FUEL SYSTEM – PETROL
As Discovery – Sec 9.4.

FUEL SYSTEM – DIESEL Tdi
As Discovery – Sec 9.4.

COOLING SYSTEM
Type. Pressurised liquid with pump and mechanical fan.
Radiator, oil coolers
V8 auto – copper and brass full face area type with twin oil coolers and single air blast gearbox oil cooler.
V8 manual – copper and brass full face area type with single oil cooler and single air blast gearbox oil cooler.
Tdi engine – copper and brass integral unit with oil cooler and aluminium intercooler.
Thermostat. 88°C.
Fan
V8 – 432 mm (17 in).
Tdi – 406 mm (16 in).
Temperature sensitive viscous drive.

ELECTRICAL SYSTEM
Battery (see also Glossary)
All models – 12v, 380/120/90.
Alternator
All models – 100 amp.

Headlamps. 60/55 watt halogen bulbs.

TRANSMISSION
Manual transmission
Clutch
Hydraulic push, reduced-load clutch operation. Asbestos-free lining. Clutch plate diam:
V8 engine – 267 mm (10.5 in)
Tdi engines – 235 mm (9.25 in)
Main gearbox. R380 manual gearbox incorporating five forward speeds and one reverse. Synchromesh on all gears – triple cone 1st, 2nd and 3rd; large single cone on 4th and 5th. Synchronised constant-mesh reverse gear train. Integral oil pump with remote cooler.
Automatic transmission
Automatic gearbox. Available on V8 engines only. ZF type 4HP22 with four forward and one reverse speed. Incorporates automatic torque converter lock-up on 4th.
Manual and auto transmission
Transfer gearbox. Borg Warner type 13-61-000-003 2-speed reduction on main gearbox output. Front and rear drive permanently engaged via a third differential – locked automatically by a viscous coupling unit (VCU) when front/rear prop shaft speed differences are sensed.
Electronic traction control – ETC
ETC is available on vehicles fitted with ABS. A spinning rear wheel is pulse braked to restore overall traction.

Differences between conventional coil springs and air suspension are shown above – viewed beneath rear axle looking forward. Note anti-roll bars in both cases, secured transversely between chassis members, curving forward to pick up beneath axle.

Range Rover 100 inch wheelbase 4-door (108 inch above)

MAIN GEARBOX RATIOS, mph per 1000 engine rpm

	Ratio	mph/1000 rpm	
		High	Low
V8 and Tdi automatic			
4th	0.728:1	26.91	10.00
3rd	1.000:1	19.59	7.28
2nd	1.480:1	13.24	4.92
1st	2.480:1	7.90	2.94
Rev	2.086:1	9.51	3.54
Tdi manual			
5th	0.770:1	25.45	9.46
4th	1.000:1	19.59	7.28
3rd	1.397:1	14.03	5.21
2nd	2.132:1	9.19	3.41
1st	3.692:1	5.31	1.97
Rev	3.429:1	5.71	2.12
3.9 l V8 manual			
5th	0.731:1	26.79	9.96
4th	1.000:1	19.59	7.28
3rd	1.397:1	14.03	5.21
2nd	2.132:1	9.19	3.41
1st	3.321:1	5.90	2.19
Rev	3.429:1	5.71	2.12

FINAL DRIVE
Axle ratios. 3.540:1
Transfer ratios
High   1.205:1
Low   3.245:1
Axles. As Discovery – Sec 9.4.

BODY
Construction. Steel monocoque, bonnet, tailgate, and rear lower quarter panels. **Aluminium panels.** Both front wings, roof, body sides, decker and upper rear quarters. All door outer panels. Side intrusion beams in doors.
Plating/painting. Zinc phosphate. Cathodic electrocoat, polyester surfacer. Colour coated either clear over metallic or alkyd for solid colours.

CAPACITIES (litres, Imp gal)
As Discovery – Sec 9.4 – except:
Engine oil, including filter
V8 – 6.66 lit
Diesel Tdi – 6.85 lit
Transfer gearbox
1.7 lit

The Land Rover Experience

9.6. Technical data – New Range Rover

Weights

Model	**4 door**				
Engine	4.0 V8	4.0 V8 Auto	4.6 V8	4.6 V8 Auto	MIX 2.5 diesel
Gross vehicle weight kg	2780				
Kerb weight	2252	2262	2252	2262	2259
Payload	603	593	603	593	596
Seating capacity	All models 4/5 seats				

New Range Rover comes as a 4-door with air suspension as standard.

Exterior dimensions – mm (ins)

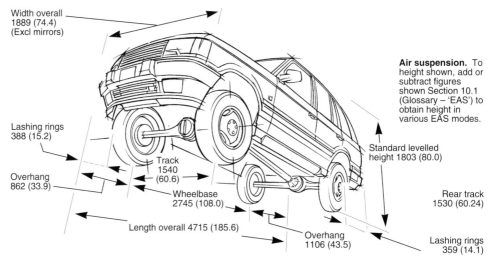

Width overall
1889 (74.4)
(Excl mirrors)

Air suspension. To height shown, add or subtract figures shown Section 10.1 (Glossary – 'EAS') to obtain height in various EAS modes.

Lashing rings
388 (15.2)

Standard levelled
height 1803 (80.0)

Track
1540
(60.6)

Overhang
862 (33.9)

Wheelbase
2745 (108.0)

Rear track
1530 (60.24)

Length overall 4715 (185.6)

Overhang
1106 (43.5)

Lashing rings
359 (14.1)

The New Range Rover has a 108 inch wheelbase. It is available with a 4.0 l or 4.6 l V8 petrol engine or a 2.5 l 6 cylinder diesel. The petrol versions are available with auto transmission.

Interior dimensions – mm (ins)

See also Section 8.1- biggest slide-in box

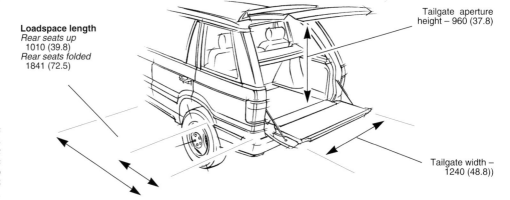

Loadspace length
Rear seats up
1010 (39.8)
Rear seats folded
1841 (72.5)

Tailgate aperture
height – 960 (37.8)

Tailgate width –
1240 (48.8))

Luggage capacity is 522 litres seats, parcel shelf in use; with seats down it is 920 litres stacked to window line, 1643 litres stacked to roof .

Geometric limitations

Minimum under
axle 214(8.43)

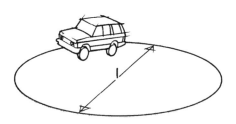

Normal wading depth 500 (19.7)

Minimum mid-chassis
under *belly*, approx:
Air Standard 302 (11.9))
Air High profile 342 (13.4)

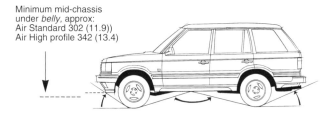

Ride height (see Glossary 'EAS')	Approach angle (to spoiler/bumper)	Ramp angle (235/70 or 255/65 tyres)	Departure angle to exhaust (pet/diesel)
Crawl/access	24 / 28°	160°	19-20°
Low	28 / 32°	156°	21-22°
Standard	30 / 34°	154°	23-24°
High	34 / 37°	151°	25-26°

Longitudinal articulation angle: 6.51° (see Glossary)
Wheel movement at GVW, bump stops 50% compressed:
Front: 159 (6.3) up, 135 (5.3) down, total 294 (11.6)
Rear: 178 (7.0) up, 153.(6.0) down, total 331 (13.01)

Minimum kerb-kerb turning circle
235/70 x 16 tyres: 11.85 m (38.9 ft)
255/65 x 16 tyres: 11.89 m (39.0 ft)

CHASSIS

Type. Box section, ladder construction. 2mm – 4mm steel; refined crash-collapse characteristics. Provision for detachable, stowable towing swan-neck using wheel nut wrench. Towing recovery eyes (one each front/rear). Lashing provision (2 each front/rear). 'Crush-can' energy absorbers at front bumpers.

Paint treatment. Zinc phosphate, cathodic electro coat followed by waxing in the box sections.

SUSPENSION

Type. Electronically controlled, variable-height air suspension – EAS (electronic air suspension). (See Section 10.1) Double acting hydraulic dampers.

Front. Beam axle located by cranked radius arms and Panhard rod; anti-roll bar.
Rear. Beam axle located by composite trailing link and Panhard rod.

Levelling and control
Automatic ride-levelling front and rear; periodic re-levelling when parked. Automatic control of normal and high speed ride height. Manual control of arduous off-road/wading, low profile and access height. Recovery from chassis-grounding off-road by automatic selection of 'extended' ride height position when wheel off-loading sensed. 'Crawl' (on the bump-stops) facility at access height up to 20 mph (alert warning at 10 mph). Fascia-mounted control switch,

Composite material trailing links for rear axle, clamped under axle and lateral-axis bolted to chassis, inhibit axle twisting so also function as an anti-roll bar. Note Panhard rod (upper left) for lateral location of axle (see Glossary).

...continued

9.6. Technical data – New Range Rover – contd

display and manual override; interface with message centre to provide suspension information. See Glossary under EAS, Section 10.1 for more detail. Ride height sensors fitted to radius arms.

STEERING

Type. Linear power assisted, recirculating ball with positive on-centre feel, hydraulic and mechanical lock stops. (PAS pump: ZF7691 petrol versions, ZF7681 diesel). Adjustable steering column (78 mm axial and 5-position tilt, 28° total); on-steering wheel options include cruise and radio controls, airbag.

Ratio, geometry.
Ratio, constant – 15.2:1
Camber angle (kerb wt) 0°
Castor angle (kerb) 4°±0.5°
Swivel pin inclination 8°±0.5°
Ground offset 17.0 mm
Front wheel toe-out 0.60-1.80 mm

Turns, lock to lock. 3.16.

Wide-span swivel pins (kingpins) and new design put front hub further into wheel, thus reducing ground offset for improved steering.

Wheels and tyres.

Alloy wheels with asymmetric safety-hump feature to aid tyre retention at blow-out. Suitable for Land Rover Parts design snowchains.
7.00J x 16 in 3-spoke, (standard), or 7.00J x 16 in 5-spoke New and Prestige style. Stainless steel capped wheelnuts. Steel spare wheel. Tubeless tyres, H-rated, 235/70 x 16 or 255/65 x 16 – see Section 8.2.

BRAKES

Type. Power-assisted, hydraulically activated disc brakes with permanently engaged dual circuit anti-lock facility (ABS). Electrically driven hydraulic pump and reservoir provide power for electronic 4-channel anti-lock braking system usable on and off-road. Optional traction control (ETC) controls wheel-spin on rear wheels (see Transmission in next spread) using ABS system. Ventilated discs front, solid discs rear.

Handbrake (parking brake). Single drum operating on transfer box rear output shaft. Handbrake not for use while vehicle in motion.

ENGINE – V8 4.0 litre, petrol

Type. V8-cylinder, aluminium construction with 5-bearing crankshaft, self-adjusting hydraulic tappets. Crankshaft-nose mounted oil pump, high-output water pump. Rigidly-mounted auxiliaries with serpentine multi-ribbed belt and dynamic spring tensioner. Fully programmed closed-loop Sagem/Lucas GEMS engine management system with double-ended coils and knock sensing. Champion RN11YCC spark plugs with 30000 mile life. Exhaust catalyst standard.
Bore. 94.0 mm (3.70 in)

Stroke. 71 mm (2.79 in)
Displacement. 3950 cc (241 cu in)
Compression ratio. 9.34:1. Low compression 8.2:1 available.
Max power. 186 bhp @ 4750 rpm (139 kw) EEC1256.
Max torque. 236 lbf ft @ 3000 rpm (320 Nm).
Rev limiter. Fuel cut-off point 5500 rpm; re-introduced 5400.

ENGINE – V8 4.6 litre, petrol

Type. Details 4.0 litre except:
Bore. 94.0 mm (3.70 in)
Stroke. 82 mm (3.23 in)
Displacement. 4554 cc (278 cu in)
Compression ratio. 9.34:1. Low compression 8.4:1 available.
Max power. 221 bhp @ 4750 rpm (164.6 kw) EEC1256.
Max torque. 278 lbf ft @ 3000 rpm (376.6 Nm).

ENGINE – BMW 2.5 litre diesel

Type. 6 cylinder in-line, intercooled and turbo-charged high speed indirect injection diesel with hydraulic self-adjusting tappets. Cast iron block with aluminium cylinder head.
Bore. 80.00 mm (3.12 in)
Stroke. 82.8 mm (3.26 in)
Displacement. 2497 cc (152 cu in)
Compression ratio. 22.0:1
Max power. 134 bhp @ 4400 rpm (100 kw) EEC1256.
Max torque. 199 lbf ft @ 2300 rpm (270 Nm).
Turbo-charger model. Mitsubishi TD04-11G4.
Maximum operating pressure. 1.2 bar (1.26 kgf/cm^2, 18.0 lbf/in^2).

FUEL SYSTEM – PETROL V8

Fuel injection type. Lucas electronic fuel injection with GEMS-ECU.
Fuel pump. Electrical, submerged in fuel tank.
Filters. In line.
Fuel tank construction. Blow moulded plastic – high density polyurethane.
Fuel. 95 RON unleaded, 91 RON unleaded on low-

compression models.
Inertia switch. Collision or sudden impact cuts off fuel supply. May be re-set via access flap in right hand footwell.

FUEL SYSTEM – DIESEL
Injection system. Bosch fully electronic control DDE 2.5.
Fuel pump. Electrical pump submerged in fuel tank, engine driven injection pump.
Fuel tank construction. Blow moulded plastic – high density polyurethane.
Filters. In line filter.
Fuel. Derv class A1 or A2. (Or fuel not exceeding 1% sulphur content.)
Inertia switch. Collision or sudden impact cuts off fuel supply. May be re-set via access flap in right hand footwell.

COOLING SYSTEM
Type. Pressurised liquid with pump and mechanical fan.
Radiator. Aluminium radiator with remote plastic header tank and bottom-hose thermostat for improved heater performance and progressive warm-up. Separate engine oil cooler. Diesel post-turbo-charger intercooler matrix mounted ahead of radiator. Diesel has 'two-pass' coolant radiator.
Gearbox oil cooler (manual and auto)
V8 engine – mounted in front of radiator.
Diesel – mounted in front of radiator.
Thermostat. 82°C.
Fan
V8 – 425 mm (16.7 in) sickle-bladed ring-fan.
Diesel – 432 mm (17 in). Temperature sensitive viscous drive.

ELECTRICAL SYSTEM
Message centre and warning system. Comprehensive driver information, system functions, diagnostic and electrical system monitoring (eg any bulb or fuse failure) are shown and graded

New Range Rover

on the instrument cluster alpha-numeric message centre and also on the warning light panel. Under-bonnet fusebox housing fuses, fusible links, control relays. Seat base fuse box with BCM (Body Control Module - EAS, ABS, Message Centre.)

Battery (see also Glossary)
V8 engine – 12 v, 380/120/90.
Diesel – 12 v, 490/170/90.
Alternator
4.0 l V8 engine – 100 amp.
4.6 l V8 engine – 120 amp.
Diesel engine – 95 amp.
Headlamps. 60/55 watt halogen bulbs.

9.6. Technical data – New Range Rover – contd

TRANSMISSION

Manual transmission

Clutch

V8 engine – AP, 267 mm (10.51 in) diam.
Diesel engine – Valeo, 242 mm (9.53 in) diam.
Hydraulic pull, reduced-load clutch operation. Asbestos-free lining.

Main gearbox. R380 manual gearbox incorporating five forward speeds and one reverse. Synchromesh on all gears – triple cone 1st, 2nd and 3rd; large single cone on 4th and 5th. Synchronised constant-mesh reverse gear train. Integral oil pump with remote cooler.

Automatic transmission

Automatic gearbox. Available on V8 engines only. ZF type

H-gate shift controls on automatic version of New Range Rover enable selection of low range gears to be achieved by moving selector lever to plane farthest from driver. See Section 2.3.

4HP24 fitted to 4.6 litre variants, otherwise ZF 4HP22. Four forward and one reverse speed. Incorporates automatic torque converter lock-up on 4th. H-gate selector – driver side of H is high range, passenger side is low range. Plus forward/aft mode selections in each plane: high range – Normal and Sports; low range – Normal and Manual. (Manual gives select-and-hold facility on gear selected.)

Manual and auto transmission

Transfer gearbox. Borg Warner chain-drive 2-speed reduction on main gearbox output with high, low and neutral positions electrically switched and selected. Transfer box range on manual vehicles controlled by in/out (lo/hi) button on fascia;

auto vehicle range controlled via 'H-gate'. (NB Transfer box neutral can only be selected – eg for towing – by adding a 5 amp fuse to position 11 in the seat-base fuse box.) Front and rear drive permanently engaged. Third differential between front/rear shafts, locked by viscous control unit when shaft speed differential sensed.

MAIN GEARBOX RATIOS, mph per 1000 engine rpm

	Ratio	mph/1000 rpm	
		High	Low
4.0/4.6 V8 manual			
5th	0.730:1	26.56	9.87
4th	1.000:1	19.44	7.23
3rd	1.397:1	13.92	5.18
2nd	2.132:1	9.12	3.39
1st	3.321:1	5.85	2.17
Rev	3.535:1	5.50	2.04
V8 automatic			
4th	0.730:1	26.7	9.93
3rd	1.000:1	19.4	7.22
2nd	1.480:1	13.14	4.89
1st	2.480:1	7.84	2.92
Rev	2.090:1	9.30	3.45
BMW 2.5 l diesel manual			
5th	0.730:1	26.56	9.87
4th	1.000:1	19.44	7.23
3rd	1.397:1	13.92	5.18
2nd	2.132:1	9.12	3.39
1st	3.692:1	5.27	1.96
Rev	3.535:1	5.50	2.04

FINAL DRIVE RATIOS

Axle ratios. 3.540:1
Transfer ratios

	All models
High	1.216:1
Low	3.271:1

Front axle. Spiral bevel crown wheel and pinion. Separate ball-joint swivel pins; external, gaitered constant velocity joints.
Rear axle. Spiral bevel crown wheel and pinion with fully floating shafts.

BODY

Construction. Inner steel monocoque, steel bonnet, roof, tailgate and door inners, and rear lower quarter panels; all exterior panels double-sided zinc coated. Side intrusion rail. Rear floor has provision for flush-fitting load-lashing cleats.
Aluminium panels. Both front wings (bolt-on), all door outer panels and lower tailgate skin.
Painting. Zinc phosphate. Cathodic electrocoat, polyester surfacer. Colour coated either clear over metallic or alkyd for solid colours.

CAPACITIES (litres, Imp gal)
Full fuel tank
Petrol:100 lit (22.0 gal)
Diesel: 90 lit (19.8 gal)
Usable fuel
Petrol: 93 lit (20.4 gal)
Diesel: 83 lit (18.2 gal)
Low fuel warning
9 lit (2.0 gal) approx
Cooling system
V8 and diesel – 11.3 lit
Engine oil, including filter
V8 – 4.9 lit (0.85 lit min to max)
Diesel – 9.5 lit (1.0 lit min to max)
Main gearbox (manual)
2.7 lit initial fill; 2.4 lit top-up to

filler plug after draining.
Main gearbox (auto)
ZF4HP22 – 9.7 lit
ZF4HP24 – 11.0 lit
Transfer gearbox
2.4 lit
Front differential
1.7 lit
Rear differential
1.7 lit
Swivel pins
N/A - packed for life
Power steering
1.65 lit
Windscreen washer reservoir
6.0 lit

Section 10

Reference

10.1. Glossary

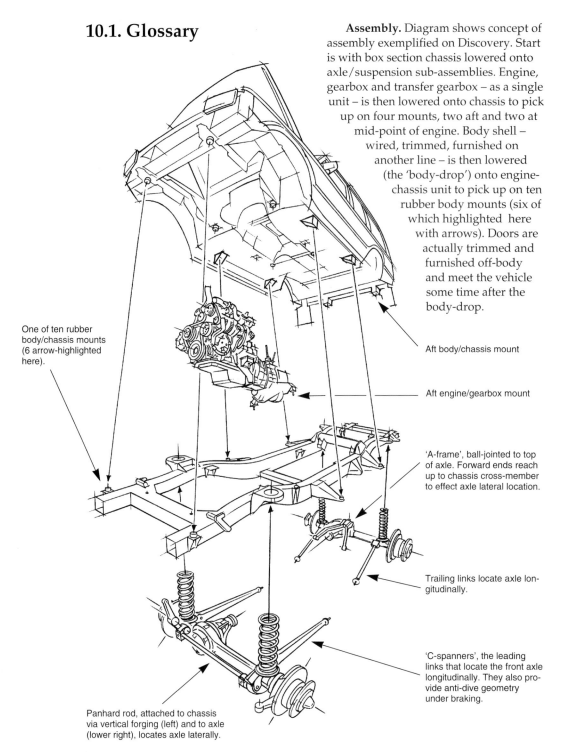

Assembly. Diagram shows concept of assembly exemplified on Discovery. Start is with box section chassis lowered onto axle/suspension sub-assemblies. Engine, gearbox and transfer gearbox – as a single unit – is then lowered onto chassis to pick up on four mounts, two aft and two at mid-point of engine. Body shell – wired, trimmed, furnished on another line – is then lowered (the 'body-drop') onto engine-chassis unit to pick up on ten rubber body mounts (six of which highlighted here with arrows). Doors are actually trimmed and furnished off-body and meet the vehicle some time after the body-drop.

Aft body/chassis mount

Aft engine/gearbox mount

One of ten rubber body/chassis mounts (6 arrow-highlighted here).

'A-frame', ball-jointed to top of axle. Forward ends reach up to chassis cross-member to effect axle lateral location.

Trailing links locate axle longitudinally.

'C-spanners', the leading links that locate the front axle longitudinally. They also provide anti-dive geometry under braking.

Panhard rod, attached to chassis via vertical forging (left) and to axle (lower right), locates axle laterally.

ABS. Anti-lock braking system; prevents wheels locking under maximum braking. Works on the principle of braking a wheel until it just begins to skid (this is the point where braking efficiency would drop off dramatically) and then releasing the brake pressure and re-applying the brakes. Wheel speed sensors identify the skid point and trigger a release in brake pressure. The cycle is repeated many times a second – with appropriate 'cobblestone' feed-back on the brake pedal to indicate you are in ABS mode. See also 'Cadence braking'.

A-frame. The means of effecting lateral location of the rear axle. Acting with the trailing links it also controls axle rotation. See diagram left and at 'Levelled suspension'.

Air suspension. – see EAS.

Anti-lock brakes. See ABS above.

Anti-roll bar (ARB). A large, U-shaped bar of steel (about 25 mm diameter) anchored to each side of the chassis in pivoting rubber mounts at the bottom of the U. The free ends of the U are attached to a front or rear axle to limit roll of the body relative to that axle. If the chassis/body is called on to move up and down parallel to the axle the ARB offers no interference; if, however body roll forces are induced by cornering, the twisting moments on the ARB tend to inhibit roll. In an off-road vehicle an ARB must be carefully designed not to limit axle articulation excessively and thus affect off-road performance. (See photos of rear axle anti-roll bars on Range Rover at Section 9.5). New Range Rover's composite trailing arms function as anti-roll bars as well as locating the axle longitudinally – 'Composite trailing arms' below.

Approach angle. In side-view, the angle between the ground and a line, ahead of the vehicle, joining the periphery of the front wheel and (typically) the front bumper or other low component. It represents the size or steepness of a slope or obstacle that can be approached or

climbed without striking bodywork. See diagram (right) and Sec 3.3.

Articulation. The ability of one axle to move – left wheel up, right wheel down or vice versa – relative to the chassis or its fellow axle. It is a measure of the ease with which wheels can stay in contact with the ground – and thus retain traction – on very 'twisty' off-road terrain. See Sec 3.3, 5.1.

Articulation angle, longitudinal. See 'Longitudinal articulation angle', p 199.

Assembly. See opposite.

Axles, one-piece, live. Also referred to as rigid or beam axles, in which the drive shafts to the wheels run within rigid casings without joints to allow vertical hinging as with independent suspension. See Sec 1.2.

Battery designation. Three figures define battery designation by encapsulating performance criteria. A '380/120/90' battery thus has a maximum rapid-discharge current at -18°C of 380 amp; it can maintain a discharge of 25 amp at 25°C for 120 minutes before reaching a terminal voltage of 10.2 volts; and its rate of voltage drop at max rapid-discharge of 380 amp (at -18°C) will be such that 5-7 seconds after commencement of discharge, voltage will have dropped to 9.0 volts. This is multiplied by 10 to give 90.

BCM. Body Control Module: and electronic module on New Range Rover, positioned under the front seats of the vehicle in which are contained the ECUs for the EAS and ABS. See p 194.

Boge unit. Self-levelling unit fitted to the rear axle of Range Rover and on Defenders fitted with optional self-levelling suspension. Unit has the function of 'self-pumping' the suspension up to a pre-determined height after the vehicle has travelled a certain distance. See diagram at 'Levelled suspension', p 199.

Bridle. A rope or cable attached to

...continued

The Land Rover Experience

two points – typically the right and left chassis members – of a vehicle and converging to a point of attachment for a tow rope. See Sec 5.2.

'C-spanner'. See 'Trailing/leading link' and diagram at 'Assembly', p 188.

Cadence braking. A method of manual braking with the foot brake to simulate the action of ABS brakes – see above. Very effective in slippery conditions where brake locking has occurred or might otherwise occur, the driver applies the footbrake in a series of very rapid jabs at the pedal taking the wheels up to the point of brake locking and then releasing them before the inevitable fall-off in braking efficiency takes place. Effects improved braking in any extremely slippery conditions such as ice, snow, wet mud, or rain. See Sec 3.2, 4.11, 6.3..

Camber. Angle at which, when viewed from the front, the front wheels of a vehicle splay out (positive camber) from the vertical – as shown in diagram; in some layouts it varies with position of suspension. Camber affects lateral control and ideally should be zero at all times. With Land Rover products, equipped with beam axles, camber angle is always zero.

Front axle

Camber angle →

Capstan winch. A winch, generally mounted on or just behind the front bumper, usually run from an engagable extension to the engine crankshaft. The active component is usually a slowly revolving drum, about 15 cm in diameter, round which a rope may be wound to effect a winching operation. Has the advantage of being powered by the engine at idling speed and being a very low-stress unit that may be used all day without overheating or high electrical load. See Sec 5.4.

Castor (or caster) angle. When the front wheels are moved right or left to steer the vehicle they each move about a steering axis. The aft inclination of this steering axis from the vertical (when viewed from the side) – about 3° in the case of most Land Rovers – is the castor angle. Like casters on a tea trolley or office chair, this puts the ground contact point of the wheels behind the pivot axis and the result is a self-centring action tending to keep the front wheels pointing forward when in forward motion. Note that in deep sand with a 'bow wave' build-up of

sand ahead of the wheels the effective ground contact point moves ahead of the steering axis and can give the effect of negative castor with 'runaway' steering. The same thing happens when vehicle is travelling in reverse – the ground contact point being 'ahead' of the steering axis and again tending to make the front wheels 'run away' to full lock – see Sec 4.4, (failed climbing of steep off-road inclines). Also see 'Steering feel', p 202.

Castor action. Tendency of front wheels to self-centre when the steering wheel is released with the vehicle going forward. NB Opposite action takes place when in reverse – see Castor angle above. Castor action is a basic ingredient of steering feel – see 'Steering feel', p 202.

Centre differential. A differential gear device – diagram Sec 1.3 – installed at the point where the transfer box splits engine power between the front and rear axles via the front and rear propeller shafts. Working in the same way as the conventional rear axle differential on a two-wheel drive car, it allows differential rotation of front and rear shafts to accommodate the small rotational differences encountered in normal running, going

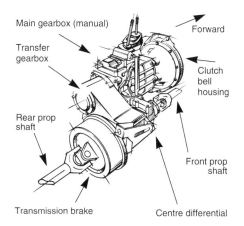

Main gearbox (manual)

Forward

Transfer gearbox

Clutch bell housing

Rear prop shaft

Front prop shaft

Transmission brake

Centre differential

round sharp corners etc. Such a device is essential in a vehicle having – for use on-road as well as off-road – full-time or permanent 4x4. Vehicles (currently by other manufacturers) fitted with part-time or selectable 4x4 are not fitted with centre differentials and thus cannot be used in four wheel drive on hard roads. See Sec 1.3, 2.5, also 'Diff lock', p 196.

Chott. Local name for salt flat or sebkha in Tunisia, Algeria and Morocco.

CLA. Coefficient of longitudinal articulation (superseded term) – see 'Longitudinal articulation angle'. A measure of 'twisty ground' capability.

Composite trailing arm. The new Range Rover rear axle uses composite material trailing arm links and a Panhard rod to locate the rear axle longitudinally and laterally (respectively) – see photo Sec 9.6. The composite trailing arm, by reason of the way it is attached to the chassis and clamped to the axle, also acts as an anti-roll bar. See also 'Trailing link'.

Continuous rolling contact. Description of a wheel in steady rolling contact with the ground without slip, wheel-spin or slide (as with locked brakes). Should be the aim at all times both on and off road. See Sec 3.2. Also see 'Discontinuity of rolling contact' below.

Co-ordinated tow. When recovering a stuck vehicle, the process by which the engine power of both the tug and the

stuck vehicle are co-ordinated – usually by a signal from an external marshaller – and the clutches of both vehicles are engaged at the same time. See Sec 5.2.

Corrugations. Deformation of an unsurfaced track taking the form of transverse, close-pitch undulations – ie at right angles to the direction of the track. Often referred to as 'washboard'. See Sec 4.9.

Coupled brakes. Brake system installed with certain large trailers whereby the trailer brakes are applied at the same time as are the brakes of the towing vehicle. Vehicles must be specifically modified to operate this system – with appropriate trailers. See Sec 4.1.

Cross-axled. See 'Diagonal suspension'.

Cross ply tyre. Tyre in which the sidewall reinforcement plies run diagonally from the bead towards the tread – each layer of textile at a different angle to its adjacent layer. Generally superseded by radial-ply tyres whose thinner, more flexible sidewalls and braced tread yield better grip and lower rolling resistance. Because of thicker, multi-ply sidewalls, not so prone to sidewall damage as radials and – see Sec 4.9, 8.2 – can have low-cost applications when operating continuously on rock. However, reduced pressures in soft going can, due to the thick sidewalls, cause overheating and possibly de-lamination of the tyre. See diagram at 'Radial ply tyres' on p 200.

De-coupled prop shaft. Feature introduced for 1995 model year on Discovery to reduce transmission of NVH (noise, vibration and harshness). Normal Hookes universal joint at aft end of rear prop shaft is replaced by a rubber doughnut joint designed to isolate vibration from the chassis.

Alphabetical sequence of Glossary items resumed on p 196 after four page insert for Electronic Air Suspension.

...continued

The Land Rover Experience

EAS: <u>AUTOMATIC</u> AIR SUSPENSION ACTIVATION – ALL RANGE ROVERS (WHERE SPECIFIED) ...contd →

NOTES

1. This sequence does not occur every time you use the vehicle. Chart shows criteria that will trigger automatic suspension changes from given start points.

2. Manually selected suspension changes, see charts facing page.

3. If you are in the condition shown at the beginning of an arrow, end of arrow is the automatically selected condition if the activation criteria shown in columns occur.

Use of diagram, examples:

a. Parked vehicle starts in 'Standard'. When it reaches 50 mph and exceeds it for 30 sec (col 8) it moves to 'Low'.

b. If it then drops to 35 mph or less for 30 secs (col 2), it automatically rises to 'Standard' .

c. If you have manually selected 'High', suspension will automatically return to 'Standard' when 35 mph exceeded (col 7).

4. 'High' and 'Access' can only be selected manually though an auto-sensed change to 'Extended' (cols 3, 4) will (if speed still under 35 mph) automatically revert to 'High' after 10 min. (col 5). Col 6, 7 if 35 mph exceeded.

5. 'Freezes':

a. 'Footbrake freeze'. Use of footbrake *during height change* inhibits attainment of any new position for 1 min (3 min New Range Rover) unless speed 1-5 mph. This obviates front/rear dip under braking in mid-change.

b. 'Door freeze'. Opening door or tailgate freezes movement to/from 'Access'. If freeze lasts more than 30 sec, further button selection required.

	CHANGE CRITERIA →	Drive off or handbrake released or auto out of Park	Under 35 mph			Exceed 35 mph	Over 50 mph 30 sec
			for 30 secs	Wheel(s) off-loaded for 7 secs	After 10 mins		
		1	**2**	**3**	**4**	**5**	**6 7**	**8**

AUTOMATIC SUSPENSION ACTIVATION – NO DRIVER INPUT

Extended
High profile
Standard
Low profile
Access

30 mm
40 mm
20 mm
60 mm

New Range Rover, if 'Access' originally selected with Inhibit button pressed.

NB. New Range Rover 'Low' and 'Access' (Crawl) are 25 and 65 mm below 'Standard', not 20 and 60 mm as on diagram.

SELECTION OF 'ACCESS' REQUIRES:
1. Vehicle stationary
2. Handbrake on or selector in 'Park' with automatic transmission
3. Doors closed
4. Footbrake off
5. Engine running or has been in previous 15 secs (40 secs, New Range Rover)

EAS – electronic air suspension. A complete summary of automatic and manual operation on both models of Range Rover is contained in the diagrams above – automatic functions on this page, manual overrides on the facing page. Introduced in the 1993 model year on certain Range Rover models and further refined as the standard fit for 1995 new Range Rover, EAS enhances standards of road noise insulation, ride and handling and off-road versatility. It substitutes air springs and a pneumatic system, (ie an electrically driven compressor, air pressure reservoir and associated controls) for the steel coil springs used on the rest of the Land Rover model range. Logic-controlled by an electronic control unit (ECU), height sensors and driver controls, the system maintains front and rear self-levelling in the five height modes shown above. These notes show details of the system and and its operating mode change criteria. However, for the casual driver, new to the vehicle, no prior knowledge or expertise is required; so

EAS: <u>MANUALLY CONTROLLED</u> AIR SUSPENSION ACTIVATION

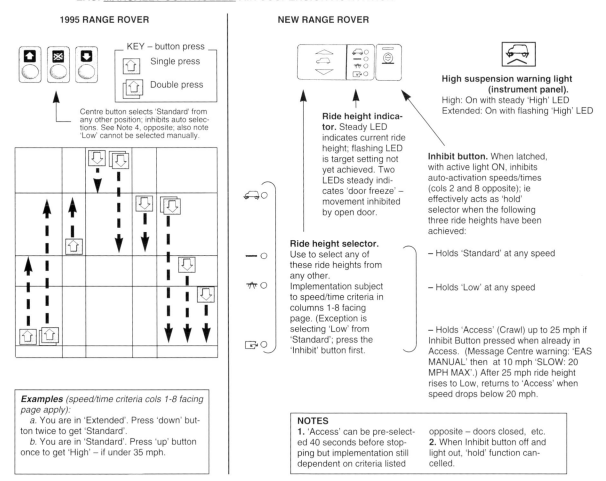

1995 RANGE ROVER

KEY – button press

Single press

Double press

Centre button selects 'Standard' from any other position; inhibits auto selections. See Note 4, opposite; also note 'Low' cannot be selected manually.

Examples (speed/time criteria cols 1-8 facing page apply):
a. You are in 'Extended'. Press 'down' button twice to get 'Standard'.
b. You are in 'Standard'. Press 'up' button once to get 'High' – if under 35 mph.

NEW RANGE ROVER

Ride height indicator. Steady LED indicates current ride height; flashing LED is target setting not yet achieved. Two LEDs steady indicates 'door freeze' – movement inhibited by open door.

Ride height selector. Use to select any of these ride heights from any other. Implementation subject to speed/time criteria in columns 1-8 facing page. (Exception is selecting 'Low' from 'Standard'; press the 'Inhibit' button first.

High suspension warning light (instrument panel).
High: On with steady 'High' LED
Extended: On with flashing 'High' LED

Inhibit button. When latched, with active light ON, inhibits auto-activation speeds/times (cols 2 and 8 opposite); ie effectively acts as 'hold' selector when the following three ride heights have been achieved:

– Holds 'Standard' at any speed

– Holds 'Low' at any speed

– Holds 'Access' (Crawl) up to 25 mph if Inhibit Button pressed when already in Access. (Message Centre warning: 'EAS MANUAL' then at 10 mph 'SLOW: 20 MPH MAX'.) After 25 mph ride height rises to Low, returns to 'Access' when speed drops below 20 mph.

NOTES
1. 'Access' can be pre-selected 40 seconds before stopping but implementation still dependent on criteria listed opposite – doors closed, etc.
2. When Inhibit button off and light out, 'hold' function cancelled.

long as the 'Inhibit' button on '95 model is not pressed (diag, facing page), EAS will cycle automatically through appropriate modes according to basic programming. The driver need not even know EAS is fitted. On engine start-up EAS assumes the last selected ride height.

1. *Standard ride height* – similar to that of coil springs; normal road use – and off-road use, keeping High in reserve. Can be 'held' as an Inhibit mode (eg for towing) cutting out automatic height changes.

2. *Low profile;* automatically activated to drop ride height by 20 mm (25 mm new Range Rover) if 50 mph is exceeded for 30 seconds. Reduces aerodynamic drag and tunes steering for high speed use by slightly increasing castor angle. If less than 35 mph is held for more than 30 seconds, standard ride height will be resumed automatically. In new Range Rover this ride height can, like Standard, be held as an Inhibit mode at any speed.

3. *High profile;* manually selected by ride height selector buttons, it raises ride height by 40 mm for occasional use off-

...continued

'High suspension' warning indicators on '95 Range Rover (above) and New Range Rover (below)

road or when wading; auto-reversion is to Standard ride height when 35 mph exceeded. Manually de-selectable. In both '95 model year Range Rover and New Range Rover, 'high suspension' warning lights show when in this mode – steady light indicating 'High' mode and flashing indications showing 'Extended' mode (see item **5.** below)

4. *Access;* manually selected by ride height buttons when stationary and doors closed. Drops ride height by 60 mm (65 mm new Range Rover) from standard. Mode cancelled and standard ride height resumed automatically when handbrake released or the automatic transmission shifter moved from 'Park' and vehicle driven away. Various requirements – see diagram – before Access position can be assumed. Opening a door during descent/ascent to/from Access position will freeze the suspension at that point. New Range Rover has Crawl mode in which Access can be 'held' up to 25 mph (see previous page). Purpose of Crawl is for manoeuvring in height-limited conditions such as multi-storey carparks. In

Access/Crawl, vehicle is actually lowered to bump stops – hence the need for speed-related automatic reversion to an air spring-supported condition when moving or moving above a certain speed.

5. *Extended;* raises ride height up to 20 mm above High Profile. Selected automatically when one or more wheels is off-loaded (eg when vehicle is bellied on a mound) for more than 7 seconds. Cannot be selected manually. Suspension reverts to High profile automatically after 10 minutes or reverts to standard ride height if 35 mph is exceeded. May be de-selected manually by one or two presses of suspension Down button which will respectively lower it to the High profile or Standard position.

EAS – basic system function. The plan-view diagram below gives a conceptual indication of the electronic air suspension (EAS) function; front of vehicle is to the right. An electrically driven air compressor supplies air at up to 10 bar (145 psi) to a reservoir mounted outboard of the left main chassis member (inboard right chassis member, New Range Rover) and thence to air springs at each corner of the vehicle. Actual air spring pressure varies between 3 bar and 7 bar according

Electronic air suspension – system operation concept

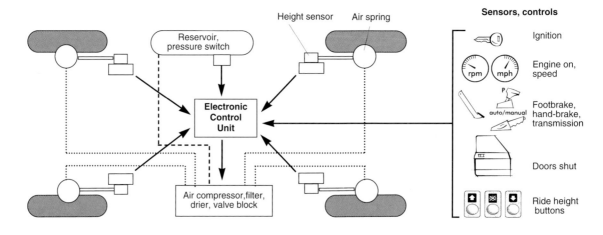

to load. An electronic control unit (ECU) housed under the front seat controls a valve block which apportions air to each spring as required. A height sensor on each longitudinal suspension link is the prime information feed to the ECU but, as shown on the diagrams overleaf, information on speed, door position, brakes-on etc are also needed and the ECU gets these from appropriate sensors as shown below. The ride height control buttons also feed direct to the ECU which puts commands through a logic check before implementing them.

EAS – functionality. Not surprisingly, the detailed functionality of the EAS, taking care of every possible combination of event and interruption by various inhibit interlocks, is very complex. The complexity need not concern an owner and is aimed only at the elimination of danger, damage or possible inconvenience – a vehicle with open doors descending to 'Access' over a high kerb that could damage the doors, ride-height changes that could cause temporary dazzle to oncoming traffic through a tail-first height change.

'Odd sensations' (and their elimination) are also catered for: a common one being arrival at traffic lights in 'Low' ride height. If you are at the lights over 30 seconds you might expect (Column 2 previous spread) the peculiar sensation of rising to 'Standard' in a stationary vehicle. This rise is postponed until the vehicle is moving. On the new Range Rover it is also postponed for a *further* 30 seconds so that, should you re-establish a speed above 35 mph in that time, the vehicle will actually remain in 'Low' – as you were when you approached the lights.

EAS – messages and faults. An 'intelligent' self-checking and fault logging system is built into the ECU to differentiate between faults that are temporary, important, those that require driver speed limitation, those that need logging for subsequent recovery and analysis by spe-

cialist equipment and those that are 'volatile' – ie will go ('evaporate') after the system has 'powered-down' (engine stopped) for two minutes or more. The main indications on the Message Centre in the New Range Rover are:

1. 'EAS MANUAL' on the Message Centre , as noted on the previous page, indicates that you have manually selected 'Access/crawl'. When your speed rises to 10 mph in this mode, since the vehicle is riding on the bump stops, the Message Centre will warn: 'SLOW: 20 MPH MAX'. If you ignore this the ride height will rise to 'Low' at 25 mph, returning to 'Access' when speed drops below 20 mph.

2. 'EAS FAULT' on the Message Centre accompanied by a bleep and return to 'Standard' ride height. If unaccompanied by further indication it is in order to continue without further action and it may well be a 'volatile' fault that on the next power-up has disappeared.

3. 'EAS FAULT' that alternates in 4 second cycle with 'SLOW: 35 MPH MAX' indicates the suspension is trapped in a position above 'Standard' or below 'Low' and the speed limit should be observed.

In cases 2 or 3 it is worth stopping, switching off and starting up again after two minutes in case the fault is a volatile one. If it is not, keep within the speed limits indicated and contact your Land Rover dealer who will use diagnostic equipment to establish detail cause.

EAS – uses of 'Inhibit'. A quick guide to the uses of 'Inhibit":

1. *Towing.* On both types of Range Rover, set suspension to 'Standard' and then select 'Inhibit' to keep it there.

2. *Sporty handling.* On new Range Rover, you may prefer the feel of the vehicle in 'Low' – taut ride and enhanced high speed steering. If not already in 'Low', select "Inhibit" first, then "Low".

3. *'Access/crawl'.* On new Range Rover when, for example, manoeuvring in a low-roof multi-storey car park select 'Access', then 'Inhibit'.

...continued

Alphabetical sequence of Glossary items resumed here from p 191 after four page page insert for Electronic Air Suspension.

Departure angle. In side view, the angle between the ground and a line, aft

of the vehicle, joining the periphery of the rear wheel and (typically) the rear chassis member or other low component. It represents the size or steepness of a slope or obstacle that can be approached or climbed in reverse without striking bodywork. See Sec 3.3.

Diagonal suspension. A manifestation occurring off-road when a vehicle is, for example, diagonally crossing a small but well-defined ridge. When the ridge is so severe that, say, the right front wheel and the rear left wheels are on full 'bump' (ie fully up in the wheel arches) and the other wheels are hanging down to the full extent of wheel travel, the vehicle may be described as being diagonally suspended or on diagonal suspension. Some also refer to this state as being 'cross-axled'. See Sec 4.3.

Diagonal wheel-spin. The wheel-spin that can take place on the fully extended (or off-loaded) wheels in a condition of diagonal suspension as described above. The presence of slippery ground under these wheels can provoke the condition. Can also occur crossing ditches diagonally; see Sec 4.3.

Diff-lock. See first 'Centre differential' above. Locking of the centre differential, activated by moving the transfer gearbox lever to the left and confirmed by illumination of the 'DIFF-LOCK' indicator light, puts the differential function on hold. Where traction conditions or grip are different front and rear there would be a tendency for the centre differential to permit the front wheels, say, to spin ineffectively while they are on wet clay and cause the rear wheels, on grippier ground, to stop

rotating. The diff-lock locks the centre differential, thus locking front and rear prop shafts together, ensuring they revolve at the same speed and enhancing traction. Diff-lock is usually engaged for difficult off-road conditions but should never remain engaged on hard grippy roads. See also 'Centre differential lock', Sec 2.5. See also 'Viscous coupling', p 205.

Differential casing. Not to be confused with the centre differential, each axle, of course, has a normal cross-axle differential at the point where the propeller shaft from the transfer gearbox meets the axle. The size of the crown wheel and pinion plus differential demands a bulge in the axle casing – referred to as the diff casing. It has special significance in off-road vehicles because it is the lowest point of the axle and thus the point of least ground clearance – Sec 3.3.

Discontinuity of rolling contact. Generic term for wheel-spin and wheel slide – as on locked brakes. See Sec 3.2 and 'Continuous rolling contact' above.

Divergent. A dynamic condition that 'gets worse of its own accord' – eg an oscillation of ever-increasing amplitude or a turn that, once initiated, tightens up on its own. See also 'Oversteer, divergent'.

EAS. See p 192.

Electric range change. Method of shifting transfer gears on the New Range Rover by pressing button or use of H-gate lever position instead of by manual lever.

Electronic air suspension. See p 192.

Electronic traction control – ETC. ETC is a standard/optional feature, available only on ABS-equipped Range Rovers. It inhibits wheel-spin by applying brake to a spinning rear wheel and thus enhances traction on ice, snow or in severe off-road conditions. It is an entirely automatic function and has no driver control or override. It utilises ABS sensors for wheel speed determination and brakes the spinning wheel to apply, through the axle differential, torque to the stationary wheel. Like ABS, it is especially effective in maintaining control when one side of the vehicle is on a more slippery surface than the other – a so-called 'split-µ' surface. A dashboard light illuminates when the system is operating. The function is inhibited above 50 kph to preclude overheating, a speed above which unintentional wheel spin is unlikely to occur. See Sec 2.1, 3.2..

Engine braking. Vehicle retardation derived from engaging a low gear and taking your foot off the throttle. See also Sec 4.5, 6.3.

Emergency flotation (tyre pressure). Very low tyre pressure (about 60% of normal road pressures), always associated with a low maximum permitted speed (20 kph or 12 mph) used for traversing or recovery from very soft ground. Such low pressures cause extreme tyre sidewall flexing – hence the speed limitation. See Sec 4.7, 8.2..

Emergency soft. Another name for emergency flotation tyre pressure – see above.

ETC . See 'Electronic traction control' above.

Fatigue life. Number of specified load reversals at which a metal component will fail. In the context of this book see fatigue life of nylon snatch-towing ropes – 'Recovery – snatch-towing', Sec 5.3.

'Fesh-fesh'. Desert terrain comprising a thin crust of fine gravel or wind-blown sand laid over deep very fine dust of powder consistency. Can be bad enough to bog a vehicle. Difficult to spot due to overlay of normal-looking sand.

Flotation. Characteristic of a vehicle, by reason of large softly inflated tyres, not to sink on soft going such as mud or sand. See Sec 4.7 and 'Optimum pressures', Sec 8.2.

Four-wheel drive (4x4). Vehicle transmission system in which engine power is applied to all four wheels. The term 4x4 (four by four) has the specific connotation that it is a four (wheeled vehicle driven) by four (wheels). See Sec 1.1.

Full-time 4x4. A transmission system on a four-wheeled vehicle in which all four wheels are driven by the engine all the time. (As opposed to a vehicle that is normally in two-wheel drive with four-wheel drive selected by a separate lever when required.) See Sec 1.1, 2.1.

Geometric limitations. A term coined for this book to describe the limitations and extent of approach and departure angles, ramp angle, steering lock, articulation and – an even newer term – longitudinal articulation angle. See 'Geometric limitations', Sec 3.3, and throughout Sec 9.

Ground clearance. Space between the ground and a given mechanical part of the vehicle. Usually, when quoted for a vehicle, taken as the least for any component on the vehicle – the space under the differential casing. But note difference between under-axle and under-belly clearance – see Sec 3.3.

Ground offset. Sometimes also called 'steering offset'. The lateral distance between the point where the extension of the steering swivel pin (or king pin) axis touches the ground and the centre line of the front wheel – also at ground level – when viewed from the front. Offset influences amount of 'drag' present at each front wheel. These cancel out, side-to-side in normal straight, hard-road driving but when cornering causes weight transfer to one side or one wheel goes through thick 'draggy' mud off-road, steering feel and feedback of shock can be affected – hence need for damper and worm/roller steering box. Zero offset is the ideal but very hard to achieve with

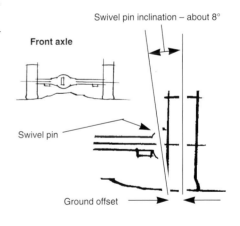

Swivel pin inclination – about 8°

Front axle

Swivel pin

Ground offset

...continued

complexities of all-wheel drive and brakes to cram into a small space; New Range Rover has reduced ground offset to 17 mm, enabling use of recirculating ball steering system. See picture Sec 9.6.

Ground stress. Term coined for this book to indicate how much strength is being asked of a particular piece of ground in terms of flotation or lateral shear to accommodate traction, braking or acceleration. See Sec 1.2, 4.7.

GVW. Gross vehicle weight – the maximum permitted laden weight of a vehicle including payload, fuel and driver.

H-gate. New Range Rover with automatic transmission uses twin selection quadrants for high and low range gears separated by centre bar at the neutral position – hence 'H-gate'. See Sec 2.3.

Handbrake. See 'Transmission brake'.

Harmonics. Here taken as relating to the natural frequency of a vehicle's suspension system that can influence the formation of transverse surface corrugations on unsurfaced tracks. See Sec 4.9.

Heel and toe wear. Jargon for the uneven front to rear wear on individual blocks of a bold off-road tyre tread when used on roads. See Sec 8.2, 'Mud tyre' and 'Sand tyre'.

High box. Transmission status when the two-speed transfer gearbox lever is in the high ratio position – for normal, on-road, day-to-day use. See Sec 1.2.

High ratio. Term to describe the transmission when the transfer gearbox lever is in the high position – high box above.

Hi-lift jack. Versatile lever-operated mechanical bumper jack capable of a lift of about a metre. See Sec 5.1.

Hi-lo lever. Term sometimes used to describe the transfer gearbox range change lever. See Sec 1.2.

High Load suspension. An option on the Defender 90 (stronger, dual-rate rear springs) enabling payload to be raised by about 150 kg – see Sec 9.1.

Hydraulic tappets. Method of operat-ing the engine cylinder valves incorporating what is in effect an oil-filled section of the operating rod. Method is 'self-adjusting', eliminates need for and noise emanating from 'valve clearances' associated with normal actuation method.

Hydraulic winch. Winch with rotational function actuated by a hydraulic motor. Power source is hydraulic pump mounted on power take off at rear of gearbox. See Sec 5.4.

Kerb weight. Empty vehicle plus full fuel plus 75 kg driver.

KERR. Kinetic Energy Recovery Rope. Descriptive term coined to describe specially specified nylon ropes capable of stretching during snatch tow. See 'Recovery – snatch-towing', Sec 5.3.

Kinetic energy. Energy of motion, proportional to total weight of the vehicle and the square of its speed. Thus if a vehicle's weight doubles its KE also goes up two times; but if its speed doubles its KE increases by two squared, ie four times. See 'Recovery – snatch-towing', Sec 5.3.

King pin. See 'Swivel pin'.

Laden. Vehicle carrying some or full payload. See also GVW above concerning loading to maximum permitted weight.

Leading link. See 'Trailing/leading link'.

Levelled suspension. (See diagram opposite page.) A means of eliminating the 'squat' of the rear suspension under load using a hydraulic self-levelling unit (see also 'Boge unit') between the chassis and the centre of the rear axle. Standard on coil sprung Range Rovers, Defender 110 Station Wagons and County; special order other Defender 110. See 'Unlevelled suspension', p 205. (Range Rovers with EAS have auto levelling front and rear.)

Longitudinal articulation angle. A single number, taking account of both wheel movement and wheelbase, that conveys the off-road, 'twisty ground' potential of an off-road vehicle. It is the angle between the ground and a line joining the front and rear hubs (or tyre

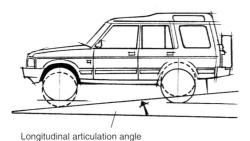

Longitudinal articulation angle

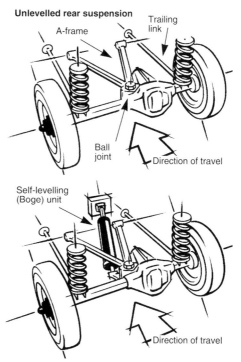

Unlevelled rear suspension
A-frame
Trailing link
Ball joint
Direction of travel

Self-levelling (Boge) unit
Direction of travel

Levelled rear suspension
(See opposite page, right hand column.)

periphery) when one wheel is on full bump and the other fully extended. A given max wheel movement enhances this capability more on a short wheelbase than on a long wheelbase vehicle. Higher values mean better articulation; small differences in articulation angle make quite large differences to performance. Vehicle values Sec 9.1 – 9.6.

Low box. Low range; when the transfer gearbox lever is in the low position – for difficult off-road conditions demanding greater traction or low speed control. See 'Traction – extra gears', Sec 1.2, and 'Low range – when and how', Sec 2.4.

Low range. Term to describe the transmission when transfer gearbox lever is in the low position. See Sec 2.1, 2.4, 2.5.

Low ratio. See 'low range'.

Marshalling. ('Marshaller' derived from ground-crew who marshal aircraft at airports.) In the context of off-road operations, taken to mean the detailed direction of a vehicle by a marshaller outside the vehicle who is able to see all four wheels and also the difficult ground being traversed. Marshalling should be undertaken when there is the danger of damaging tyre sidewalls or the underside of the vehicle on rocks or other obstacles. See 'Look before you leap', Sec 3.4.

Mechanical sympathy. In the context of this book, concern for and empathy with the structural stress, durability of, and possible damage to mechanical components of your vehicle. In a phrase, caring about your Land Rover. See 'Mindset – mechanical sympathy', Sec 3.1.

Message centre. Alpha-numeric information readout on New Range Rover instruments showing systems status, faults, fuse/bulb failures, suspension and transmission status. See Sec 9.6, 2.1, 2.3.

M+S tyres. Mud and snow tyres. A generic term for 4x4 tyres with a road-oriented, not especially bold, tread pattern suitable for mild snow and mud conditions. See Sec 8.2, 'Tyres'.

Mode. Method or regime of operation of a system – eg fast or slow, high or low, manual or auto. Hence its use in the context of (and see) 'EAS' (p 192-195) and 'H-gate automatic transmission' (Sec 2.3).

Mud tyres. Bold, open-tread tyres optimised for mud with disadvantages on hard roads. See Sec 8.2, 'Tyres'.

Multi-purpose tyre.
Combination/compromise between on-road and mud tyres. See Sec 8.2, 'Tyres'.

...continued

NATO towing hook. Large, robust, four-bolt attachment towing pintle with top-closure originally specified for NATO 7.5 tonne military vehicles. Suitable for off-road towing ; noisy, due to trailer towing eye not being a close fit over the hook. See 'Towing – on-road', Sec 4.1 and 'Towing off-road', Sec 6.4.

Nose load. Trailers should be nose heavy; the nose-load is the amount of nose-heaviness measured at the tow-hitch and must be considered part of the towing vehicle's payload. See 'Towing – on-road', Sec 4.1.

NVH. Abbreviation for 'noise, vibration and harshness', an affliction the chassis and engine engineers try very hard to eliminate by the likes of carefully tuned power train mounts, suspension isolation pads, de-coupled prop shafts and air suspension.

OE. Abbreviation for 'original equipment', usually referring to tyres as supplied on a vehicle when bought from the factory.

On-foot recce. Inspecting a difficult off-road obstacle on foot before committing your vehicle to it. See 'Look before you leap', Sec 3.4.

Overrun brakes. Trailer brakes activated by the tendency of the trailer to overtake – or overrun – the towing vehicle when the vehicle brakes or slows down. See 'Towing- on-road', Sec 4.1.

Oversteer, divergent. Tendency for an initiated steering command to 'run away' toward full lock or (Sec 4.1) for an extremely nose-heavy trailer to cause this condition on a fast, sharp bend.

Over-torque. Used in this book to convey the concept of applying too much torque (or power) to the wheels so that they break their grip with the ground and spin.

Panhard rod. A suspension component, of the order of 30 mm diameter and a metre long, that laterally locates a front or rear axle relative to the chassis. One end is attached and pivoted to the (say,

right hand) chassis member and the other end to the (in this case, left hand) end of the axle. The arrangement permits vertical movement of the axle, and articulation, whilst constraining lateral movement. See diagram at 'Assembly' (p 188), and photo of New Range Rover at Sec 9.6. Panhard rods are used for front axle lateral location on all Land Rover products and, on New Range Rover, for the rear axle too. (For rear axles on other models, see 'A-frame'.) Together with the trailing or leading links, the Panhard rod is thus part of a linkage system that locates an axle fore and aft as well as laterally.

Part-time 4x4. See 'Selectable four-wheel drive' next page.

Permanent four-wheel drive. See 'Full-time 4x4' above.

Power take off. Attachment to rear of gearbox for running accessories such as hydraulic pumps or shaft drives to winches and saws. Approved versions available for Land Rover products.

PTO. See power take off.

Radial ply tyre. A type of tyre construction in which sidewall structural plies run radially out towards the tread

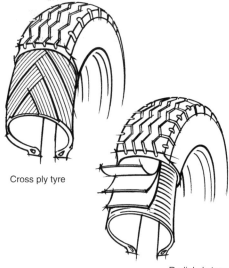

Cross ply tyre

Radial ply tyre

instead of criss-cross diagonally. With their thinner, more flexible sidewalls, radial tyres have lower rolling resistance than cross-ply tyres (yielding better fuel consumption) as well as giving longer tread life. They can accommodate the use of low inflation pressures without over-heating, due to their flexible sidewalls, but are sometimes more prone to sidewall damage when operating in rocky or stony conditions. Because radial tyres invari-ably also have a braced tread area of great dimensional stability, they 'track-lay' the tread (like a bulldozer), do not suffer from 'tread shuffle' and so achieve more traction in limiting off-road conditions. See also Sec 4.7.

Ramp angle. A measure of vehicle under-belly clearance or the ability to drive over a sharp ridge or ramp without touching the underside of the vehicle on the obsta-

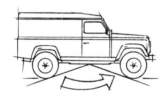

cle. The ramp angle is the angle measured from the lowest part of the chassis at mid-wheelbase down to the periphery of front and rear wheels. Obviously a short wheelbase vehicle with large wheels will have the smallest ramp angle and best under-belly clearance; a Defender 90 will be better than a Defender 130 in this respect. See Sec 3.3.

Ramp breakover angle. The fuller title of 'Ramp angle ' above.

Range change. Term sometimes used for the transfer gearbox lever. See Sec 2.1.

Reduced inflation. Lowering tyre pressures to increase flotation in soft ground conditions such as mud or soft sand. See Sec 4.7 and Sec 8.2, 'Tyres'.

Rolling contact – see 'Continuous rolling contact'.

Sand ladders. A pair of aluminium ladders, about 170 cm long, specially made with rungs closer than normal, to lay beneath the vehicle wheels in soft sand to give grip and flotation. See 'Self-recovery', Sec 5.1.

Sand tracks. Generic name sometimes given to any item fulfilling the role of a sand ladder. May be PSP (pierced steel planking). See 'Self-recovery' and dia-gram Sec 5.1.

Sand channels. Term often inter-changeable with sand tracks, derivative from the days when metal channels were used for this purpose. Can include articu-lated sand planks, see 'Self-recovery' and photo Sec 5.1.

Sand tyres. Term often used to mean desert tyre – which implies an ability to cope with desert rock and stones as well as sand. These tyres are characterised by tread blocks of a gentle, shouldered pro-file with no bold, right-angled edges such as a mud tyre would have. Radial con-struction is far more suited to the low inflation pressures sometimes used in sand. Despite their appearance, 'balloon' tyres with circumferential groove treads are considerably less effective in sand than a radial such as the Michelin XS. See Sec 4.8 and Sec 8.2, 'Tyres'.

Salt flat. Salt marsh (also known as 'chott' or 'sebkha') of very unreliable con-sistency and bearing strength found in desert regions and characterised by a top crust of varying thickness and strength with soft salt mud of great depth beneath it. See Sec 4.8.

Sebkha. See Salt flat above.

Selectable four-wheel drive. A four-wheeled vehicle which proceeds normally in two-wheel drive but on which, by means of a lever control, four-wheel drive may be selected. It is important to remem-ber that such vehicles in four-wheel drive do not have the benefit of a centre differ-ential (see p 190 above) so should not be used on hard roads or firm grippy sur-faces in this mode. See Sec 1.3.

Self centring. The characteristic of front (steered) wheels to resume the

...continued

straight-ahead position due to castor angle (See 'Castor angle', p 190 above) when the steering wheel is released. This characteristic can be utilised to enhance safety when driving in deep wheel ruts on slippery ground. See 'Driving on tracks', Sec 4.2 and 'Steering feel' this page.

Self-levelling suspension. See 'Levelled suspension' p 198.

Sidewall. The external 'walls' of a tyre between the tread and the bead or wheel rim. This area is particularly vulnerable on radial ply tyres to damage in off-road operations from oblique rubbing contact with side-swiping sharp rocks. Driver awareness essential. See Sec 4.9.

Sidewall awareness. Awareness by sensitive drivers of the susceptibility to damage of the tyre sidewall. An attribute worth developing. See 'Rocks, stones, corrugations', Sec 4.9.

Sidewall deflection. Outward movement of the tyre sidewall in the region of the ground contact patch due to low inflation pressures or hitting a sharp bump with excess speed. It is important not to run tyres at less than recommended inflation pressures for given maximum speeds and loads (see Sec 8.2, 'Tyres') since by doing so you will exceed the manufacturer's specified limits for sidewall deflection and thus cause overheating and serious damage to the tyre.

Top section

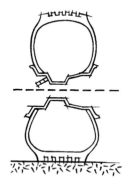

Ground level section

Shock loading. In the context of this book, taken to mean the arrest of mechanical motion in an excessively abrupt way or the application of sharp load reversals in a such a way as to risk structural fail-ure. For example, the application of the handbrake whilst the vehicle is in motion – important, see 'Traction controls', Sec 2.1 – can cause unacceptable shock loading of the rear axle half-shafts. (See 'Transmission brake' next page.) Engaging diff lock whilst one or more wheel is spinning could also result in severe and damaging shock load to the transmission (See also 'Viscous coupling' p 205 and 'Mechanical sympathy', p 199.)

Small gear lever. Don't be embarrassed if you can't remember the name for the transfer gear lever..! (See p 204.)

Snatch tow. A method of recovering a stuck vehicle in which the towing vehicle is in motion before taking up the slack in the tow rope. Use only special-purpose stretch ropes and specified procedures for this, See 'Recovery – snatch towing', Sec 5.3.

Steering lock. The extent to which the steering wheel may be moved to the right or left. Thus 'full lock' implies movement of the steering wheel as far as it will go right or left.

Steering feel. Steering feel is a vital and safety-relevant ingredient of the feedback between vehicle and driver. The communication is achieved almost entirely by assimilating the amount of self-centring or castor action present and how it compares with normal on-road conditions. (See first Castor action and Castor angle above – p 190.) It is important for drivers always to be alert to variations in steering feel and to know what may cause them. A very brief summary follows:

1. *Power steering.* On Land Rover products this is power assisted steering so feel is retained at all times. The centre 6°, ie 3° either side of straight ahead, is not power assisted and this aids straight-ahead feel. Be alert to the possibility of inexperienced mechanics having adjusted this out.

2. *In slippery ruts* accurate feel will be lost and you will find it hard to know exactly which way your wheels are pointing. It is essential to check visually until back on normal ground – see Sec 4.2, Railway lining effect.

3. *In soft sand*, as noted above, the effective ground contact point may well be ahead of the pivot axis and this can give 'negative castor action' effect – ie a tendency for the wheels to run away to full lock. This will be particularly – and dangerously – apparent when descending the slip face of a sand dune. Grip the steering wheel firmly with both hands and, down a sand-fall, have a marshaller guide you: and watch the marshaller – he is the only one who can tell which way your front wheels are pointing.

4. *Rock or rough ground.* Whilst the worm and roller steering design and power assisted steering of Land Rover vehicles is ideally suited to off-road driving, be aware of the potential for serious kick-back from the steering when traversing rough ground, rocks and boulders. Grip the steering wheel firmly and keep your thumbs outside the rim so that sudden, unexpected kickback does not cause injury.

5. *Range Rover with electronic air suspension.* One of the additional benefits of EAS is that variations in suspension height also cause slight variations in castor angle. Low profile, automatically selected above 50 mph, increases castor angle by just over 1° and produces exceptional stability and enhanced self-centring – exactly what is required for high speed motorway driving. Conversely, when on high profile or extended suspension settings, steering castor is reduced, making the steering inherently lighter over difficult ground.

6. *Ice, snow, slippery conditions* – on road. This will be well-enough known to experienced 4x2 drivers but is still worth mentioning here since the same laws of physics apply to 4x4s. When grip is at a premium obviously the self-centring of the front wheels will be dramatically diminished and the heart-sinking 'lightness' of the steering wheel will be experienced. As in a surprising number of off-road situations, delicate 'finger-tip' steering and 'the midwife's touch' are the order of the day.

Stretch limit (KERR ropes). The extent to which a kinetic energy recovery rope or strap will stretch before it is in danger of breaking. A guide for the Marlow Ropes Recovaline is 40% stretch; this limit should never be approached. See 'Recovery – snatch towing', Sec 5.3.

Survey on foot. Inspect before you drive. See On-foot recce above and 'Look before you leap', Sec 3.4.

Swivel pin. Sometimes known as king pin. The axis about which a front wheel pivots in order to effect steering. Swivel pin axes are invariably inclined aft to achieve a castor angle or trail thus providing self-centring. When viewed from the front, the lower end is further outboard than the top end which helps reduce ground offset and improves steering in other respects. See diagram at entry for 'Ground offset', p 197.

Swivel pin inclination. See above and Sec 9.1 – 9.6 for individual vehicle values.

Toe-in / toe-out. Amount by which front wheels, in plan view, are not parallel to each other. This is a designed-in feature that affects handling and steering feel and there are defined limits for each vehicle.

Traction. In the context of this book the concept of achieving grip between the wheels and the ground without slip, skid or sinkage. See Sec 1.2, 3.2.

Traction Control. See 'Electronic Traction Control, ETC'.

Traction controls. Here taken to mean the lever controlling the transfer gearbox and centre differential lock, see 'Traction controls', Sec 2.1.

Tractive effort. The amount of 'pull' exerted by a vehicle as a result of traction.

Trailer preponderance. Sometimes used to denote down-load on the vehicle towing hitch – see 'Nose load' p 200 above and 'Towing – on-road', Sec 4.1.

...continued

Trailer nose-load. See 'Nose load' p 200 above.

Trailing link / leading link. Trailing links, fitted to all current Land Rover vehicles, are structural members of the order of a metre long each side of the chassis linking (at their forward end) the chassis to (at their aft end) the rear axle. They thus locate the axle fore and aft relative to the chassis, allowing it to rise and fall as required whilst also transmitting braking loads and thrust from the wheels. See diagram at 'Levelled suspension'. Forward-pointing *leading links* do the same thing for the front axle; here they are forgings – often referred to as 'C-spanners' because of their shape and each bolted to the front axle by two rubber-bushed bolts (see diagram at 'Assembly'.)

Transfer gearbox. Originally the name implied the transfer of power from the main gearbox to the front axle as well as the rear axle on a four-wheel drive vehicle. In all Land Rover products a two-speed transfer box is fitted so it has the additional role of permitting power from the gearbox to go to the axles at normal 1:1 gearing (high ratio) or geared down by nearly 2:1 (low ratio). See 'Traction – extra gears', Sec 1.2, 'Low range – when and how', Sec 2.4 and diagram below.

Gearbox, transfer box, hand brake

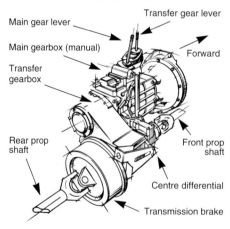

Transfer gear lever

Main gear lever

Main gearbox (manual)

Transfer gearbox

Forward

Rear prop shaft

Front prop shaft

Centre differential

Transmission brake

Transfer gear lever. The 'small gear lever', in the cab next to the main gear lever. It controls whether the transmission is in 'high ratio' or 'low ratio' in the transfer box. The same lever also controls the engagement of the diff lock – see above – except in the Range Rover where a viscous coupling fulfils this requirement automatically. See 'Traction controls', Sec 2.1 and 'Viscous coupling' opposite.

Transmission brake. The handbrake on all Land Rovers operates by gripping the rear propeller shaft at the point where it leaves the transfer gearbox and is thus called a transmission brake. It should be used as a parking brake only and should never be operated whilst the vehicle is in motion except in emergency - see 'Traction controls', Sec 2.1 and drawing left.

Transmission wind-up. Read first 'Centre differential', p 190 above. A 4x4 with no centre differential or one driven with the centre diff locked (ie in both cases the front and rear propeller shafts locked together) is unable to accommodate the small differences in distance normally travelled by the front wheels compared to the rear wheels. The diff-lock ensures both propeller shafts rotate exactly the same amount despite the small differences in distance actually travelled. This results in some wheel slip and skid which, on loose ground, can take place without any harm. On hard roads, however, the superior wheel grip makes it difficult for the wheels to slip much and in the process of trying to do so considerable torsional stress builds up in the transmission. This is known as transmission wind-up and can sometimes exert so much stress that the diff-lock gears will not disengage when so selected. You will also sense very heavy steering. If this occurs due to your forgetting to de-select diff-lock on hard ground (or at any other time) and the diff lock will not disengage, the solution is to reverse the vehicle some distance until the diff-lock warning light extinguishes.

Tyre nomenclature. Details of all information inscribed on the sidewalls of tyres is contained in Sec 8.2, 'Tyres', final page.

'Two-pass' radiator. Engine coolant radiator type fitted to diesel version of New Range Rover; radiator is effectively split vertically by an internal baffle forcing coolant to follow a U-shaped path. Coolant enters upper left, passes down the left half, across the bottom and up the right side to exit upper right.

Unladen. Vehicle carrying fuel, driver but no payload or other load – see 'Kerb' above.

Unlevelled suspension. Defender 110 rear suspension without the self-levelling option as described at 'Levelled suspension', p 198 above.

Viscous coupling unit (VCU). A unit fitted as standard to all Range Rovers across the centre differential (not instead of it) automatically to effect locking of the differential when a significant speed difference between front and rear propeller shafts is sensed. Conceptually it comprises a cylinder attached to the rear prop shaft into which an extension of the front prop shaft is introduced. Discs are attached alternately to the front prop shaft and the inside of the cylinder so that

they interleave very closely within the cylinder. The cylinder is sealed at both ends and is filled with a special silicone fluid which has the characteristic of markedly increasing its viscosity when stirred. Thus when one prop shaft rotates relative to the other one – the situation of front (or rear) axle wheel-spin – the fluid increases its viscosity enough to lock the shafts together. When relative rotation ceases the viscosity changes back to its original value and the shafts are unlocked. The viscous coupling unit (VCU) has the advantage of being automatic on both engagement and disengagement and its action is gradual and without shock-loading to the transmission.

Wading plugs. Oil drain holes are provided in the bottom of the clutch housing (and the camshaft drive-belt housing on Tdi and 2.5D engines) to preclude the possibility of the clutch or cam belts becoming contaminated in the event of oil leaks from the adjacent bearings. Wading plugs should be fitted to block these holes when driving through water over 30 cm deep and subsequently removed. See 'Wading' and photo, Sec 4.10 (covers R380 gearbox).

Wheel-slide. See above 'Discontinuity of rolling contact' p 196. A condition in which one or more wheels slide over a slippery surface rather than rolling over it; can be provoked by brake lock up or excessive engine braking. See 'Gentle right foot', Sec 3.2.

Wheel-spin. See Discontinuity of rolling contact p 196. A condition in which a stationary or moving vehicle has power applied to the transmission in conditions of poor grip and one or more wheels spins without associated forward motion (or rearward if in reverse). See 'Gentle right foot', Sec 3.2.

10.2 Index

...continued

A Defender 110 County on an expedition in the Sahara desert. There are few regions where meticulous vehicle operation and mechanical sympathy could be more important.